BY KURT ANDERSEN

Fantasyland

True Believers

Reset

Heyday

Turn of the Century

The Real Thing

FANTASYLAND

FANTASYLAND

How America
Went Haywire

A 500-YEAR HISTORY

KURT ANDERSEN

RANDOM HOUSE  NEW YORK

Published in the United States by Random House,
an imprint and division of Penguin Random House LLC, New York.

RANDOM HOUSE and the HOUSE colophon are registered trademarks
of Penguin Random House LLC.

Some passages in *Fantasyland* were originally published in different forms in
The New Yorker, New York, Time, and *The New York Times.*

Library of Congress Cataloging-in-Publication Data
Names: Andersen, Kurt, author.
Title: Fantasyland : how America went haywire : a 500-year history / Kurt Andersen.
Description: New York : Random House, 2017. | Includes index.
Identifiers: LCCN 2017016052 | ISBN 9781400067213 |
ISBN 9781588366870 (ebook)
Subjects: LCSH: National characteristics, American. | United States—Civilization. |
Popular culture—United States—History.
Classification: LCC E169.1 .A543 2017 | DDC 973—dc23
LC record available at https://lccn.loc.gov/2017016052

Printed in the United States of America on acid-free paper

randomhousebooks.com

4 6 8 9 7 5

Book design by Susan Turner

For the people who taught me to think—

Jean and Bob Andersen,

and the teachers of Omaha's District 66

"The easiest thing of all is to deceive oneself; for we believe whatever we want to believe."

— DEMOSTHENES

"Unceasingly we are bombarded with pseudo-realities. Reality is that which, when you stop believing in it, doesn't go away."

— PHILIP K. DICK

"You are entitled to your own opinion, but you are not entitled to your own facts."

— DANIEL PATRICK MOYNIHAN

CONTENTS

PART III
A Long Arc Bending Toward Reason: 1900–1960

PART IV
Big Bang: The 1960s and '70s

PART V
Fantasyland Scales: From the 1980s Through the Turn of the Century

PART VI

The Problem with Fantasyland: From the 1980s to the Present and Beyond

FANTASYLAND

1

Now Entering Fantasyland

THIS BOOK HAS BEEN GERMINATING FOR A LONG TIME. IN THE LATE 1990S I wrote a few articles pointing toward it—about American politics morphing into show business and baby boomers trying to stay forever young, about untrue conspiracy theories being mainstreamed and the explosion of talk radio as it became more and more about the hosts' wild opinions. In 1999 I published a novel about a TV producer who created two groundbreaking shows— a police drama in which the fictional characters interact with real police arresting real criminals, and a news program featuring scenes of the anchors' private lives.

But the ideas and arguments really started crystallizing in 2004 and 2005. First President George W. Bush's political mastermind Karl Rove introduced the remarkable phrase *reality-based community*. People "in the reality-based community," he told a reporter, "believe that solutions emerge from judicious study of discernible reality. That's not the way the world really works anymore." He said it with a sense of humor, but he was also deadly serious. A year later *The Colbert Report* went on the air. In the first few minutes of his first episode, Stephen Colbert, playing his right-wing populist character, performed a feature called The Word in which he riffed on a phrase. *"Truthiness,"* he said.

> Now I'm sure some of the "word police," the "wordinistas" over at Webster's, are gonna say, "Hey, that's not a word!" Well, anybody who knows me knows that I'm no fan of dictionaries or reference books. They're elitist. Constantly telling us what *is* or *isn't* true. Or what *did* or *didn't* happen. Who's *Britannica* to tell me the Panama Canal was finished in 1914? If I wanna say it happened in 1941, that's my right. I don't trust books—they're all fact, no heart. . . . Face it, folks, we are a divided nation . . . divided between those who think with their head and those who *know* with their heart. . . . Because that's where the truth comes from, ladies and gentlemen—the gut.

Whoa, yes, I thought: *exactly.* America had changed in this particular, peculiar way, I realized. Until the 2000s, *truthiness* and *reality-based community* wouldn't have made much sense as jokes.

My understanding of how this change occurred became clearer a few years later, when I started work on a novel about a group of kids who in the early 1960s role-play James Bond stories, and then in 1968, as college students, undertake a real-life Bond-like antigovernment plot. During the 1960s, reality and fantasy blurred problematically, for my characters and for plenty of real Americans. In the course of researching and thinking through that story, I came to understand the era and its impacts in a new way. For all the fun, and all the various positive effects of the social and cultural upheavals, I saw that it was also the Big Bang moment for truthiness. And if the 1960s amounted to a national nervous breakdown, we are mistaken to consider ourselves over it, because what people say about recovery is true: you're never really *cured.*

I realized too that this complicated American phenomenon I was trying to figure out had been not just decades but centuries in the making. In order to understand our weakness for fantasy of all kinds, I needed to follow the tendrils and branches and roots further back—all the way back, to America's beginnings.

You're not going to agree with me about all the various mental habits and beliefs and behaviors I classify here as imaginary or fantastical. You may find me too judgmental about matters of deep personal conviction. As I pass by fish in barrels, I will often shoot them. But I don't consider all religion or all alternative belief systems or all conspiracy theories or all impossible dreams misguided. Each of us is on a spectrum somewhere between the poles of rational and irrational. We all have hunches we can't prove and superstitions that make no sense.

What's problematic is going overboard, letting the subjective entirely override the objective, people thinking and acting as if opinions and feelings were just as true as facts. The American experiment, the original embodiment of the great Enlightenment idea of intellectual freedom, every individual free to believe anything she wishes, has metastasized out of control. From the start, our ultra-individualism was attached to epic dreams, sometimes epic fantasies—every American one of God's chosen people building a custom-made utopia, each of us free to reinvent himself by imagination and will. In America those more exciting parts of the Enlightenment idea have swamped the sober, rational, empirical parts.

Little by little for centuries, then more and more and faster and faster during the last half-century, Americans have given ourselves over to all kinds of magical thinking, anything-goes relativism, and belief in fanciful explanation, small and large fantasies that console or thrill or terrify us. And most of us haven't realized how far-reaching our strange new normal has become. The cliché would be the frog in the gradually warming pot, oblivious to its doom until too late.*

Much more than the other billion or two people in the rich world, we Americans believe—*really believe*—in the supernatural and miraculous, in Satan on Earth now, reports of recent trips to and from Heaven, and a several-thousand-year-old story of life's instantaneous creation several thousand years ago.

At the turn of the millennium, our financial industry fantasized that risky debt was no longer risky, so many tens of millions of Americans fantasized that they could live like rich people, given our fantasy that real estate would always and only increase in value.

We believe the government and its co-conspirators are hiding all sorts of monstrous truths from us—concerning assassinations, extraterrestrials, the genesis of AIDS, the 9/11 attacks, the dangers of vaccines, and so much more.

---

* In real life, frogs jump out before the water gets too hot. In the nineteenth-century experiment that apparently generated the idea, however, a frog was boiled to death—but its brain had been removed beforehand. Which was humane and, in the present context, makes the metaphor more apt.

We stockpile guns because we fantasize about our pioneer past, or in anticipation of imaginary shootouts with thugs and terrorists. We acquire military costumes and props in order to pretend we're soldiers—or elves or zombies—fighting battles in which nobody dies, and enter fabulously realistic virtual worlds to do the same.

And that was all before we became familiar with the terms *post-factual* and *post-truth,* before we elected a president with an astoundingly open mind about conspiracy theories, what's true and what's false, the nature of reality.

We have passed through the looking glass and down the rabbit hole. America has mutated into Fantasyland.

How widespread is this promiscuous devotion to the untrue? How many Americans now inhabit alternate realities? Any given survey of people's beliefs is only a sketch of what people in general really think, but from reams of research, drilling down and cross-checking and distilling data from the last twenty years, a rough, useful census of American belief, credulity, and delusion does emerge.

By my reckoning, the more or less solidly reality-based are a minority, maybe a third of us but almost certainly fewer than half. Only a third of us, for instance, believe with some certainty that CO_2 emissions from cars and factories are the main cause of Earth's warming. Only a third are sure the tale of creation in Genesis isn't a literal, factual account. Only a third strongly disbelieve in telepathy and ghosts.

Two-thirds of Americans believe that "angels and demons are active in the world." At least half are *absolutely certain* Heaven exists, ruled over by a personal God—not some vague force or universal spirit but a *guy.* More than a third of us believe not only that global warming is no big deal but that it's a hoax perpetrated by a conspiracy of scientists, government, and journalists.

A third believe that our earliest ancestors were humans just like humans today; that the government has, in league with the pharmaceutical industry, hidden evidence of "natural" cancer cures; that extraterrestrials have recently visited (or now reside on) Earth.

A quarter believe vaccines cause autism and that Donald Trump won the popular vote in the 2016 general election. A quarter believe that our previous president was (or is?) the Antichrist. A quarter believe in witches. Remarkably, no more than one in five Americans believe the Bible consists mainly of legends and fables—around the same number who believe that "the media or the government adds secret mind-controlling technology to television broadcast signals" and that U.S. officials were complicit in the 9/11 attacks.*

When I say that a third believe X or a quarter believe Y, it's important to understand that those are *different* thirds and quarters of the U.S. population. Various fantasy constituencies overlap and feed each other—for instance, belief in extraterrestrial visitation and abduction can lead to belief in vast government cover-ups, which can lead to belief in still more wide-ranging plots and cabals, which can jibe with a belief in an impending Armageddon involving Jesus. Fantasyland operates like the European Union, a collection of disparate domains of various sizes overlaid with a Schengen Area that allows citizens of any of the dozens of lands to travel freely among the others, the way Hungarians and Maltese can visit France or Iceland at will.

And like intra-European antipathies, the mutual contempt among Fantasyland regions can be as intense as their contempt for the reality-based. To many evangelicals, Pentecostals are heretics, and to evangelicals and Pentecostals, Mormons are heretics; Pat Robertson has called Scientology satanic; the Vatican considers Oprah's apostles misguided fools; different kinds of truthers regard each other as deluded. A lot of the people certain that GMOs are unsafe to eat, despite overwhelming scientific consensus to the contrary, deride deniers of climate science. Indeed, the history of Fantasyland could be rendered bracketologically, like college basketball, centuries of continuous playoffs, with particular teams losing (Puritans) and winning (Mormons) along the way and continuing to fight it out today.

Why are we like this?

That's what this book will explore. The short answer is *because we're Americans,* because being American means we can believe any damn thing we want, that our beliefs are equal or superior to anyone else's, experts be damned. Once people commit to that approach, the world turns inside out, and no cause-and-effect connection is fixed. The credible becomes incredible and the incredible credible.

The word *mainstream* has recently become a pejorative, shorthand for bias, lies, oppression by the elites. Yet that hated Establishment, the institutions and forces that once kept us from overdoing the flagrantly untrue or absurd—media, academia, politics, government, corporate America, profes-

---

* In this chapter, I've relied on survey data collected between 2000 and 2017 by the Pew Research Center, NORC at the University of Chicago (General Social Survey), the International Social Survey Programme, Gallup, Ipsos, YouGov, the Cooperative Congressional Election Study, Qualtrics, Public Policy Polling, Opinion Research Corporation, Scripps, Harris, and the Project on Climate Change Communication.

sional associations, respectable opinion in the aggregate—has enabled and
encouraged every species of fantasy over the last few decades.

A senior physician at one of America's most prestigious university hospitals promotes miracle cures on his daily TV show. Major cable channels air
documentaries treating mermaids, monsters, ghosts, and angels as real. A
CNN anchor speculated on the air that the disappearance of a Malaysian
airliner was a supernatural event. State legislatures and one of our two big
political parties pass resolutions to resist the imaginary impositions of a New
World Order and Islamic law. When a political scientist attacks the idea that
"there is some 'public' that shares a notion of reality, a concept of reason, and
a set of criteria by which claims to reason and rationality are judged," colleagues just nod and grant tenure. A white woman *felt* black, pretended to be,
and under those fantasy auspices became an NAACP official—and then,
busted, said, "It's not a costume . . . not something that I can put on and take
off anymore. I wouldn't say I'm African American, but I *would* say I'm black."
Bill Gates's foundation has funded an institute devoted to creationist pseudoscience. Despite his nonstop lies and obvious fantasies—rather, *because* of
them—Donald Trump was elected president. The old fringes have been
folded into the new center. The irrational has become respectable and often
unstoppable. As particular fantasies get traction and become contagious,
other fantasists are encouraged by a cascade of out-of-control tolerance. It's a
kind of twisted Golden Rule unconsciously followed: *If those people believe
that, then certainly we can believe this.*

Our whole social environment and each of its overlapping parts—
cultural, religious, political, intellectual, psychological—have become conducive to spectacular fallacy and make-believe. There are many slippery slopes,
leading in various directions to other exciting nonsense. During the last several decades, those naturally slippery slopes have been turned into a colossal
and permanent complex of interconnected, crisscrossing bobsled tracks with
no easy exit. *Voilà*: Fantasyland.

THE SCOPE OF THIS BOOK extends way beyond the contagion of clear-cut, fact-
checkable untruths. America's transformation finally clicked into focus for
me when I stepped back and broadened my field of vision. I saw that the
proliferation of delusions and illusions concerning the large subjects that
people have always debated—politics, religion, even science—is connected
to the proliferation and glut of the fictional and quasi-fictional coursing
through everyday American life.

What I'm calling Fantasyland isn't only a matter of falsehoods fervently believed but of people assembling make-believe *lifestyles* as well. Both kinds of fantasy—conspiracy theories and belief in magic on one hand and fantasy football and virtual reality on the other—make everyday existence more exciting and dramatic. And the modern tipping points for both kinds were the result of the same two momentous changes.

The first was that profound shift in thinking that swelled up in the 1960s, whereby Americans ever since have had a new rule set in their mental operating systems, even if they're certain *they* possess the *real* truth: *Do your own thing, find your own reality, it's all relative.* The paradigm can be explicit or implicit, conscious or unconscious, but it's the way we are now.

The second big enabling change was the new era of information and communications. Digital technology empowers real-seeming fictions of both types, the lifestyle and entertainment kinds as well as the ideological and religious and pseudoscientific kinds, in subtypes bright and dark. Among the one billion websites, believers in anything and everything can find thousands of fellow fantasists who share their beliefs, with collages of facts and "facts" to back them up. Before the Internet, crackpots were mostly isolated and surely had a harder time remaining convinced of their alternate realities. Now their devoutly believed opinions are all over the airwaves and the Web, just like actual news. Now all the fantasies look real.

Computers make fantasies that we (mostly) understand to be fantasies seem much more authentic as well. We can pretend we're anybody or anything from any time or galaxy. But online fantasy doesn't end when we exit the CGI realms of Dr. Ludvig Maxis and Lady Jaina Proudmoore. There's an immense gray zone outside the obvious fictions of games. Because we are anonymous online, we can become fictionalized versions of ourselves in real life, real people interacting with other real people in ways that not long ago we'd never dream or dare to do.

Each of the small fantasies and simulations we insert into our lives is harmless enough, replacing a small piece of the authentic but mundane here, another over there. The world looks a little more like a movie set and seems a little more exciting and glamorous, like Hitchcock's definition of drama—life with the dull bits cut out. Each of us can feel like a sexier hero in a cooler story, younger than we actually are if we're old or older if we're young. Over time the patches of unreality take up more and more space in our lives. Eventually the whole lawn becomes AstroTurf. We stop registering the differences between simulated and authentic, real and unreal.

In the old days, if you wanted a shot at becoming instantly rich, you had to travel to Las Vegas. In order to spend time walking around a razzle-dazzling fictional realm, if you weren't psychotic, you had to go to Disneyland. *Theme* was not a verb. Pornography was not ubiquitous. Cosmetic surgery was rare; breasts were not preternaturally large and firm, faces artificially smooth and tight. We didn't reenact military battles with realistic props for days on end. We hadn't yet fabricated the mongrel of melodrama and pseudodocumentary called reality TV.

Of course, having fake boobs or playing League of Legends probably doesn't make any individual more inclined to believe that she needs a dozen semiautomatic rifles for self-protection or that vaccines cause autism or that the Earth is six thousand years old. But we are freer than ever to custom-make reality, to believe whatever or to pretend to be whomever we wish. Which makes *all* the lines between actual and fictional blur and disappear more easily. Truth in general becomes flexible, a matter of personal preference. There is a functioning synergy among our multiplying fantasies, the large and small ones, the toxic and the individually entertaining ones, the ones we know to be fiction, the ones we kinda sorta believe, and the religious and political and scientific ones we're convinced aren't fantasies at all. Scientists warn about the "cocktail effect" concerning chemicals in the environment and drugs in the brain, where various substances "potentiate" other substances. I think it's like that. We've been drinking bottomless American cocktails mixed from all the different fantasy ingredients, and those various fantasies, conscious and semiconscious and unconscious, intensify the effects of the others.

We *like* this new ultrafreedom to binge, we insist on it, even as we fear and loathe the ways so many of our wrong-headed fellow Americans abuse it. When John Adams said in the 1700s that "facts are stubborn things," the overriding American principle of personal freedom was not yet enshrined in the Declaration or the Constitution, and the United States of America was itself still a dream. Two and a half centuries later the nation Adams cofounded has become a majority-rule de facto refutation of his truism: "our wishes, our inclinations" and "the dictates of our passions" now apparently *do* "alter the state of facts and evidence," because extreme cognitive liberty and the pursuit of happiness rule.

THIS IS NOT UNIQUE TO America, people treating real life as fantasy and vice versa, and taking preposterous ideas seriously. We're just uniquely immersed. In the *developed* world, our predilection is extreme, distinctly different in the breadth and depth of our embrace of fantasies of many different kinds. Sure, the physician whose fraudulent research launched the antivaccine movement was a Brit, and young Japanese *otaku* invented cosplay, dressing up as fantasy characters. And while there are believers in flamboyant supernaturalism and prophecy and religious pseudoscience in other developed countries, nowhere else in the rich world are such beliefs central to the self-identities of so many people. We are Fantasyland's global crucible and epicenter.

This is American exceptionalism in the twenty-first century. America has always been a one-of-a-kind place. Our singularity is different now. We're still rich and free, still more influential and powerful than any nation, practically a synonym for *developed country*. But at the same time, our drift toward credulity, doing our own thing, and having an altogether uncertain grip on reality has overwhelmed our other exceptional national traits and turned us into a less-developed country as well.

People tend to regard the Trump moment—this post-truth, alternative facts moment—as some inexplicable and crazy *new* American phenomenon. In fact, what's happening is just the ultimate extrapolation and expression of attitudes and instincts that have made America exceptional for its entire history—and really, from its prehistory. What I'm trying to do with this book is define and pin down our condition, to portray its scale and scope, to offer some fresh explanations of how our national journey deposited us here.

America was created by true believers and passionate dreamers, by hucksters and their suckers—which over the course of four centuries has made us susceptible to fantasy, as epitomized by everything from Salem hunting witches to Joseph Smith creating Mormonism, from P. T. Barnum to Henry David Thoreau to speaking in tongues, from Hollywood to Scientology to conspiracy theories, from Walt Disney to Billy Graham to Ronald Reagan to Oprah Winfrey to Donald Trump. In other words: mix epic individualism with extreme religion; mix show business with everything else; let all that steep and simmer for a few centuries; run it through the anything-goes 1960s and the Internet age; the result is the America we inhabit today, where reality and fantasy are weirdly and dangerously blurred and commingled.

I hope we're only on a long temporary detour, that we'll manage somehow to get back on track. If we're on a bender, suffering the effects of guzzling too much fantasy cocktail for too long, if that's why we're stumbling, manic and hysterical, mightn't we somehow sober up and recover? You would think. But first you need to understand how deeply this tendency has been encoded in our national DNA.

PART I

The Conjuring of America: 1517–1789

"The entire man is . . . to be seen in the cradle of the child. The growth of nations presents something analogous to this; they all bear some marks of their origin. If we were able to go back . . . we should discover . . . the primal cause of the prejudices, the habits, the ruling passions, and, in short, all that constitutes what is called the national character."

—ALEXIS DE TOCQUEVILLE,
Democracy in America (1835)

2

I Believe, Therefore I Am Right: The Protestants

IN THE BEGINNING, IT DIDN'T EVEN HAVE A REAL NAME: *THE NEW WORLD* WAS a placeholder, like the generic proxy NewCo that corporate lawyers nowadays temporarily assign to businesses their clients are creating. To its prospective white residents, the New World was practically an imaginary place. For them, America *began* as a fever dream, a myth, a happy delusion, a fantasy. In fact, it began as multiple fantasies, each embraced around 1600 by people so convinced of their thrilling, wishful fictions that most of them abandoned everything—friends, families, jobs, good sense, England, the known world—to enact their dreams or die trying. A lot of them died trying.

Ours was the first country ever designed and created from nothing, the first country *authored*, like an epic tale—at the very moment, as it happened, that Shakespeare and Cervantes were inventing modern fiction. The first English people in the New World imagined themselves as heroic can-do characters in exciting adventures. They were self-fictionalizing extremists who abandoned everything familiar because of their blazing *beliefs,* their long-shot hopes and dreams, their please-be-true fantasies.

But to extend Tocqueville's metaphor, if the first English undertakings in the New World constituted newborn America, the cradle of the nation, then let's go back a bit further and try to see how this singular infant came to be conceived.

A DEVOUT, KNOW-IT-ALL YOUNG THEOLOGY professor at a new provincial university south of Berlin disagrees with Christian doctrine and practice in some important ways. He's especially upset that the regional archbishop, in order to cover the costs of celebrating his elevation to cardinal, has encouraged local Christians to pay money to be forgiven their sins (and the sins of deceased loved ones), thereby reducing or eliminating the posthumous wait in purgatory. In addition to paying, the buyers of forgiveness were required to troop through the local church on All Saints' Day to admire its thousands of holy relics, most if not all of them fake. These included a piece of straw from baby Jesus's manger, threads from His swaddling clothes, a bit of Mary's breast milk, a hair from adult Jesus's beard, a piece of bread from the Last Supper, and a thorn from His crucifixion crown. The young theologian, appalled by the church's merchandising, writes an impassioned three-thousand-word critique in proto-PowerPoint form, nails it to the door of the church on All Saints' Eve, Halloween, and for good measure sends a copy of his screed to the archbishop himself.

If all this had happened in 1447, say, the episode might now be an obscure historical footnote. But because this young preacher, the Reverend Father Martin Luther, went public in 1517, a good half-century into the age of mechanical printing, his manifesto changed everything. The Ninety-five Theses were immediately printed, translated from Latin into local languages, distributed throughout Europe, and reprinted ad infinitum. Protestantism had been launched, an organized alternative to the Christian religious monopoly, Roman Catholicism.

After the launch of this new Christianity, the new printing enabled its spread. Luther's main complaint had been about the church's sale of phony VIP passes to Heaven. "There is no divine authority," one of his theses pointed out, "for preaching that the soul flies out of the purgatory immediately [when] the money clinks in the bottom of the chest." Within a few decades that was moot anyhow, because the Vatican ended the practice of selling salvation. However, Luther had two bigger ideas, revolutionary ideas, that became foundational both to his religion and to America.

He insisted that clergymen have no special access to God or Jesus or truth. *Everything* a Christian needed to know was in the Bible. So every individual Christian believer could and should read and interpret Scripture for him- or herself. Every believer, Protestants said, was now a priest.

This would have been a doomed, quixotic dream any earlier. According to the Vatican's long-standing regulation, only priests were permitted to own Bibles, particularly Bibles translated from Latin into modern languages. It was a rule easy to enforce, because Bibles were extremely rare and expensive. In the 1450s, when Johannes Gutenberg printed the first book—a Latin Bible—there were only thirty thousand books *of any kind* in all of Europe, about one for every twenty-five hundred people. But by the time Luther launched the Reformation in 1517, sixty years later, twenty *million* books had been printed—and more of them were Bibles than anything else.

Print it, and they will come. During the century after printed English Bibles appeared, the literacy rate among English people tripled. Now millions of Christians were able to make good on Luther's DIY Christianity. The Catholic Church and its priestly elite were disintermediated. Disruptive innovation? No new technology, during the thousand years between gunpowder and the steam engine, was as disruptive as the printing press, and Protestantism was its first viral cultural phenomenon.

Apart from devolving religious power to ordinary people—that is, critically expanding individual liberty—Luther's other big idea was that belief in the Bible's supernatural stories, especially those concerning Jesus, was the *only* prerequisite for being a good Christian. You couldn't earn your way into Heaven by performing virtuous deeds. Having a particular set of beliefs was all that mattered. (And in strict early Protestantism, even those didn't guarantee you entry.)

The original Protestant grievance seems like a strike on behalf of reason—that paying money or staring at (fake) relics couldn't expedite souls into Heaven. But it's only more fair and logical, not really more rational. It's like arguing whether the miller's daughter in Rumpelstiltskin, if she had mispronounced the dwarf's name, would have been set free. The disagreements dividing Protestants from Catholics were about the internal consistency of the magical rules within their common fantasy scheme.

However, out of the new Protestant religion, a new proto-American attitude emerged during the 1500s. Millions of ordinary people decided that they, each of them, had the right to decide what was true or untrue, regardless of what fancy experts said. And furthermore, they believed, passionate fantastical *belief* was the key to everything. The footings for Fantasyland had been cast.

3

All That Glitters: The Gold-Seekers

DURING THE 1500S TOO, EUROPEAN FANTASIES OF *WORLDLY* SPLENDORS HAD just acquired a thrilling new inspiration and focus. In 1492 Columbus had sailed west in search of a shorter route by sea from Europe to Asia that might replace the overland Silk Road trip—an impossible dream then and for four hundred years afterward. Instead of Japan, he got the Bahamas. But he had discovered a New World. It was a blank slate on which fantastic wealth and glory could be imagined from three thousand miles away.

More European explorers quickly followed and would keep coming, many of them pursuing the dream of a Northwest Passage. That was the dream of Captain John Smith at the beginning of the 1600s when he sailed to the New World, funded by English investors. Imagining that the Potomac River led all the way to the Pacific Ocean, Smith got only as far as Bethesda, Maryland. Passage to Asia was also the dream in 1609 of the Englishman Henry Hudson, who got only as far as Albany. A year later English investors who wanted to believe the Arctic-trade-route dream financed Hudson to try again. This time instead of China, he made it to Ontario; when Hudson

wanted to keep going west, his crew, not as enraptured by the fantasy, muti-
nied; Captain Hudson was never seen again.

But the Spaniards who followed Columbus, instead of searching in vain
for a Northwest Passage to Asia, headed southwest. There they discovered
advanced civilizations with cities, the Aztec in Mexico and the Inca in South
America. And there too they found the Aztecs' and Incas' gold—which they
stole and mined for more than a century, thereby establishing a transatlantic
empire.

The English envied the suddenly powerful Spanish—and their New
World gold in particular.

If there was so much treasure for the taking in the southern reaches, why
not thousands of miles closer, in the north, in the lands closest to England?
Thus the quest for gold became a fetish for would-be English colonists as the
1500s turned into the 1600s. It also established a theme we'll encounter
again and again: around some plausible bit of reality, Americans leap to con-
coct wishful (or terrified) fictions they ardently believe to be true.

A young Oxford graduate and royal factotum named Richard Hakluyt
was among the most excited and influential of England's America enthusiasts
during the 1580s and '90s. He cherry-picked the reports of earlier explorers,
many of them second- and thirdhand, to depict a perfectly ripe paradise. All
those probes into eastern North America, he wrote in a forty-thousand-word
manuscript, "prove infallibly unto us that gold, silver . . . precious stones, and
turquoises, and emeralds . . . have been by them found" up and down the
coast. The southern part "had in the land gold and silver"; a bit to the north
there was also sure to be gold because "the colour of the land doth altogether
argue it"; and farther north too "there is mention of silver and gold." At the
time, England's population was growing faster than its economy, so Hakluyt
proposed shipping off "idle men" to America and "setting them to work in
mines of gold."

It was inconvenient that humans already inhabited the northern New
World. However, Hakluyt reported that the natives were "people good and of
a gentle and amiable nature, which willingly will obey." And North America's
population density was less than 5 percent of Britain's, so to the newcomers
it appeared essentially empty, a tabula rasa ready to be transformed into some
brand of English utopia.

Hakluyt's breathless chronicle of America had been commissioned by
the thirty-year-old aristocrat, poet, rake, adventurer, zealous Protestant, and
gold-mad New World enthusiast Walter Raleigh. He was a charming, larger-
than-life up-and-comer—a stereotypical go-go American before English

America even existed. As soon as he'd had Hakluyt write his report on the
New World, meant to convince Queen Elizabeth to colonize, Raleigh over
the course of just three years became *Sir* Walter Raleigh; got the royal franchise to exploit and govern the eastern coast of North America; and sent
three separate expeditions of Englishmen to get the gold. They found none.

Although Raleigh never visited North America himself, he believed that in
addition to its gold deposits, his realm might somehow be the biblical Garden
of Eden. English clergymen had calculated from the Bible that Eden was at a
latitude of thirty-five degrees north—*just like Roanoke Island,* they said. And
there was still more fresh (hearsay) evidence of divine magic in Virginia: a
botanist's book, *Joyful News of the New Found World,* reported that various
plants unique to America cured all diseases. A famous English poet published
his "Ode to the Virginian Voyage," calling Virginia "Earth's only Paradise" where
Britons would "get the pearl and gold"—and plenty of English people imagined
that it was literally a new Eden.* Alas, no. A large fraction of the first settlers
dispatched by Raleigh became sick and died. He dispatched a second expedition of gold-hunters. It also failed, and all those colonists died.

But Sir Walter continued believing the dream of gold. He failed to find
the legendary golden city of El Dorado when he sailed to South America in
1595, but that didn't stop him from propagating the fantasy in England. He
published a book about it that consisted of secondhand historical anecdotes
meant to make the dream seem real. Raleigh helped invent the kind of elaborate pseudoempiricism that in the centuries to come would become a permanent feature of Fantasyland testimonials—about religion, about quack
science, about conspiracy, about whatever was being urgently sold.

In 1606 the new English king, James, despite Raleigh's colonization disasters, gave a franchise to two new private enterprises, the Virginia Company of London and the Virginia Company of Plymouth, to start colonies.
The southern one, under the auspices of London, they named Jamestown
after the monarch. Their royal charter was clear about the main mission: "to
dig, mine, and search for all Manner of Mines of Gold . . . And to HAVE and
enjoy the Gold." As Tocqueville wrote in his history two centuries later, "It
was . . . gold-seekers who were sent to Virginia. No noble thought or concep-

---

* More than a century later an English land promoter trying to kick-start Georgia was
still using the same selling points: it was "the most delightful country of the Universe," at
least as nice as biblical "Paradise [and] lies in the same latitude with Palestine herself . . .
pointed out by God's own choice, to bless . . . a favorite people." Also: it had *silver mines,*
he was certain.

tion above gain presided over the foundation of the new settlements." Two-thirds of those first hundred gold-seekers promptly died. But the captain of the expedition returned to England claiming to have found "gold showing mountains."

Hakluyt, a director of the London Company, never managed to get to America but never stopped believing in the gold. Sure, none had been found *yet,* he admitted in a presentation to fellow executives in 1609, but an Englishman who spoke Indian languages and had been on earlier expeditions said that "to the southwest of our old fort in Virginia, the Indians often informed him . . . there was a great melting of red metall. Beside, our own Indians have lately revealed either this or another rich mine . . . near certain mountains lying" just a bit west of the failed settlement.

No gold was found. Captain John Smith, looking for a navigable westward route to the Pacific rather than gold, was not completely exempt from gullibility—he reported as fact a native's claim that people on Chesapeake Bay hunt "apes in the mountains." But he famously did not believe in the dream of instant, easy mineral wealth. "There was no talk, no hope, no work, but dig gold, work gold, refine gold, and load gold," Smith wrote of his fellow Jamestown colonists, "golden promises [that] made all men their slaves in hope of recompense." In fact, Jamestown ore they dug and refined and shipped to England turned out to be iron pyrite, fool's gold.

Anxious investors in London demanded the colonists produce at least one chunk of real gold. In 1610, three years into the operation, they dispatched a new man to set things right, who arrived just as the surviving colonists finally abandoned the dream and set sail home for England. Lord De La Warr persuaded them to disembark and buck up; he led a team inland to search for another rumored Indian gold mine, where De La Warr's men killed some Indians, and finally . . . found no gold.

The gold fantasy wasn't limited to colonists in the South. Those dispatched at the same time by the Plymouth Company, 120 of them, landed up on the Maine coast, also looking for gold and a faster route to Asia. They found signs of neither. But their desperation to believe the impossible is funny and sad. No gold so far, the colony president wrote home, but "the natives constantly affirm that in these parts there are nutmegs, mace and cinnamon." Tropical spices growing in New England? "They [also] positively assure me that . . . distant not more than seven days' journey from our fort [is] a sea large and wide and deep . . . which cannot be any other than the Southern Sea, reaching to the regions of China." Unlike their Virginia compatriots, however, the English colonists in Maine quickly accommodated reality and admitted defeat. Half left a few months after arriving, the rest six months later. They were not credulous or imaginative enough to become Americans.

But . . . maybe they just hadn't talked to the *right* natives! Or looked in the right places! In 1614 yet another Plymouth Company expedition sailed to New England, this one exclusively in pursuit of gold. They had an inside man aboard, a native who'd been captured and enslaved by an earlier Plymouth Company ship off Cape Cod. The Indian had spent his time in captivity in London learning English and the nature of his captors' shiny-metal fixation, so he concocted a story just for them: *There's a gold mine on my own island,* he lied, *and I'll take you back there to claim it.* When the English anchored off Martha's Vineyard, he jumped ship, and his tribal brothers covered his escape with bow-and-arrow fire from canoes. The Englishmen realized they'd been played and sailed home.

Down in Virginia, meanwhile, more than six thousand people had emigrated to Jamestown by 1620, the equivalent of a midsize English city at the time. At least three-quarters had died but not the abiding dream. People kept coming and believing, hopefulness becoming delusion. It was a gold rush with no gold. *Fifteen years* after Jamestown's founding, a colonist wrote a friend to request a shipment of nails, cutlery, vinegar, cheese—and also to make excuses for why he hadn't quite yet managed to get rich: "By reason of my sickness & weakness I was not able to travel up and down the hills and dales of these countries but doo now intend every day to walk up and down the hills for good Minerals here is both gold [and] silver."

The sickness and weakness and death continued. Gold remained a chimera. Two decades into the seventeenth century, English America was a failing start-up, a vaporware tragedy and farce. But back in England the investors and their promotional agents continued printing posters, hyperbolic testimonials, and dozens of books and pamphlets, organizing lotteries, and fanning out hucksterish blue smoke. Thus the first English-speaking Americans tended to be the more wide-eyed and desperately wishful. "Most of the 120,000 indentured servants and adventurers who sailed to the [South] in the seventeenth century," according to the University of Pennsylvania historian Walter McDougall's history of America, *Freedom Just Around the Corner,* "did not know what lay ahead but were taken in by the propaganda of the sponsors." The historian Daniel Boorstin went even further, suggesting that "American civilization [has] been shaped by the fact that there was a kind of natural selection here of those people who were willing to believe in advertising." Western civilization's first great advertising campaign was created in order to inspire enough dreamers and suckers to create America.

As a get-rich-quick enterprise, Virginia was a bust. The colonists who stayed resorted to the familiar drudgery of agriculture, although the cash crop that saved them was a harbinger of a certain future America—it was indigenous, novel, glamorous, inessential, psychoactive, and addictive: tobacco.

Another leader of the colonization enthusiasts was Francis Bacon, the English government official and philosopher, who at the time was also laying foundations for science and the Enlightenment. He was bracingly clear-eyed about the New World project, and he seemed to understand better than any of his proto-American contemporaries the distorting power of wishful belief, how fantasy can trump fact. "The human understanding," he wrote in 1620,

> when it has once adopted an opinion (either as being the received opinion or as being agreeable to itself) draws all things else to support and agree with it. And though there be a greater number and weight of instances to be found on the other side, yet these it either neglects and despises, or else by some distinction sets aside and rejects; in order that by this great and pernicious predetermination the authority of its former conclusions may remain inviolate. . . . And such is the way of all superstition, whether in astrology, dreams, omens, divine judgments, or the like; wherein men, having a delight in such vanities, mark the events where they are fulfilled, but where they fail, though this happen much oftener, neglect and pass them by.

In his London circles, Bacon said, it was all "gold, silver, and temporal profit" driving the colonization project, not "the propagation of the Christian faith." For the imminent next wave of English would-be Americans, however, propagating a particular set of Christian superstitions, omens and divine judgments were more than just lip-service cover for dreams of easy wealth. For them, the prospect of colonization was *all about* the export of their supernatural fantasies to the New World.

4

Building Our Own Private Heaven on Earth: The Puritans

THE FIRST ENGLISH COLONIZERS' VISIONS OF GOLD AND A NORTHWEST Passage were not totally mad. Two hundred years later gold *was* discovered and mined in Virginia. Three hundred years later a tiny ship *did* reach the Pacific by means of a Northwest Passage through the Canadian Arctic. But in the 1620s, after four decades of English failure in the New World, reasonable people wouldn't have continued risking their lives and fortunes pursuing impossible dreams. The original hypotheses, gold for the plucking and a maritime route to Asia, were "falsifiable," as logicians say—and were finally falsified by the evidence. No gold. No shortcut to China and India. European emigrants might be able to make livings in the New World, occasionally even get rich, but only in ways they'd done in the Old World, by raising and making and selling stuff. So in seventeenth-century Virginia, as they gave up gold-hunting for tobacco-growing, empiricism and pragmatism beat back wishfulness and fantasy.

On the other hand, most supernatural religious beliefs aren't falsifiable. The existence of a God who created and manages the world according to a fixed eternal plan, Jesus's miracles and resurrection, Heaven, Hell, Satan's presence on Earth—these can never be disproved.

Queen Elizabeth had been the first Protestant English monarch. Her successor James was a Protestant too. As soon as he took the throne, he ordered up a new official English translation of the Bible—the King James Version, which four hundred years later remains the most popular Bible in America. Its creation was under way when King James, supreme governor of the Church of England, chartered those two companies to start a British empire in America. So naturally the companies' mission statements included evangelism—the "propagating of Christian Religion to such People as yet live in Darkness and miserable Ignorance," the native "Infidels and Savages." By the early 1600s, most people in England (and a third of Europeans) were Protestant. In less than a century, an anti-Establishment sect, the Protestants, had become the Establishment.

Yet unlike Roman Catholicism, with its old global hierarchy and supreme leader, the new Protestant Christianity was by its nature fractious and unstable, invented almost within living memory by uncompromising rebels who couldn't abide interpretations and rules issued by expert super-clergy. It was an innovative new religion successful at a time when innovations were transforming the rest of Europe's cultures and economies. Protestantism was thus part of an exciting tide of novelty, along with the printing press, global trade, the Renaissance, the beginnings of modern science, and the Enlightenment. Its unique selling proposition was radical. When official leaders lose their way, pious anybodies can and must decide the new improved truth on their own—that is, by reading Scripture, each individual determines the correct meaning of the Christian fantasies. The Protestants' founding commitment to fierce, decentralized, do-it-yourself truth-finding and spiritual purity naturally led to the continuous generation of self-righteous sectarian spin-offs.

The first extremists emerged as an English movement when Protestantism was only a few decades old. They considered the new Establishment and its priests both too dictatorial and too loose. Too dictatorial for demanding that every local church and every believer strictly adhere to headquarters' interpretations of the biblical stories, and too loose for letting people get away with ignoring the Bible and God when they weren't in church. Like Luther and the original Protestants who'd rejected the Catholic Establishment, these English ultra-Protestants considered themselves holier, godlier, and more unsullied than the new church Establishment. The Christians in charge ridiculed them as "Puritans," and the term stuck.

The theological disagreements between the Puritans and the Church of England were fairly slight. They were nearly all Calvinists—that is, they agreed with the rules of the game as formulated by John Calvin, a theologian a generation younger than Luther who had, not coincidentally, trained as a lawyer: only a small minority of people go to Heaven, he adjudicated, and those "elect" were chosen by God before they were born, before the beginning of time, so nothing anybody did in life could change his or her probably hellbound trajectory.

Because their (fantastical, terrifying) basic beliefs were so similar, historians tend to cast the disputes as nothing but a power struggle, interest-group politics in the guise of holier-than-thou one-upmanship. But rationalists and cynics—that is, most modern scholars—are comfortable imputing only rational and cynical motives. What really distinguished the Puritans from the mainstream were matters of personality, demeanor. To be a Puritan was to embody uncompromising zeal. (They were analogous to certain American political zealots today, who more than disagreeing with their Establishment's ideas just can't stand their reasonable-seeming manner.) Moreover, a good Christian life, the Puritans believed, was one *consumed* by Christianity.

The most extreme of the extremists were the Separating Puritans, who wanted to form their own separate churches apart from the Church of England. Among this hard core were a pair of ministers and their congregants in and around the perfectly named village of Scrooby. They decided to go further, separating not just from the Church of England but from England itself. In 1609 they exiled themselves to the closest foreign place where Protestantism was on the rise, the Netherlands.

But changing where they lived didn't change who they were—sticklers and malcontents. They lived in Leiden, a place full of all the normal real-world ungodliness of a large Dutch city. Leiden was also the center of a liberal sect of Protestants. In other words, the English Puritans in Holland were surrounded by a new species of disgusting heresy. For them, hell for now was other people who didn't share their beliefs with full fervor. Returning home was out of the question, especially given the rise of anti-Puritan forces in the Church of England.

So now they would go all the way. Ferociously believing every miracle and myth in an ancient text wasn't enough. They were no longer just a group of rash, disapproving English rustics living in a European city. They were a tribe wandering for years in exile, just like in Exodus, determined to find a promised land, as prophesied in the Book of Revelation. Because, really, once you are free—no, *obliged*—to figure out the fantastical truth on your own, and then create your own new religious species around that truth (Protestantism), and then a new subspecies (Puritanism), and then a sub-subspecies (Separating Puritanism), what's stopping you from realizing the ultimate dream of conjuring your own utopian nation dedicated to your perfect new religion?

Where to go? Swampy Virginia was already occupied by the money-grubbing nominal Christians who'd failed to find gold and now grew tobacco. But Britain's northern American parts, still unoccupied by white people, sounded perfect. After John Smith had had enough of Virginia's gold freaks and they of him, he sailed north on a reconnaissance mission and in 1616 published an account of what he found. He raved about the cornucopia of stone and timber for building and fish to eat, as well as the "moderate" climate. (He visited in spring and summer.) "Who can but approve this a most excellent place, both for health and fertility? And of all of the four parts of the world that I have yet seen not inhabited"—not counting as inhabitants the natives he'd mentioned earlier in this very account—"I would rather live here than anywhere." Four years later the several dozen Leiden ultra-Puritans sailed away from corrupt, contentious Europe for this latest Edenic piece of the New World, to create their New Jerusalem in New England.

In other words, America was founded by a nutty religious cult.

When I was taught American history as a child, I must have learned about Jamestown, but it made no impression on me. I knew almost nothing about the failed Virginia gold rush until I began this book. In school and in popular culture, the invention of America was and still is focused on the later, northern group of English settlers—the Pilgrims, the *Mayflower,* Plymouth Rock. Jamestown is tucked away, an unimportant out-of-town tryout or failed beta test.

It's telling that Americans know and celebrate Plymouth but Jamestown hardly at all. The myth we've constructed says that the first nonnative new Americans who *mattered* were the idealists, the hyperreligious people seeking freedom to believe and act out their passionate, elaborate, all-consuming fantasies. The more run-of-the-mill people seeking a financial payoff, who abandoned their dream once it was defunct? Eh. We also prefer to talk about *Pilgrims* rather than *Puritans,* because the former has none of the negative connotations that stuck permanently to the latter.

The Pilgrims—at least the most vehemently true-believing half of them—were the Puritan pioneers in America.* One of the Pilgrim leaders stayed at Plymouth only a couple of weeks before returning home to encour-

---

* Their less pious fellow travelers they called the Strangers, one of whom, arriving in 1623, a year and a half after the *Mayflower,* was evidently an ancestor of mine.

age other Separatists to come. His 1622 pamphlet, *Reasons and Consider-ations Touching the Lawfulness of Removing out of England into the Parts of America,* explained that the New World was what Israel had been for the ancient Jews, the promised land for God's new chosen people, the Puritans. It was "a vast and empty chaos" where the natives did nothing useful or civi-lized, and their "imperial governor," the local Indian chief, conveniently "hath acknowledged the king, majesty of England, to be his master and com-mander." Yet even after half the Pilgrims managed to survive, their exodus scheme didn't exactly take off. After a decade of existence, Plymouth Planta-tion had only three hundred residents; the population of Jamestown was more than ten times as large.

The next king, Charles I, was even less enamored of his annoying Puri-tan subjects than his father James had been. After he married a very Catholic French woman whom he shamelessly called Maria, the feeling was com-pletely mutual. The Church of England was moving in an even more anti-Puritan direction, becoming theologically more reasonable and stricter about church ritual—in other words, more *Catholic.*

Right around the time Plymouth's Pilgrims started calling themselves Pilgrims, a larger group of Puritans—extremists of a better social station—talked themselves into leaving England and creating their own American re-ligious utopia. And they talked the king's deputies into giving their Massachusetts Bay Company a royal charter. They negotiated a 2 percent share of any precious metals they might find in their piece of America, which was kind of a feint. The king and his royal bureaucrats were fine doing busi-ness with men who fantasized about gold—whereas this new set of Puritan colonists' true fantasy was creating a *better* theocracy a short sail up the coast from Plymouth. Eight ships had arrived in Plymouth from 1620 to 1628. During 1629 and 1630 alone, more than two dozen sailed into Massachusetts Bay, from which a thousand Puritans disembarked. To the People of God, as they called themselves, the Zion in the wilderness they'd imagined now seemed real.* Dreams could come true.

"What is it that distinguisheth New England from other Colonies and Plantations in America?" a Massachusetts Bay Colony minister asked in a sermon two generations on. It was a rhetorical question. Tocqueville made the same point about the defining oddness of these early white Americans with a vision and a plan to realize it, noting a century and a half later that they

---

* The word *wilderness* first got currency by means of the first English translations of the Bible, in which it appears 280 times.

didn't "cross the Atlantic to improve their situation or to increase their wealth. It was a purely intellectual craving that called them from the comforts of their former homes; and in facing the inevitable sufferings of exile, their object was the triumph of an idea. . . . New England was a region given up to the dreams of fancy." Back then, "dreams of fancy" meant *fantasy*.

The fantasy endured, and the fantasists spread out. Several decades after the first Puritans arrived, a pastor in New Hampshire delivered a sermon warning that normal folks were unwelcome in these parts. "It concerneth New England always to remember," he said, "that they are a plantation *religious*, not a plantation of *trade*. . . . Let merchants, and such as are increasing . . . remember this, that *worldly gain* was not the end and design of the people of New England, but *religion*."

The Puritans are conventionally considered more "moderate" than the Pilgrims. This is like calling al-Qaeda more moderate than ISIS.* The Massachusetts Bay Colony Puritans' theology was really no less mad. The second-wave Puritans were more posh and educated than the Pilgrims, less contemptuous of the ruling English swells. Their self-identity, before they came to America, was not quite so wrapped up in being off the Church of England reservation. They seemed moderate then and now because they were the Man—well spoken, well dressed, sober, intellectual, accustomed to power. But they were moderate in style, not in substance. If tolerance is part of what we mean by moderation, the Pilgrims in Plymouth were actually more moderate—they managed to coexist with the Strangers. *Theocracy* had just entered the English language—and to the Puritans, it was a good concept. They forbade Church of England clergy from setting foot in their new American theocracy in Boston and Salem, hung Quakers, and passed a law to hang any Catholic priests who might dare show up.

The Middle Ages are generally reckoned to have ended at least a century before America's founding. By the 1620s in the Old World, literal belief in biblical end-time prophecies was fading, along with other medieval artifacts.

But not among the Puritans. They took the Bible as literally as they could, especially this most spectacular piece of it. That the Catholics had for centuries downplayed end-of-the-world prophecies was, for Puritans, all the more reason those prophecies must be true. An influential Puritan scholar at Cambridge University published *Key of the Revelation Searched and Demonstrated* in 1627. He explained that the Antichrist's big move had not already

* In fact, the first governor of the Massachusetts Bay Colony tried to pass a law requiring that women wear veils in public.

occurred, as Protestant conventional wisdom had it, taking over the Vatican. No, it was going to happen in the future—the near future. Plus, Christ's return and reign wouldn't be some airy-fairy symbolic spiritual thing but a *real* kingdom on *real* Earth. And ground zero of the coming Apocalypse, God versus Satan, would be *in America*.

Even before he'd arrived here, the Boston Puritans' first leader, John Winthrop, was talking to his shipmates about the end-time. The famous bit of his sermon, "We are as a city upon a hill," has endured because that *as* makes it a simile, endlessly adaptable as a happy, self-flattering metaphor for America. But three sentences later Winthrop's end-is-near scenario isn't metaphorical at all. "As the latter days begin to unfold," Winthrop said, "this may indeed be the city, the new Jerusalem that's unfolding." His most important successor as a leader of the New England theocracy, Increase Mather, also preached "that the coming of Christ to raise the dead and to judge the Earth" might happen any minute now. Mather even had evidence: meteors or comets visible in the skies over Boston, for instance, could be signs of God's unhappiness and "presage great calamities." As the religious historian Paul Boyer says, "The Puritans really expected the end of time to come very, very soon."

When Mather took over as president of America's first college, Harvard, his twenty-two-year-old son, Cotton, who'd been preaching sermons since he was sixteen, took over for his father as pastor of Boston's main church. The younger man soon began issuing specific dates for the end of days and kept doing so for the rest of his life. *Six years from now! Okay, thirty-nine years from now—no, wait, fewer than twenty!* And when that year passed normally, Cotton Mather announced it would actually be the *following* year.

If one has enough belief in the supernatural plan, if one's *personal faith* is strong enough, false prophecies are just unfortunate miscalculations that don't falsify anything. If you're fanatical enough about enacting and enforcing your fiction, it becomes indistinguishable from nonfiction.

But what made the Puritans so American, as they self-consciously invented America, wasn't just the Protestant zealotry. Rather, it was the paradoxical combination of their beliefs and temperament. They were over-the-top magical thinkers but also prolific readers and writers. They were excruciatingly rational fantasists who regarded theology as an elaborate scientific endeavor. They were whacked-out visionaries but also ambitious bourgeois *doers,* accomplished managers and owners and makers. They were theologically medieval—but traveling three thousand miles to create a utopia led by university-educated gentlemen was a radically modern endeavor. They were crazed *and* pragmatic, Quixotes with know-how who went to find a place where nobody would mock them for their delusions and dreams.* So the seeds of America in New England were a peculiar hybrid generated from the cusp of the Middle Ages and the Enlightenment, containing elements of both—as the Harvard historian Samuel Eliot Morrison wrote, "the Englishmen who had accepted the Reformation without the Renaissance."

And their peculiar beliefs and peculiar real-world situation also made them—made Americans—exceptional in another way. If you're extremely religious people who are determined to understand everything factually and precisely; who hate allegorical or metaphorical interpretations of the Bible—and hate art because it could lead you to consider the Bible a book of allegory and metaphor; who love scientific scholarship; and who are personally responsible for your own daily survival in an unforgiving wilderness, aren't you pretty much bound to become the most *literal-minded* fantasists ever?

* The first English translation of *Don Quixote* was published in 1620, the year the Pilgrims started their American adventure.

5

The God-Given Freedom to Believe in God

THE MASSACHUSETTS BAY COLONY GREW FAST, FROM A POPULATION OF A thousand to forty thousand in its first decade or so. One of them was Anne Hutchinson, daughter of a minister, wife of a well-to-do merchant, mother of a dozen children, Boston neighbor of Governor Winthrop, and a charismatic, *extremely* impassioned Puritan. She promptly set herself up as a de facto preacher. Every week dozens of women came to the Hutchinsons' big house to hear her critiques of the previous Sunday's church sermons and ask questions about sin, salvation, and God. *Since the Lord decided before the beginning of time which of us will spend eternity with Him,* she explained to her listeners, *any one of us might hold a winning ticket, regardless of our status in the here and now. The clergy's learning and degrees and titles give them no special lock on godliness.*

But she didn't just argue the logic and quibble over the fine points of the beliefs they all shared. No, she gleamed with an absolute conviction, *knew* she was Heaven-bound, *felt* the truth in her gut. The Puritans in Massachusetts "were the first Americans to enact the paradigm that underlies all romantic projects," as the historian Andrew Delbanco says: they "dared to assert the direct apprehension by the believer of the divine." Hutchinson took that paradigm and upped the ante, calling the leaders' bluff. People "look at her as a prophetess," Governor Winthrop anxiously wrote in his journal. She claimed to have some kind of sixth sense for divining who was or wasn't a member of God's special elect.

Men began attending the gatherings as well, and she added a second weekly session. Enlightened and emboldened, her followers took to walking out of church in the middle of sermons by ministers they weren't *feeling*. Anne Hutchinson, resident in America for only a thousand days, was leading a movement to make her colony of magical thinkers even more fervid. Protestantism had started as a breakaway movement of holier-than-thou zealots—and in the even-holier-than-thou zealots' state-of-the-art utopia, they now had a *still-holier*-than-thou mystic militant in their midst.

Once a faction of the colony's leaders signed on to Hutchinson's more magical, passionate, extra-pure Puritanism, she became problematic. Sure, individuals sometimes overflowed with the Holy Spirit. And yes, everybody's a Bible-reading amateur theologian; the "priesthood of all believers" made Protestants Protestants rather than sheeplike Catholics or crypto-Catholics. *But come on, we've got a brand-new theocracy to run here* (and at that moment a war to wage against a native tribe in Connecticut). Anne Hutchinson had gone rogue.

She was charged and tried for defaming ministers. Governor Winthrop served as chief judge. On the first day of her testimony in November 1637, she stayed within the bounds of Puritan intellectualism, batting scriptural references back and forth, arguing that her religious meetings weren't public events. She didn't *quite* tell them she was godlier than they, but her contempt was clear. "We are your judges," Winthrop told her, "and not you ours." She fainted.

When her trial resumed the next day, she let it all hang out. It wasn't just the Bible that guided her but the Holy Spirit—that is, God, speaking to her personally, just as He had spoken to people in the Bible. It was, she told them, "an immediate revelation. . . . by the voice of his own spirit to my soul. . . . God had said to me . . . 'I am the same God that delivered Daniel out of the lion's den, I will also deliver thee.'" Governor Winthrop and his forty fellow judges had assembled to convict her of something, and now she'd made it easy. Furthermore, she threatened them and their misguided regime with God's own wrath: "Therefore take heed how you proceed against me—for I know that, for this you go about to do to me, God will ruin you and your posterity and this whole state."

"*This* is the thing that has been the root of all the mischief," Winthrop bellowed, pointing at her. And also: "I am persuaded that the revelation she brings forth is *delusion.*" *We're* all *irritating, self-righteous Christian nuts,* he did not add, *but good God, woman, even we have our limits.*

"Mistress Hutchinson," a once and future Massachusetts governor among the judges said during the trial, "is deluded by the Devil." And a witness against her, one of her fellow shipmates on the passage from England, testified that she'd made "very strange and witchlike" pronouncements when they'd landed in America three years earlier. The court might have brought a conviction for witchcraft and executed her. Instead, they threw her out of the colony.

In the modern era, Anne Hutchinson is inevitably portrayed as the first great American heroine, a feminist crusader for religious liberty and the victim of a show trial. Undoubtedly her gender made her freelance shamanism even more appalling and unacceptable. The trial transcript, dozens of male judges and witnesses versus one female defendant, is a horrible, hilarious episode of mansplaining. One minister testified that she "had rather been husband than a wife; and a preacher than a hearer."

But the intolerance she experienced isn't what makes Anne Hutchinson a prototypically American figure. Protestant communities in Europe surely would've punished or exiled her as well, and by global standards, Massachusetts was not an unusually oppressive place for women. No, Hutchinson is so American because she was so confident in herself, in her intuitions and idiosyncratic, subjective understanding of reality. She's so American because, unlike the worried, pointy-headed people around her, she didn't recognize ambiguity or admit to self-doubt. Her perceptions and beliefs were true *because they were hers* and because she felt them *so thoroughly* to be true. They weren't mere theories and opinions delivered by her Oxford- and Cambridge-educated antagonists. Hutchinson didn't have to study any book but the Bible to arrive at the truth. Because she *felt* it. She *knew* it. The great historian of Puritanism Perry Miller refers to her "fanatical anti-intellectualism"—in other words, a prototypical Fantasyland American.

The American Puritans were the Protestant avant-garde, and she was the most avant of all—a dissident persecuted and banished by a corrupt and self-serving elite, a self-righteous individual whose individual imagination was all that mattered. By claiming she had personal access to God, Hutchinson took a big piece of the nonconformist Protestant idea to an even more fantastical and perfectly American extreme.

It's hard for us to understand or empathize with our founding Puritans, not because of their wild religious beliefs—many of which a great many Americans still share—but because of their ferocious insistence on discipline. Alone among the Puritans, Anne Hutchinson is the one with whom American sensibilities today can connect, because America is now a nation where every individual is gloriously free to construct any version of reality he or she devoutly believes to be true. American Christianity in the twenty-first century resembles Hutchinson's version more than it does the official Christianity of her time.

In other words, Anne Hutchinson lost her battle in Cambridge but would finally win the war. For the Puritan leaders, it was their way or the highway. But in America there was an infinity of highways and new places not so far away where outcast true believers could move.

While Quaker Pennsylvania soon welcomed Christian zealots of almost every kind, the Quakers' famous civic reasonableness—tolerant, democratic, pacifist, protofeminist, abolitionist—tends to obscure their own founding zealotry: each person could directly commune with God, which variously took the form of prophecies, trancelike rants, and convulsions.

Hutchinson's fellow charismatic Massachusetts Puritan, the young minister Roger Williams, claimed no wizardly superpowers. Nevertheless, he was also problematic for the Boston theocrats—he disapproved of theocracy, and his hatred of the Church of England was a bit too self-righteously fervent. They convicted him of heresy and sedition shortly before they banished Hutchinson. He moved forty miles south to start a new colony, which he named for God's blessed omnipotence, Providence. Williams and Hutchinson were thus both key inventors of American individualism. He disagreed with the religious nonsense you spouted, but he would defend to the death your right to spout it; she was the crackpot case study for extreme freedom of thought and speech, insisting she be allowed to believe and tell people she had magical powers. Which Williams was willing to let her do in Providence, where she moved.

Today we tell ourselves a story of America's progress toward freedom of thought and a happy ending. Williams in Rhode Island and the Quaker William Penn in his new colony were indeed heroic progressives, separating the state from any one church.* The Massachusetts theocracy softened and eventually dissolved. Then a century later came Thomas Jefferson's Virginia Statute for Religious Freedom, the Constitution, and the First Amendment.

---

* Despite the official tolerance, however, no Catholic church was built in Rhode Island for the first two centuries of its existence.

All that was indeed progress. Disbelief was eventually permitted, at least legally.

But during our founding 1600s, as giants walked in Europe and the Age of Reason dawned—Shakespeare, Galileo, Bacon, Isaac Newton, René Descartes, Thomas Hobbes, John Locke, Baruch Spinoza—America was a primitive outlier. Individual freedom of thought in early America was specifically about the freedom to believe whatever supernaturalism you wished. Four centuries later that has been a freedom, revived and unfettered and run amok, driving America's transformation.

6

Imaginary Friends and Enemies: The Early Satanic Panics

AMERICANS HAVE ALWAYS BEEN DEVOUT BELIEVERS IN THE HIGHLY IMPLAUSI-
ble and impossible. And those beliefs, Christian and otherwise, always come
in both blissful and fearful forms. Fantasyland is both a deliriously happy and
nightmarishly scary place.

On the one hand, you might get eternal life, and America itself is at the
heart of God's plan for His forthcoming earthly kingdom. *Fantastic.* On the
other hand, you're definitely going to Hell if you're not a Christian and probably even if you are—and God is already angry at us for bungling America.
Uh-oh.

But an afterlife in Hell wasn't the only imaginary satanic problem America's pious Christian founders faced. The devil was already tormenting them
now, right where they were pursuing their happy fantasy of building God's
kingdom. Even before the new colonies in Massachusetts were established, a
Puritan minister had warned that "Satan visibly and palpably reigns" in
America "more than in any other known place of the world." What? Yes, another Puritan leader explained, as Christianity had spread through Europe

during the previous fifteen hundred years, taking market share, the devil at some point arranged for a swarm of Asian infidels to cross the Pacific Ocean to America—"had decoyed those miserable savages in hopes that the Gospel of our Lord Jesus Christ would never come here to destroy or disturb His absolute empire over them." The American Indians, in other words, weren't merely unbelievers—they were Satan's soldiers.* And even though the tribes were highly distinct entities, always fighting each other, they were sure to band together eventually to annihilate the colonists.

The Puritans, who had been conspiracy-fearing truth-tellers even before they turned themselves into Americans, became more fantastically so. They'd escaped one unholy conspiracy—the Antichrist and his popish confederates running the English churches—only to find themselves on the western front of the global holy war. They'd made their difficult (but thrilling!) pilgrimage from the frying pan into a terrible (but thrilling!) fire. Governor Increase Mather's son Cotton, after his father the most famous American Puritan minister, described the "Droves of Devils in our way" as "demons in the shape of armed Indians."

In *A Narrative of Troubles with the Indians,* another Harvard-educated minister and Puritan leader wrote that he'd seen from the start that the Indian troubles were a satanic plot: two chiefs in Maine he'd never met were "not without some show of a Kind of Religion, which . . . they have learned from the Prince of Darkness." Even the Indian-loving liberal wimp Roger Williams was appalled by their "hideous worships of . . . devils." Fortunately, the Almighty served up miracles to kill a lot of them—in the form of disease unwittingly carried by the white saints themselves. "It pleased God to visit these Indians with a great sickness and such mortality that a thousand . . . of them died," the governor of the Plymouth colony gratefully recorded.

For their first sustained war on Indians, however, the colonists recruited other presumed demons to help them exterminate a tribe of definite demons, the Pequots. The Pequot War's most famous episode was a one-day massacre in 1637 of hundreds of native people, including women and children. According to Increase Mather, his side won this war fought before he was born due "to the wonderful Providence of God."

---

* Not many decades earlier the founder of Protestantism had literally demonized an ethnic group of infidels. In *On the Jews and Their Lies,* Martin Luther wrote of "the unbearable, devilish burden of the Jews. . . . Wherever they have their synagogues, nothing is found but a den of devils." In order "to save our souls from the Jews, that is, from the devil," he recommended burning all synagogues and destroying Jews' houses, and that even "safe-conduct on the highways be abolished completely for the Jew."

Over the next two generations, as the English population quintupled, exceeding the Indians', the natives naturally grew . . . restless. As a result, after a half-century the settlers' long-standing fantasy of a pan-Indian conspiracy became self-fulfillingly real: the natives finally did form a multitribal alliance to fight back. The public case for wiping out the newly militant Indians remained supernatural, however. For Christians who imagined themselves battling satanic beasts, conventional rules of war no longer applied. Yet another Harvard-educated minister, serving as chaplain to one of Massachusetts's military units, exhorted his soldiers to "kill, burn, sink, destroy all sin and Corruption . . . which are professed enemies to Christ Jesus, and not to pity or spare any of them." The year of pitiless killing from the summer of 1675 through the summer of 1676 was among the most concentrated bloodbaths in American history. And a dozen years later came another, longer war that made good on the second part of the earliest American conspiracists' fears—that the pope's forces (the French) and Satan's (the Indians) would merge. Cotton Mather happened to see a cabbage root with two branches, which looked to him like swords and an Indian club—*clearly a warning from God* of this imminent new battle against the hounds of Hell, he preached, a "prodigious war *made* by the spirits of the invisible world upon the people of New-England . . . [by] the Indians, whose chief[s] . . . are well known . . . to have been horrid sorcerers, and hellish conjurers, and . . . conversed with demons."*

In Europe, the learned had entered The Age of Reason. In the New World, however, unreason had made a ferocious comeback.

IN ADDITION TO DEPLOYING INDIANS (and Catholics) against them, the early Americans understood that Satan might also enlist traitors among the good white English people themselves. Today most of us think of witches as a kind of independent magical species—a folk superstition, not part of the Christian scheme. And for the thousand years or so that Catholics ran Christianity, the church agreed: witchcraft officially didn't exist during the Middle Ages. But as soon as Protestantism emerged, so did alleged witches and witch hunts.

---

* God, like Satan, could also employ the Indians to do His hideous bidding. After a few years in Rhode Island exile, Anne Hutchinson moved south to New Netherland, building a house in what's now the Bronx. Local natives promptly slaughtered her and six of her children. It was an epic irony, given that Hutchinson's dovishness toward Indians had been another point of contention in Massachusetts. The Hutchinson massacre, those New England leaders reckoned, was perfect divine punishment—God smiting "this great imposter, an instrument of Satan."

Once the Puritans were in their wonderful and horrifying new promised land, fulfilling God's plan and fighting Satan, witches were probably inevitable. In the 1640s the Puritans in Connecticut and Massachusetts began indicting a couple of people each year for witchcraft. But they fined and banished and acquitted more witches than they hung, thus proving to themselves their moderation. That early hysteria over sorcery subsided, and for two generations New England wasn't executing witches.

But then in 1689, at the conclusion of decades of religious struggle back in England, parliament passed the Act of Toleration, which obliged the Puritans in America to allow their fellow Americans to believe and practice almost any version of Protestantism. The grandchildren of the original great dissenters now had to permit some dissent—and therefore to become just one more Christian sect among burgeoning Christian sects. Some of them detected Satan's hand in this existential demotion. But . . . witches: *witches* didn't need to be tolerated. Young Reverend Cotton Mather had recently published an essay describing the slippery slope of faithlessness: once you started disbelieving in witches, what was to stop you from disbelieving in God? The year the Toleration Act became law, he published another book, *Memorable Providences, Relating to Witchcrafts and Possessions,* about a recent episode of witchcraft and enchanted children in Boston.

Mather's handy guide was a bestseller, and one of its readers was the minister of the First Church in Salem, the New England Puritans' oldest. In the winter of 1691, his nine-year-old daughter began acting strangely— screaming, barking, burning up with fever. After other girls displayed similar "distempers," the cause became clear—witchcraft—and some sorceresses were identified: the minister's Caribbean servant, plus two other local women, one very poor and the other a nonchurchgoer. More girls turned weird, a few other women were accused, then men, then dozens more people.

Cotton Mather, the golden-boy witch expert in Boston, weighed in. He declared that "spectral evidence," tricky as it was, should be allowed at the trials—that is, prosecution witnesses' accounts of their dreams and supernatural visions of ghostly witches and demons. After the first convicted witch was hung, Mather suggested the court use spectral evidence carefully, but it continued to be prime evidence, and he encouraged the judges in their "speedy and vigorous prosecutions." Most of the several dozen accusers were girls. In four months more than two hundred trials produced dozens of guilty verdicts, mostly of women, and at least twenty witches and sorcerers (and two satanic pet dogs) were executed. A few others died in jail. The total population of the towns of Salem and Andover was only 2,400.

Our contemporary understanding of the Salem episode has been shaped significantly by *The Crucible,* Arthur Miller's 1953 play. Which is too bad, because *The Crucible* doesn't mainly portray early Americans' beliefs in magic as sincerely mad. Rather, the play's villains, accusers, and judges, are cynically and selfishly using the witchcraft panic as a pretext for exercising power. No doubt there was cynicism among accusers, girls who pressed cases they probably knew were false, and among defendants who confessed to save themselves. But my strong hunch is that the Salem trials were not mainly a willful sham. I'm sure Cotton Mather believed the nonsense he wrote. And many or most of the other principals in Salem in 1692 surely believed what they said. The girls did have dreams and hallucinations they thought had been induced by witches and sorcerers. The judges did think they were battling Satan. And many among the fifty people who confessed to witchcraft believed they really had made personal pacts with the devil—such as the accused witch who, at trial, asked Satan out loud to whisk them away from their Puritan tormentors.

As the madness reached its peak that summer, the Reverend Increase Mather, a leader of the colony, returned from a trip to England and promptly hit the brakes. After eight witches and sorcerers were hanged in Salem in one day, the most so far, he wrote a tract called *Cases of Conscience* and had it approved by the Puritan clerical association. Presently his friend the governor disbanded the Salem witchcraft court.

Ever since, *Cases of Conscience* has been regarded as the great turning point in the restoration of reason in colonial America. Its title seems appealingly liberal, and its most famous line makes us think Salem was a completely anomalous moment of temporary insanity: "It were better that ten suspected witches should escape than one innocent person should be condemned." But the seldom-quoted complete title of the book is a giveaway: *Cases of Conscience concerning evil SPIRITS Personating Men, Witchcrafts, infallible Proofs of Guilt in such as are accused with that Crime.* It's an explanation of how Satan actually works, filled with secondhand tales of evil magic from around the world, such as a new report of "a Venetian Jew" who knew "how to make a Magical Glass which should represent any Person or thing according as he should desire." For Increase Mather, the problem in Salem was that Satan had bewitched some of the accusers into making false accusations— the devil made the good people do it. As the historian Edmund Morgan has written, "In 1692 virtually no one in New England . . . disbelieved in witches."

Although the special witchcraft court adjourned, the chief judge from Salem was also the chief judge of a replacement court. And although to his great disappointment spectral evidence was no longer admissible, for months his new court continued trying people for witchcraft, and he signed the death warrants for three more convicted witches. The following year he was elected governor of Massachusetts.

Increase Mather never fully condemned the Salem episode, and his son backpedaled hardly at all. Although mistakes were made, Cotton eventually admitted—decades later, deep into the eighteenth century, in the lifetime of his neighbor Ben Franklin—he did not stop defending the witchcraft trials and executions.

THE BIG PIECE OF SECULAR conventional wisdom about Protestantism has been that it gave a self-righteous oomph to moneymaking and capitalism— hard work accrues to God's glory, success looks like a sign of His grace. But it seems clear to me the deeper, broader, and more enduring influence of American Protestantism was the permission it gave to dream up new supernatural or otherwise untrue understandings of reality and believe them with passionate certainty.

Science was being invented at the time. Like science, Protestantism was powered by skepticism of the established religious paradigms, which were to be revised or rejected—but unlike science, the old paradigms were to be replaced by new fixed truths. The scientific method is *unceasingly* skeptical, each truth understood as a partial, provisional best-we-can-do-for-the-moment understanding of reality. In their travesty of science, Protestant true believers scrutinized the natural world to deduce the underlying godly or satanic causes of every strange effect, from comets to hurricanes to Indian attacks to unusual illnesses and deaths. For believers in the new American religion, the truth was out there: everything happened for a purpose, and the purpose wasn't so hard to suss out.

This country began as an empty vessel for pursuing fantasies of easy wealth or utopia or eternal life—a vessel of such spaciousness that an assortment of new fantasies could be spun off perpetually. That had never happened before. Ordinary individuals took the initiative and improvised a country out of a wilderness, reshaped the world. That had never happened before, either. In just a century, the (white) American population grew from a few thousand to a million people, and it continued doubling every couple of decades. This improbable and peculiar new place thrived. The dream—that is, any of several and then dozens and finally hundreds of coexisting American fantasies—seemed to be coming true.

7

The First *Me* Century: Religion Gets American

IT WAS ALMOST TWO CENTURIES AFTER THEIR FOREBEARS' ARRIVAL, IN THE late 1700s, that the new inhabitants of the continent started calling themselves *Americans*. In the popular imagination today, that's also when America starts to seem intelligible, imaginable, modern-ish. The God-crazed Puritans and gold-crazed Virginians might have founded the place in the seventeenth century, but the people we call the Founders all came along in the eighteenth. They were rationalists and pragmatists, men who liked money and fine living but didn't expect to get rich overnight by stumbling into some North American El Dorado. They produced our national mission statement (the Declaration of Independence) and operating manual (the Constitution). The war those documents book-ended was a modern one, concerning politics rather than religion, to replace a monarchy with a republic. The steamboat, the cotton gin, bifocals, a newspaper that still publishes today—all American innovations of the late 1700s.

But that standard version of our eighteenth century, the march of progress starring Franklin, Adams, Jefferson, Washington, Hamilton, and (the atheist) Thomas Paine, is only part of the story, the most respectable part. It tends to obscure the big, weird, equally important narrative strands that explain our four-hundred-year American journey.

In post-Puritan America of the 1700s, the great Christian thinker was the Massachusetts minister Jonathan Edwards. He's revered today by everyone from theologians at Bob Jones University to scholars at Yale, from which Edwards graduated at sixteen. One understands why Yale and its ilk still embrace Edwards. He was a bona-fide intellectual who made sophisticated attempts to reconcile rationality with his absolute faith in an omniscient creator. He promoted new science and technology. He didn't talk about witchcraft or predict the end of the world or see warnings from God in random cabbage roots.

It's also understandable why contemporary evangelicals love him. He was celebrated and successful—but *also* a gospel preacher whose beliefs were like theirs. He had the ecstatic transformative experience of being born again—as a teenager, after an epiphany about the interconnectedness of existence: he took the feeling as proof not just of God but of the Bible and its Protestant interpretations. His contemporaries like Franklin and Jefferson resorted to a hazy belief in some kind of higher power and got on with their lives, but Edwards was all about obsessively *believing* and *feeling* the *magic*. He was, Mark Twain wrote to a pastor friend, a "resplendent intellect gone mad."*

Edwards's best-known sermon, "Sinners in the Hands of an Angry God," is famous for its vivid depiction of the fire (mentioned 17 times) and flames (11 times) in the pit (18) of Hell (52) where the wicked were headed for eternity. But in fact, this wasn't typical of him. He preached and wrote much more about Heaven than Hell. A good Christian's job now was to sin less, clean up the mess, and make the world as Christian as possible. By these means, the perfect future "shall be gradually brought to pass." Very, *very* gradually: according to Edwards's reading of Revelation, the golden age of Christianity wouldn't begin for hundreds of years, and Jesus would still be the absentee overlord until he returned as the king of the remade planet another thousand years after that.

Yet under such a "post-millennial" scheme, the glorious happy ending is so *far* in the future it might as well be . . . imaginary, metaphorical. Which is

---

* Edwards also retailed the wild old Puritan idea that Satan, alarmed by Christianity's early success, had led the Indians from Asia to America "that they might be quite out of the reach of the Gospel, that here he might quietly possess them, and reign over them as their god."

to say, for a lot of Americans, too boring. A religion that doesn't get the believer's blood pumping *right now* can be like a marriage without sex.

Edwards's enormous success was not mainly due to his nicer end-days scenario. Or to his thoughtful erudition—famous American ministers who preceded him had been intellectuals too. Rather, although Edwards is known as the Last Puritan, he was also somewhat Anne Hutchinsonian, a mystic visionary, consumed by the Bible but also by the totally subjective visionary *experience* of holiness.

Despite his low-key sobriety, he had a knack for making believers go wild, and he was at the center of what eventually became known as the Great Awakening. Five generations after the first Puritans arrived, the zealotry had diminished. Americans still read the Bible and went to church, but the religious boil had become more of a simmer. Reverend Edwards found he could turn up the heat, whipping proper New Englanders into ecstatic and agonizing deliriums that he and they took to be miraculous proofs of God.

Especially the kids. The Great Awakening got started as America's first youthquake.* In his town of Northampton, Massachusetts, the thirty-year-old Reverend Edwards found "a very unusual flexibleness . . . in our young people. . . . It seemed," he wrote, "almost like a flash of lightning upon the hearts of young people," then "became universal . . . among people of all degrees, and all ages. . . . Other discourses than of the things of religion, would scarcely be tolerated in any company. The minds of people were wonderfully taken off from the world."

More preachers awakened more congregations. Their listeners didn't just pledge to stop sinning and believe more strongly in God. They didn't just read and discuss the Bible and the sermons. In the middle of church services, respectable people felt the Holy Spirit, which produced "the Affections"—moaning, weeping, screaming, jerking, fainting.

Reverend Edwards, the Yale intellectual, was sometimes ambivalent about these "bodily effects," as the Mathers of Harvard fifty years earlier had been ambivalent about relying on "spectral evidence" to find witches. But he was sure that a lot of the shrieks and convulsions were indeed "distinguishing marks" of a supernatural presence, God shaking and slapping a sinner to make him or her see the light, or possibly Satan's violent resistance to God's embrace. In any case, it was an exciting innovation in the salvation process.

* By the way, in the 1960s, after the editor of *Vogue* coined *youthquake* as a catchword for countercultural fabulousness, it became the name of the fashion-forward division of— yes—the *Puritan* Dress Company.

Literal-minded Americans want *evidence*. This looked like evidence. And in a country shaping itself around the idea of individualism in all senses, whose people were already known abroad for their expressiveness, a histrionic and absolutely individual experience of holy magic was perfect.

To Edwards, this sudden madness of the crowd was also evidence of the supernatural big picture manifesting. "'Tis not unlikely," he wrote, "that this work of God's Spirit, that is so extraordinary and wonderful, is the dawning, or at least a prelude, of that glorious work of God, so often foretold in Scripture"—that is, the slow-but-sure final act. "There are many things that make it probable that this work will begin in America."

Edwards took his show on the road around New England, and other new-style itinerant evangelists of his generation did the same throughout the colonies. Just as ambitious English fantasists had invented America in Virginia and Massachusetts, a century later American evangelicalism was cofounded in a *new* New World wilderness by a pair of energetic young militant true believers over from England.

When John Wesley was five, his church boarding school in London caught fire. Getting plucked from the blaze became for him miraculous proof that God had special plans for him. He began praying constantly. He started a club of ultra-Christians at Oxford, got ordained, and arrived in the new colony of Georgia to serve as priest for its first town, Savannah. "My chief motive" in coming, he wrote, was "to learn the true sense of the Gospel of Christ by preaching it to the heathen."

He and the Church of England didn't see eye to eye, however. Like the Puritans a century earlier, he felt so much more *committed* and so much *holier* than fellow Anglicans who just went through the motions. For instance, he decided that the baptism of infants was a rubber-stamp symbolic ritual.* Only adults could properly choose to join the church. Which at first glance seems reasonable. But the point wasn't really the freedom to *decline* to join or to *disbelieve*: rather, Wesley's demand was that church members, as thinking adults, were obliged to abandon skepticism, declare themselves true believers, and feel "the Spirit of God immediately and directly." Dreams, for instance, could be messages from God, according to Wesley.

---

* Three centuries later, when and how and if baptism is an essential part of Christian magic remains a principal argument among the various Protestant denominations, as the new sects came to be called in the 1700s. This is another of the bitter fantasist-versus-fantasist debates that baffle or fascinate outsiders.

Wesley stayed in America only a couple of years.* He passed the baton to a young Oxford pal and protégé named George Whitefield, his cofounder of the Methodist movement. Unless you're a scholar or serious Methodist, you've probably never heard of him. But the subtitle of a recent biography—*America's Spiritual Founding Father*—isn't an overstatement. Whitefield was born to be an American.

Unlike Wesley, he had already experienced his "new birth." He also believed he received messages directly from God. During the two years between his ordination and his arrival in America, the "boy preacher" became an overnight star in England. He loved his celebrity and his rock 'n' roll impact on crowds. After his very first sermon, at age twenty-one, he wrote in his diary that "most of those present seemed struck, and"—1735 humblebrag—"a complaint has been made to the Bishop that I drove fifteen mad at the first sermon."

In America they loved him even more. He was young, like the country, and good-looking. He had natural charisma and experience as a schoolboy actor. His sermons weren't disquisitions read from the pulpit but were *performed* without a script or notes. He *portrayed* Jesus, the apostles, sinners arriving in Hell, and women as well as men. He knelt, he shouted, he stamped his feet. "I would give a hundred guineas," said David Garrick, the most important English actor of the century, "if I could say 'Oh' like Mr. Whitefield." A Whitefield appearance was fabulous theater—but his was apparently *authentic* emotion, a channeling of the Holy Spirit, a reality show. Most of his audience arrived with disbelief presuspended, and his performances let them believe the fantasy. At least as much as Edwards's and Wesley's sermons, Whitefield's preaching made people involuntarily twist and shout.

In 1740 he preached to Jonathan Edwards's congregation in Massachusetts. By Whitefield's own account, he killed: "Preached this morning, and good Mr. Edwards wept during the whole time of exercise. The people were equally affected." And when he wasn't welcome in established churches, that was fine too—he didn't need their religion's "dry, dead carcass." He'd preach to crowds outdoors, in fields and town squares, with bonfires burning. Which was a new sort of spectacle. As "the Grand Itinerant," traveling through the colonies, he could acquire a national audience.

---

* At thirty-four, after he broke up with his teenaged American girlfriend, he essentially kicked her out of the church, she sued him, and he escaped back to England, where he finally had his own grown-up born-again experience and continued cofounding Methodism.

Whitefield was the pioneering multimedia evangelical marketer of himself. Newspapers advertised his sermons and published accounts of the ecstatic mobs he attracted. He published a successful autobiography at twenty-six—the first of several. Within a couple of years of his arrival, Whitefield may have been the most famous person in America.*

By quoting again and again the biblical passage where Jesus tells a chief rabbi that "except a man be *born again,* he cannot see the kingdom of God," Whitefield implanted in American Christianity one of its big ideas and terms of art. And enabling an intense supernatural *feeling* of being born again was the ticket. "He makes less of the doctrines than our American preachers generally do," Jonathan Edwards's wife noted, "and aims more at affecting the heart."

As the Great Awakening spread, the Christian Establishment loathed all the embarrassing emotional displays of *me me me* fanaticism—as one critic at the time wrote, these awful "perturbations of mind, possessions of God, ecstatic flights and supernatural impulses." Sure, the religion was founded on stories of miracles and individual visions and revelations, but whoa . . . miracles and revelations right here, right now? To which the delirious mob responded *yes, exactly.* Whitefield wrote that the "screamings, tremblings" that he and other evangelists provoked were surely just like the "sudden agonies and screamings" that Jesus provoked among His converts. "Is not God the same yesterday, today, and forever?" It was Anne Hutchinson's argument all over again. *Give us the magic now!*

He reveled in the criticism, like Br'er Rabbit in the briar patch. Mainstream rejection served to reinforce his and his followers' certainty. The uncomprehending critics were jealous because they'd never had the euphoric personal experience of Jesus and the Holy Spirit. America was a sequel to biblical history and fulfillment of prophecy, so *of course* American Christians would be derided, like the early Christians. For Protestants as for Americans— well north of 90 percent of colonial Americans were Protestant—persecuted righteousness was central to their self-identities.

Edwards, Wesley, and Whitefield were all ordained Anglican priests. Their success was due in part to the fact that they weren't freelance crackpots but men of the Establishment who challenged that Establishment, like

* His media mastermind and traveling companion, William Seward, was a former London stockbroker who had been an executive of the investment company most famous for creating the disastrous financial fraud known as the South Sea Bubble. Returning to England after Whitefield's first American tour, he became an evangelist himself—and was presently stoned to death while preaching in Wales.

America's political founders. Their new, ultrademocratic American Christianity incorporated the founding Protestant antagonisms—to official holy men, stable doctrine, and fixed protocols—but went much further. As this mode became the norm among Baptists and other new denominations, it got even more extreme.

Anybody could become a preacher. A preacher could preach anywhere, in any way he wanted. The more evident the passion, the better. And all believers could find or start a sect or congregation that permitted them to express their faith in any way they wished—to achieve what felt like the optimal "personal relationship with Jesus Christ." "The most distinctive characteristic of early American Methodism," according to one of its modern historians, was "this quest for the supernatural in everyday life." Early American Methodists thus put "great stock in dreams, visions, supernatural impressions, miraculous healings, speaking in tongues." Of course, each preacher and believer of every sect knew that his or her idiosyncratic version of the truth was *the* truth.

As we let a hundred dogmatic iterations of reality bloom, the eventual result was an anything-goes relativism that extends beyond religion to almost every kind of passionate belief: *If I think it's true, no matter why or how I think it's true, then it's true, and nobody can tell me otherwise.* That's the real-life reductio ad absurdum of American individualism. And it would become a credo of Fantasyland.

8

Meanwhile, in the Eighteenth-Century Reality-Based Community

THE TWENTY-FOUR-YEAR-OLD PHENOM GEORGE WHITEFIELD ARRIVED IN America for the first time just before All Saints' Day, Halloween 1739. The first major stop on his all-colonies tour was Philadelphia. Crowds equal to half the inhabitants of the city gathered to see each performance. Among them was the not-so-religious young printer and publisher Benjamin Franklin.

Franklin was astonished by how Whitefield could "bring men to tears by pronouncing *Mesopotamia*," and "how much they admired and respected him, notwithstanding his common Abuse of them, by assuring them they were naturally half Beasts and half Devils." The publisher introduced himself on the spot and signed up to print a four-volume set of Whitefield's journals and sermons, which became an enormous bestseller. But Franklin's only awakening during the Great Awakening was to the profits available by pandering to American religionists. Over the next three years, he published an evangelical book almost monthly. With Whitefield himself, Franklin wrote, he formed "no religious Connection."

Franklin and his fellow Founders' conceptions of God tended toward the vague and impersonal, a Creator who created and then got out of the way. The "enthusiasts" of the era—channelers of the Holy Spirit, elaborate decoders of the divine plan, proselytizers—were not their people. John Adams fretted in a letter to Jefferson that his son John Quincy might "retire . . . to study prophecies to the end of his life." Adams wrote to a Dutch friend that the Bible consists of "millions of fables, tales, legends," and that Christianity had "prostituted" all the arts "to the sordid and detestable purposes of superstition and fraud." George Washington "is an unbeliever," Jefferson once reckoned, and only "has divines constantly about him because he thinks it right to keep up appearances." Jefferson himself kept up appearances by attending church but instructed his seventeen-year-old nephew to "question with boldness even the existence of a god; because, if there be one, he must more approve the homage of reason, than that of blindfolded fear." He considered religions "all alike, founded upon fables and mythologies," including "our particular superstition," Christianity. One winter in the White House, President Jefferson performed an extraordinary act of revisionism: he cut up two copies of the New Testament, removing all references to miracles, including Christ's resurrection, and called the reassembled result *The Life and Morals of Jesus of Nazareth*. "As to Jesus of Nazareth," Franklin wrote just before he died, "I have . . . some doubts as to his Divinity; though it is a question I do not dogmatize upon . . . and I think it needless to busy myself with it now, when I expect soon an opportunity of knowing the truth with less trouble."

When somebody asked Alexander Hamilton why the Framers hadn't mentioned God in the Constitution, his answer was deadpan hilarious: "We forgot."

Yet ordinary American people were apparently still much more religious than the English. In 1775 Edmund Burke warned his fellow members of Parliament that the X factor driving the incipient colonial rebellion was exactly that, the uppity Americans' peculiar ultra-Protestant zeal. For them, Burke said, religion "is in no way worn out or impaired."

Thus none of the Founders called himself an atheist. Yet by the standards of devout American Christians, then and certainly now, most were blasphemers. In other words, they were men of the Enlightenment, good-humored seculars who mainly chose reason and science to try to understand the nature of existence, the purposes of life, the shape of truth. Jefferson said Bacon, Locke, and Newton were "the three greatest men that have ever lived, without any exception." Franklin, close friends with the Enlightenment *philosophe* Voltaire,* was called "the modern Prometheus" by the Enlightenment philosopher Immanuel Kant, and Adams was friends with the Enlightenment philosopher David Hume, whose 1748 essay "Of Miracles" was meant to be "an everlasting check to all kinds of superstitious delusion." America's political founders had far more in common with their European peers than with the superstar theologians barnstorming America to encourage superstitious delusion. "The motto of enlightenment," Kant wrote the year after America won its war of independence, "is . . . *Sapere aude!*" or Dare to know. "Have courage to use your own understanding!"

For three centuries, the Protestant Reformation and the emerging Enlightenment were strange bedfellows, symbiotically driving the radical idea of freedom of thought, each paving the way for the success of the other. Protestants decided they could reject the Vatican and start their own religion, and they continued rejecting the authority and doctrines of each new set of Protestant bosses and started their own new religions again and again. Enlightenment thinkers took freedom of thought a step further, deciding that people were also free to put supernatural belief and religious doctrine on the back burner or reject them altogether.

But the Enlightenment part of this shift in thinking was a double-edged sword. The Enlightenment liberated people to believe *anything whatsoever* about every aspect of existence—true, false, good, bad, sane, insane, plausible, implausible, brilliant, stupid, impossible. Its optimistic creators and enthusiasts ever since have assumed that in the long run, thanks to an efficient marketplace of ideas, reason would win. The Age of Reason had led to the Enlightenment, smart rationalists and empiricists were behind both, so . . . right?

No. "The familiar and often unquestioned claim that the Enlightenment was a movement concerned exclusively with enthralling reason over the passions and all other forms of human feeling or attachment, is . . . simply false," writes the UCLA historian Anthony Pagden in *The Enlightenment: And Why It Still Matters.* "The Enlightenment was as much about rejecting the claims of reason and of rational choice as it was about upholding them." The Enlightenment gave license to the freedom of *all* thought, in and outside religion, the

---

* "As long as there are fools and rascals," Voltaire wrote in 1767, "there will be religions. [And Christianity] is assuredly the most ridiculous, the most absurd . . . religion which has ever infected this world."

absurd and untrue as well as the sensible and true. Especially in America. At the end of the 1700s, with the Enlightenment triumphant, science ascendant, and tolerance required, craziness was newly free to show itself. "Alchemy, astrology . . . occult Freemasonry, magnetic healing, prophetic visions, the conjuring of spirits, usually thought sidelined by natural scientists a hundred years earlier," all revived, the Oxford historian Keith Thomas explains, their promoters and followers "implicitly following Kant's injunction to think for themselves. It was only in an atmosphere of enlightened tolerance that such unorthodox cults could have been openly practiced."

Kant himself saw the conundrum the Enlightenment faced. "Human reason," he wrote in *The Critique of Pure Reason,* "has this peculiar fate, that in one species of its knowledge"—the spiritual, the existential, the meaning of life—"it is burdened by questions which . . . it is not able to ignore, but which . . . it is also not able to answer." Americans had the peculiar fate of believing they *could* and *must* answer those religious questions the same way mathematicians and historians and natural philosophers answered theirs.

PART II

United States of Amazing: The 1800s

"The perfect good-nature with which the American public submits to a clever humbug."

—P. T. Barnum,
The Life of P. T. Barnum (1855)

"We all do no end of feeling, and we mistake it for thinking. It is held in reverence. Some think it the voice of God."

—Mark Twain,
"Corn-Pone Opinions" (1901)

9

The First Great Delirium

REASON AND LEARNING AND SCIENCE DID INDEED BECOME PROUD PARTS OF the American march of progress during the nineteenth century. In the 1700s the Enlightenment had been all hopeful theory and writing and talk, an intramural discourse among the elite. But in the 1800s it was authentically and democratically realized. Education became free and compulsory in the United States. The literacy rate climbed to 90 percent. Newspapers and books multiplied, public libraries appeared, then public colleges and universities. As modern science begat modern technology, the proof was irrefutably in the pudding: we got telegraphy, high-speed printing presses, railroads, steamships, vaccination, anesthesia, more. We were rational and practical. We were modern.

If you were a devout American Christian, it had all turned out so well because—obviously—God was with us. We were fulfilling biblical prophecy, creating a virtuous new Christian nation that would pave the way for the millennium. But you didn't need to be very religious to consider the

Revolution and Constitution a consummation of some kind of providential plan. Like prophets creating new religions or novelists creating fictional worlds, Americans together had, astoundingly, created a new nation from scratch—a nation that guaranteed personal liberty above all, where citizens were officially freer than ever before to invent and promote and believe anything. So Americans promptly began believing almost everything.

We started to believe attractive falsehoods about our founding. Successful leaders had been glorified always, but America's mythologizing happened immediately and had a particular sanctimonious flavor. The best-known fact about Washington's first forty-five years, concerning the cherry tree—"I can't tell a lie, Pa. . . . I did cut it with my hatchet"—was a lie in a bestselling biography that appeared months after he died. One of the best-known facts about his war service, the time he knelt in prayer at Valley Forge, was almost certainly untrue. A bestselling work of fiction in the 1800s, *The Legends of the American Revolution, 1776,* included a story called "The Fourth of July, 1776." A quasi-angel—"a tall slender man . . . dressed in a dark robe"—mysteriously appears among the Founders in Philadelphia and delivers a five-minute speech ("God has given America to be free!") that makes them finally stop arguing and sign the Declaration. Then he mysteriously disappears. Americans from across the religious spectrum chose to regard that fantasy as historical fact, and they still do today.*

Instead of turning all Americans into reasonable, rational Ben Franklins, the onslaught of newness and amazing technology drove many citizens more deeply into fantasy, Christian and otherwise. As much as the nineteenth century was an American age of incredulity and wisdom, it was also an age of belief and foolishness. Cultural historians have focused on the religious side, the invention and expansion and growing emotionalism of Protestant denominations. But that frame is too narrow. As the Yale religious historian Jon Butler has written, the early United States was an "antebellum spiritual hothouse," Christian faith blending freely with folk magic—belief in the occult, clairvoyance, shamanic healing, and prophetic dreams, much of it old folk superstition no longer constrained by Puritan

---

* A century later, in a commencement address at his alma mater, a celebrity alumnus told the story as actual eyewitness history, attributing it to Thomas Jefferson. The 1957 commencement speaker was Ronald Reagan. Later, as president, when he repeated the story at length in a Fourth of July essay he published, his handlers evidently persuaded him to call it a "legend" and delete the Jefferson attribution.

doctrine and order. America was ripe for and rife with magical thinking of every kind.

Indeed, I'm proposing that the Second Great Awakening in the first half of the 1800s was just one part of something larger—the Great Delirium. During this First Great Delirium, new fantasies of *every* sort erupted—not just religious but cultural, pseudoscientific, utopian, and political, all variously radiant and lurid, feeding one another in a synergistic national crucible. Over the next few chapters, I'll discuss each domain. But first, let's look at how American Christianity wildly reinvented itself.

IN THE THREE CENTURIES SINCE its founding, dissident, hot-blooded Protestantism had spun off dissident sects of believers who wanted to remain hot. In England and Europe, the new denominations faded away or got absorbed by state churches. For Christians in Europe, one's official religious choice was essentially binary—subscribe to a state-sanctioned church, Protestant or Catholic, or to no organized religion at all.

But America was different. We had got started as a land of excitable escapees (and of hustlers and the hustled) determined to spread and devise fantastic new truths, and those origins defined us. While most of the thirteen colonies had a state church before the Revolution, afterward the Constitution outlawed them. Every set of beliefs and practices—old or new, more or less reasonable or plainly nuts—was officially equal to every other. In other words, a new American culture and psychology emerged during the 1600s and 1700s—which the new government then codified, allowing our native peculiarities to continue. Here in the land of homespun truth-finding and institution-making, Protestants' founding impulse—nonconformist, dissenting, *protesting*—waxed and waned but never went dormant. Established leaders were regarded with chronic resentment and renegade leaders with cultish devotion, individual believers determined to experience and radiate holiness. American Protestantism remained fully, perpetually fissile. As soon as a church's leadership got too high and mighty, or its doctrine and worship too reasonable and abstract and boring, the denomination was apt to explode and spin off new sects . . . which could grow and cool and then explode, on and on.

Nowadays the South is our most vehemently Christian region. But it was not always thus. In 1785 Thomas Jefferson created one of the first charticles, summarizing for a French aristocrat friend America's regional differences. He included this, about religion:

In the North they are . . .	In the South they are . . .
superstitious and hypocritical in their religion	without attachment or pretensions to any religion but that of the heart

Back then probably a minority of colonial Southerners attended church. Compared to New Englanders, they tended to be cavalier about sin and Jesus and Satan and Heaven and Hell and the Apocalypse. In the South, the governments jettisoned state churches during and right after the Revolution, but it took New England another half-century of argument to separate and privatize its churches entirely.

Throughout the South, *church* had meant the Church of England, before its post-Revolution rebranding as the Episcopal Church. Religious life was more about priests leading neighbors in the repetition of ancient communal ceremonies—scripted prayers and assertions, music, bread and wine. During the 1700s all over America, including the South, preachers like George Whitefield had planted the seeds of a new, wilder religion—what came to be called evangelical Christianity. The Southern Anglican mainstream rejected gung-ho mystical enthusiasts, such as the new Baptists and Methodists determined to enact their personal relationships with Jesus and *publicly demonstrate* the supernatural effects of the Holy Spirit. Particularly in Virginia, breakaway evangelical religious services were interrupted, attendees roughed up, preachers arrested. As ever for American true believers, persecution by the benighted was proof of their own righteousness.

As the century turned, the dam broke. By reputation, Presbyterian ministers were stiff-necked boors—*Methodists* did the arousing. But it was a young Presbyterian whose North Carolina preaching provoked less godly locals to burn his pulpit and deliver a death threat written in blood. He moved six hundred miles to the far western reaches of Kentucky. On the frontier, nobody much objected to one more freak. Everyone was a newcomer, so there were no established churches. And his sermons rocked. They were the only regularly scheduled entertainment within a day's ride.

Like an ambitious show business impresario, the Kentucky minister decided to expand. In the summer of 1800 he turned his regular annual communion-feast weekend into a regional festival of supercharged preaching and conversion. Hundreds came to his Red River Meeting House to watch and hear a half-dozen different preachers preach, including a Methodist. People shouted, people cried, people *freaked out.* "The power of God was strong upon me," the Methodist recalled afterward. "I turned again and, losing sight of the fear of man, I went through the house shouting and exhorting with all possible ecstasy and energy, and the floor was soon covered with the slain"—that is, individuals on the floor, experiencing improvised fits of hysteria.*

Something huge had been unleashed, and everyone realized it immediately. It was crazier than what Jonathan Edwards and George Whitefield had incited in their grandparents' day. God had *entered* people. They were not just enthusiastic, they were living the dream. "On Monday," the organizer wrote, "multitudes were struck down under awful conviction; the cries of the distressed filled the whole house. . . . There you might see little children of ten, eleven and twelve years of age, praying and crying for redemption, in the blood of Jesus, in agonies of distress." His young friend and fellow Presbyterian minister was astonished too. "Many, very many . . . continued for hours together in an apparently breathless and motionless state. . . . After lying there for hours . . . they would rise, shouting deliverance."

The fantasy had been contagious. At the repeat performance organized the next month at a nearby church, people camped out, and the contagion erupted again. Hundreds gathered. Dozens were "slain."

A year after the astonishing prototypes, the two entrepreneurial pastors decided to go even bigger. For the 1801 event at the second minister's church in Cane Ridge, Kentucky, they booked dozens of ministers to preach, Presbyterians and Methodists and Baptists. Like the first extravaganza, it was scheduled around an annual Holy Fair, the first weekend in August. Cane Ridge was in the more populous eastern part of the state, only a day's ride from the booming little city of Lexington (pop. 1,759), so maybe they would attract not just hundreds of people but a thousand or two thousand. No more than five hundred, tops, could fit into the bamboo-covered meetinghouse, so they erected a tent and outdoor stage as well.

They were overwhelmed. Instead of three days, it continued for nearly a week. As many as twenty thousand people arrived and stayed to hear the gospel, to be saved, to be part of a once-in-a-lifetime human carnival, an unprecedented lollapalooza. For a few days, Cane Ridge was among the several most populous places in America, bigger than Providence, as big as Charleston.

---

* It was a high-strung time and place. Two miles away and six years later, former U.S. senator and future president Andrew Jackson won a duel with a man who'd called him a coward and suggested his wife was a slut.

Things really got rolling twenty-four hours in, as Saturday afternoon turned to dusk. Campfires and bonfires burned. Darkness descended. Preachers preached from trees and wagons, several at once. Dozens of ordinary people—women, children, *anyone* moved by the Holy Spirit—were self-appointed "exhorters," shouting the truth of the gospel as they believed or felt or imagined or otherwise *knew* it. People screamed uncontrollably. People ran and leaped, barked and sang uncontrollably. People laughed and sobbed uncontrollably. Hundreds were overcome by "the jerks," convulsive seizures of limbs and necks and torsos that sometimes resolved into a kind of dance. And of course, hundreds or thousands of sinners found Christ and repented—including one of the gang of drunken local blasphemers who had ridden into the throng at full speed to make trouble, fell from his white horse, knocked himself out, and finally awakened more than a day later, smiling . . . saved. The wonder and chaos ebbed and flowed as dawn broke and the sun rose and set again, but it never stopped, day and night after August day and night.

An equivalent American gathering today, as a fraction of the U.S. population, would be more than a million people. As the Vanderbilt historian Paul Conkin and Harold Bloom of Yale have both noted, Cane Ridge was the Woodstock for American Christianity, an anarchic, unprecedented August moment of mass spectacle that crystallized and symbolized a new way of thinking and acting, a permanent new subculture. "The drunk, sexually aroused communicants at Cane Ridge," Bloom writes in *The American Religion*, "like their drugged and aroused Woodstockian descendants, participated in a kind of orgiastic individualism." The improvised acting-out at Cane Ridge and subsequent camp meetings apparently descended from the religious fringes, such as those of African-American Baptists.*

More Baptist and Methodist preachers organized more camp meetings all over the country, but especially in the South, and more mobs of people assembled to go over the top and out of their minds. It had gone viral. As a mass-market phenomenon in the 1800s, widespread and frequent, it was unique to America. A new and fully American Christianity had been invented, more fantastic and unsubtle than any other, strictly subjective and individual—as Bloom says, an "experiential faith that called itself Christianity while possessing features very unlike European or earlier American doc-

---

* Which suggests a further elaboration of the Woodstock rhyme: white Americans mixing English folk culture with black culture in order to leave reason and respectability behind, wild and emotional Christianity at the beginning of the nineteenth century, wild and emotional rock 'n' roll in the second half of the twentieth.

trinal formulations." The new mode quickly spread from the frontier back east to civilization. During the year after Cane Ridge, a third of the students at Yale were converted, born again.

New, Cane Ridgier denominations were started. Along with the Baptists and Methodists, they committed to a version of Christianity more thrilling and magical right now, as well as a sure-thing payoff for eternity. Thus the new American way: it was awesome, it was democratic, you're a winner if you believe you're a winner.

In the years after Cane Ridge, Methodism rode the wave, growing faster than any other denomination. Church attendance probably doubled during the first half of the century, and by the 1850s two-thirds of churchgoers were Methodists or Baptists, emotional and enthusiastic. Christianity became more and more synonymous with this *evangelical* Christianity: sinners walking to the altar to be saved and experience an all-consuming feeling of a personal relationship with Jesus. A generation after Cane Ridge, Christian emotionalism no longer seemed so kooky in America.

One night in the autumn of 1821, for instance, a twenty-nine-year-old small-town lawyer in western New York had what sounds like a panic attack: "I had become very nervous, and . . . a strange feeling came over me as if I was about to die . . . [and] sink down to hell." The next day "God's voice" spoke biblical passages to him in the woods outside town. After praying and weeping until after dark, Charles Finney closed himself in a room at his offices, prayed some more, and then . . . *shazam*. The room "appeared to me as if it was perfectly light," and then "it seemed as if I met the Lord Jesus Christ *face to face* . . . as I would see any other man. . . . It seemed to me a reality that He stood before me." After Finney sobbed, "the Holy Spirit descended upon me . . . *like a wave of electricity,* going through and through me," a wave that, it seemed, "literally *moved my hair like a passing breeze.*" The next morning he was a new man: "My sense of guilt was gone, my sins were gone."

Finney promptly became a Presbyterian minister and was soon *the* flashy-but-respectable Christian superstar of his time, its Billy Graham, preaching to huge camp meetings all over the country. But he didn't dwell on the Presbyterians' buzzkill doctrine of predestination or on doctrine generally. The only point was for rationalists, like the young professional he'd been, to *experience* Jesus, as he'd done, and thereby—presto—become free of sin and guilt, with guaranteed passage to Heaven. Like his pioneering predecessor Whitefield a century earlier, he understood that in America Christianity should be a kind of show business: "to expect to promote religion without excitements," Finney wrote, "is . . . absurd."

The new Christian revivalist fire never caught in the Old World the way it did here. "In modern times," sympathetic evangelicals wrote in a Yale quarterly at midcentury, "revivals of religion have been more or less peculiar to the churches of the United States." They understood that that was because Christianity here was so high-strung from the start, with Americans hankering for religious contagions, so those expectations became self-fulfilling. "In England," they noted, "it has been far different. To a great extent there, churches and ministers have been without the expectation."

At the height of the Second Great Awakening, in 1831, the first American studies scholar from abroad, age twenty-five, happened to arrive in America from France for his famous nine-month tour. "On every side in Europe," Tocqueville wrote in *Democracy in America,* "we hear voices complaining of the absence of religious faith, and inquiring the means of restoring to religion some remnant of its pristine authority." But he wasn't in the land of Voltaire anymore.

> The philosophers of the eighteenth century explained the gradual decay of religious faith in a very simple manner. Religious zeal, said they, must necessarily fail, the more generally liberty is established and knowledge diffused. Unfortunately, facts are by no means in accordance with their theory. . . . America one of the freest . . . nations in the world fulfils all the outward duties of religious fervor. . . .
>
> There is no country in the whole world in which the Christian religion retains a greater influence over the souls of men than in America. . . .
>
> You meet with men, full of a fanatical and almost wild enthusiasm, which hardly exists in Europe.

The religious divergence of Europe and America became more pronounced, as Europeans swung toward the calm and reasonable, Americans toward the excited and fantastical. Here in improvisation nation, the individual liberty empowered by the Enlightenment led to a certain fanaticism when it came to finding God.

Yet as the born-again revivalists entered the American mainstream during the 1800s, the Methodists and Baptists and fired-up Presbyterians like Finney weren't really going nuts *theologically.* Methodists were more and more encouraged to emulate the historical Jesus rather than his frenzied disciples, evangelizing against slavery and other injustice, doing good. The world would become a Christian wonderland gradually and subtly, as Jonathan Edwards had taught a century earlier during the First Great Awakening. Finney had seen the light and met Jesus, but he preached that Christians' duty was to "make the world a fit place for the imminent return of Christ." By *imminent,* he meant *eventual.* He became president of Oberlin College, a fount of social progressivism.

American Christianity was now filled, uniquely, with ecstatic conversions in church but not wild excitements about Götterdämmerung scheduled for the week after next. Among theologians and ministers, prophetic beliefs really had faded away since the Puritan 1600s. The nightmarish "tribulations" in the Bible, battles between black magic and holy miracles—the experts had decided those *already happened,* ages ago. Armageddon, Gog and Magog, end of days—all that was inspired allegory, not meant to be taken at face value, and certainly not subject to a countdown, the way Cotton Mather used to do.

But it turned out that a lot of Americans, being Americans, still wanted a promise of the adventure tale to end all adventure tales. They wanted to see Jesus for real, here on Earth, sooner rather than later, actually leading them in a sensational battle against monsters from Hell, a war they were guaranteed to win.

In the mid-1800s, thanks to two little-known pioneers, those beliefs revived in America and became a central feature of the Christian faith of many millions of Americans. And then they never went away.

The first of these crucial end-time heralds was William Miller, like Finney an ordinary upstate New York guy who'd been iffy about religion as a young man. Like John Wesley, he'd miraculously escaped fiery death (in a War of 1812 bombardment), which convinced him that God had intervened on his behalf. He became a born-again Baptist preacher, obsessed with a bit of the Bible attributed to the apocalyptic seer Daniel. After Daniel watched a multihorned flying goat defeat a multihorned ram, the angel Gabriel told him that in "two thousand and three hundred days; then shall the sanctuary be cleansed." After a decade of calculating, Miller had it all worked out. He figured the angel must have issued the prophecy in 458 B.C.E. and that those 2,300 *days* actually meant 2,300 *years.* And the final cleansing of the sanctuary actually referred to the moment Christ would return. Which meant—do the math—the world was going to end in the spring of 1843. It was scholarship, completely scientific.

By means of hundreds of end-is-nigh pamphlets and books and periodicals and tent meetings, Miller acquired almost a million American believers, as many as one in ten northeasterners. After 1843 came and went normally,

Miller and company decided they'd miscalculated the date and changed it to the following April—no, wait, *October,* 1844. But October 22 turned out to be just another Tuesday. The disappointed masses who kept the faith broke into different factions, one of which was the Seventh-day Adventists.

But the big, long-lasting impact was the mainstreaming of the belief among modern American Christians that they might personally experience the final fantasy—the end of days, the return of Jesus, Satan vanquished. Around the same time, another Protestant minister was devising an even more complicated version of end-of-the-world prophecy. The Reverend John Nelson Darby, by means of two decades of cross-country preaching tours, permanently embedded the Bible's end-time prophecies into the heart of American Christianity.

There are a few reasons why Darby's version of the end-time endured. First, he preached the end was coming . . . soon*ish,* but he wasn't a date-setter, so his prophecy could never be proven false. Second, he recast the apocalypse in a far more appealing light—for believers. All so-called pre-millennialists agree that an ugly period of worldwide tribulation will be humankind's existential denouement—war, famine, pandemic disease. But Darby more or less invented the idea of "the rapture," a moment just before all hell breaks loose when Jesus will arrive incognito and take Christians away to heavenly safety to wait out the earthly horrors. Then He and the lucky saints return to Earth for the happy ending. Third, Darby wasn't trying to forge a whole new denomination, just offering new features that could be attached to any church's existing theology.

Finally, Darby was not some crank but a legitimate scholar, a Brit educated at the best schools, author of an original translation of the New Testament. Americans often resist the idea that educated experts can tell them what is and isn't true, but from the Puritans on, we've also been more than happy for scholarly *fellow believers* to confirm our beliefs and make them more impressively complicated. It is a modern wish for proof of one's premodern fantasies. "The enduring appeal of prophecy belief for evangelicals," as the historian Paul Boyer has written, is its "quasi-empirical 'scientific' validation of their faith." Explainers like Darby "explicitly portrayed their endeavor . . . as a science." In an increasingly scientific age, Christians could thrive by treating the Bible as an unimpeachable data set.

Although the Catholic Tocqueville didn't attend a camp meeting during his tour, he noted in *Democracy in America* that "strange sects arise which endeavor to strike out extraordinary paths to eternal happiness. Religious insanity is very common in the United States." One of the best known was the sect founded by an English émigré fanatic who'd made herself unwelcome among her fellow Quakers in England and moved with a few disciples to upstate New York. Ann Lee was repulsed by sexuality, obsessed with the Second Coming, had visions, made prophecies, spoke in tongues, and magically cured the sick. Her celibate followers came to consider her the returned Jesus. Long before Methodists and Baptists and other revivalists normalized worshippers' convulsions in America, Ann Lee's followers were regularly doing so—so other people called them Shakers. After she died, her communal sect grew and spread during the 1800s from the Northeast to the western frontier.

The Shakers' maximum membership coincided with their maximum hysteria beginning in the 1830s, their so-called Era of Manifestations, when members—especially young female ones—had fits during which they believed they traveled to Heaven and communicated with the dead. That's just when Tocqueville attended a Shaker service. He was flabbergasted and privately appalled. "Can you imagine, my dear mother," he wrote home, "what aberrations the human spirit can fall into when it's abandoned to itself? There was a young American Protestant with us who said as we left, 'Two more spectacles like this one and I'm turning Catholic.'"

The Shakers were among the more successful of dozens of smaller American sects and cults in this period, each led by an electrifying individual who claimed to have a direct line to God or His angels. A large fraction of Americans wanted or needed to believe they lived in an enchanted time and place, that the country swarmed with supernatural wonders, and that mid-nineteenth-century America was like the Holy Land of the early first century, when Jesus was only one among many itinerant prophets and wizards and healers wandering the eastern Mediterranean. And indeed, at the height of the First Great Delirium, the strangest and most astoundingly successful new American religion arose.

10

The All-American Fan Fiction of Joseph Smith, Prophet

LIKE HIS CONTEMPORARIES FINNEY AND MILLER BEFORE THEY BECAME SUPER-star preachers and prophets, Joseph Smith was a young nobody living in rural western New York. He grew up in a middling family that dipped in and out of various churches, and his father reported having prophetic dreams. Joseph attended school for only a couple of years, but he was a charming and popular boy who found he could make easy money indulging a particular folk fantasy. Many of his neighbors, like lots of Americans at the time, had come to be-lieve the landscape was studded with buried loot—old Spanish or Indian gold, tranches of robbers' cash, lost jewels. Teenage Joseph hired himself out to help find underground treasure. He claimed to do this supernaturally, using two magic "seer stones."

When he was fourteen, he said later, God appeared to him one day in a pillar of light in the woods (also, he remembered even later, Jesus). God told him his sins were forgiven and that the existing churches had Christianity all wrong. Three years afterward, at seventeen, around the time he became a freelance magical treasure-hunter, he was praying at home and saw an angel floating above the floor, again in a column of light. The angel was named Moroni, a name that doesn't appear in the Bible. Moroni told him that the heretofore unknown remainder of the Bible, its text engraved in Egyptian hieroglyphs on golden plates, happened to have been buried fourteen centuries earlier four miles south of the Smiths' house, along with two ancient seer stones with which Joseph would be able to translate it. Moroni left the house through "a conduit open right up into heaven," but then immediately returned and repeated everything he'd said earlier, this time adding—right, sorry, one more thing—that the Apocalypse was coming soon. The angel returned to Heaven but presently came back a third time, repeating everything once more—and then the next day reappeared and repeated everything yet again.

Four years later Smith finally succeeded in unearthing the tablets, then began "translating" them. His friends and his wife were often at his side as he performed the translations. He would place a seer stone in a hat beside one of the golden plates, bury his face in the hat, and then speak the English words he "saw," a sentence at a time. During the period he was translating the tablets, he said, he received additional revelations directly from God, in his mind, which he also transcribed.

The result, after "reading" and talking five days a week for three months, was the Book of Mormon. Smith said it was the third chunk of the Christian Bible, containing revisions to both the Old and New Testaments among its quarter-million words.* He published the book in 1830, the year after he dictated it. It's a doozy. A heretofore unknown prophet named Lehi escaped besieged Jerusalem in the sixth century B.C.E. and sailed with his family and friends to the Americas, where their descendants founded a civilization. The civilization split into two warring peoples, one white and the other dark-skinned. The freshly resurrected Jesus Christ appeared among the white half, appointed twelve of them as his new, second set of apostles, and re-peated the Sermon on the Mount. Thanks to Jesus's visit, the light- and dark-skinned American nations reunited for a while, but then in the fifth century A.D. they went to war again, the darker people annihilating the whiter people. Smith's interlocutor Moroni was one of the last whites alive when he buried the plates. (Smith said later that God told him American Indians are de-scended from the dark-skinned group.) For the rest of his life, Joseph Smith continued reporting revelations from God, which he both published as inde-pendent scripture and used to correct the Bible.

* Put another way: the Book of Mormon is more than twice as long as *The Hobbit* but not as long as *The Lord of the Rings*.

As I've described, American Christians from the start tended toward the literal and hysterical and collectively self-centered. Joseph Smith met that bid and raised it a million. Like the American Puritans as well as the new millennialists of his own era, he prophesied that Armageddon was coming soon. "The heavens shall shake and the Earth shall tremble," he said God had informed him, and for the unlucky, "flesh shall fall from their bones, and their eyes from their sockets." One night in 1833 at four A.M., he saw what he took to be a providential meteor shower: "I arose and beheld to my great Joy the stars fall from heaven . . . a sure sign that the coming of Christ is close at hand."

The grandiose anything-goes literalism of his theology knew no bounds. He said that "God . . . has flesh and bones," and he suggested that Jesus was conceived by means of literal sexual congress between God and Mary. American Christians had always nudged the Bible in the *direction* of America, imagining their cities upon hills to be at least *like* Jerusalem, and themselves to be God's chosen people at least *analogous* to the ancient Israelites. Smith made America a literal second Holy Land, settled by literal Israeli émigrés and visited by the literal Jesus Christ. The new kingdom he'd create in the American West would literally be the center of the reborn Christian world.

If one considers the Bible, in the main, to be historical fiction, then what Joseph Smith produced was a monumental and pioneering work of fan fiction, the most successful ever.* Fan fiction, as one scholar has written, is created by fans to "fill the need" among other fans for "narratives that expand the boundary of the official source products." Smith's official source products were the Old and New Testaments. Jewish and Christian theologians—in particular, American Protestants during their first two centuries—had previously indulged a bit of biblical fan-fiction impulse, but they'd limited it to interpretation and annotation. (One could argue that the New Testament itself was a collaborative anthology of fan fiction inspired by the Old Testament— *We'll give Jehovah a son, part god and part human!*) But it took hubris of a particularly entrepreneurial American kind for an individual to produce such a comprehensive work of fan fiction over the course of just a few years, one purporting to have been dictated in part by the original author, God himself.

According to Smith, according to God, Adam and Eve's banishment from the Garden of Eden was not the tragic Fall of Man but a *good thing,* because

---

* More than 150 million copies of his Book of Mormon have been printed since 1830. The second most successful work of fan fiction in history, the *Fifty Shades of Grey* books, inspired by the bestselling vampires-and-werewolves *Twilight* novels, have sold more than 100 million copies.

it enabled ordinary pleasure and joy, let humans be human. Jesus's physical appearance here in the New World made Christianity more *relatable;* a defining trait of Americans from the start was a parochial and narcissistic interest in America. In theological tales, unlike fiction written as fiction, readers are meant to become characters in the story, and the new happy ending in Smith's fan fiction was fabulous. The term *fan fiction* was coined in the 1960s to describe stories written by fans of a science fiction series, and Smith's Heaven is very sci-fi. It has distinct quality levels, like American Express cards—one for run-of-the-mill people who don't deserve Hell, one for good Christians, and a superpremium level for Mormons. There you're not just one of a mass of a billion indistinguishable souls in some ethereal netherworld, but a king or queen of your personal planetary fiefdom as a resurrected immortal physical being, continuing to produce princes and princesses. God lives near an actual celestial object called Kolob, a definite number of miles away from Earth. Plus, any dead friends or relatives can be posthumously baptized and sent along to Heaven as well. Better history, better future—and at least for men, a better present, now that sex with multiple women was no longer a sin but a holy commandment.

So much about the founding of the church seems so comic, even at the most fine-grained level. When Smith asked a disciple to serve as church historian, for instance, the man said he'd do it only if *God* asked him. So Joseph repeated the order, this time using more God-like language: "Behold it is expedient in me that my servant John should write and keep a regular history."

Rough Stone Rolling is the recent definitive biography of Joseph Smith. Its author, Richard Lyman Bushman, is a Columbia University history professor emeritus and a lifelong member of the Church of Latter day Saints, in which he has served as a clergyman. His ancestors knew and followed Smith and his apostles across America in the 1800s. "What is most interesting about Joseph Smith," Bushman writes in a sentence of breathtaking understatement, "is that people believed him." Bushman never really answers the question he raises. How can he? One of Smith's disciples said that he and Smith spoke with John the Baptist in Wayne County, New York, and with Jesus Christ near Cleveland. Two others said they too, alongside Smith, met with angels. Bushman reports all these as factual events.

Was Joseph Smith a prophet who spoke to God and Jesus, an extraordinarily successful charlatan, or sincerely delusional? My strong hunch is option three. "I don't blame anyone for not believing my history," Smith said near the end of his life. "If I had not experienced what I have, I should not have believed it myself."

As ever, when true believers are persecuted for their beliefs, it can fuel their zeal. When the fourteen-year-old Smith told a Methodist pastor about his first visitation by God, the man was appalled and dismissive. At age twenty, after one of his treasure-hunting clients complained that Smith's magic was fraudulent, he was arrested and tried—and a year later had the golden tablets. And of course, he and his followers were harassed, driven out of towns, genuinely persecuted.

Which didn't stop the heresy from catching on. In its first decade, the church grew from fewer than three hundred members to almost twenty thousand. After Smith (and then his followers) obeyed an angel's long-standing order to become polygamous or die, he married thirty women in two years, eight of them during one three-month period, six of those teenagers. The official and unofficial persecution naturally went into overdrive—and the church grew faster, by more than half in just three years. In one of his last sermons, not long after he announced his candidacy for U.S. president, Smith bragged to his people that he'd kept them more loyal than Jesus had his disciples. "I glory in persecution," he told them. Shortly thereafter, still in his thirties, he was indicted, arrested, and then killed while in custody—*like Jesus Christ*. During the two years after his murder, church membership increased by another third, and the members undertook their exodus—into a desert, just like the ancient Israelites—to establish their own Jerusalem in Utah.

Joseph Smith was a quintessentially American figure. Whether he was a heartfelt believer in his delusions or among the greatest confidence men ever, his extreme audacity—his mind-boggling *balls*—is the American character ad absurdum. America was created by people resistant to reality checks and convinced they had special access to the truth, a place founded to enact grand fantasies. No Joseph Smiths emerged elsewhere in the modern world. And if they had, where else would so many responsible people instantly abandon their previous beliefs and lives and risk everything on the say-so of such a man making such claims?

On Easter Sunday in 1800 at St. Paul's in London, the main cathedral of the Church of England, only six people received communion. The nineteenth-century awakenings in Britain and Europe and Australia were altogether different phenomena. The revivalists were quieter, nerdier, more about returning to stripped-down Protestant piety, less about the individual emotional convulsions of spiritual crisis and rebirth, let alone radical new theological twists. They remained blips, important not for propagating supernatural (and selfish) fantasies but for establishing organizations like the YMCA and Salvation

Army to practice Christ-like generosity toward the needy, the poor, and the lame. They were a sideshow to the secularization of Europe and, except for the United States, the rest of modernizing Christendom.

In the United States, meanwhile, supernaturally focused sects arose and boomed, some of them soon dominating whole regions—the Baptists in the South, the Mormons in Utah. They were really new religious species, Harold Bloom argues in *The American Religion,* as different from the Christianity that preceded them as Christianity had been from Judaism when it began. America was still exceptional and growing more so.

11

Quack Nation: Magical but *Modern*

THE NEW AMERICAN CHRISTIANITY EMPHASIZED NOT JUST THE ANCIENT miracles but miracles right now, feeling the supernatural by believing in it strongly enough. We had become a country where millions of evangelical Christians were rising up breathlessly from the sinners' "anxious bench" to channel the Holy Spirit and be born again *instantly.* We were a practical country, so along with moral lessons and promises of an eternal afterlife, churches in the early 1800s were providing instant solutions, miracle cures for feelings of meaninglessness and emptiness.

The revived belief in magic appeared simultaneously with astounding new technology—high-speed travel and nearly instant mechanical pictures and communication. Only four years after Samuel F. B. Morse sent the first electric telegram (quoting an Old Testament verse: "What hath God wrought?") in 1844, the United States had two thousand miles of sparking, glowing wires carrying messages from Maine to Missouri, Chicago to Savannah. "On the first of January, 1848, of the Christian era," *The New York Herald* declared, "the new age of miracles began." Which was among the greatest illustrations of Arthur

C. Clarke's famous third law: "Any sufficiently advanced technology is indistinguishable from magic." But in this book Clarke's aphorism has a converse meaning as well: technology that seems magical and miraculous can encourage and confirm credulous people's belief in make-believe magic and miracles.

A few months after the *Herald* announced this new age of miracles, Americans were therefore inclined to believe when a pair of sisters, twelve and fifteen, announced they had communicated with a ghost haunting their house by means of a kind of knock-knocking Morse code. (Like so many of my nineteenth-century characters, they were in western New York State, the next town over from where Joseph Smith first spoke to God.) The Fox sisters became famous mediums and helped launch a national movement of "spiritualists" communicating with the dead. Respectable Americans attended séances. Horace Greeley, the great journalist of the era, defended and promoted the girls. (Fortunately for him, he wasn't alive forty years later when they admitted it had all been a fraud.) The Shakers chronicled in detail their intercourse with spirits and ghosts, and one of their religion's books breathlessly reported that electrical transatlantic communication was "proof of a telegraphic communication established between the two worlds" of the living and the dead. On the other hand, Reverend Darby, the end-time evangelist and rapture inventor, considered the telegraph a "harbinger of Armageddon."

In America during the First Great Delirium, the marvels of science and technology didn't just reinforce supernatural belief by analogy or as omens—they inspired sham science and sham marvels. Especially when it came to medicine. Many nostrums were the products of knowing charlatans, but many of the most successful inventors and promoters were undoubtedly sincere believers themselves. If the patients also had faith in the miraculous treatments, they could even seem to work. The term *placebo* had just come into use as a medical term.

Looking back from the present, stories of forgotten pseudoscientific medical fads—there are dozens, hundreds—reassure us that the authentic eventually drives out the wishful and fake. In the 1800s America had hundreds of water-cure facilities, for instance. But then we lost faith in hydropathy and stopped wrapping people in sheets drenched in cold water in order to cure rheumatoid arthritis, heart and kidney and liver disorders, smallpox, gonorrhea, and dysentery. Yet from this nineteenth-century miasma emerged one school of quackery that became huge in America and never faded away.

Homeopathy was the original "alternative medicine." Quinine, a bonafide treatment for malaria, led to its inventor's eureka moment: ingesting it made him feel as if he *had* malaria, so he extrapolated—deciding that "that which can produce a set of symptoms in a healthy individual, can treat a sick individual who is manifesting a similar set of symptoms." Again, so nice and *simple*—and he made his theory even simpler: "Like cures like." As with many newly constructed fantasies in the new age of reason and science, homeopathy employed a travesty of science, analogy with a superficial sheen of logic, to make its argument: like-cures-like was imagined as a universalized version of vaccination, the new technique by which a bit of cowpox virus successfully immunized people against smallpox.

Dozens of different substances were mixed up into batches of homeopathic medicine—flowers, barks, metals, arsenic. The inventor disparaged nonhomeopathic fellow fantasists: "superstition, impure observations, and credulous assumptions," he warned, "have been the source of innumerable falsely ascribed remedial virtues of medicines."

Of course, swallowing arsenic or other poisons could harm patients, but homeopathy had that figured out. The medicines were made by diluting the ingredients in water or alcohol, shaking the mixture (that is, "potentizing" and "dynamizing" their "immaterial and spiritual powers"), then diluting it again, shaking, diluting some more, on and on. The dilution ratios were (and are still today) so extreme—billions and trillions to one—that the finished elixirs are just water or alcohol, containing essentially none of the named ingredient. A typical recommended dilution is literally equivalent to a pinch of salt tossed into the Atlantic Ocean.

Homeopathy, its fake medicines prescribed to cure *every* disease, is a product of magical thinking in the extreme. After it was exported from Germany to America during the so-called Era of Good Feelings, it swept the country and continued booming for the rest of the 1800s. In 1848 the Homeopathic Medical College was founded in Philadelphia, eventually becoming the Drexel University College of Medicine. Homeopathic M.D. degrees were issued by schools across the country to many thousands of homeopathic physicians.

The upside was that homeopathy inherently fulfills the Hippocratic Oath: *First, do no harm.* Homeopathic medicines contain negligible active ingredients. If thousands of homeopaths and millions of patients, as Mark Twain said, wanted to "bribe death with a sugar pill to stay away," that was their problem.

The other two most important pseudoscientific medical protocols that excited and entranced Americans in the mid-1800s were mesmerism and phrenology. Both attracted masses of celebrated and respectable American believers. In fact, although phrenology and mesmerism were, like homeopathy, imported from Europe, their popularity and impact were larger and longer-lasting in the United States than anywhere else. And a century later, starting in the 1960s and '70s (see Chapter 22), homeopathy would have its all-American comeback.

Mesmerism, also called magnetic healing and electrical psychology, attributed *all* disease and illness to a single cause—in the words of one of its most successful American practitioners, "the electricity of the system [is] thrown out of balance." (He addressed the U.S. Senate on the subject.) By using magnetized rods or their mysteriously "energized" hands, mesmerists convinced people they could clear the blockages in patients' internal electrical flows. Some claimed to heal fractures, make the lame walk, and cure insanity. Many Christians considered it witchcraft, but the "electro-psychological" theorist and practitioner who addressed the Senate said that Jesus had used mesmerism to accomplish His miraculous blindness cures. Around the same time mesmerism was dreamed up, a Yale-educated physician had enormous success with his own version of the same basic pseudoscience and his own apparatus to "draw off the noxious electrical fluid that lay at the root of suffering." He and other practitioners stroked patients with his three-inch metal rods—which received the first U.S. patent ever granted to a medical device. Despite but also because of opposition by the elite—the inventor was expelled from the Connecticut Medical Society—people believed his "tractors" worked to relieve their pain. Because he figured they could cure all sorts of diseases, he volunteered to treat yellow fever patients during an epidemic in New York City; there he contracted yellow fever and died.

The craze for cure-all mesmerism qua mesmerism peaked during the 1800s. However, one mesmerist school was all about inducing trances, which around 1880 came to be known as hypnosis, a genuine neurological phenomenon in which the subjective distinctions between imaginary and real are muddled. A century later it would become a powerful mischief-maker—a means by which many Americans, for instance, become convinced they've been enslaved by satanists (see Chapter 37). But even the magic-wand and magic-hand versions of mesmerism were just the supersuccessful trial run for the various mystical healing practices involving "energies" that would become central to the alternative medical establishment of the late twentieth and twenty-first centuries (see Chapter 34).

Like so much pseudoscience, mesmerism was faulty science fiction, a fantasy inspired by a misunderstood bit of reality—scientists had recently demonstrated that muscles are indeed activated by electrical signals. A similar sci-fi leap produced phrenology, which madly extrapolated from the actual fact that the mind is all in the brain and the brain, in the words of its founder, "an aggregate of mental organs with specific functions." According

to phrenologists' imaginary diagnostic scheme, however, each psychological trait corresponded to a particular bit of the brain and—the totally bogus
extrapolation—could be "read" by scrutinizing and feeling the topographical
details of a person's skull through the scalp. Phrenology got its American foot-
hold in Boston in the early 1830s, then quickly became a highly respectable
national craze. Phrenologists were *the* American mental health professionals
for most of the nineteenth century, with multiple societies and journals. Every
city and many towns had practitioners. One of the best-known phrenologists
supposedly examined the heads of three hundred thousand people during his
career—a number equal to more than one percent of all Americans in 1850.

Such pseudoscientific practices harmed healthy people no more frequently than they cured sick people, but their popularity derived from and
fed the big American idea that opinions and feelings are the same as facts.
"The phrenological cult," Gilbert Seldes wrote in *The Stammering Century* in
1928, not so long after it faded away,

> had a profound effect on the development of American character.
> First it favored the cult of the individual. Or it would be equally ac-
> curate to say that phrenology drew from the American atmosphere
> certain tendencies to individualism and adapted itself to the Ameri-
> can character. . . . Phrenology and mesmerism both made man more
> interesting to himself, as psychology and psychoanalysis did half a
> century later. . . . Had phrenology come to America before Method-
> ism began its fermentation, it would have been persecuted as a her-
> esy and possibly rejected entirely.

In other words, the various fantasies, religious and pseudoscientific,
cross-fertilized. Methodism's cofounder Wesley published a bestselling self-
help compendium of remedies, subtitled *An Easy and Natural Method of Curing Most Diseases*—onions and honey cure baldness, apples prevent insanity.
A Presbyterian minister named Sylvester Graham (of the eponymous cracker)
led a movement based on his conviction that meat and spices were unhealthy
and, maybe worse, sexual stimulants. The cofounder of the new Seventh-day
Adventist denomination, who'd had visions of the end of the world, also had
a vision of a hospital devoted to water cures and hired an Adventist physician
named Dr. John Kellogg (of the eponymous corn flakes) to run it.*

---

* One of the patients at Kellogg's Seventh-day Adventist sanitarium was C. W. Post, who
got the idea there for Grape Nuts, which made him rich. Among Grape Nuts' advertised

Out of this cross-fertilization of pseudoscience and spirituality came new sects and eventually one whole new American religion. In the 1830s in Maine, a clockmaker and inventor with the irresistible name Phineas P. Quimby found out about mesmerism. He became a practitioner, hypnotizing sick and unhappy people and persuading them to feel better. Quimby's work and philosophy were a wellspring of the New Thought movement, a nineteenth-century American precursor to both Scientology and the New Age movement of the twentieth and twenty-first centuries. New Thought believers figured that belief conquers all, that misery and bliss are all in your head. Some disciples were specifically Christian, some weren't, but they all pitched themselves as scientific as well as mystical, providers of practical tools for individual perfection.

In 1862, a few years before he died, Quimby took on a patient named Mary Patterson, a sickly fellow New Englander who'd tried homeopathy and water cures (and communicating with the dead) before the mesmerism seemed to work. Around the time Quimby died and her husband abandoned her, Mrs. Patterson hurt her back in an accident. After reading the Bible's account of Jesus curing a paralytic, she found her own injury cured. She set about inventing her own quasi-Christian pseudoscientific belief system, which she presented in a book called *Science and Health*. There's only "*belief* in pain.*" "We say man suffers from the effects of cold, heat, fatigue. This is human belief, not the truth of being, for matter cannot suffer," and "what is termed disease does not exist." And not just pain, not just illness, but dying and matter itself—none of it is real. What's more, "evil is an illusion, and it has no real basis. Evil is a false belief" that "has no reality." Over the next few years, she married for a third time and retook her maiden name, becoming Mary Baker Eddy, and founded the Church of Christ, Scientist. Her followers, forming more than a thousand Christian Science churches in America within thirty years, were called not believers but *scientists*.

An individual mesmerist or phrenologist or hydropathist could make a decent living, but selling professional services was not really scalable as a national business. Inventing a religion, as Mary Baker Eddy did, was one way to scale. Manufacturing and selling miraculous products was another, as American wheeler-dealers figured out in the 1830s and '40s, when branded miracle cures became an industry. Small and large businesses started selling all sorts of elixirs, tonics, salves, oils, powders, and pills. The principal ingre-

---

health benefits was curing appendicitis. As it happened, Post later had an apparent appendicitis attack, and when surgery didn't end his distress, he shot and killed himself.

dient of many so-called patent medicines was sugar or alcohol; some contained opium or cocaine. (Dr. Thomas' Electric Oil contained alcohol, opium, *and* cocaine, although it probably did not, as claimed, cure "deafness in 2 days.") But they were mostly sold as secret potions of exotic ingredients collected from nature—literally root of hemlock and slips of yew, if not eye of newt and toe of frog.

"There is no sore it will not heal," the sellers of Hamlin's Wizard Oil promised, "no pain it will not subdue. Pleasant to take, magical in its effects." There was Swaim's Celebrated Panacea, Dr. Dix Tonic Tablets ("Make Sick People Well"), and Dr. Worden's Female Pills for Weak Women, prescribed to cure "hunchbacks," "acquired deformities," and "early decay" as well as menstrual cramps. To cure "asthma, diabetes, epilepsy and cancer," patients were to wear the Electro-Chemical Ring on a finger.

One typical small-time nineteenth-century medicine-seller was a man from upstate New York who traveled the country selling nostrums. "Dr. William A. Rockefeller, the Celebrated Cancer Specialist," his sign announced. "Here for One Day Only. All cases of cancer cured unless too far gone and then can be greatly benefited." (His sons John D. and William Jr. became businessmen of a different kind, founding the Standard Oil Company.) Another of the elder Rockefeller's medicines, dried berries picked from a bush in his mother's yard, was prescribed to women; the berries' important contraindication—*not* to be taken during pregnancy—appears to be a perfect con man's way to market fake abortifacients.

Rockefeller was a typical small-time grifter. On the other hand, Microbe Killer, a mass-marketed pink elixir, which came in large jugs and consisted almost entirely of water, sounded plausibly scientific, the way mesmerism and phrenology and homeopathy had science-y backstories: germ theory was new science, and *microbe* a new coinage. Microbe Killer's claims were extreme, simple, ridiculous: "Cures All Diseases." The inventor built Microbe Killer factories around the world and became rich.

Benjamin Brandreth got even richer. At twenty-five, as soon as he'd inherited his English family's patent medicine business, he moved it and his family—of course—to America. Brandreth's Vegetable Universal Pills were supposed to eliminate "blood impurities" and were advertised as a cure for practically everything: colds, coughs, fevers, flu, pleurisy, "and especially sudden attacks of severe sickness, often resulting in death." One ad describes "a young lady" who'd been ill for years, "her beauty departed," but after two weeks of swallowing Brandreth's Pills, "her health and good looks recovered." Brandreth advertised extensively and constantly in America's new cheap newspapers. A few years after his arrival, a contemporary wrote that "Dr. Brandreth figures larger in the scale of quackery, and hoists a more presuming flag, than all the rest of the fraternity combined." A decade later Brandreth was elected to the New York Senate, founded a bank, and had his pills mentioned in *Moby-Dick.*

Fortunately, American skepticism was still exceptionally robust and correctly focused. In fact, it was as if the First Great Delirium and its outbreaks of wishful fantasy triggered antibodies. In a single generation, Americans came up with the terms *holy roller, double-cross, confidence man, bunkum,* and *sucker.* In 1838 a prominent physician and public health innovator published *Humbugs of New York,* savaging "the fashion of delusion, the reign of humbug," "those who seek to make proselytes to any creed, however absurd, or to find believers in any pretensions, however incredible, or miraculous. They have taken the pills of foreign and domestic quacks by the thousands. . . . They have swallowed . . . homeopathia; and are now equally busy in bolting down Phrenology and Animal Magnetism." The good doctor also rolled his eyes at anticoffee and antiliquor fanatics and saw that what he called "ultraism" extended beyond his field—he ragged on ultra-Protestants, anti-Catholics, these nutty new Mormons, and newspaper hoaxes. And he understood that in America, criticism and debunking were unfortunately fuel for the madness. "Persecution only serves to propagate new theories, whether of philosophy or religion," he wrote. "Indeed, some of the popular follies of the times are indebted only to the real or alleged persecutions they have suffered . . . even for their present existence."

The author of another book of the era, *Quackery Unmasked,* nailed patent medicines as that industry headed toward its peak:

> The American people are great lovers of nostrums. They devour whatever in that line is new, with insatiable voracity. Staid Englishmen look on in astonishment. They call us pill-eaters and syrupdrinkers, and wonder at our fickleness and easy credulity; so that we have almost become a laughing-stock in the eyes of the world.

Brandreth could never have succeeded in his own country, but he saw that the people of the United States, like young birds in their nest, were holding their mouths wide open for something new. He embraced the opportunity and presented himself here, ready to supply their cravings.

In its demand for life-changing miracles, America's exceptionalism was undeniably real.

12

Fantastic Business: The Gold Rush Inflection Point

THE PATENT MEDICINE INDUSTRY EMERGED NOT LONG AFTER AMERICA OFFI-
cially decided that in this new country, ignorant dupes were on their own.
The end of the War of 1812 meant the British naval blockade of U.S. ports
would also end, meaning in turn that southern tobacco could start shipping
again, and the price would thus skyrocket. The Saturday morning in 1815
that news of peace reached New Orleans, a guy who heard it early made a
deal to buy fifty tons of tobacco from a man who didn't yet know the blockade
was ending. The seller, feeling cheated afterward, sued the buyer, but in one
of its most important early opinions, the U.S. Supreme Court unanimously
decided the plaintiff had no recourse: sorry, sucker, in this free market, buyer
and seller beware. Telling less than the whole truth—hustling—had received
a blanket indemnity. In commerce as in the rest of life, when it came to truth
and falsehood, America was a free-fire zone.

"History doesn't *repeat* itself," Mark Twain allegedly said, "but it does
rhyme." In the main features of that story from 1815 New Orleans—greed,
caveat emptor, the South, tobacco—the rhyme I hear is with 1600s Virginia,

that misguided first generation betting their lives on a false promise of gold, finally forced to face reality and become tobacco growers. After that, tobacco became the main cash crop all over the South, and over time that original dream of gold-free-for-the-plucking mostly faded away.

Except finally, two centuries later, the gold fantasy started coming true, first in North Carolina in the early 1800s, after a boy stumbled across a seventeen-pound chunk (which his father sold for a thousandth of its value), then in 1829 in Georgia. Prospectors rushed in. But they were small, essentially regional rehearsals for *the* Gold Rush, the one that started in California in 1848.

Why was one rush among the most transformative events of the century, and the others tiny historical footnotes?

By 1848, Americans' appetite for the *amazing* and the *incredible* had been whetted by two decades of transformative technologies and by the manic fabulism of dime museums and medicine shows and newly sensationalist newspapers. A credulity about E-Z self-improvement—swallowing pills or feeling the Holy Spirit to end one's suffering magically—had been normalized during the First Great Delirium.

At the beginning of 1848, twelve thousand white Americans lived in Oregon, and maybe a thousand in the adjacent Mexican state of Alta California. Then came a piece of preternaturally fortunate timing, luck heaped upon luck: on a Monday morning in January an American building a sawmill in Alta California found a piece of gold in the mill creek, and on the following Wednesday, the treaty ending the Mexican War was signed, instantly making California and all its gold American. The original New World fantasy was validated: El Dorado had appeared.

History doesn't repeat, but it rhymes. Excitable people abandoning settled lives and civilization to travel thousands of miles west to a wilderness utopia? And a wilderness that was truly garden-like, a western Eden occupied by a few exceptionally docile natives? And *gold* for the plucking? The rush to California in the 1800s was unmistakably a mythic replay of America's invention, providential adventure redux. As in the early 1600s, the route was freshly charted, and pioneering expeditions had just undertaken the first journeys west, this time in wagon trains.

For a thousand days, life in the California gold fields was topsy-turvy, an enchanted alternate reality. Without any title to land or expensive machinery, you really could find gold in the gravel of streambeds, sitting in the dirt, knotted in tree roots. Just an ounce, a bit smaller than a penny, was worth the equivalent of a good weekly wage back east, and in the early days it wasn't unusual for one man to find several *pounds* of gold a week. It was the dream-iest possible version of the American Dream: absolutely anybody really could get rich overnight; their background and social station were irrelevant; there were no bosses, merely notional government and laws; the countryside and climate were magnificent. For the first ten thousand Americans who happened to be close to California or quick enough to get there right away, life in the foothills of the Sierras was as much like a fairy tale as anything anywhere before or since.

At the beginning of 1849, a year after the discovery, *The New York Herald* reckoned the prospect of free and easy gold in California had "set the public mind almost on the highway to insanity." Over the next several years, as many as 5 percent of America's young men rushed west to look for gold, maybe 100,000 in 1849, perhaps another 200,000 in 1850. For the whole half-century or so from the founding of the United States through 1847, total national gold production had been thirty-seven tons. During the decade after gold was discovered in California an average of seventy-six tons *per year* were mined there.

For Americans, I believe, the Gold Rush was an inflection point, permanently changing the way we thought about impossible dreams and luck and the shape of reality. Maybe there would be an eternal heavenly reward, but life right here could become a fabulous romance, reality as marvelous as any tall tale. Personal reinvention was not just theoretically possible but suddenly happening wholesale. Soft Boston clerks and daydreaming Pennsylvania farmhands were lighting out for the territories and turning themselves into colorful Wild West characters. *Bonanza* and *pay dirt* entered the language.

These giddy new habits of mind became central to the ethos of the West, of course, but the Gold Rush also triggered a shift in the psychology of Americans at large. Gold in California resurrected the distinctly un-Puritan ambition of the first Virginia settlers—the individual and piratical freedom to grab for instant wealth, with little or no adult supervision. Where our founding seventeenth-century mindsets overlapped—the Massachusetts religious die-hards and the get-rich-quick Virginians—was in their common determination to believe the unbelievable, live enchanted lives, be characters in their own adventure stories, make their fantasies real. The Gold Rush was all that, no waiting required. Something like magic could suddenly sweep aside common sense. Miracles actually happened in America.

This dream-come-true celebration of individualism was brief. The flood-tide of luck in northern California receded. An average miner's take in 1849 was a third of what it had been in 1848 and continued shrinking. In the end, the unlucky outnumbered the superlucky by ten or a hundred to one. Just four years after gold was discovered, total output peaked and mining was industrialized, requiring capital, deeds, bosses, entrepreneurs.

THE JOB CATEGORY OF ENTREPRENEUR, not-necessarily-rich men with access to capital who enlisted other men to create a business out of nothing, came into being at the same time as America, itself a business conjured out of nothing. The organizers of the Virginia Companies, which funded the first colonies in the 1600s, were early entrepreneurs. But when the word entered English in the 1800s, *entrepreneur* was a synonym for *showman* or *impresario,* a creator and promoter of spectacles. Right around the time Tocqueville arrived and the Gold Rush happened, its meaning expanded to encompass people starting every sort of business. "I know of no country where the love of money has taken stronger hold on the affections of men," Tocqueville observed. "Love of money is either the chief or secondary motive in everything Americans do."

Individual anybodies with good ideas and grit and luck could imagine and then create new businesses and industries. The entrepreneurial instinct has served America well. But as with the three hundred thousand California gold-seekers in 1849–50 who followed the fortunate ten thousand in 1848, as with the American habit of wishfulness in general, a confirmation bias kicks in: from Ben Franklin to Mark Zuckerberg, the stories of the supremely successful entrepreneurs obscure the forgotten millions of losers and nincompoops. The fabulous successes seem like proof of the power of passionate belief in oneself, our American faith in faith.

Entrepreneurs exist on a smoke-and-mirrors spectrum, from small-time fabulists to legitimately world-changing visionaries. But part of every entrepreneur's job is to persuade and recruit others to believe in a dream, and often those dreams are pure fantasies. A defining feature of America from the start, according to McDougall's *Freedom Just Around the Corner,* was the unprecedented leeway and success of its hucksters —"self-promoters, scofflaws, occasional frauds, and peripatetic self-reinventors," as well as "builders, doers, go-getters, dreamers." He writes that "Americans are, among other things, prone to be hustlers," which "is simply to acknowledge Americans have enjoyed more opportunity to pursue their ambitions, by foul means or

fair, than any other people in history." For a large pool of hustlers to be successful, of course, requires a large population of easy believers.

The California Gold Rush accelerated the westward migration of dreamy
Americans. Many people had solid reasons to go west. But once there was an
industry based on moving Americans west—the transcontinental railroads—
a large and continuous stream of travelers and settlers was required to sustain
those new entrepreneurial businesses. Which meant that the railroads and
their allies needed to sell the settlers fantasies, as the original New World
speculators had done to prospective Americans back in the 1600s. Occasional new discoveries of gold and silver could pull the most excitable, but the
main lure was land, cheap or even free, and not just to tediously farm. All
over the empty West, the promoters promised, *land* could make you *rich*. An
1874 guidebook called *New Homes: Or, Where to Settle* reported, for instance,
that land in central Nebraska—the middle of nowhere then, the middle of
nowhere still—had increased in value a dozen-fold in the previous dozen
years. My first Nebraska ancestors arrived from rural Tennessee and Missouri in the 1860s and '70s, and bought land. They did not get rich.

A generation later more of my ancestors arrived in Nebraska from Denmark, right before the Panic of 1893. That financial panic, which triggered a
huge economic depression, was caused in part by the unsustainable over-
building of the western railroads and the popping of that railroad bubble.
Which had been inflated by the western real estate bubble. Which happened
even though just twenty years before, the Panic of *1873* had been caused by
the popping of a *previous* railroad bubble. Americans, predisposed to believe
in bonanzas and their own special luckiness, were not really learning the
hard lessons of economic booms and busts.

You know the story of the ant and the grasshopper? The ant is disci-
plined, the grasshopper parties as if the good times will last forever—but
then winter descends; the ant was correct. Americans were always energetic
grasshoppers *as well as* energetic ants, a sui generis crossbreed, which is why
we have been so successful as a nation. Our moxie always came in the two
basic types. We possessed the unexciting virtues embodied by the Puritans
and their secular descendants like Ben Franklin: steady hard work, frugality,
sobriety, and common sense. And then there's our wilder, faster, and looser
side, that packet of attributes that also makes us American: impatient, overexcited gamblers with a weakness for stories too good to be true. Ant mode
consistently tempered grasshopper mode.

A propensity to dream impossible dreams is like other powerful tendencies, okay when kept in check by common sense, at least in the aggregate and over the long run. For most of its history, America had exactly such a dynamic equilibrium between fantasists and realists, mania and moderation, credulity and skepticism. But as much as we wish for a natural and inevitable balance between those competing forces, like the laws in physics, there's no such mechanism governing civilizations. Societies and cultures can lurch out of balance. As ours eventually would do.

13

In Search of Monsters to Destroy: The Conspiracy Theory Habit

CONSPIRACIES EXIST. SOMETIMES GROUPS SECRETLY EXECUTE AGENDAS TO achieve or maintain or expand their power and wealth. In the 1700s militants in America, fearing a conspiracy in London to eliminate their liberty, formed their own conspiracy to resist it. When shooting began in 1775, the English general in Boston called John Adams "as great a conspirator as ever subverted a state," and two months later King George III, not yet mad, said the rebellion was the result of a "desperate conspiracy." The Declaration of Independence consisted mainly of the colonials' hyperbolic catalog of complaints about the king's conspiracy to enslave his American subjects, his "design to reduce them under absolute despotism."

Americans thereby started off having some reason to believe that conspiracies importantly drive politics and history. It's out of such precedents and bits of reality that myths often grow and endure: "its power," the cognitive psychology pioneer Jerome Bruner wrote of myth, "is that it lives on the feather line between fantasy and reality." As it turned out, the recipe for what came to be America—our peculiar history, our peculiar psychology, the symbiosis between them—was also specifically a recipe for a tendency to believe in conspiracies.

For starters, consider Protestantism—an alternative system of truth-telling to replace the Vatican conspiracy's false and corrupted version. The Puritans, oppressed by conniving elites, developed a self-identity focused on victimhood that sent them into American self-exile. When the Dissenters' new American society promptly produced its own dissenters, the subversives and oppressors each saw the other as a conspiracy.

Christian religiosity itself, in particular our pseudo-hyperrational kind, amounts to belief in the grandest and greatest conspiracy of all: God the mastermind plotting and executing His all-encompassing scheme, assisted by a team of co-conspirators, the angels and prophets. Like religious explanations, conspiratorial explanations of the world tend to connect all sorts of dots, real and imaginary, drawing lines to impute intention and design and purpose everywhere, ignoring the generally greater power of randomness and happenstance.

Fantastical conspiracy theories tend to imagine secret plots of colossal scale, duration, and power. Beliefs in American conspiracies in the 1800s, the Yale historian David Brion Davis has written, usually consisted of

> hard grains of truth connected with a mucilage of exaggeration and fantasy. But the central theme, which is so central to the paranoid style, is the conviction that an exclusive monolithic structure has imposed a purposeful pattern on otherwise unpredictable events. One suspects this conviction is a product of the liberal faith, inherited from the Enlightenment, that history can be shaped in accordance with a rational plan. . . . When the irrationality of events proves that the children of light have lost control, then the children of darkness must have secretly seized the levers of history. . . . The illusion of American omnipotence . . . easily leads to a fear of un-American omnipotence.

Another result of America's Enlightenment roots is that thick strain of skepticism. That reflex, to disbelieve official explanations, seems antithetical to religious belief and faith in hidden purposes and plans. *Skepticism,* after all, is an antonym for *credulity.* But when both are robust and overheated, they can fuse into conspiracy-mindedness. Take nothing on faith—except that the truth is deliberately hidden and can be discovered and precisely diagrammed.

During their first century, Americans believed themselves beset by satanic conspiracies of witches and Indians. During their second century, there were panics about foreign conspiracies—despotically inclined leaders in league with European monarchs, other despotic leaders in league with European revolutionaries. Americans learned of the all-powerful master cabal controlling the European subversives from a 1797 book called *Proofs of a Conspiracy,* about the Freemasons and Illuminati. One of its overexcited readers was a prominent Massachusetts minister, a former student of Jonathan Edwards's named Jedediah Morse, who delivered sermon after sermon about the evil global Illuminati conspiracy. *Dangerous nonsense,* other conspiracy theorists insisted—the Illuminati conspiracy was imaginary, concocted by Alexander Hamilton in conspiratorial league with the British to incite American panic. In 1798 Congress passed and President John Adams signed the Alien Acts, giving him the power to imprison or deport any suspicious foreigner—especially French ones, whose recent revolution, people said, had been an Illuminati undertaking.

Besides, the French were nearly all Catholic, and paranoia about the Vatican conspiracy to destroy our nation went into overdrive during the 1800s. The pope's agents in America—that is, Catholics—were doubling every decade. Jedediah Morse's son, a New York City painting professor and tinkerer, developed a sideline as a hysterical anti-Catholic crusader just as he was about to invent his telegraph. Samuel F. B. Morse's 1835 book, *Foreign Conspiracy Against the Liberties of the United States,* was an exposé of "the cloven foot of this subtle foreign heresy . . . the existence of a *foreign conspiracy* against the liberties of the country."

At the same moment, Americans also awoke, finally, to the elder Morse's warnings about the Freemason conspiracy. Masonic lodges, which had started in England, were then more or less what they are now: adult fraternities, clubs where public-spirited men gathered to eat, drink, network, and perform goofy secret rituals. George Washington and dozens of signers of both the Declaration and the Constitution had been Masons. "Their Grand Secret," the young Freemason Ben Franklin said, "is that they have no secret at all." The members were disproportionately upscale and well connected. As religious frenzy swept the country in the 1820s and '30s—the so-called Second Great Awakening—so did a panic, particularly among the very religious, about an all-powerful Freemason conspiracy supposedly running America.*

---

* To be fair, a conspiracy of Masons in upstate New York in 1826 apparently did murder an ex-Mason who'd written an exposé of the organization's secret oaths, and a conspiracy of Masons apparently did cover up that crime.

They were said to be debauched, depraved, satanic operators of a hidden government. The principal fear-mongers were, first, Christian clergy riding the national fantasy wave, then resentful common folk and the opportunists pandering to them, then even an ex-president. "There is no fouler stain upon the Morals of this nation," declared John Quincy Adams, "than the Institution of Freemasonry." *No fouler stain,* said the man crusading against slavery, who'd also famously said that the rational, peaceful United States "goes not abroad in search of monsters to destroy."

Maybe the simultaneous mass hysterias over Catholic immigrants and native-born Masonic snobs was partly what Freud called displacement—in place of anxiety about the looming national crackup over slavery, it was simpler and easier to vent about imaginary fears. The great irony, as Davis noted, was that in America, "actual conspiracies from Aaron Burr to the American Communist Party have seldom been as significant social realities as the movements against alleged conspiratorial groups." He was writing about the Northern belief, before the Civil War, in a "Slave Power conspiracy." When the actual, epochal crisis over slavery finally became undeniable, however, each side naturally saw the other as the deluded pawn of evil puppet-masters.

14

The War Between States of Mind

THE CIVIL WAR RESULTED FROM LARGE AND REAL DISAGREEMENTS BETWEEN people in the South and the North—about two different political economies, two different cultures, and two irreconcilable moral understandings. The causes were not imaginary. But during the decades leading up to the war, those authentic causes became wrapped in self-serving fictions on both sides—moral and cultural and political fantasies.

As I've said, some conspiracies are real, especially ones with particular, narrow purposes. In Virginia in 1831, Nat Turner and his enslaved co-conspirators killed dozens of white people over two days, and in 1859 John Brown and his abolitionist co-conspirators staged a raid on a federal arms depot, intending to incite and equip a slave rebellion. The Underground Railroad was the work of an ongoing national conspiracy. And at the end of the war, a short-lived conspiracy was behind the assassination of President Lincoln. None of those were just theories.

Acknowledging actual, specific conspiracies makes sense. But reflexive conspiracism can become a bad habit and a misguided way of making sense of current events. In 1836, when anti-Masonic paranoia was burning itself out and abolitionism was still a fringe idea, for instance, an aging American revolutionary from South Carolina published *The South Vindicated from the Treason and Fanaticism of the North Abolitionist*. "The efforts of these conspirators," he wrote, "at their midnight meetings, where the bubbling cauldron of abolition was filled with its pestilential materials, and the fire beneath kindled by the breath of the fanatics has often reminded us of the witch scene in *Macbeth*."

The abolitionists were just as convinced of an all-powerful conspiracy on the other side. In 1852 the abolitionist party's presidential candidate saw that "the inexplicable labyrinths of American politics for the last sixty years," including the War of 1812 and the dismantling of the national bank, were *all explained* as parts of the slaveholders' perfect plot, because "the Slave Power, like the power of the pit, never lacks for a stratagem."

In the 1850s it seemed obvious to many Northerners that the current president and previous president had conspired secretly with the chief justice of the Supreme Court to entrench the Slave Power conspiracy. "We cannot absolutely know that all these exact adaptations are the result of preconcert," Abraham Lincoln said in his famous "House Divided" speech, during his failed run for the Senate in 1858. He figured his opponent, the incumbent Democrat, was another of the co-conspirators. *We can't absolutely know*—but then Lincoln proceeded to draw a bright evidentiary line in the murk between motive and result. "When we see a lot of framed timbers, different portions of which we know have been gotten out at different times and places and by different workmen"—he then cutely gave only the first names of each of the alleged co-conspirators, including the U.S. senator from Illinois who was about to defeat him.

> And we see these timbers joined together, and see they exactly make the frame of a house or a mill, all the tenons and mortices exactly fitting, and all the lengths and proportions of the different pieces exactly adapted to their respective places, and not a piece too many or too few . . . in such a case we find it impossible not to believe that [the workmen] all understood one another from the beginning, and all worked upon a common plan or draft drawn up before the first lick was struck.

Honest Abe, conspiracy theorist. In their speculations and theories, habitual believers in conspiracy do exactly what they imagine conspirators somehow do in the real world—make the tenons and mortices and lengths and proportions of different pieces fit *exactly*.

After secession happened and fighting broke out, conspiracy theories multiplied, most of them crazily implausible, like the one in an 1863 exposé called *Interior Causes of the War: The Nation Demonized and Its President a Spirit-Rapper*. The author, a "resident of Ohio," said it was no coincidence that abolitionism and the craze for communicating with the dead had taken off simultaneously during the late 1840s and 1850s. The spirits, dead people, "have a magnetism peculiar to themselves, fired with vengeance [and] hatred." In other words, ghosts and their living American interlocutors— the spiritualists—were scheming to destroy the nation. "For a number of years before the war, the spiritualists were promised, by spirits, a president of their own faith." Lincoln "sprang mysteriously from the prairies," "selected by spirits for the very work—the equalization of white men and negroes—which he is now endeavoring to perform." "These spirits . . . are now in control" of the Union. By means of "a secret hole in the White House, a rapping table," "Mr. Lincoln, and at least a portion of his cabinet . . . are now holding spiritual circles in the executive mansion, and consulting spirits in regard to the prospects and conduct of the war." The spirits had essentially hypnotized Lincoln and the Union leaders into thinking they'd win the Civil War in order to send America "down the broad road to ruin."

THEN THERE WERE THE POWERFUL religious rationales for annihilating one's fellow Americans. Each side was sincerely convinced that it was carrying out God's orders. In the North and the South, soldiers and ministers and civilians believed and said again and again, "God is on our side."

Sermons on both sides depicted the war as part of the divine plan, a holy battle on the way to Armageddon and Christ's reign. In fact, coming not long after the Second Great Awakening, the war made religion matter even more to Americans, bringing the grand Christian fantasy vividly back to life. "Repeatedly," Davis writes of Northerners in *The Slave Power Conspiracy and the Paranoid Style,* "the opponents of the Slave Power likened their stand to that of Protestant reformers from Luther to Wesley, and thought of their crusade as a reenactment of the sacred struggles against the Kingdom of Darkness."

And each accused the other of being fanatics hijacking Christianity. An Alabama newspaper editor wrote that war-hungry, self-righteous New

Englanders "exhibit those severe traits of fanaticism which had ever marked their history," such as "burning witches."

Early in the war, after things went badly for the Union armies, plenty of Northerners thought that was the result not of bad generals and bad luck but of God punishing the North for not yet outlawing slavery. Two years in, an evangelical mania—mass baptisms, battlefield revival meetings, thousands of conversions—swept through both armies, especially the Confederates, who were starting to lose. Weeks before the war ended, Lincoln delivered his second inaugural address, beloved today for its even-handed suggestion that the Lord was *neither* side's commander-in-chief: "Both read the same Bible and pray to the same God. . . . let us judge not that we be not judged."

However, between there and the lovely end ("With malice toward none"), Lincoln's next couple of hundred words, rarely quoted, conclude that God *is* in charge and essentially *is* on the Union side. And three months later, with the war won, the sermon of a New York minister was typical: God had "yoked the whirlwinds of carnage and of civil war to the chariot of his own predestined triumph." Victory (and 750,000 deaths) had been the divine plan all along.

IN ADDITION TO FIGHTING ON behalf of a religious dream, the Confederacy fought to preserve an elaborate secular dream, maybe more powerful—the fantasy that the South was the last outpost of the old-fashioned virtues of chivalry, honor, grace, and charm.

This myth too was extruded from a germ of historical reality. Following the first colonists in Virginia, the ones whose dreams of gold came to nothing, a generation of aristocrats arrived from England with titles to large American estates. They came because they'd been on the losing side in the English Civil War against . . . the Puritans. Just as *Puritan* was originally a slur against Protestants, the Puritans in turn had denigrated their opponents as imperious and snobbish *Cavaliers,* who adopted the name themselves. The transplanted Southern Cavaliers set about re-creating feudal Olde England in the New World, with black slaves instead of white serfs.

By the 1800s, of course, not many Southerners were either well-to-do or aristocratic, but the myth endured. And as the North grew still more *northern*—urban, calculating, censorious, grasping—and started phasing out slavery, the Southern myth was fomented and believed more devoutly than ever. In American books, according to Google's Ngram—the database of mil-

lions of digitized books—the frequency of the word *cavalier* quintupled between 1810 and 1840.* All kinds of people in the South came to think of
themselves as civilized gentlemen and ladies who had been opposed forever
by the same breed of unromantic fanatics and gradgrinds.

Southerners' fictionalized self-conception was encouraged and shaped
for decades by novels that enshrined the Cavalier myth and depicted the
plantation system as idyllic. *Swallow Barn,* published in 1832, was immensely
popular. "I am quite sure they could never become a happier people than I
find them here," the narrator says of the fictional slaves on a Virginia plantation. "No tribe of people has ever passed from barbarism to civilization
whose . . . progress has been more secure from harm, more genial to their
character, or better supplied with mild and beneficent guardianship, adapted
to the actual state of their intellectual feebleness, than the Negroes of Swallow Barn." The author revised and reissued the novel in 1852, he explained at
the time, as "an antidote to the abolition mischief."†

But even more influential in feeding Southerners' self-glorifying fantasy
of the South were novels not quite so on the nose, set neither in America nor
in the present day. Walter Scott's books—such as *Ivanhoe, Waverley,* and
Woodstock, or The Cavalier—are overwrought, sentimental historical fictions
of English and Scottish knights and lords and ladies of centuries past. There
had never been an author more popular. He published a new novel every eighteen months between 1814 and 1832, just as Southerners became desperate
to justify and romanticize their slave-based neofeudalism. "The appearance
of a new novel from his pen caused a greater sensation in the United States
than did some of the battles of Napoleon," an American publisher and contemporary of Scott's wrote after he died. "Everybody read these works; everybody."

Everybody especially in the South, where children and steamboats and
plantations and dozens of towns were named after Scott's fictional and fictionalized characters and olden-times and imaginary places. Shortly after the
Civil War, another famous novelist, a former Southerner, specifically blamed
the great catastrophe of the South and of America's nineteenth century on
Scott's novels. The region had been modernizing along with the North during
the decades after the Revolution, Mark Twain wrote in *Life on the Mississippi,*

* Throughout this book, I cite quantified historical rises and falls in the use of words and
phrases; they're all derived from Google Ngram.
† The views of the author, a friend of many of the most celebrated novelists of his day,
evolved, as we now say of politicians: he was proposed to be Lincoln's vice president in
1860 and during the war became an abolitionist.

but things changed: "Then comes Sir Walter Scott with his enchantments," and

> the change of character can be traced rather more easily to Sir Wal-
> ter's influence than to that of any other thing or person. By his single
> might [he] checks this wave of progress, and even turns it back; sets
> the world in love with dreams and phantoms; with decayed and
> swinish forms of religion; . . . with the sillinesses and emptinesses,
> sham grandeurs . . . and sham chivalries of a brainless and worthless
> long-vanished society. He did measureless harm; more real and last-
> ing harm, perhaps, than any other individual that ever wrote. . . . It
> was Sir Walter that made every gentleman in the South a Major or a
> Colonel, or a General or a Judge, before the war. . . .
>   Sir Walter had so large a hand in making Southern character, as
> it existed before the war, that he is in great measure responsible for
> the war.

Twain was a hyperbolist, for sure, but his conclusion still bears repeating: a particular set of historical fictions and fantasies led to secession and Civil War.

15

Ten Million Little Houses on the Prairie

THE HOUSE WHERE I GREW UP IN NEBRASKA SAT ON AN ACRE OF LAND COV-
ered with big trees and studded with ruins—a tiny rectangular pond with a
fountain, a brick rose arbor, a small greenhouse, sheds. Next door was a wild,
empty acre my parents didn't own but that my siblings and I treated as our
own Neverland. As kids, we spent days and nights on adventures, pretending
to be cowboys, trappers, and outlaws, climbing trees and digging foxholes,
smoking cigarettes and blowing stuff up. For our annual vacations, my parents took us on camping trips to isolated northern forests and lakes and rivers, where the family more or less pretended to be pioneers. Today my wife
and I own a house hours outside New York City where we hunker for days
without seeing other houses or people or hearing cars, staring at sunlit hedge-
rows and forests and the occasional bear, half-pretending we're settlers or
gentry, different people living in a different century, or characters in a novel.
For a few years, we really went overboard, raising sheep.

In other words, I have fully and consistently indulged in the great American pastoral fantasy.

Of course, at the turn of the seventeenth century, while Englishmen back in England promoting emigration gushed about the physical magnificence of the New World they'd never seen, the actual emigrants' reactions tended more toward dread and misery, seeing the place as a horror to be suffered as part of their Christian adventure, a replay of the ancient Israelites' humbling and testing for forty years in Exodus. In 1662 a prominent young Massachusetts minister published a poem called "God's Controversy with New-England," reflecting the standard Puritan view of the place to which his parents had brought him—"a waste and howling wilderness" and "dark and dismal western woods."* That "howling wilderness" was the Puritans' standard term, from the Bible. But within a few generations, with a lot of the wilderness cut back and ordered by walls, roads, farms, and towns, the American attitude had changed.

We discovered that our wild mountains and forests and rivers were *sublime*—a word that quintupled in American books during the 1700s. We were defined by our romantic landscapes, untamed and tamed, terrifying and glorious, as painted by Thomas Cole and Albert Bierstadt and the Frederics Church and Remington, and by the endless little pictures of nature-nestling homes mass-produced by Currier & Ives. The same wild and pastoral America was romanticized in the novels of James Fenimore Cooper, Washington Irving, and William Cullen Bryant and in dime novels about the West—and later by Laura Ingalls Wilder. American pictures and stories helped embed specifically *American nature* deep in the American dream.

In the past, for aeons, as Leo Marx writes in *The Machine in the Garden*, dreams of withdrawing "from the great world [to] begin a new life in a fresh, green landscape" had been a genre of pure fantasy, "a poetic theme, not to be confused with the way poets did in fact live." But in America by the late 1700s, "the dream of a retreat to an oasis of harmony and joy was removed from its traditional literary context. . . . The effect of the American environment . . . was to break down commonsense distinctions between art and life." In this infinite new place, land of the literal, you could live this fantasy.

A century after the first English settlers came west to a howling wilderness, a family of persecuted English Quakers came and built a cabin farther west, to avoid persecution by Quakers who'd preceded them, in the howling

---

* The same minister the same year also published *Day of Doom*, America's first bestseller, an extremely long and cheerfully terrifying poem about Judgment Day: "However fair, however square, your way and work hath been . . . Earth's dwellers all . . . suffer must, for it is just, Eternal misery."

wilderness of Pennsylvania, and then moved deeper into the wilderness, to North Carolina. From there, one of their middle-aged middle sons led settlers even farther west into a fresh piece of wilderness. On his fiftieth birthday, an eight-thousand-word memoir of his first dozen years living on the new frontier was published, possibly written by him. "No populous city, with all the varieties of commerce and stately structures, could afford so much pleasure to my mind, as the beauties of nature" in "Kentucke, lately an howling wilderness . . . become a fruitful field." The little book made Daniel Boone world famous, turning him into an emblematic American, a real-life superhero. Another bestselling as-told-to memoir featured him wrestling a bear and escaping natives by swinging on vines.

Boone lived thirty-seven years as a celebrity, surviving and thriving on the edge of the American wilderness as he made it progressively less wild, more pastoral. His English contemporary Lord Byron, the romantic poet, devoted four stanzas to Boone in his final masterwork in the 1820s: "When they built up unto his darling trees,— / He moved some hundred miles off, for a station / Where there were fewer houses and more ease." Which was just the kind of stuff Boone claimed to despise: "Nothing embitters my old age," he wrote, like "the circulation of absurd stories that I retire as civilization advances." But in fact, he leveraged his living-legend frontiersman celebrity to become a successful politician and less successful land speculator. His life, authentic and extraordinary but also fictionalized even as he lived it, became for his fellow citizens a real-time, real-life fantasy of the ultimate American Natural Man, an early version of the kind of supercelebrity that Buffalo Bill would fictionalize and monetize a half-century after Boone died.

The American pastoral ideal also grew out of the new Christianity that considered itself more perfect because it was more pure and primitive. Americans' loathing of Catholicism and later of monarchy devolved into a loathing of Europe and of cities as well. All of which made it easier for Americans to turn the lemon of the New World—the horrifying wilderness—into lemonade, to make the new nation one in which (tamed) nature was ever present. Americans wanted it both ways, the prosperity and comfort that required towns and cities and factories and railroads, but also the picturesque fantasy that one was still Boone-like, living near where the buffalo roam and the deer and the antelope play.

For all the actual miseries and life-and-death threats the wagon-train generations endured, they moved west equipped with fantasies as well as pans and axes and guns, real-life characters in a narrative jury-rigged out of the romantic tales and biblical stories they'd read and heard and the pictures they'd seen. Those pioneers were a tiny minority of Americans. But forests and mountains and vast grassy vistas were now a key piece of the national story—"a cultural and moral resource and a basis for national self-esteem," as Roderick Frazier Nash writes in *Wilderness and the American Mind*. Americans living in towns and cities, in order to feel truly, virtuously American, needed nearby *reminders* of wild nature, needed to pretend they were pioneers living at the edge of the untamed.

If you had the American fantasy knack, enough belief in your own beliefs, you could feel immersed in nature without traveling far or risking a thing. When I was sixteen, in 1970, I read *Walden* and adored it. *I* believed in civil disobedience to oppose an unjust war of aggression on impoverished foreigners, and so had this guy a century earlier. *I* had briefly lived in a tent by a pond in the woods by myself—and he had published a famous book about doing pretty much the same thing.

Henry David Thoreau invented a certain kind of entitled, upper-middle-class extended adolescence. After college he hung around the nice Boston suburb where he'd grown up, taught some school, wrote the occasional essay, networked, became personal assistant and protégé to a famous local writer (Ralph Waldo Emerson), decided eating meat was bad, and on a camping trip with a local rich kid accidentally burned down three hundred acres of forest.

Then, at twenty-seven, in 1844, he hatched a high-concept plan for a project that epitomized the pastoral fantasy that American suburbanites and hippies and country-home owners have reenacted ever since. On a wooded lot that Emerson owned, young Henry built a one-room cabin. He moved in on the Fourth of July—nice touch—and imagined he was an American hinterlander, rustic and self-reliant, fully communing with nature, pure and virtuous. *Walden* was the book of *pensées* he published chronicling his two years "in the woods, a mile from any neighbor, in a house which I had built myself . . . and earned my living by the labor of my hands only. . . . I wanted to live deep and suck out all the marrow of life. . . . Instead of no path to the front-yard gate in the Great Snow—no gate—no front-yard—and no path to the civilized world."

In fact, his cabin, which his friends helped him build, was barely a half-hour walk from the prosperous old town where his mom and dad and a couple of thousand other people lived, and only a seventeen-mile trip on the new railroad from the third-largest city in America. John Muir, the nature-worshipping American who actually walked the walk a generation later, mocked Thoreau as a poseur pretending to "see forests in orchards and patches of huckleberry brush" a "mere saunter" from Concord. Indeed, when

Thoreau left Walden Pond to spend a couple of weeks in the true wilderness of northern Maine, he was horrified—"grim and wild," "vast, Titanic, inhuman Nature." After eight hundred days living deep and sucking out all the marrow of existence, he returned to town, helping run his father's pencil-making business, living for the rest of his life at his parents' big house on Main Street. Thoreau epitomized this particular have-your-cake-and-eat-it American fantasy, a life in harmony with nature as long as it's not too uncomfortable or inconvenient.

In addition, Thoreau believed in fairies and astrology and thought the full moon enabled him to have out-of-body experiences. He and Emerson were Transcendentalists, the lightly Asian-flavored link between the bland, educated Protestantism of the American Enlightenment and the spicy pot-luck animism and mysticism efflorescing when I first read *Walden*. "Standing on the bare ground," Emerson told an audience shortly before Thoreau published *Walden*, "my head bathed in the blithe air, and uplifting into empty space,—all mean egotism vanishes. I become a transparent eyeball. I am nothing. I see all. The currents of the Universal Being circulate through me; I am part or particle of God." *Humans are essentially good. All creation exists in a magnificent web of interconnection. Nature is God and God is nature.* What's not to like?

Right around that time, thirty-two-year-old Herman Melville wrote a letter to his friend Nathaniel Hawthorne about this wave of romantic giddiness. Melville appreciated the delicious, seductive power of their peers' transcendental ecstasies, but he also understood them to be on a slippery slope toward a very American solipsism. "'Live in the all,'" Melville wrote to Hawthorne.

> What nonsense! . . .
>
> This "all" feeling . . . there is some truth in. You must often have felt it, lying on the grass on a warm summer's day. Your legs seem to send out shoots into the earth. Your hair feels like leaves upon your head. This is the <u>all</u> feeling. But what plays the mischief with the truth is that men will insist upon the universal application of a temporary feeling or opinion.

That is, it only becomes problematic when people refuse to let blissful epiphanies remain mostly obscure and evanescent.

This American impulse to *live* a pastoral fantasy, as Leo Marx writes, also "was embodied in various utopian schemes for making America the site of a new beginning for western society." History was rhyming again. Just as religious dissenters like the Quakers and Shakers had split off into their own fantasy communities during the 1600s and 1700s, citizens in the 1800s with idiosyncratic ideals—political, economic, nutritional, sexual—set out into the countryside to form better, more perfect micronations within their new nation. More than a hundred utopian communities were established across the American countryside during the First Great Delirium. Among the most famous were Fruitlands and Brook Farm, organized by well-to-do Transcendentalists outside Boston. The other settlements ranged in size from a dozen to hundreds of people, ridiculous and fascinating and adorable American fantasias. Except for the free-love Oneida Community, which had multiple branches in the Northeast and lasted for decades before morphing into a major cutlery and tableware company, they were short-lived—but in the late 1960s, at the birth of modern American Fantasyland, they reincarnated as communes.

At the beginning of the 1800s, 94 percent of Americans lived in rural places. By 1900, nearly half lived in towns and cities. The population had grown fourteen times as large, and the economy seventy times. But the American Dream required living in a little house on the prairie, in the big woods, on the banks of a creek or shores of a lake. Or rather, as the twentieth century proceeded, in some plausible facsimile of such a place. It was a perfect amalgam, nostalgia for the pioneer life along with a sense of spiritual purity. And so, going on two centuries after Thoreau played backwoodsman, most Americans today live in suburbs, if not in pastoral simulacra actually called Walden Pond (in Indianapolis, near Cleveland, near Detroit, in Durham, North Carolina, sea to shining sea), then in Maple Creek, Witherspoon Meadow, Oak Run, Eagle Valley, Elm Lake, Barrington Brook, or Turtle Knoll.*

But I'm getting ahead of myself.

* Apart from the subdivisions actually called Walden Pond, the others are the product of the Suburban Development Name Generator, an entertaining app.

16

Fantasy Industrialized

IN HIS BOOK ABOUT THE LIVING-OFF-THE-GRID STUNT, WHICH HE WROTE after moving back to town, Thoreau declared that he was choosing "not to live in this restless, nervous, bustling, trivial Nineteenth Century." From his high ground, he looked down on all the American clamor and vulgarity. "What are men *celebrating*?"

He had a point. At that *Walden* moment, modern media and advertising and show business, all interdependent, were busy being born in America. The second quarter of the nineteenth century was when Americans began using the phrases *show business, celebrities, ad, brand,* and *salesmanship*. It suddenly seemed possible and irresistible to advertise and sell almost anything, to make fictions seem real, to spread entertainment into other parts of American life.

Consider the selling of the president 1840. William Henry Harrison was the first fully merchandised candidate. He had grown up rich and was the nominee of the elites' Whig Party. But his spin doctors sold him to voters as the opposite—a common man, a rough regular guy, with on-message campaign songs and chants, one about his "homespun coat" and "no ruffled shirt." They branded him with life-size and miniature log cabins, and they gave out whiskey in bottles shaped like log cabins and shaving soap called Log-Cabin Emollient. Harrison had fought Indians in the West forty years earlier, so his handlers had the candidate perform Indian war cries at campaign events. His opponent's upbringing really had been humble, but he was the incumbent president and thus could be framed as an elitist. Harrison won by a landslide.

What was working for patent medicines also worked for a political candidate. And essential to both were the new, large-circulation newspapers and magazines that much faster, bigger, steam-powered presses had made possible. These cheap daily papers didn't scruple about the advertising they published, and they had loose standards of accuracy and truth in their news reports as well. They were beacons of a new American audacity about blurring and erasing the lines between factual truth and entertaining make-believe.

The New York Sun was the great pioneer penny paper, and in 1835 it published an extraordinary six-part, sixteen-thousand-word series. Every day for a week, a battalion of newsboys—also an invention of the two-year-old Sun—shouted the extraordinary news on the streets of America's largest city: famous astronomers at a new superpowerful telescope in South Africa had discovered life on the moon!

The moon had forests, oceans, lakes, rivers, birds, tiny bison and zebras, blue unicorns, giant shellfish, beavers walking upright and carrying young in their paws. It had a magnificent seventy-foot-high temple of polished blue stone with a golden roof. It was inhabited by winged, hairy humanoids, "man-bats," evidently "rational beings," happy vegetarians who "appeared impassioned and emphatic" and "capable of producing works of art." There were dark man-bats and others "of larger stature . . . less dark in color, and in every respect an improved variety of the race."

The Sun sold a hundred thousand copies that week in a city of three hundred thousand people. "The credulity was general," the editor of another paper recalled. "All New York rang with the wonderful discoveries. . . . There were, indeed, a few sceptics; but to venture to express a doubt of the genuineness of the great lunar discoveries, was considered almost as heinous a sin as to question the truth of revelation." The news was believed not just by the rabble. "The promulgation of these discoveries," wrote Horace Greeley, "creates a new era in astronomy and science generally." Up at Yale, a writer noted, the campus "was alive with staunch supporters . . . Students and professors, doctors in divinity and law—and all the rest of the reading community, looked daily for the arrival of the New York mail with unexampled avidity and implicit faith. . . . Nobody expressed or entertained a doubt as to the truth of the story." Three years later, long after the story had been exposed as an entirely fictional hoax, a New York writer remarked that "very many in our city [still] regard those revelations with more of reverence and confidence than any of the established truths in physics."

The story was believed not just because Americans were predisposed to believe exciting untruths, but because it contained shards of plausibility. The articles were intelligently written and filled with detail. A new Royal Observatory did exist on the Cape of Good Hope; there was an amazing forty-foot telescope in England; Mars had just been mapped.

Not long before, the editor of a Connecticut newspaper had received a letter from a local teenager warning about the larger, ongoing part of the Great Delirium—his "fears" of "the evils resulting from undue religious excitement" going on around him. After the newspaper declined to publish it, the boy started his own newspaper. As he recalled the fervor years later, "by means of systematized effort, large numbers of people of all ages, but especially the young, were converted" to born-again Christianity. "So great was the alarm awakened in the minds of some of these converts, that they became victims of religious frenzy. . . . Many thousands of our citizens were influenced by the religious enthusiasm which was sweeping like a tornado through our land."

That young man was Phineas Barnum, known as P.T., who by his early twenties was earning a living in Connecticut selling lottery tickets. Coming of age during this period of avid belief in the unbelievable, Barnum had had his career-making, world-changing epiphany: he realized "the perfect good-nature with which the American public submits to a clever humbug."

As other states were doing at the time, Connecticut outlawed lotteries. Nearly broke, he wrote in his autobiography, young Barnum moved to New York City "to 'seek my fortune.'" In the summer of 1835, just as the *Sun* was preparing its series on lunar bat-men and unicorns, he read in another paper about an enslaved African-American woman—blind, toothless, paraplegic, but "very sociable," he soon discovered—who said she'd been George Washington's "mammy" a century earlier. She also claimed she was 161 years old. "The story," he decided, "seemed plausible." He bought her for a thousand dollars, printed handbills and posters, notified the newspapers, and took his slave on the road until she died some months later, "carrying out my new vocation of showman."

During the six years it took for his new vocation to achieve momentum, the first American advertising agency opened, and Barnum also worked as an ad copywriter. In 1841 he opened his American Museum, a big, multistory, multimedia entertainment complex in the center of Manhattan. Among its most notorious and popular early attractions was the corpse of what he called the Feejee Mermaid. It was a taxidermied construction combining a primate and a fish that Barnum had acquired. Before he put it on exhibit, he recalled in his autobiography, the naturalist he employed said he knew of no ape with such teeth or arms and no fish with such fins. "'Then why do you suppose it is manufactured?' I inquired. 'Because I don't believe in mermaids,' replied the naturalist. 'That is no reason at all,' said I, 'and therefore I'll believe in the mermaid, and hire it.'"

P. T. Barnum was the great early American merchandiser of exciting secular fantasies and half-truths. His extremely successful precircus career derived from and fed a fundamental Fantasyland mindset: *If some imaginary proposition is exciting, and nobody can prove it's untrue, then it's my right as an American to believe it's true.* Barnum's response to his naturalist was a perfect perversion of Enlightenment empiricism and logic: *Disbelieving in mermaids isn't proof that this creature isn't a mermaid.* The exhibits and performances at his American Museum freely mixed and confused the authentic with the fake artifact, the didactic with the imaginary, the real with the dubious with the totally counterfeit. "If I have exhibited a questionable dead mermaid in my Museum," Barnum wrote, "I should hope that a little 'clap-trap' occasionally . . . might find an offset [from] the wonderful, instructive, and amusing realities."

But the American Museum's combination of fake and real was more pernicious than if he'd exhibited sideshow humbug exclusively. For decades, it was at the respectable center of the new popular culture, reflecting and reinforcing Americans' appetite for entertaining fibs and a disregard for clear distinctions between make-believe and authentic. And as Neal Gabler notes in *Life: The Movie*, "by the mid-nineteenth century the popular culture here was much vaster than in Europe and had permeated society much more deeply." Barnum's humbuggery was influential.

The pseudopharmaceutical industry, already booming, took his pop cultural big idea and made it both narrower and broader. Each traveling medicine show was devoted to selling a particular manufacturer's patent medicines, but the shows appeared all over the country, especially in small towns. Whereas Barnum's business model was straightforward and traditional—buy a ticket, be entertained—the innovation of the medicine show was closer to that of the advertising-dependent penny press: *pay nothing* to be entertained by musicians, magicians, comedians, and flea circuses in exchange for watching and listening to interstitial live advertisements for dubious medical products.

Entrepreneurialism had become the default American mode. What succeeded in business succeeded in religion and vice versa, charismatic visionaries persuading people to believe golden dreams. Medicine shows were revivalist camp meetings selling a different form of instant salvation. Both were conducted by itinerant showmen appealing to Americans' hunger for magic and drama. In fact, when the Hamlin's Wizard Oil medicine show arrived in a new town, it always offered donations to local churches.

Probably the grandest patent medicine shows were those staged by the Kickapoo Indian Medicine Company, a company in the Northeast that appropriated the name of an actual southwestern tribe. Why Indians? White Americans had just begun the last chapter of their three-hundred-year war against them. This time, instead of literally demonizing natives, the European-Americans turned to the noble savage idea. More and more popular books and paintings depicted the natives as the doomed but beautiful losers in the inevitable modern sprawl from sea to shining sea, the romantic collateral damage of American manifest destiny.

The Kickapoo Indian Medicine Company's marketing concept went way beyond brand names. As the final Indian wars took place—the Battle of Little Bighorn, Geronimo's War, the Wounded Knee Massacre—corporate headquarters sent out traveling encampments of tents and teepees with as many as a dozen acts in each show—and medicine salesmen—appearing on a twenty-foot stage. They sold a fictional cure-all called Sagwa, as well as Kickapoo Indian Oil, Kickapoo Buffalo Salve, Kickapoo Indian Cough Cure, and Kickapoo Indian Worm Killer.* A whole genre of Indian-themed medicine shows emerged, impersonations of the original impersonation.

The Kickapoo company arranged to have its fictional Indian backstory for its Sagwa brand—a "blood, liver and kidney renovator" consisting mainly of water and alcohol—endorsed by someone who knew Indians, William F. Cody, stage name Buffalo Bill. "An Indian," he agreed to be quoted in ads,

---

* Worm Killer pills were large and embedded with string, so that after digesting and excreting them, people were convinced that they had indeed been cured of intestinal worms.

"would as soon be without his horse, gun or blanket as without Sagwa." Celebrities as we now know them were a new breed, and celebrity product endorsements even newer.

Barnum was America's first great commercial blurrer of truth and make-believe, the founder of infotainment, but the second was Cody. (They were acquaintances.) The true story of Cody's life is like a work of fiction. For a dozen years, from boyhood into young manhood, he was a scout, soldier, buffalo hunter, and Pony Express rider on the Plains and in the West. Then at twenty-three, he featured as the title character in a highly fictionalized "true" story, "Buffalo Bill, King of the Border Men," published in a New York newspaper. And starting at twenty-six, the year he won the Congressional Medal of Honor for leading a squad of cavalry against some Sioux, Cody became a theatrical performer: he played himself in a play called *Scouts of the Prairie*—written by the author of the earlier newspaper story, who also published dime novels about Cody. Buffalo Bill had become a star. In his late twenties, he started publishing his own dime novels starring himself, and he toured the East in more theatrical productions playing Buffalo Bill—even as he continued working off and on in the far West as an Indian fighter.

In the summer of 1876, three weeks after General George Custer's catastrophic defeat, Cody was riding the Plains with the army a few hundred miles to the southeast of Little Bighorn. One day, wearing his Buffalo Bill stage outfit—black velvet, red and lace trim, silver buttons—he killed and scalped a Cheyenne warrior called Yellow Hair. Within a few months, Cody was back east, touring a new play based on that event, *The Red Right Hand; or Buffalo Bill's First Scalp for Custer.* Yellow Hair's weapons and scalp were exhibited in each town where the show played. According to Cody, the show provided "ample opportunity to give a noisy, rattling, gunpowder entertainment, and to present a succession of scenes in the late Indian war." Buffalo Bill was thirty, and from then on, for forty more years, he devoted himself exclusively to live-action cartoon portrayals of the "settlement" of the West.

Cody's own extraordinarily successful traveling pageant, *Buffalo Bill's Wild West,* featured Indians playing Indians and white performers playing soldiers and settlers. Each reenactment of Custer's Last Stand was immediately followed by Buffalo Bill—the actual person—riding in to reenact his killing of a particular Indian, played by an Indian. The show started in Omaha, in eastern Nebraska, in 1883; in the western part of the state, the Indian Wars continued. Cody enlisted the Lakota Sioux chief Sitting Bull, who'd been one of the commanders of the forces at Little Bighorn, to be his co-star. Buffalo Bill became the most famous personality in America and probably the world. Barnum advised him to take the show to Europe, to "astonish the Old World," and he did.

His *Wild West* was the prototype from which movie westerns evolved. But the shows were even more importantly peculiar and unprecedented, a key milestone in our national evolution. Practically in real time, Cody—no, *Buffalo Bill!*—turned news and history into entertainment, turned real-life figures of historic consequence (himself, his pal Wild Bill Hickok, his enemy Sitting Bull) into simulated versions of themselves, riding real horses and firing real guns outdoors.

Until the twentieth century, *nostalgia* still had a specific quasi-medical meaning—extreme personal homesickness, the melancholy of soldiers and exiles missing their towns and countries and old friends. But during the nineteenth century, a new form of nostalgia emerged as an important tic in Americans' psychology, an imaginary homesickness for places and times the nostalgists had never experienced and that had in some cases never existed.

In politics, just when Americans started using the phrase *olden times,* Democrats were driven by nostalgia for the America of their youth, before large-scale capitalism. Then Southerners were driven by nostalgia for the time before slavery started becoming untenable. The overriding theme of the first great popular songwriter, Stephen Foster, was nostalgia for a South that he imagined from up north in Pennsylvania and Ohio. Fenimore Cooper, the first famous American novelist, specialized in nostalgia for the earlier American wilderness, and Twain wrote his greatest books about the bygone America of his antebellum youth.

So by the time Buffalo Bill became a professional fabulist in the 1870s, Americans were completely ready to accept the virtual reality of his *Wild West* tableaus. The nostalgia he stoked and served was new in several ways. It was jolly, giddy. It was *instantaneous,* the day before yesterday made heroic and larger than life. And it was also *anticipatory,* nostalgia for the end of a western frontier that hadn't yet ended—like the nostalgia of Southerners years before the Old South passed away. Buffalo Bill distilled the previous half-century of the Old West into a montage using actual participants and artifacts, for audiences who had mostly never been west of the Mississippi. Forever and everywhere in the world, the popular imagination tends to blur reality and fantasy over time, but now the two were being immediately and systematically fused.

*   *   *

BUFFALO BILL SCALPED THAT LAST Indian and took to the stage in the year the United States turned one hundred, which was the pretext for the first great U.S. world's fair. Like Cody's show, the Centennial Exposition in Philadelphia mixed the real and the unreal—there was a reproduction "New England Farmer's Home" as if from the 1600s, a leather bag containing George Washington's actual field tent, an ersatz colonial windmill.

Seventeen years later in Chicago, at the Columbian Exposition, the fantastic quasi-reality was full tilt, practically the whole point of the fair. The center of the faux-European sector, the White City, was an urban dreamland—more than a dozen neoclassical buildings, but all temporary, disposable, full-size facsimiles covered in plaster of Paris, open for six months, then gone. The White City was a new thing, not obviously inauthentic like a stage set but not authentic either. It was a fantasy *and* it was real.

The rest of the fair was an almost-anything-goes collection of simulacra and a few bits of reality. There were reproductions of three different famous medieval Irish buildings mashed up into one, reproductions of particular foreign city blocks (Vienna, Constantinople), and generic foreign village streets (Java, Lapland). There was a full-scale reproduction of the New Jersey mansion that had served as Washington's headquarters in the Revolution. There was a fake-old-fashioned log cabin, paid for by young Theodore Roosevelt as a commemoration of Daniel Boone and Davy Crockett. And there was the actual North Dakota cabin in which Sitting Bull, after quitting show business, had been arrested and shot dead three years earlier.

On the Midway, extending west from the fair proper, a Jewish teenager born in Hungary and raised in Wisconsin performed tricks as a magic Hindu yogi, calling himself Harry Houdini. A new milling company founded by a Missouri newspaper editor was marketing a new branded pancake mix called Aunt Jemima, its trademarked avatar a character plucked from a popular minstrel song. At the Chicago fair, the millers incarnated her for the first time, hiring an African-American woman, formerly enslaved, *to be* Aunt Jemima, which she continued doing for the rest of her life. Patent medicines were on sale, the most memorable a concoction by a former Texas cowboy who claimed that a Hopi shaman had taught him the recipe. In front of audiences, Clark Stanley eviscerated live rattlesnakes, boiled them, and sold his cure-all elixir as Stanley's Snake Oil.

The fair's organizers had turned down Buffalo Bill's request to install his *Wild West* show on the fairgrounds, so he set up camp next door and made a fortune. Chicago was a *world's* fair, so Cody used the opportunity to expand his narrative, renaming the show *Buffalo Bill's Wild West and Congress of*

Rough Riders of the World. And five years later life imitated art: a U.S. Army cavalry regiment sent to wage the Spanish-American War in Cuba, commanded by the fair patron Teddy Roosevelt, named itself after Buffalo Bill's fictional warriors, the Rough Riders.

The U.S. population was 65 million at the time. In six months, the Chicago fair was visited by more than 27 million people, for whom there must have been one big takeaway: fantasy seems superior to reality—and, by the way, is there any important difference between the two?

The gatekeepers of respectability and guardians of reality had given the fantasyland their imprimatur. They gathered at the fair in 1893 for a Congress of Mathematics and Astronomy, a Parliament of Religions—and the annual convention of the American Historical Association, where a thirty-one-year-old professor from Wisconsin named Frederick Jackson Turner delivered an hour-long talk a week after the Fourth of July called "The Significance of the Frontier in American History." During the "four centuries from the discovery," he said, Americans had invented and reinvented themselves on successive frontiers, in proximity to wild nature. "A steady movement away from the influence of Europe" had defined our new national character "on American lines," making of us "a new product that is American." The latest national census, he noted, showed there was no longer a clear western frontier line in America—that is, white people now lived at every U.S. longitude from the Atlantic to the Pacific. "The frontier has gone, and with its going has closed the first period of American history."

Around the corner from where he spoke were simulated artifacts of that disappearing frontier—the fake log cabin for Boone and Crockett, the former cowboy selling snake oil, Buffalo Bill himself simulating the Old West. Turner's history paper, more important and widely known than any before or since, didn't foresee the next period. But he certainly teed up the twentieth and twenty-first centuries, when simulations of our frontier past fully replaced the real thing, like a chronic phantom-limb syndrome, and continued shaping our national character.

Over the course of the nineteenth century, when masses of Americans began believing in miracle cures and a civilization of lunar batmen and George Washington's 161-year-old nanny; when panics over Masons and Catholics erupted and revived; when millions suddenly subscribed to urgent end-of-the-world prophecies and believed God or Satan had taken control of their bodies and minds; when new churches were splitting off helter-skelter from almost-new ones, modern American Christianity *and* the modern

American news media, advertising, entertainment, politics, and pharmaceutical industries all got their starts. Each was predicated on freewheeling blends of the fanciful and the real. Selling ourselves dreamy fabrications on a national scale became routine, part of the American way. What had been founded, in other words, was a synergistic and unstoppable fantasy-industrial complex.

PART III

A Long Arc Bending Toward Reason: 1900–1960

"The way to deal with superstition is not to be polite to it, but to tackle it with all arms, and so rout it, cripple it, and make it forever infamous and ridiculous."

—H. L. MENCKEN,
in the Baltimore *Evening Sun* (1925)

"The early advocates of universal literacy and a free press . . . did not foresee . . . the development of a vast mass communications industry, concerned in the main neither with the true nor the false, but with the unreal. . . . In a word, they failed to take into account man's almost infinite appetite for distractions."

—ALDOUS HUXLEY,
Brave New World Revisited (1958)

17

Progress and Backlash

THE UNITED STATES IS A SELF-CONSCIOUSLY MODERN COUNTRY. DURING THE
first three decades of the first self-consciously modern century, the twentieth, rationality and reasonableness seemed to be winning the war against
magical thinking and backwardness. The amazing material progress accelerated, with cars and nationwide electrification. Medical science advanced,
and the American Establishment decided to put an end to large-scale quackery. The new mass-market magazine *Ladies' Home Journal* stopped accepting ads for patent medicines, and *Collier's* published a game-changing
eleven-part investigative series on the "'tonics,' 'blood purifiers' and 'cures'"
racket—and a year later the Pure Food and Drug Act became federal law,
putting most of that industry out of business. The U.S. Supreme Court ruled
in 1905 that states and towns could legally require citizens to be vaccinated
against smallpox and other infectious diseases—that Americans' constitutional right to believe and promote whatever they wished did not give "an
absolute right in each person to be, in all times and in all circumstances,
wholly free from restraint."

The government established national food and public health rules and the Federal Reserve. The NAACP was founded. Fair-minded and responsible new national news media emerged. Universities thrived, and science and scientists were revered. The rest of the world acknowledged that Americans were creating world-class literature and music and art. When Henry Luce, the founder of *Time* in 1923, declared that the American Century had begun, it seemed inarguable.

No surprise—there was some backlash to the march of progress. Of course! It was a free country! We'd been a rough frontier nation the day before yesterday. From the turn of the century through the 1920s, new spiritual fads and kooky religious denominations arose, along with aversion to migrating hordes—Italians and Jews over from Europe, African-Americans up from the South. But to the self-confident mainstream, all those reactionary outbursts looked like last gasps, rear-guard actions by primitives, exceptions to smart-set modernity that proved the rule.

In the 1920s, Gilbert Seldes wrote *The Stammering Century* as a rationalist's good-riddance epitaph for the last vestiges of America's ridiculous magical-thinking 1800s. Psychics and séances had a revival—the young wife of a Boston socialite physician became an illustrious medium, in part because she often disrobed during séances—but spiritualism was definitively debunked during the 1920s by Houdini and other skeptics. Nearly all of the big spiritualist communities that had sprung up during the late 1800s disappeared. Theosophy, a hot turn-of-the-century American mishmash of occultism, mysticism, astrology, alchemy, and magic, splintered and declined into obscurity starting in the 1920s.

On the worldly and political front, Americans gave themselves over once again to panics about conspiratorial aliens in their midst—but the hysterias were brief. During World War I, people of German ancestry became suspect. Nearly one in ten Americans was a German immigrant or the child of one. There were riots, a lynching, and between 1910 and 1920, the miraculous disappearance of almost a million German-born Americans from the census rolls. But the sheer number of German-Americans also made it harder to indulge the panic fully, and the United States was officially at war for only nineteen months.

The first big anti-Communist panic, in the 1910s and '20s after the Soviet Union was established, promptly edged into anti-Semitism and vice versa. And by the way, weren't a lot of those German-Americans who worried us during the war also Jewish? Fear of Jewish influence had its American moment as soon as the Jewish population hit 2 percent—about the same threshold at which American anti-Catholic hysteria kicked in a century earlier. Henry Ford, America's most esteemed and successful industrialist, became a superfan of *The Protocols of the Elders of Zion*—the Russian book originally published as fiction, now purporting to be a nonfiction account of a secret meeting of the leaders of a global Jewish conspiracy plotting world domination. In the 1920s he underwrote the U.S. publication of a half-million copies. He also conceived and published a four-volume set called *The International Jew: The World's Foremost Problem;* the young Joseph Goebbels and Adolf Hitler read the German translation and became Henry Ford superfans. But after Americans condemned Ford and started boycotting his company, he promptly apologized and backed off, and U.S. anti-Semitism began its steady twentieth-century decline.

THE PERNICIOUS AND COMPLICATED FANTASIES that underlay white supremacy were not so easily banished when the war over slavery ended. After our Civil War, the fever never entirely broke, because the losing side in its heart and mind never entirely surrendered. The North forgave, but the South didn't, and neither side completely forgot.

You'd think the war would've rendered the Old South myths obsolete in the North, or at least eliminate the power of fictions of happy slaves to charm and beguile a nation that had lost almost a million sons, husbands, fathers, and friends fighting over it. But at the turn of the twentieth century, just three decades after the tragedy and the slaughter, an amazing slavery theme park was erected in Brooklyn. Its mastermind was William Cody's producer, who installed the inaugural iteration of what he called Black America in a semirural park where he and Buffalo Bill had performed the *Wild West* the previous summer. His partner on Black America was a black performer and impresario who had recently staged a theatrical reenactment of the Battle of Vicksburg on Coney Island.

For Black America, they recruited five hundred "Southern Colored People"—"actual field hands from the cotton belt," an advertisement promised—to occupy the 150 brand-new reproduction rustic slave cabins, and for two months they pretended to be enslaved, picking cotton bolls from a recently planted acre and processing them in a real cotton gin. Tens of thousands of white people watched "the labors that the Negroes of slavery days engaged in, and the happy, careless life that they lived in their cabins after work," a *New York Times* reporter wrote. "A fat black mammy, with a red handkerchief on her head, sits outside one of the little cabins, knitting." The

Times also found the make-believe slaves' make-believe talismans entertaining, the rabbits' feet and the "musk bag" whose "mysterious ingredients . . . protect against . . . the wiles and deceptions of the Evil One." The show included a detachment of active-duty black soldiers from a segregated U.S. Army regiment. Black America was a hit, and it toured the Northeast.

At the same moment, Robert Love Taylor, Tennessee's former governor and future U.S. senator, was lecturing throughout the country on the glories of the Old South. "Every sunrise of summer was greeted by the laughter and songs of the darkies as they gathered in gangs and went forth in every direction to begin the labors of the day," he'd say. "I never shall forget the white-columned mansions rising in cool, spreading groves. And stretching away to the horizon were the cotton fields, alive with the toiling slaves, who, without a single care to burden their hearts, sang as they toiled from early morn till close of day." This was typical of the treacly, long-sigh fantasy visions of Old Dixie being propagated in the early 1900s.

Nostalgia had been turned back into a pathology. In 1915 the director D. W. Griffith released a motion picture that was more cinematically ambitious, sophisticated, and compelling than any so far—the movie of the year, of the decade, hugely profitable. It was *The Birth of a Nation,* a shameless three-hour-long piece of propaganda for the mythical Old South and its Ku Klux Klan redeemers. It was the first movie to be shown at the White House, and it played in New York City for almost a year. And then life proceeded to imitate art. During the next decade, the popularity of the revived Klan exploded. Along with the hideous nostalgia for unquestioned white supremacy, the Klan now had standardized spooky-fantasy-figure costumes (the white robes, the conical hats) and new fantasy nomenclature—officers were Imperial Wizards and Grand Goblins, and local Klan groups became "klaverns." It had spread beyond the former Confederacy. As a million and a half black people migrated from South to North during the 1910s and '20s, four of the five states with the largest Klan memberships were Indiana, Ohio, Pennsylvania, and Illinois. At its peak in the early 1920s, probably 5 percent of white American men were in the KKK. But what happened next is a measure of how much the moderating, modernizing forces of reason were nevertheless in control of the culture: within just a few years, by the end of the decade, the Klan's membership had shriveled from many millions to tens of thousands. Which reassured respectable Americans that they'd seen the farewell performance of the most fantastical and vicious bigots.

The meteoric rise and fall of the Klan aside, white Southerners' myth of their own special goodness—honorable, honest, humane, and civilized guardians of tradition, unlike the soulless Yankees—did not wither. It endured in new forms in the new century, with Daddy's and Granddaddy's Civil War a noble and glorious Lost Cause that tragically failed to preserve their antebellum golden age. Slavery qua slavery? No, no, *no,* the war hadn't really been about that; slavery was a detail. In fact, white Southerners had fought the war to defend their right as Americans to believe *anything* they wanted to believe, even an unsustainable fantasy, even if it meant treating a class of humanity as nonhuman.

Many Southern historians of the South agree that a defining quirk of Southerners had been a weakness for illusion and delusion. A young North Carolina journalist named Wilbur Cash in 1941 published the single most influential twentieth-century book on his region's cultural psychology, *The Mind of the South.* It began as an essay for H. L. Mencken's magazine, where Cash wrote that the South's

> salient characteristic is a magnificent incapacity for the real, a Brobdingnagian talent for the fantastic. The very legend of the Old South, for example, is warp and woof of the Southern mind. . . .
>
> Unpleasant realities were singularly rare, and those which existed, as, for example, slavery, lent themselves to pleasant glorification. Thus fact gave way to amiable fiction. . . .
>
> Everywhere [the Southerner] turns away from reality to a gaudy world of his own making.

For a century after the Civil War, writes the University of Virginia historian Paul Gaston in *The New South Creed: A Study in Southern Mythmaking* (1970), the conventional wisdom was "that the South would be absorbed into the mainstream [as] its socioeconomic system and moral views became standard 'American.'" In other words, the vanquished would become Northernized, less myth-addled, more reality-based. *Progress!* As a military and legal fact, the Confederacy lost the Civil War, and the United States remained united and joined the rest of the developed world in ending slavery. But in other ways, the question of which side won is more ambiguous. Slavery's spread was stopped, but not the nationwide spread of certain unfortunate Southern habits of mind, along with increasingly berserk versions of Christianity.

18

The Biggest Backlash: Brand-New Old-Time Religion

FOR BOTH NORTH AND SOUTH, THE OUTCOME OF THE CIVIL WAR, RESPECTIVELY winning and losing, reinforced the trajectories of their Christianities. Before the war, Christianity below the Mason-Dixon Line had started to resemble the older Yankee Christianity—purely Protestant, ultra-orthodox, and insular, with church and community practically synonymous. Afterward, as they wallowed in their tragic nobility and persecution, Southerners turned ever more to their churches for definition as Southerners. Revised hymns and new stained-glass windows conflated Christian and Confederate imagery and themes. White Southern religious culture became kind of a rump Confederacy. Believers doubled down on the supernatural, looking toward a miraculous do-over, an ultimate victory on Judgment Day and in the hereafter. Instead of squarely facing the uncomfortable facts—slavery was wrong, secession a calamitous mistake—they shifted into excuse-and-deny mode. For a great many white Southerners, defeat made them not contrite and peaceable (like, say, Germans and Japanese after World War II) but permanently pissed off. Which in turn led them to embrace a Christianity almost as medieval as the Puritans'.

For Northerners, victory had confirmed they were on God's side, fortifying their besetting smugness, and their religion resolved more and more into a pretty, reassuring background hum. Going to church meant sitting quietly and listening to lectures about virtue. America's religious Establishment, headquartered in the North, kept moving toward reasonableness, along with the rest of Christendom, recasting the miracles of the past and prophecies for the future as illustrative allegories.

In the first year of the twentieth century, *modernism* became a word in this discourse—as a catchall for the fuzzier, more intellectual, more plausible version of Christianity that was becoming mainstream. "The advance of liberalism, so-called, in Christianity, during the past 50 years," William James wrote, "may fairly be called a victory . . . within the church over the morbidness [of] the old hell-fire theology. We now have whole congregations where preachers . . . ignore, or even deny, eternal punishment." The New Theology emphasized personal goodness and downplayed the supernatural. Reducing history to a battle between God and Satan was foolish. The Bible was an extraordinary construction, divinely inspired but the product of fallible ancient authors.

The seminal modern work of sociology, Max Weber's *The Protestant Ethic and the Spirit of Capitalism* (1905), wasn't much interested in our American religion qua religion. Weber's idea was that certain Protestant mental habits happen to jibe well with ambition and industriousness. Thus they'd come along at exactly the right time to train Europeans and Americans to create and operate the market economies emerging at the same time. He reckoned, and everyone agreed, that in the twentieth century and beyond, modern societies no longer needed that original religious catalyst to keep thriving and would eventually slough off the supernatural parts as vestigial bunk. Essentially, Weber said, Protestants' capitalism-friendly theology had evolved into modern rationalism.

But in America, and pretty much only in America, that rationalism was viscerally opposed by lots and lots of people who didn't cotton to the inrushing newness—fancy foreign art and ideas, jazz, movies, sexual looseness, racial equality, women's suffrage—let alone science that contradicted their understanding of the first book of the Bible.* In America, even as the mod-

---

* In 1920, just before the Constitution was amended to give women the vote, all but one of the seven states without any female suffrage were in the South, and most of the states that had been Confederate refused to ratify the Nineteenth Amendment until the 1960s or later.

erns declared victory, the committed magical thinkers weren't giving up. And they fell back on one of the original Protestant and Puritan reflexes: if the decadent elite was stigmatizing believers as bumptious zealots, persecuting them for their unfashionable faith, the believers would go even more hard-core.

During the first three decades of the twentieth century, millions of back-lashing Americans became more invested in the idea that God had dictated the Bible, that it was 100 percent nonfiction, and that reading between the lines was permissible only if it confirmed their belief that Christ would return soon to stop the torrent of modern demonic corruption once and for all.

They already had the beginnings of a counter-Establishment. Dwight Moody, a shoe salesman turned celebrity preacher, had opened his influential Moody Bible Institute, a college and correspondence school, as well as a publishing house. He insisted that every sentence in the Bible was literally true, no more metaphorical than the Sears, Roebuck catalog, and he helped revive a scriptural fetishism in American Christianity. To make even the most poetic parts like Revelation understandable, he popularized Reverend Darby's end-time schedule—along with his rapture add-on, the apocalypse escape route to a supernatural VIP waiting room. Moody called this new improved theology the "old-time gospel." The final masterstroke was making his institute and theology nondenominational: as long as you were evangelical and opposed to open-mindedness, you were welcome. Which meant this brand of zealotry could spread freely through almost every Protestant denomination and serve as a seedbed for new sects.

Moody's most important protégé was a corrupt and alcoholic Kansas lawyer and politician named Cyrus Scofield. After deserting his wife and children, he became an evangelical minister, cofounding his own Bible schools, launching his own correspondence course, and finally, in 1909, publishing his own Bible. This wasn't a new translation; rather, he took the King James Version and, in his lawyerly way, filled almost half of each page with explanatory text, publishing his take on the new evangelical take on the meaning and timing of the scriptural stories and prophecies—including the calculation that God created the world in the autumn of 4004 B.C.E. All those footnotes made the most outlandish versions of Christian myth appear more bona fide. It was published by Oxford University Press and became a phenomenal bestseller.

Around the same time in Los Angeles, the elderly founder of Union Oil, a conservative Presbyterian upset about modernizing Presbyterianism, commissioned a paperback set of antimodernist essays called *The Fundamentals* and spent the equivalent of seven million dollars distributing millions of free copies. Baptists too were flipping out over what looked like the final triumph of Enlightenment reason. At their 1920 annual convention, not even the *Northern* Baptists used the euphemistic new term *modernism* to declare what they were against: "We view with increasing alarm the havoc which rationalism is working in our churches." They explicitly endorsed the irrational. And the Brooklyn-based editor of the Northern Baptists' weekly newspaper, working off the title of the recent paperbacks, gave the movement of alarmed Christian superfantasists a name:

> Fundamentalism is a protest against that rationalistic interpretation of Christianity which seeks to discredit supernaturalism. This rationalism . . . scorns the miracles of the Old Testament, sets aside the virgin birth of our Lord as a thing unbelievable, laughs at the credulity of those who accept many of the New Testament miracles . . . and sweeps away the promises of his second coming as an idle dream. . . . In robbing Christianity of its supernatural content, they are undermining the very foundations of our holy religion. They boast that they are strengthening the foundations and making Christianity more rational and more acceptable to thoughtful people. Christianity is rooted and grounded in supernaturalism, and when robbed of supernaturalism it ceases to be a religion and becomes an exalted system of ethics.

Fighting to keep the big Protestant denominations from drifting toward the rational was hard work. But in twentieth-century America, celebrity was totally fungible, entrepreneurialism the winning way, and show business exploding. Thus the most famous evangelical preacher of the era hadn't been ordained and wasn't affiliated with any one church but was already a *star* (in major league baseball), preached the old-time religion in an all-American Iowa accent, did so entertainingly (jumping, whirling, flailing, cracking wise), and had a perfect name: Billy Sunday. He called the Protestant upper crust a "pack of pretentious, pliable, mental perverts . . . dedicated to the destruction of religion and one and all are liars." The righteous, regular American people by the million loved him.

Science had proved that humans descended from animals—which is tough to reconcile with a literal reading of Genesis, in which God forms man from the dust of the ground by breathing into his nostrils the breath of life. In the half-century since Darwin's *The Descent of Man*, intellectually supple

Christians around the world—the "modernists"—had reconciled Scripture with scientific evidence: the astronomers, geologists, paleontologists, and biologists were simply discovering the operational details of God's miraculous creation. Even orthodox theologians were showing flexibility. "'Evolution,'" an essayist wrote in *The Fundamentals,* was "but a new name for 'creation,'" and thus "the Bible and science are . . . in harmony." So God in his amazing way created man, but not in a single day, and not by blowing on a dirt statue.

A large fraction of American Christians, however, refused to move beyond the picture of human creation they'd had as children. "I don't believe your own bastard theory of evolution," Billy Sunday snarled. "I believe it's pure jackass nonsense." In the winter of 1925, he preached for two weeks in Memphis, where 250,000 people (in a city of 200,000) turned out to hear him rail against Darwin and godless biology. Immediately the state of Tennessee enacted the strictest of several (Southern) laws that criminalized science's bastard theories, making it "unlawful for any teacher in any of the Universities . . . and all other public schools of the State . . . to teach any theory that denies the Story of the Divine Creation of man and to teach instead that man has descended from a lower order of animal."

A BIG, STARK AMERICAN INFLECTION point had arrived. Modern science or ancient myth? Reason or magic? Reality or fiction? The argument over evolution had finally come to a head, each side coalescing and arming for battle during the same decade. A ferocious sector of Christians arose and named itself, and anti-evolution-education laws were enacted. Among the seculars, the American Civil Liberties Union was created, the biggest newspapers became national, influential weeklies (*The New Republic, Time, The New Yorker*) were founded, and newsreels and regular radio newscasts began. This new set of conditions resulted, in the summer of 1925, in the so-called Monkey Trial, the first great national smackdown between fantasists and rationalists.

"We are looking for a Tennessee teacher who is willing to accept our services in testing this law," announced the ACLU ad in the *Chattanooga Daily Times* on the first Monday in May. An hour up the Tennessee Valley in the town of Dayton, a well-born young Methodist engineer recently transplanted from New York City, and his group of local boosters, immediately saw an opportunity—a way to put little Dayton on the map *and* to make full-throated public cases for both science *and* fundamentalism with the whole world watching. They persuaded another young local newcomer—John Scopes, a year out of college and teaching science at the local high school—to be indicted and tried. (Actually, Mr. Scopes had been out sick the day his class was taught evolution, but . . . whatever.)

All over America, earnest partisans, cynical impresarios, and regular spectacle-loving folks instantly recognized what a crackerjack show this might be. Each side brought in its own celebrity ringer. The lawyer Clarence Darrow, fresh off saving the rich teenage Chicago murderers Leopold and Loeb from the gallows, joined the ACLU's defense team. For the prosecution, it was William Jennings Bryan, the three-time Democratic presidential nominee who was making a late-life career out of stirring up popular rage against evolutionary biology. For weeks before the trial, *The New York Times* published articles on the case, one headlined BRYAN IS ARRAIGNED AS RELIGIOUS BIGOT. Barely one hundred days after the law's enactment, *State of Tennessee v. John Thomas Scopes,* conceived and cast as a show trial, was under way.

The county courthouse was freshly painted, and they'd installed new bathrooms and telephone lines, a platform for newsreel cameras, and five hundred additional seats for spectators—two hundred of whom were reporters from around the country and the world. The *Chicago Tribune*'s new radio station sent a crew to broadcast the trial live. "We're like moon men here," the announcer marveled. "We're the radio guys from outer space!" Outdoors, concession stands sold snacks and drinks and stuffed toy monkeys, and a local butcher showed off a pair of kittens with rabbit-like hind legs, what he called "cabbits," proof of genetic inheritance if not of evolution. A celebrity chimpanzee wearing a plaid suit, fedora, and spats was offered up as a defense exhibit; Darrow declined. The owner of a different chimp offered his to the prosecution, and the jury, led by "the juror who looks like Buffalo Bill," as *The New York Times* described him, visited a hotel room for an audience with the ape.

Clergy rushed to Tennessee to join the show. A Mississippi minister passed out antievolution pamphlets with alliterative titles ("Hell and the High Schools," "God or Gorilla"). A rabbi from Nashville arrived, offering to explain Genesis in Hebrew. An outdoor preacher from Oregon made himself up to look like a popular funny-papers character. A man from Michigan whose business card identified him as an "Independent Free-Thinker and Lecturer" was arrested, and police also prevented a Unitarian minister from Manhattan's Upper West Side from speaking. When the pastor of a local Methodist church invited the Unitarian to address his congregation, the uproar prompted his immediate resignation.

At the end of the trial's second day, Darrow delivered a long speech laying out his legal and philosophical case. Is there a word meaning the opposite of *pander*? Bryan's years of antievolution militancy, Darrow said, were "responsible for this wicked, mischievous and foolish" new law. As "almost impossible as it is to put my mind back into the sixteenth century, I am going to argue as if it was serious, and as if it was a death struggle between two civilizations." It was absurd that "the book of Genesis, written when everybody thought the world was flat," should refute science, and what Tennessee had done was "as plain religious ignorance and bigotry as any that justified . . . the hanging of the witches in New England."

When he finished, a journalist from the Baltimore *Sun* reported, "the morons in the audience . . . simply hissed it." The *Sun,* three states and six hundred miles away, was a co-producer of the show. The paper had agreed in advance to pay Scopes's bail and his fine if he was convicted. To report on the trial and hullabaloo, it had dispatched a five-man team led by H. L. Mencken, its star writer whose columns—including the one referring to "the morons in the audience"—were nationally syndicated. In rural Tennessee, he wrote, "Darwin is the devil with seven tails and nine horns. Scopes, though he is disguised by flannel pantaloons and a Beta Theta Pi haircut, is the harlot of Babylon. Darrow is Beelzebub in person."

But it wasn't just Mencken: the reams of *straight* news coverage also treated Bryan and the trial as comedy and fundamentalism as exotic and senseless. "Here comes William Jennings Bryan," the courtroom color commentator for Chicago radio said on the air. "He enters now. His bald pate like a sunrise over Key West." During the trial, the *Times* ran several stories a day, often leading page one, almost all with tendentious headlines—such as FARMERS WILL TRY TEACHER . . . ONE IS UNABLE TO READ, NONE BELIEVES IN EVOLUTION and DAYTON'S REMOTE MOUNTAINEERS FEAR SCIENCE. In the words of one *Times* reporter, "Dayton believes in a Christ born of a virgin and resurrected from the tomb, a real Adam and a real Eve and a real serpent and a real angel with a flaming sword." And so, he wrote, they "had to have an antievolution law. Such firmness, such bigotry, if you will, is bone of their bone and flesh of their flesh." *That* was an age of mainstream media with a liberal bias.

The celebrity principals were acting as attorneys but were mainly just *acting,* performers in America's first great multimedia reality show. For a week, Darrow and Bryan joshed and derided each other in and out of court. On the trial's penultimate day, it was reconvened outside on the courthouse lawn, so everyone could attend the improbable and fabulous denouement.

Bryan agreed to take the stand as a hostile defense witness, willing to be righteously martyred. "These gentlemen," he said of the blasphemer Darrow and company, "came here to try revealed religion. I am here to defend it." The crowd loved that.

"Great applause from the bleachers!" Darrow cracked, commenting on the show in real time.

"From those whom you call 'yokels,'" Bryan retorted. "*Those* are the people whom you insult."

Now Darrow lost his temper: "*You* insult every man of science and learning in the world because he does not believe in your fool religion." He asked about various Old Testament miracles—did Bryan believe that Jonah *actually* survived three days in a whale's belly, that God *actually* created Eve out of Adam's rib, that a crafty talking snake *actually* convinced her to disobey God? And on and on.

Yes, Bryan testified, he believed everything in the Bible. He testified that he believed the flood in Genesis happened around 2348 B.C.E.

Again, incredulity from Darrow. "You believe that every civilization on the Earth and every living thing, except possibly the fishes . . . were wiped out by the flood? And then, whatever human beings . . . that inhabited the world . . . and who run their pedigree straight back, and all the animals have come on to the Earth since the flood?"

BRYAN: Yes.
DARROW: Don't you know that the ancient civilizations of China are six or seven thousand years old at the very least?
BRYAN: No. . . .

An hour or so into this, the official chief prosecutor objected—what's the *purpose*? "The purpose," his comrade Bryan declared from the witness stand, "is to cast ridicule on everybody who believes in the Bible." Darrow grandstanded right back: "We have the purpose of preventing bigots and ignoramuses from controlling the education of the United States."

The next day, after deliberating for nine minutes, the jury found Scopes guilty. The judge fined him $100. And as if the whole episode were not already theatrical enough, a few days later in Dayton—on the following *Sunday*—Bryan dropped dead.

DURING HIS TIME IN TENNESSEE, Mencken had done some reporting beyond the courthouse "here in the Coca-Cola belt." One night he attended an outdoor religious service. "Suddenly," he wrote, one of the men "rose to his feet, threw back his head and began to speak in tongues—blub-blub-blub, gurgle-gurgle-gurgle. His voice rose to a higher register. The climax was a shrill, in-articulate squawk, like that of a man throttled. He fell headlong across the pyramid of supplicants." Then another man "leaped into the air, threw back his head and began to gargle as if with a mouthful of BB shot. Then he loos-ened one tremendous stentorian sentence in the tongues and collapsed."

Tongues. Mencken had witnessed the defining voodoo artifact of the newest species of fantastical Christianity. It had occasionally bubbled up here and there in America for a century or two before finally becoming a sustained geyser in the early 1900s.

As grassroots Christian *beliefs* grew more implausible in opposition to the liberalizing mainstream, some of the grass roots yearned for more implausible and flamboyant Christian *practice*. Since the Civil War, the force field of the new Holiness Movement had swept up higher-keyed zealots from the big denominations. They were pushed from more respectable congregations, es-pecially Methodists, forming their own churches, one-off and regional opera-tions that shared a brand (the Church of God), but even more decentralized than the Baptists, with no national leadership or headquarters, every church free to do its own thing. This kind of self-franchising felt correct, more righ-teous and American. Members wanted to live strictly virtuous lives—without liquor or tobacco, without singing or dancing, without theater or movies. And at their services, they weren't content just to hear sermons, get baptized, and pray. Indeed, maybe to compensate for the everyday asceticism, the lack of intoxicants and fun, they sought another sort of mind-altering and mind-altered entertainment: camp meetings, traumatic and ecstatic public conver-sions, faith healing. They were Americans, so they wanted *more*. They'd read in the Bible's Book of Acts that some weeks after Jesus's crucifixion, His apostles were temporarily granted supernatural powers to perform "wonders and signs"—the so-called Pentecost. Among those miraculous powers had been the ability "to speak with other tongues"—instant fluency in all the languages spoken at that time in multicultural Jerusalem. A little later in the Bible, the apostle Paul mentions Christians who "speaketh in an unknown tongue."

Twenty centuries later Americans decided they wanted that delirious Pentecostal experience for themselves, every week. Not until then had glos-solalia, as it became known, served as the defining fantasy of any Christian religion. Four hundred years after Luther said that "we are all priests," Amer-icans took the notion a hysterical step further: every believer could now be a prophet as well, each equal to one of Jesus's apostles, commissioned to perform and reveal miraculous wonders and signs, and not just temporarily.

The two main founders of Pentecostalism were a pair of young evangelists, former Methodists by way of the Holiness Movement. Charles Parham had set up a little Bible college in Topeka for people "willing to forsake all, sell what they had, give it away, and enter the school," where he taught that the end-time was near. On the very first day of the twentieth century, this twenty-seven-year-old put his hands on a student, a thirty-year-old woman, and, according to him, "a halo seemed to surround her head and face, and she began speaking in the Chinese language and was unable to speak English for three days." Although a local Chinese person said that what she spoke wasn't Chinese at all, the believers *believed,* and soon more Topekans, including the minister and his clerical peers, were excitedly speaking dozens of different made-up foreign languages.

Then he went on the road, in Houston enlisting a talented African-American protégé, William Seymour, whom he dispatched to spread the magic to booming Los Angeles. The new L.A. church, in a ramshackle building in Little Tokyo, was instantly successful. Thousands made their way downtown for the nonstop performances. Two weeks into the madness, the great 1906 earthquake leveled San Francisco and shook L.A.—a coincidence that encouraged the believers on Azusa Street to believe they were receiving bulletins from God about Armageddon and Christ's return.

It may go without saying, but I'll say it: "tongues" are gibberish. The authoritative contemporary scholar of glossolalia, William Samarin of the University of Toronto, is charitable. After witnessing, recording, and studying dozens of episodes, he rejected "psychopathological explanations." However, the "languages" spoken are sham improvisations: "strings of syllables, made up of sounds taken from all those that the speaker knows, put together more or less haphazardly" with "a facade of language" but "without having consistent [sentence] structure." English-speakers speaking in tongues, he found, tend to avoid uttering sounds that make the fake language sound too similar to English.

Shortly after Seymour began leading services on Azusa Street, the *Los Angeles Daily Times* ran a skeptical page-one story. NEW SECT OF FANATICS BREAKING LOOSE, the headline announced. "Night is made hideous in the neighborhood," read the story, "by the howlings of the worshippers who spend hours swaying forth and back in a nerve-racking attitude of prayer and supplication. They claim to have 'the gift of tongues'; and to be able to comprehend the babel. Such a startling claim has never yet been made by any company of fanatics, even in Los Angeles, the home of almost numberless creeds."

Word of the outpourings spread. A North Carolina preacher who'd recently switched from Methodist to Holiness in order to accommodate his beliefs in faith healing and the imminent end-time crossed the country to witness the free-for-all in L.A. Immediately converted, he returned home and barnstormed the South to recruit other evangelical ministers for the new sect—who in turn set up Pentecostal denominations that endure today.* Within a decade, the main Pentecostal denominations had millions of American members.

ALTHOUGH RATIONALISTS LOST THE LEGAL battle at Scopes's 1925 trial in Tennessee, it seemed to almost everybody at the time that they were winning the wider war. "Two months ago," Mencken wrote from Dayton, "the town was obscure and happy. Today it is a universal joke." In fact, thanks to the new national media—which, as Mencken said, "show[ed] the country and the world exactly how the obscene buffoonery appeared to realistic city men"— Christian fundamentalism and Holy Roller theatricality had become a national joke as well.

And an international joke. "In the 1920s," the Notre Dame historian George Marsden writes in *Fundamentalism and American Culture,* "when the American fundamentalists were fighting their spiritual battles, few in England rallied to the battle cry." And not just England: "Almost nowhere outside of America did this particular Protestant response to modernity play such a conspicuous and pervasive role in the culture."

Yet while the United States was a twentieth-century straggler, it did seem to be catching up with the rest of the world, taking two steps forward for every one back. In the big U.S. denominations, the Baptists and Presbyterians and Methodists based in the North, the liberals definitively won their fights against their fundamentalists during the 1920s. The prestigious Princeton Theological Seminary, the final fortress of biblical inerrancy, was taken over by modernists. The new king of the Protestant Establishment, featured on the cover of *Time,* was Reinhold Niebuhr, a New Yorker and bona-fide intellectual comfortable with nuance and ambiguity who didn't believe in the

* For the Reverend Gaston Barnibus Cashwell, that founding spree was apparently a midlife crisis, a phase: four years later he returned to the Methodists.

biblical miracles, including Jesus's bodily resurrection, or even in individual heavenly eternal life.

The fundamentalist resistance, according to respectable opinion at the time, was the last hurrah of atavistic know-nothings. To metropolitan Americans, the fundamentalists and Pentecostals (and Mormons) were embarrassments, to be mocked or ignored until they finally disappeared once and for all. The three superstar evangelists of the period—Billy Sunday, the Reverend Major Jealous Divine, and Aimee Semple McPherson—were figures of fun everywhere in the new national news media.

Time, a fair proxy for upper-middle-class sensibility, referred to "the farmer-jurors" of the Scopes trial. "Billy Sunday," the magazine said, "on a lower intellectual plane," had Americans debating "whether he did more harm than good." The magazine described him "leaping and snarling like a small, vivacious cougar." Father Divine, an African-American based in and around New York City, said he was God incarnate. *The New York Times* assumed his and his followers' insanity: 16 OF DIVINE'S CULT SHOW MENTAL ILLS, one article was headlined; ONLY 2 OUT OF 18 OBSERVED AT BELLEVUE FOUND FREE OF WELL-DEFINED PSYCHOSES. McPherson, known as Sister Aimee, was a faith-healing, tongues-speaking Pentecostal divorcée preaching in a five-thousand-seat church in L.A. with a giant animated-electric-light billboard inside. After she went missing for five weeks in 1926, claiming she'd been kidnapped, *Time* described "her 'disappearance,'" the way it referred to Billy Sunday's "sermons," with disparaging quotation marks. The bestselling novel of 1927 was Sinclair Lewis's *Elmer Gantry,* a satire about a Billy Sunday–esque evangelist and his McPhersonian lover. In 1933 *Time* happily reported that "U.S. evangelists find their circles narrowing, embracing smaller and smaller towns."

As a constitutional matter, the Monkey Trial didn't resolve the conflict in America between science and creationist fantasy. On appeal, the state supreme court nullified Scopes's standing to appeal to the U.S. Supreme Court. For the next several decades, oddly, the ACLU pursued no more big test cases. A kind of de facto truce prevailed. Only a few Southern states kept antievolution laws on the books, and even those statutes began to be repealed. In most places, the principles of biology were taught without any asterisks.

The cultural impact of the Scopes trial, however, was enormous. Each side was confirmed in its beliefs. It allowed the mainstream to write off Christian true believers as hillbilly dead-enders and to imagine that reason was inexorably triumphing in America. Thought leaders and cosmopolites and middle-class *Time*-reading conservatives, such as my grandparents and parents in Nebraska, could almost forget that many millions of gung-ho Christian fantasists still existed. And the fantasists—especially in the South, for whom the Yankees' twentieth-century national cultural victory was a rerun of their Civil War victory—could go on believing and telling their children that science was untrue when it contradicted the Bible.

A hyperfantastical Christianity had blazed in America for a quarter century. After the Scopes trial, the official chroniclers figured the fires were dying. National attention was no longer much paid. But in the South and outside big cities, the coals were still red hot and banked, never extinguished, ready to rekindle in the second half of the twentieth century, bigger than ever.

19

The Business of America Is Show Business

CITIZENS OF OUR ETERNALLY NEW NATION ARE SUCKERS FOR NOVELTY AND astonishment, whether the thing is newfangled "old-time religion" featuring in-church miracles, or miraculous technological contraptions—electricity! telephones! X-rays! airplanes!—that turned the present into a science fiction future. Yet while the curious new U.S. religions were very successful—Mormonism, Christian Science, Pentecostalism, fundamentalism—as the twentieth century rolled out, the vast majority of Christians were sticking with the familiar, sensible, plain-vanilla churches.

Which isn't to say they weren't still fantasy-hungry Americans who loved being amazed, loved believing that exciting secular fictions were real. The foundations laid in the 1800s by impresarios and hucksters of thrills and bliss were fully built out during the 1900s into a far-flung fantasy-industrial complex. Entertainments that had been for most people a rare and occasional diversion—the odd play, a medicine show, a visit to Barnum's American Museum, *Buffalo Bill's Wild West,* a world's fair—were now presented perpetually, in myriad forms. Starting in the 1900s, from coast to coast and seven days a week, Americans more than anyone on Earth could immerse in the virtuosic fantasies created and sold by show business and the media. This was a new condition. As we spent more and more fabulous hours engaged in the knowing and willing suspension of disbelief, experiencing the unreal as real, we became more habituated to suspending disbelief unconsciously and involuntarily as well.*

"The chief business of the American people is business," President Calvin Coolidge, freshly reelected, told a convention of newspaper editors in 1925, as business boomed on every front. But in a larger sense the business of Americans had become the business of fantasy, in all its iterations.

America went world's-fair-crazy, mounting a new, giant, year-long extravaganza in a new city every few years. The two big Christian religious holidays had acquired their own official, nondenominational supernatural (and highly commercial) fantasy figures, Santa Claus and the Easter Bunny. Magicians entered their golden age, with a half-dozen American superstars and dozens more who were merely well known. Houdini was one of the most famous people on Earth during the first quarter of the century, his shows a seamless intermingling of true and false—one day he escaped from manacles by sheer tenacity, the next he appeared to make a five-ton elephant vanish from a giant Broadway stage, his audiences believing or half-believing the fake as well as the real. (If you could now communicate wirelessly, then why *not* mind reading and giant beasts dematerializing?) Between 1910 and 1930, nearly all of today's Broadway theaters were built, and Coney Island, reachable by the new subway, suddenly had *three* big amusement parks.

For a century, people had been dumbfounded again and again by amazing new devices. But when an advanced technology came along that was indistinguishable from magic and dedicated to making the pretend seem real *and* the basis of a big business—that is, movies—a kind of quantum change occurred in the culture. The difference between fantasy and reality narrowed suddenly, viscerally, profoundly. Movies made it easy for almost anyone anywhere, literate or not, imaginative or not, to enter a magical realm where they were teleported everywhere to see anything—not paintings of exotic places or descriptions of imaginary characters but actual people in actual places, alive and moving. No previous medium seemed so powerfully and uncannily

* During the 1920s, use of the phrase *suspension of disbelief* suddenly quadrupled in American books, even though it had been coined a century earlier by the English writer Samuel Taylor Coleridge, arguing for a revival of supernatural fantasy in fiction. Coleridge, an opium addict, helped found the Romantic Movement as a reaction against Enlightenment rationalism.

real. Watching a movie, the suspension of disbelief was easier than watching a play; it was simply more *astounding* than watching flesh-and-blood people pretend on a stage. Going to the movies wasn't like reading a novel at home, privately imagining a fictional world, but more like going to church—quietly gathering for an hour or two in a special hall every week with a crowd of neighbors to experience a magical, dreamlike virtual reality simultaneously.

In 1915, when the movies became a culture-shaping art and industry— the year Charlie Chaplin became a huge celebrity, the year of *Birth of a Nation—Scientific American* published a three-volume encyclopedia called *The Book of Progress*. About movies, its writer (who later became a science fiction author) was agog.

> Wonderful as is the magic of the prestidigitator . . . it is as nothing to the magic which we see upon the screen when we watch a motion picture. . . . Here, at last, is the magic of childhood—appearances, disappearances, apparitions . . . objects possessed of the power of movement and of intelligence. . . .
>
> For the motion picture does for us what no other thing can do save a drug. . . . It eliminates the time between happenings and brings two events separated actually by hours of time and makes them seem to us as following each other with no interval between them.

A Harvard psychology professor who worked under William James loved this new means of confusing the fantastic and authentic. "The close-up," he wrote the following year in *The Photoplay: A Psychological Study*, "far transcends the power of any theater stage," and movies produce "hallucinations and illusions" as "vivid as realities." Indeed, watching movies makes it seem "as if reality has lost its own emphasis," that the "outer world . . . has been freed from space, time and causality."

Moviemaking was not exclusively American, of course, but America quickly became its headquarters, with a sunny new city devoted to it. The people creating the movie industry had utilitarian reasons for moving from the east coast to L.A. in the 1910s—it had just become a big city, land was cheap, and the sun shone six days out of seven. In 1907 there were five thousand U.S. movie theaters; seven years later there were eighteen thousand. In 1911 only two American feature-length films were released; in 1919 there were 646. After the World War, 90 percent of movies were American movies.

When talkies arrived at the end of 1927, the viewers' suspension of disbelief became still easier, the simulated reality of cinema even more intensely and unprecedentedly persuasive. In a 1929 book called *The Film Finds Its Tongue,* the author was gobsmacked by the first sound film he'd seen: it was "like watching a man flying without wings. It was uncanny. . . . No wonder the next day a scientist called it: 'the nearest thing to a resurrection.'" Color film made the fantasy still more realistic, which was what people, especially American people, wanted.

My argument here is that movies (and then television, and then video-games and video of all kinds) were a powerful and unprecedented solvent of the mental barriers between real and unreal—not that that was Hollywood's explicit intent (although sometimes it was, as in the case of *The Birth of a Nation*).

Although Hollywood suddenly became a new epicenter of show business, Emerald City West, the fantasy-industrial complex was extending well beyond movies. Americans were now being entertained and fooled and fed fantasy on several fronts.

Such as advertising. *Marketing* had just acquired its modern meaning, and *advertise,* until recently a general term for publishing information, came to mean only the paid promotion of products (and ideas and people) by whatever mix of facts and fiction and dazzle did the trick and made the sale. Advertising became ubiquitous, produced by a huge, formal, American-dominated industry essential to almost every other industry. Patent medicines had been fantasy products advertised as cures for serious problems, but in the twentieth century, advertising gave mundane problems like hygiene new fantasy subtexts. When advertisements for Woodbury's Facial Soap in 1911 began promising "skin you love to touch," the unique selling proposition was sex, not cleanliness, and in the 1930s Woodbury soap ads featured a nude woman sunbathing. Once advertising successfully used fantasies as a way to glamorize products that satisfied basic needs, it began using them to arouse new desires—products to make you happier and better in all kinds of intangible ways—and then to make those wishes feel like urgent needs.

Newspapers and most magazines had always sold advertising space, but the ads had been pretty strictly informational, small and printed in small type, and not the main revenue source for most publications—until the 1900s. The exceptions had been the papers of the penny press, which were also happy to publish fantasies as news. But most papers and magazines scrupled to distinguish fiction from nonfiction, and advertisements were uncomfortably in between—exaggerations, hyperbole, sometimes altogether fantastical (as when selling patent medicines). *Harper's Weekly*, the first American newsmagazine, refused to take ads when it started in 1857. Then it sold a half page per issue, which grew to three pages in the 1870s—and then, the more the merrier, at least ninety pages in each issue during the early 1900s. Between 1900 and the late 1920s, annual spending by American advertisers increased from the contemporary equivalent of $6 billion a year to $48 billion.

Until the 1920s, providers of entertainment and information almost never gave their products away. Even cheap newspapers cost a few cents. So when the magical new medium of radio came along, because there was no way to charge listeners, its founding American impresarios required some time to figure out a business model. The wheel they reinvented was the medicine show: they could broadcast a mixture of entertaining fiction (*Amos 'n' Andy, Mystery House, Let's Pretend*) and occasional information (news) and *give it all away*, because their actual business would be—d'oh!—charging companies to broadcast mixtures of information and entertaining fiction in the form of advertisements.

Maybe radio plays weren't as amazing and immersive as the movies, but you didn't have to leave home or buy a ticket to experience them. And it was so convenient to have everything—dramas, comedies, music, vaudeville, news—come out of a single wireless spigot. A decade after the CBS Radio Network was founded in the late 1920s, its weekly *Mercury Theater of the Air*, just a few months old, broadcast an episode that took brilliant advantage of the new medium's commingling of entertainment and news. Its whole perverse point was to erase the lines between fantasy and reality.

After a weather report—"A slight atmospheric disturbance of undetermined origin is reported over Nova Scotia"—the regular announcer calmly returned: "We now take you to the Meridian Room in the Hotel Park Plaza in downtown New York." A tango played, but then after a while a different announcer broke in: "Ladies and gentlemen, we interrupt our program of dance music to bring you a special bulletin from the Intercontinental Radio News. . . . Professor Farrell of the Mount Jennings Observatory, Chicago, Illinois, reports observing several explosions of incandescent gas, occurring at regular intervals on the planet Mars . . . and moving towards the Earth with enormous velocity." It was, of course, twenty-three-year-old Orson Welles's live *War of the Worlds* broadcast, which proceeded with an hour of fake on-location news reports chronicling a Martian invasion that concluded with the destruction of New York City. In real life during the previous few weeks, the

Munich Agreement had been signed and Germany had invaded the Sudeten-land; some listeners that night figured the "Martians" bombing and burning America were actually Nazi invaders.

The first decades of the twentieth century were also, not coincidentally, when celebrity assumed its modern, quintessentially American form. Fame had existed forever, of course: in every culture, a few talented and powerful people were well known. But before the United States existed, there was hardly any cultural machinery for making private individuals famous, or for encouraging the populace to talk and think and fantasize about them. News papers and magazines, the first foundations of modern celebrity, came into existence simultaneously with America. Photography emerged, and almost immediately celebrity photographers of celebrities, such as Mathew Brady. In 1850 Barnum whipped up so much advance newspaper publicity for Jenny Lind, a young Swedish singer whose first American tour he was promoting, that a tenth of New York's population gathered on piers simply to watch her arrive. That was the moment when *celebrity* came to mean a famous indi-vidual, and after that Americans coined the slang word *fan* for people besot-ted by particular celebrities.

In the early 1900s, the print-media substrate for celebrity and fandom grew wildly: in two decades the number of daily papers doubled, and the combined circulation of magazines tripled. More of them featured more and more photographs of famous people, which starting in the 1920s could be instantly transmitted everywhere over electric wires. In the 1910s a newspa-per started the first Hollywood gossip column, and they multiplied, becoming nationally syndicated in the 1920s, when the fan magazine *Photoplay* took off. The grand new photo-centric weekly *Life,* amazingly, put no Hollywood star on the cover for its first six months, but resistance was futile: there were four in 1937, then ten in 1938. They'd begun to open the floodgates of mod-ern celebrity culture.

Just a couple of decades earlier, before radio and the movies, there had been no flood to hold back. National fame was rare, and the celebrated were almost never so familiar and protean as radio and film stars. Before movies and radio, most Americans had surely never heard the voice of more than a single major celebrity in their lifetimes. In the 1910s and '20s and '30s, the number of celebrities and their visibility increased by orders of magnitude. No more than a million Americans saw the biggest theatrical superstar of the 1800s, Edwin Booth, perform his signature role, Hamlet, over the course of his entire career—whereas twenty million would see Charlie Chaplin in just one movie. And because the multiplying new stars were creatures of these uncanny new media, they were more phantasmagorical, like supernatural beings, making fandom in the age of radio and cinema (and then television) an inherently more fantastical state of mind.

For the first time, most of the most famous Americans were not politicians or military men or writers or painters but actors—people renowned for pretending to be people they weren't. My grandparents understood that Chaplin was just a man, but after seeing him in films didn't they inevitably regard him as partly fictional as well, both a real person and the Little Tramp? (And don't we still today?) Movie stars were a new species of fantasy figure, demigods among us, beings whom the new news media allowed us more than ever to imagine we practically *knew*.

20

Big Rock Candy Mountains:
Utopia in the Suburbs and the Sun

THE NEW AMERICAN FAME-MAKING APPARATUS COULD TURN EVEN A MIDDLE-aged midwestern architect into a glamorous international celebrity. At forty-seven, Frank Lloyd Wright was familiar among architects (and around Chicago for abandoning his wife to skidoo with a client's wife), but his was not a household name. In August 1914, as the outbreak of World War I otherwise dominated the news, *The New York Times* made room for his (and his mistress's) first appearance in the paper:

WILD NEGRO CHEF KILLS 6, WOUNDS 4
FORMER MRS. C. H. CHENEY OF
CHICAGO MURDERED IN COTTAGE
OF FRANK LLOYD WRIGHT.

He was instantly famous and kept getting more so (with more girlfriends and scandals and constant media coverage) during the second half of his long life. Celebrity as much as genius put Wright on the cover of *Time* at sixty-eight and gave him an hour of CBS prime time at ninety and, when he died at ninety-one, a *Times* obituary at the top of page one with another five articles about him inside.

But Frank Lloyd Wright has not barged into this book only as an exemplar of the new celebrity culture that exploded in the early twentieth century. He's here because he was a principal author of another all-American fantasy coming to full fruition—the suburb. America's century of wholesale suburbanization was another part of its happy fictionalization, a nation morphing into Earth's biggest theme park.

When Wright was a little boy, not far from where he'd later live outside Chicago, the prototypical built-from-scratch American suburb appeared—Riverside, Illinois, designed and created by Frederick Law Olmsted and Calvert Vaux. Their model was explicitly nostalgic, "the more agreeable rural characteristics of a New England Village." Before long, as the Columbia University historian Kenneth Jackson writes in *Crabgrass Frontier*, "detached housing had clearly emerged as the suburban style," and "the ideal house" in America "came to be viewed as resting in the middle of a manicured lawn or picturesque garden"—as if in a pastoral landscape from a previous American century. *Suburbia,* apparently a conflation of the terms *suburb* and *utopia,* became a word.

For his first twenty years of adulthood, at the turn of the century, Frank Lloyd Wright lived in a bucolic Chicago suburb—then returned north to Wisconsin, where he was born and raised, to build Taliesin, his first royal residence, complete with an artificial lake. In other words, he pursued and was a primary promoter of the American pastoral fantasy, having it both ways: working in modern cities—where stature, celebrity, and big money are available—but living the pseudorustic dream of countrified isolation and independence. "Urban life [has] served its term," he declared in 1932, the city a "monster aggregation," a "Moloch," a "tumor grown malignant," and "a menace to the future of humanity." Wright's hatred of cities was part of what made him so American. And all of a sudden there was a lot more urban America to hate. During the first four decades of the century, U.S. population growth actually slowed, but the big cities doubled and tripled or quintupled in size.

For a people whose adoring self-conception was wrapped up in its *Little House on the Prairie* past—Laura Ingalls Wilder published those novels in the 1930s and early '40s—urbanization caused some cognitive dissonance. Wright learned to despise big cities as a young architect working in Chicago for a decade. L. Frank Baum was living there at the same time when he wrote *The Wonderful Wizard of Oz,* and the world's fair's White City clearly inspired his Emerald City. Over the next few decades, after Baum decamped to Hollywood as soon as possible and wrote a dozen more Oz novels, the portion of the U.S. population living in central cities increased by half. America's most fantastic urban skyline—the Flatiron, the Woolworth, Chrysler, and Empire State buildings, plus Rockefeller Center—became fully Oz-like. But of course, at the end of the story Dorothy leaves the magical city and returns to her true American home, the humble farm on the Great Plains.*

Now, however, there was a new means for middle-class Americans to have it both ways, to *work* downtown in the real world but otherwise *live* the old dream: the suburb. As Leo Marx writes, "The psychic root of all pastoralism—genuine and spurious" is one that "our experience as a nation unquestionably has invested . . . with peculiar intensity. The soft veil of nostalgia that hangs over our urbanized landscape is largely a vestige of the once dominant image of an undefiled, green republic, a quiet land of forests, villages, and farms dedicated to the pursuit of happiness."

In fact, the suburb was a twofer, fantasy-wise. Loathing cities had always been a defining American impulse, but as cities rapidly filled up with millions of black and Catholic and Jewish and otherwise not-quite-white immigrants, a lot of native-born people found cities even more loathsome. So in addition to nostalgia for the undefiled green republic, suburbs could also satisfy white people's nostalgia for a time when they lived almost exclusively among other white (and Christian, preferably Protestant) people. Just as Americans in the 1600s and 1700s left towns where they found the dominant religious cast obnoxious and started new towns, Americans in the 1900s could leave cities where they found the ethnic and demographic cast obnoxious and move to new towns not very far down the road.

Automobiles (and electricity) enabled the suburban dream to become the new norm. Between the two world wars, cars went from rare novelties, one for every hundred adults, to one per family. In 1907 only 8 percent of American homes had electricity; by 1930, 70 percent did. Now you could drive yourself in your own dreamy roadster to your faux homestead in your simulated New England village. In the 1930s Frank Lloyd Wright was not only channeling Americans' disgust with the big bad city—"throw it away," he

---

* Another moral of the Oz story, what the con man/wizard teaches the lion and scarecrow and tin man, is an underlying theme of this book: for Americans, wishfully *believing* that something is true, even when it's false, makes it effectively true.

said—but grandiloquently giving his stamp of approval to suburban life. "Our pioneer days are not over," he wrote, because our new manifest destiny was to make America a coast-to-coast suburbia, what he called Broadacre City, "the only possible city of the future," "this city for the individual," with no higgledy-piggledy downtowns at all, each family in its own house on its own acre, every American transformed into "landed gentry," the Jeffersonian fantasy realized at last. "Birds sing, rain falls for him, the rain falls on his growing garden," and he thinks great thoughts all alone. "Individuality is his." If Wright hadn't existed, Ayn Rand would have had to invent him.*

The central-city-dwelling fraction of Americans reached a third—and never rose above that again. Meanwhile the suburban population more than doubled in three decades and kept on doubling. As it turned out, most Americans (and industry and federal policy makers) shared the fantastic retro vision of a nation covered by brand-new old-timey homesteads and ranches and small towns, and themselves as pioneers redux.

Suburban life was surely better than life in the city for lots of people in lots of ways—less racket and stink, more room and obvious order. But for almost everyone, in ways they seldom put into words, it also looked and felt like a dreamier, uniquely *American* way of life, a happy facsimile of the quiet green land of olden times. So along with America's extreme passions and knacks for religion and show business, the suburb became yet another fantasy-driven facet of the "divergence of the American experience," as Jackson writes in *Crabgrass Frontier*, "from that of the rest of the world."

I've confessed to living my own version of the American pastoral fantasy, and I'm very grateful that at the turn of the twentieth century, the federal government began creating national parks and preserving wilderness. But it is telling that the first director of the national parks was a Barnumesque former *New York Sun* reporter who'd made his fortune inventing the pioneering pioneer-nostalgia brand 20 Mule Team Borax. And no less than Sigmund Freud saw such parks as the perfect metaphor for fantasy in a psychiatric sense. "The creation of the mental domain of phantasy," he wrote in *A General Introduction to Psychoanalysis,* published in 1916, "has a complete counterpart in the establishment of 'reservations' and 'nature parks' in places where the inroads of agri-

---

* Actually, she sort of did. "I am writing a novel about the career of an architect," Rand told Wright in a 1937 letter, megalomaniac to megalomaniac, which will be the "story of human integrity. . . . That is what you have lived . . . the only one among the men of this century who has lived it." That turned into *The Fountainhead,* her first bestselling fantasy of a glorious superindividualist, which became a foundational text for American libertarians (see Chapter 40).

culture, traffic, or industry threatened to change the Earth rapidly into something unrecognizable. . . . The mental realm of phantasy is also such a reservation reclaimed from the encroaches of the reality principle."

A few years later, in the 1920s, over in a different part of the emerging fantasy-industrial complex, a singer-songwriter called Haywire Mac recorded the great ballad of American utopian pastoral fantasy: "Big Rock Candy Mountain." That was the place of "cigarette trees" and "lemonade springs" and hens laying soft-boiled eggs, where "the handouts grow on bushes" and "you can slip right out" of jail. It rose to number one on *Billboard*'s Hillbilly Hits chart, and a subsequent cover version made it a fixture in the folk music canon. The lyrics I learned and loved as a child in the 1960s had "a lake of stew and ginger ale too"—not Haywire Mac's original "lake of stew and a gin lake too." But the most radical revision was the deletion of the last verse. Rather than ending on the hobo's happy-happy reverie, a younger hobo undercuts it all with a funny reality-based finale:

> I've hiked and hiked till my feet are sore
> And I'll be damned if I hike any more
> To be buggered sore like a hobo's whore
> In the Big Rock Candy Mountains.

In fact, America was starting to bowdlerize in various ways at the time, trying to make everything not just more fantastic but *nicer*. Suburbanization was partly that, as were Hollywood's new codes to make sure movies weren't too salty or salacious. You can see it in our very language—particularly where it comes to discriminating between the actual and the unreal and ridiculing fantasies purporting to be authentic. For a century, Americans had a wide-ranging, well-established vocabulary for this, talking about *suckers* falling for *hogwash*. After the 1920s, however, we invented fewer and fewer such disparagements. Soon words like *balderdash, humbug,* and *bunkum* were shoved to the back of the language attic and semiretired or eliminated, along with *hooey, claptrap,* and *malarkey*. We also did a strange thing to a certain set of older words. For as long as they'd been English, *incredible, unbelievable, unreal, fabulous,* and *fantastic* were either derogatory or neutrally descriptive, different ways of calling claims unlikely, imaginary, or untrue. But then they were all redefined to be terms of supreme praise, synonyms for *wonderful, glorious, outstanding, superb*. It was a curious linguistic cleansing and a convenient prelude to the full unfettering of balderdash, bunkum, hooey, humbug, and malarkey later in the century.

* * *

EXACTLY ONE PIECE OF THE Big Rock Candy Mountain's paradise was becoming real: the narrator is "bound to go where there ain't no snow" and "the sun shines every day." Earlier migrations to and within America were inspired by visions of religious liberty, financial possibility, and self-reinvention. In the twentieth century, those reasons still applied. But now, as the fantasy-industrial complex expanded, millions of Americans picked up and moved simply because everyday life elsewhere looked prettier, easier, dreamier. That could mean a short hop to one of the new suburbs. And now it could also mean moving to suddenly urbanizing southern California or South Florida, both invented in the first few decades of the century as real-life Shangri-Las.

It was gold, the possibility that any lucky knucklehead could get rich overnight, that first sucked people to California and allowed America to fulfill its manifest destiny. But the remarkable climate and fecundity were also part of the original appeal, a dream-come-true whether or not you'd hit pay dirt (yet). The place might as well have been the Garden of Eden—warm, fertile, soft, fragrant. Anything could grow there, and California after the Gold Rush, filled with hundreds of thousands of uprooted seekers, became a place for cultivating every sort of wishful fantasy. Maybe It wasn't *inevitable*: San Francisco's early bohemia, Pentecostalism, Hollywood, and all the various wellsprings of utopianism and lifestyle perfectionism—as well as, still to come, the Beats, Scientology, Big Sur, Disneyland, Ronald Reagan, the Summer of Love, and Silicon Valley. But what other place on Earth has been more congenial to believers and promoters of mad dreams and schemes of so many kinds? California is America squared.

Between 1900 and 1930, the population doubled every decade—and Los Angeles grew even faster, ballooning from a hundred thousand to more than a million. For everyone rushing in, movie moguls as well as random try-anything wildcatters, southern California had a fundamental American quality—it was a blank slate, culturally as well as physically. "In Los Angeles," the *New Yorker* film critic Pauline Kael once wrote, "you can live any way you want (except the urban way); it's the fantasy-brothel, where you can live the fantasy of your choice."

Back east at the turn of the century, the Coney Island amusement parks were built adjacent to America's largest city. In southern California in the early 1900s there was no huge existing city, so an ambitious new entertainment zone instead became urban protoplasm: just southwest of Los Angeles, by the beach, a real estate developer (and eccentric utopian) named Abbot Kinney

built an amusement park around an artificial lagoon, with canals and gondo-
liers, calling it Venice of America. Other developers extended the conceit,
building more canals; the whole storybook confection quickly started becoming an actual town, Venice, and in the 1920s officially part of Los Angeles.

If amusement parks could morph into cities, why not vice versa? Coca-
Cola, until recently a patent medicine for headaches and impotence, had
been rebranded around looser dreams of refreshment and fun, so in the
1930s its downtown L.A. bottling plant was refashioned to look like an enormous cruise ship, with portholes and a catwalk. A five-minute walk away was
one of two remarkable giant local cafeterias that featured artificial indoor
streams, waterfalls, rain, rock formations, and groves of redwoods and palms.

The movie tycoons invented studio lots, towns within a town—offices,
workshops, restaurants, and bungalows, but inhabited by *celebrities*—that
also contained full-scale reproductions of fragments of other cities and towns.
These promptly provided a de facto model for domestic life in Los Angeles,
gated stage-set neighborhoods where the movie people could live: the Malibu
Beach Motion Picture Colony, Beverly Crest, its entrance marked by a pair of
"medieval" "English" stone "castle" towers, and Laughlin Park in Los Feliz,
where the houses let you pretend you were living in Italy or France or
seventeenth-century England or the nineteenth-century American Midwest.
The new American dream home became a small private back lot for enacting
one's lifestyle fantasy of choice.

South Florida was the other warm, sunny, mostly empty piece of America where the extended fantasy-industrial complex manufactured a large-
scale paradise. Miami and Palm Beach had come into being in the 1890s as
a citrus-business hub and resort, respectively. Miami was still a small town
when promoters started calling it the Magic City, then started marketing the
whole region as an idyllic place for living as well as vacationing. A real estate
boom and building frenzy started around 1915, with swamps drained to make
buildable land. Miami Beach was created by a developer who dredged up
sand from the ocean and imported thousands of tons of soil. Addison
Mizner—who'd grown up in an old California Gold Rush town and taken off
for the Klondike during its gold rush—was South Florida's defining architect,
and picturesque fantasies of European glamour were de rigueur: imitation
Côte d'Azur and Costa del Sol, faux Paris and Venice.*

---

* One such Mediterranean fantasia was Mar-a-Lago—built at the height of the first Florida real
estate bubble in the 1920s by the daughter of the founder of Post cereals (see Chapter 11), now
owned by a high lord of Fantasyland and president of the United States (see Chapter 46).

One way to track the nation's transmutation into Fantasyland is to look at where Americans moved during the twentieth century. In 1900 only two of the twenty largest cities, New Orleans and San Francisco, had temperatures that seldom got below freezing. Today, fourteen of the twenty largest cities are places where there ain't no snow and the sun shines every day.

21

The 1950s Seemed So Normal

I WAS BORN IN THE MIDDLE OF THE CENTURY IN THE MIDDLE OF THE COUNTRY to middle-class parents. My dad was a small-town Nebraskan and a veteran of the Pacific war who wore a tie to work every day; my mom was a lifelong Omahan and college graduate who'd worked in army cryptography but whose occupation was raising my three siblings and me. I grew up on a busy street lined with old Dutch elms on the prosperous suburban edge of town, where the houses and yards were neither huge nor tiny, neither old nor new. Six blocks west was a cornfield. Where I lived it seemed nobody was rich, and nobody was poor. I walked to school, where my classmates were exclusively white. When I wasn't at school, I spent most of my time watching television.

As a stereotype, it is close to perfect. At the time and certainly in retrospect, that era did and does seem like a pure and total embodiment of *normal*. But for all the supposed placidity and tameness, I have a different take now.

The 1950s were freaky and fantastical.

Start with two defining pieces of the stereotypical American 1950s—TV and the suburbs. Both were expressions and enablers of our American appetites for immersive make-believe. After suburbia and TV became so pervasive so fast—Currier & Ives on the outside, private electric cinemas inside—we lost any sense of the radical peculiarity of our new fantasy-drenched postwar way of life.

When my eldest sister was born, just seven years before me, a fraction of 1 percent of Americans had TVs; by the time I started school, there was a TV in practically every household. Television's supply of superrealistic fantasies (including the ads) was free and abundant and required no reading, no trips to theaters, not even the imaginative work of listening to radio plays. By the end of the decade, the average American spent a third of his or her waking hours watching TV. Nowhere and never had more people spent more time consuming fictions and advertising, and never in such a continuous quasi-hypnotic state.

From the end of World War II to 1960, the fraction of Americans living in suburbs doubled, faster than ever before or since. All at once we spread out over the countryside, replaying our westward-ho! past, déjà vu all over again. At the beginning of the century, two-thirds of Americans still lived in old small towns and on farms. By 1960, only a third did—and another third now lived in suburbia's new simulations of old-time countrified America. As the land closest to cities became built up and saturated and more distant parcels developed, the implicit nostalgic model shifted from the New England village to the pioneer homestead. Suburbia became the nearly mandatory ideal, one's own separate house on one's own acreage the requisite embodiment and expression of American individualism. No other developed country has such a huge fraction of its people living at such low densities on such massive amounts of land.

At the time, America's total embrace of TV and suburbia during the 1950s didn't seem like symptoms of a national immersion in fantasy. To the contrary, all serious observers saw reason and rationality cruising to victory on most fronts, led by America. The United Nations was established. Colleges and universities were growing fast. Science was unchallenged, the genetic code was broken, computers and transistors were invented, government and big business and even the big churches were run by technocrats, and ideology seemed passé. "Our culture is unique," a historian and sociologist of the period declared, "in its . . . outlawing of the irrational." *The Secret Life of Walter Mitty* became a box office hit in 1947 by satirizing an American freak who fictionalized himself as a dashing hero, living in his own private dream-world. Yet the new normal—driving in and out of suburban pastoral fantasies, immersing in endless new televised fantasies—was turning all Americans into Walter Mittys without them realizing it.

The 1950s, that stereotypically homogenous and conformist and *regular* American decade, generated extraordinary new alternate realities as well. To people then, they looked like bits of strangeness and pizzazz on the side, but they turned out to be prototypes for what would become mainstream American life. In this chapter, I'll look closely at a half-dozen creations of that era that became important foundations for ultimate Fantasyland—including Las Vegas, *Playboy,* the Beats, Scientology, McCarthyism, and revived Christian evangelicalism. Most promulgated happy fantasies, some of them scary fantasies. Some were hedonistic, others not hedonistic but nevertheless countercultural—and thus were attacked by Establishment antibodies that tried to quarantine or co-opt them. One was happy and hedonistic but not remotely countercultural, a synthesis of confabulated small towns and television, a manufactured city on a hill inspired by P. T. Barnum and Buffalo Bill devoted to weaving together reality and fiction: Disneyland.

WALT DISNEY WAS BORN AT precisely the right moment (1901) and had precisely the right skills (drawing, storytelling) and sensibility (high-quality populist) and instincts (entrepreneurial) to do what he did. His father had worked as a carpenter on Chicago's Columbian Exposition, and during Walt's childhood, America had three big world's fairs—in Buffalo, St. Louis, and San Francisco. Suddenly too the whole country was thick with amusement parks, hundreds of them. However, they were just better-capitalized versions of a familiar, itinerant form—bigger rides, more freaks, supercarnivals permanently installed on a piece of real estate the operator owned.

By the 1930s and '40s, when Walt Disney was busy turning a peripheral show business medium, animation, into an ambitious, high-end popular art, amusement parks had regressed to their seedy, quick-buck carnival roots. For Disney and other middle-class Americans, they were too *urban,* not enough like the new, orderly suburban ideal. They were, he said as he started imagining Disneyland, "so honky tonk with a lot of questionable characters running around, and they're not too safe. They're not well kept. I want to have a place that's as clean as anything could ever be, and all the people in it are first-class citizens."

His initial idea was one that any other show business executive might have had—a dinky eight-acre Mickey Mouse Park in Burbank next to the studio where he made his animated movies. But no, he decided, that was too modest, and too small potatoes. He was now the mogul *Walt Disney,* so his second act would need to wow people. The Tivoli Gardens amusement park in Copenhagen was suitably tasteful and influenced his vision, but it wasn't big enough, just twenty acres crammed into the middle of an old city. America needed something more incredible, more fabulous, more fantastic.

In the 1940s there were newly hatched models in America on which Disney drew as well, museum-like tourist attractions that mixed and matched the actually old and the pretend old. One was just south of L.A. in Orange County. A farmer named Walter Knott had started growing a freakishly large new berry, which he named the boysenberry and sold at his farmstand—and then built attractions to get more money out of the fruit buyers: a nineteenth-century hotel hauled in from Arizona, a fake ghost town and saloon, a reproduction Old West theater. In Virginia, the Rockefellers had just funded the rebuilding of Williamsburg as it had been in the 1760s, a who-can-tell-the-difference mélange of hundreds of restored old and new fake-old buildings. And in Michigan on some acreage near an automobile factory, Henry Ford had created Greenfield Village, consisting of the actual buildings, transplanted from Pennsylvania and Ohio and Illinois, where Stephen Foster and the Wright brothers and Abraham Lincoln had lived and worked. It was a totally new species, "a dream of assorted history as might have come out of 'Alice in Wonderland,'" an astonished *New York Times* reporter wrote in 1931. "It is a kind of history unknown to school textbooks, for it has small reminder of politics and none of war," filled with "actors, carrying on all kinds of American crafts," performing an "archaic theatrical show" amid "objects . . . [that] are not to appear as antiques corrupted by moth and rust, but as when new." There were also plans, he reported, for a "Jules Verne house of the future."

Walt Disney visited all those places during the decade he was dreaming up Disneyland. He was the Steve Jobs of his era, a visionary impresario taking pieces created by others and integrating them to make a shiny new branded invention greater than the sum of its constituent parts. In 1953 he bought an orange grove in Orange County—160 acres, a quarter-section, the elemental American land parcel—just south of Knott's Berry Farm.

The Disneyland that Disney envisioned was even more fantastic than the one he could afford to build. He wanted voice-activated doors that would "obey . . . like a Genie," a "working farm operated with real live miniature horses, cows, oxen, and donkeys," plus a "Lilliputian Land" with tiny talking robots. Nowadays we take it for granted when we encounter people walking around in costumes, playing beings from movies or TV shows or comic books or the past or the future. We routinely shop and eat in spaces designed and built to look like "authentic" places from other times and other countries. Before Disneyland, these were not routine experiences.

When it opened, Disneyland had five thematic zones, only one of them called Fantasyland. At the time, Hollywood studios didn't routinely let tourists in to see their fake-neighborhood sets—and Disney had created back lots with none of the seams and gears showing and *all* the employees acting. Main Street USA, while the most naturalistic of the "lands"—an old-fashioned town center, with real shopkeepers selling real merchandise—was Disney's single most world-changing 3-D fiction of all. It was more or less a replica of Marceline, Missouri, the small town where he'd grown up—indeed, an amazing dream version of the sort of place where only a few decades earlier three-quarters of Americans had lived and shopped. It wasn't just a story or show about the good old days—it practically *was* the good old days.

On Main Street USA, there were no giant twirling teacups or mechanical crocodiles: it was imaginary—always bright and clean, charming and happy—but it seemed uncannily real, life with the dull and charmless bits cut out. One's disbelief approached complete suspension. The illusion was brilliantly reinforced by design tricks such as forced perspective: in each pseudo-nineteenth-century building, each story was slightly smaller than the one below it, which made the streetscape both friendlier and grander than the real things. Just as the century of American rail travel was coming to an end, diesel replacing steam and freight replacing people, at the foot of Main Street was an old-fashioned station, the head end of Disneyland's own steam-powered passenger railroad.

When the Disneyland opening ceremonies were televised like a prime-time news special in 1955—*Dateline: Disneyland* on the ABC network, a major investor—who was one of the on-air celebrity hosts? The movie star Ronald Reagan, a decade before he was transmogrified into the governor of California and then president of the United States.

Walt Disney, the Disneyland-loving novelist Andrew O'Hagan has written, was "king of the irresistible falsehood." Photographs often show Disney with the index and middle finger of his right hand together as though he's about to give the Cub Scout salute: he chain-smoked (and died of lung cancer), but every time they could, he and his handlers had photographs retouched to eliminate the Lucky Strike. "With Disneyland," O'Hagan says, "Walt Disney felt he was giving America a better version of itself. . . . What he created was a new way of thinking about life and dreaming, a kind of American Eden." After Disneyland opened, the term *theme park* was coined, and more and more of America proceeded to be themed. That bit of Anaheim may have been the Most Magical Place on Earth, but . . . why stop there?

DISNEYLAND AND MODERN LAS VEGAS were born simultaneously. Disneyland had been inspired by disapproval of "questionable characters" and "honky-tonk" atmosphere. In the badlands three hundred miles across the Mojave Desert, Vegas was *created* by questionable characters *to be* honky-tonk, the Pottersville to Disneyland's Bedford Falls. Just as Disney did with amusement parks, the creators of the new Vegas took seedy American artifacts—gambling halls and roadhouses—and reinvented them as something grand. It was Adventureland for people who hungered after a different hormonal and neurotransmitter mix, one requiring high-stakes indeterminacy—the chance of getting instantly rich or laid, going broke or on a bender. Vegas and Disneyland were just two different new brands in the expanding line of the fantasy-industrial complex.*

Like the agricultural towns of Los Angeles and Miami before their reinventions, Las Vegas in the early 1900s existed as a nub of its future self. Nevada had uniquely permissive laws concerning gambling, matrimony, and prostitution, but in the 1920s and '30s, Las Vegas was still a shabby little burg where men working in mines and on Hoover (*né* Boulder) Dam could gamble and screw, nationally known only as a place where movie stars and millionaires sometimes visited to marry or divorce quickly.

The proof of concept for its transformation into a satanic Disneyland happened during World War II, as tens of thousands of aviators came through for training at the Las Vegas Army Airfield. At first, the fantasy references were strictly local and nostalgic. The Hotel Last Frontier, its architect and manager explained, "was conceived to be as near western as we could make it," by which he meant convincingly and fictionally pseudowestern. "The ceilings were of hewn timbers—logs—rough-sawed boards antiqued in such a way as to look many years old." He installed an old bar from the local red-light district, to which he added custom-designed bar stools in the shape of horse

---

* A decade after Disneyland opened, it capitulated a bit: its first new "land," New Orleans Square, was Disney's own version of louche, with a private "speakeasy" that was the only place in the park serving alcohol, and the Pirates of the Caribbean, in which money-mad mechanical men cracked jokes about rape.

saddles. He built an adjacent Last Frontier Village, another pastiche of real and fake: an 1870s jail and an 1860s Chinese-railroad-workers' temple were trucked in from northern Nevada, with a church and a Texaco station in brand-new nineteenth-century-style wooden buildings. Guests could travel to and from the airport in horse-drawn stagecoaches.*

During the decade after the war, Vegas took off, and its theming purview expanded from the Old West to the desert in general to anywhere hot and exotic to . . . any era anywhere at all. The New Frontier opened just before the space age with the slogan "Out of this World," chandeliers shaped like spacecraft and a mural of extraterrestrials heading for Vegas. In the Venus Room after the late show on Saturday nights, the fantasies on offer switched from worldly to metaphysical: a Roman Catholic mass was performed at four-thirty A.M. every Sunday morning. By the way, the Strip and most of what we know as Las Vegas are not technically in the city of Las Vegas. Rather, they are even today located in the unincorporated town of Paradise, Nevada.

YOU COULD HAVE YOUR FILL of naughty fantasies in Las Vegas in the 1950s, but southern Nevada was a long way from anywhere. A copy of *Playboy,* however, was available on newsstands everywhere and cost only fifty cents. At the moment when Vegas was becoming the branded hub of American bacchanalianism and construction was about to begin on Disneyland, *Playboy* was created by an American, Chicago born, the twenty-seven-year-old advertising copywriter Hugh Hefner.

Like Walt Disney with animation and Disneyland, and Bugsy Siegel and his associates with Las Vegas, Hefner took a disreputable thing and reinvented it as something modern and classy and singular. Existing girlie magazines were grotty black-and-white pulps, furtively sold, with minuscule circulations. *Playboy*'s first issue, in 1953, featured a fancy two-page color picture of Marilyn Monroe, nude, in its centerfold (a word coined by Hefner); three years later American men were buying a million copies each month.

---

* If time travel were possible, the Ramona Room at the Last Frontier would be on my itinerary, twice. On Christmas in 1944, with Army Air Force men and officers in the audience (maybe including members of the *Enola Gay* crew, training nearby for their mission to drop the A-bomb on Hiroshima), the twenty-five-year-old Liberace was performing, his first Vegas gig. And then on Washington's Birthday in 1955, not long before he introduced Disneyland to TV viewers, Ronald Reagan was paid the equivalent of $130,000 a week to perform with chimps. "What about the hoods and hookers in the ringside seats?" he'd fretted to his promoter beforehand. "What about my image?"

Photographs of naked women had never before been the raison d'être of such a large publication. Of course, like its skeevier print-porn predecessors, every copy of *Playboy* was a masturbation facilitator. But *Playboy*'s dream girls weren't the poorly photographed victims in *Pep!* and *Spot*.

Hefner's genius was not just in providing more upscale make-believe—color pictures of unequivocally beautiful women shot by good photographers, skillfully retouched and printed on glossy paper—but in building out a 360-degree fantasy that seemed normal, an aspirational template for his wankers to reimagine their everyday lives fantastically. "The Playmate," he instructed his staff in 1956,

> should be posed in a *natural* setting. . . . The model herself should look relaxed and natural. . . . Some simple activity like reading, writing, mixing a drink, trying on a new dress. . . . We like a healthy, intelligent American look—a young lady that looks like she might be a very efficient secretary or an undergrad at Vassar. . . . Playmates are real people and they are one of the good things in life that you can enjoy.

One of Hefner's brilliant innovations was to provide a few details about Playmates' lives, the more banal the better—their hobbies, their favorite books and foods. The fantasy seemed more real. And the rest of the magazine allowed its readers (and "readers") to imagine themselves living fantastically sexier lives. *You are not a scared, lonely chump with dreary domestic responsibilities and a crappy job,* every page told them. *You are masculine and sophisticated and witty and suave and well dressed and cool, with good taste, in a fun America full of women eager to have no-strings sex with you.*

James Bond was a new model of manhood in the 1950s. The first Bond novel was published the same year Hefner published the first *Playboy,* and a new book appeared every year. "I'm sure James Bond, if he were an actual person," Hefner said, "would be a registered reader of *Playboy*." Indeed, as soon as Hefner created Playboy Clubs in the actual world—in order to "let people get a glimpse of what the fantasy world was all about," as his brother explained—Ian Fleming wrote Playboy Clubs into his fiction, making Bond a member.

While reading *Casino Royale* or *Goldfinger,* one knew that James Bond wasn't real, whereas *Playboy* was mainly, nominally *non*fiction. Its photo spreads of naked women, its advice columns, its articles about (and ads for) hot cars and cool bachelor pads and hi-fi and hep new cultural products, constituted an imaginary world presented as perfectly real and available. Reality and fiction were a total blur for Hefner. He donated to John F. Kennedy's presidential campaign, he said, because he figured he would be "a *Mr. Smith Goes to Washington, Meet John Doe* president." Plus, Kennedy was the ultimate *Playboy* man—urbane, Ivy League, great-looking, oversexed, a real-life fantasy figure. JFK, Hefner said, "was one of us." (And as soon as he became president, Kennedy confirmed that, announcing that one of his favorite books was the Bond novel *From Russia with Love*.)

A few years after inventing a magazine that allowed men to fictionalize themselves, Hefner stepped through his looking glass, turning his own life into a full-blown public fiction, with himself as its main character: the pipe, the bathrobe, the friendship with the Rat Pack, the Playboy Mansions, the harem of permanently youthful Playmates in residence, the whole shebang.

IN THE LATE 1950S *PLAYBOY* paid Jack Kerouac to write an article called "The Origins of the Beat Generation." The following month the centerfold featured their "Beat Playmate," an actress and daughter of jazz musicians the editors claimed to have discovered in one of "the beat coffee houses of Hollywood." Her interests included "ballet, the poetry of Dylan Thomas, classical music ('Prokofiev drives me out of my skull!'). She has strong opinions and is more than a bit of a rebel, frowning prettily on conformity," and "confesses to being 'somewhat of a nut' about health food," which she eats at "an 'organic food restaurant' called The Aware Inn."[*]

Hefner and his magazine were ambivalent about the Beats. They were members of adjacent new Fantasyland denominations—sex! booze! bennies! jazz! selfishness!—but mutually contemptuous, not unlike the two-way suspicion between Christian evangelicals and Pentecostals. Hefner even coined and used the term *Upbeat Generation* to distinguish his affluent go-go sophisticates from the slackery beatniks.

We think of the Beats as un-American creatures, the anti-1950s exceptions who proved the rule. But they were *highly* American. For one thing, the founders became enduring pop celebrities. More important, their animating

---

[*] The Beat Playmate was Yvette Vickers; you might recall the 2011 news of the discovery of her "mummified" corpse in her house in Beverly Crest—the L.A. neighborhood built in the 1920s with fake English castle towers. Her *Playboy* photos had been shot by Russ Meyer just before he became the soft-core-porn auteur of movies such as *Faster, Pussycat! Kill! Kill!* The owner of the Beat Playmate's "organic food restaurant" was Jim Baker, who in the 1960s and '70s, as Father Yod, led an L.A. cult called the Source Family.

impulses grew out of that old American search for a sense of meaning that devolved into dreamy, grandiose unreasonableness. Kerouac first spoke the phrase *Beat Generation* to a novelist who—in 1952 in *The New York Times,* of all places—published a mission statement. Being a Beat wasn't about having a bohemian way of life, he wrote: "A man is beat whenever he goes for broke and wagers the sum of his resources on a single number." Members of the Beat Generation "have an instinctive individuality," a "lust for freedom" that dug "bebop, narcotics, sexual promiscuity" but also William F. Buckley's *God and Man at Yale.* "Unlike the Lost Generation, which was occupied with the loss of faith, the Beat Generation is becoming more and more occupied with the need for it . . . busily and haphazardly inventing totems for [God] on all sides. . . . This almost exaggerated will to believe in something . . . a *will* to believe . . . a perfect craving to believe."

This is what made the Beats such an American phenomenon. They were all about their mystical, individualist beliefs, and all in. They rejected bland rules to live lives of antimaterialist and quasi-religious purity. They were like some freaky renegade Protestant sect who didn't focus on Jesus but otherwise took the original priesthood-of-all-believers idea to the max. The Beats' self-conception descended from a particular American lineage—mountain men, outlaws, frontier cranks, lonely individualists, and narcissistic outsiders sounding their barbaric yawps over the rooftops of the world. The hippie dream that followed drew as well from a parallel lineage—Cane Ridge, the communes of the 1830s and '40s, Transcendentalism, pastoralism, Thoreau. Both were enactments of classic American fantasies.

Kerouac, the king of the Beats, nicely embodied a couple of recurrent themes in this history—mythologizing the good old days, living life as if it were a piece of fiction. "Nostalgia," the Harvard cultural historian Louis Menand has written of *On the Road,* was "part of its appeal in 1957. For it is not a book about the nineteen-fifties. It's a book about the nineteen-forties," the "dying . . . world of hoboes and migrant workers and cowboys and crazy joyriders." What's more, the novel was not a fictionalization of adventures Kerouac just happened to experience—rather, "the trips in *On the Road* were made for the purpose of writing *On the Road.*"*

The novel's fictional avatars of Kerouac and his buddy Neal Cassady visit

---

* Considered in this light, with William F. Buckley as a crypto-Beat, it starts to make sense that Ayn Rand's didactic novel *Atlas Shrugged,* a founding text of libertarianism, appeared in the same 1957 publishing season as *On the Road.* The heroes of both are extreme, do-their-own-thing American individualists who reject the comfy Establishment.

the fictional version of their friend William Burroughs, the noir fantasy writer. The Burroughs character, the narrator tells us, has a "sentimental streak about the old days in America . . . [when] the country was wild and brawling and free, with abundance and any kind of freedom for everyone," and says that "mankind will someday realize that we are actually in contact with the dead and with the other world."

The character, like Burroughs himself, was in the thrall of an "orgone accumulator" that he'd built, a wooden box on which "he tied bush bayou leaves and twigs" and then sat naked inside. The fictionalized Kerouac explains that "orgones are vibratory atmospheric atoms of the life-principle. People get cancer because they run out of orgones."

Like mesmerism and homeopathy in the nineteenth century, orgone therapy was an import from German Europe. Its inventor was the psychoanalyst Wilhelm Reich, a protégé of Freud—who finally concluded Reich was nuts: he "salutes in the genital orgasm," Freud wrote a colleague, as "the antidote to every neurosis." He got nuttier, announcing he'd discovered fundamental new substances—"bions" and, after he emigrated to the United States, "primordial, pre-atomic cosmic orgone energy," the very source of human vitality. In America he was taken seriously for a while and not just by the Beats. His work was cited in the major medical journals. Cancer victims came to be cured in his orgone accumulators. Farmers paid him to point his "cloudbuster" at the sky to unleash atmospheric orgone energy and make it rain, and he also said it'd work to ward off extraterrestrial invaders. He believed a secret cabal of highly placed allies in the federal government would save him from his various enemies—the Rockefeller family, Communists, the FDA, the Justice Department. The feds ordered him to stop advertising and selling his quack medical devices; he refused; they prosecuted and finally imprisoned him. A month after the Soviet satellite *Sputnik* began orbiting Earth and two months after *On the Road* was published—coincidence?—he died in a federal penitentiary.

Drug use would become part of the Fantasyland transformation, and the Beats started making drugs cool during the 1950s. Burroughs loved his junk, Kerouac his speed, Ginsberg his weed. Regular Americans also discovered and embraced new, legal psychotropic drugs in the 1950s. The synthetic amphetamine Benzedrine was available over the counter in the United States until 1959, and its more powerful sibling Dexedrine had just been introduced. By 1960, amazingly, Americans' legal-speed dosage averaged one hit per person per week. People also started taking tranquilizers by the barrel. In 1957, two years after the miracle "nerve pill" Miltown appeared in pharmacies, it accounted for a third of all U.S. drug prescriptions.

Like so many of their American predecessors and successors, the Beats cobbled together a patchwork doctrine that included exotic religious belief. Cassady, Kerouac, and especially Ginsberg considered themselves Buddhists, and Burroughs became a devotee of Scientology, proselytizing his pals.

Ah, Scientology. The entrepreneurial fabulism of L. Ron Hubbard—L.A. science fiction and fantasy author turned pop psychologist turned religious prophet—was another artifact of the American 1950s that belies the decade's stereotype. Hubbard may have been a knowing charlatan, but to me, at least at the beginning, he seems more like Joseph Smith, a true believer who thought he'd discovered a singular "mix of Western technology and Oriental philosophy" that offered the secret to human happiness. Does a con artist submit his findings to the *Journal of the American Medical Association*? His book *Dianetics: The Modern Science of Mental Health* was a national bestseller for two years running in the 1950s. Then he expanded and transformed the whole thing from a pseudoscience into a religion, the Church of Scientology.

Like Reich with the orgone accumulator, Hubbard put a gadget at the center of his purification scheme—the patented electropsychometer, or e-meter, transistorized and battery-powered, totally 1950s-modern. And as a spiritual leader, he was ahead of his time. Decades before New Age therapists/shamans started hypnotizing people to fantasize past lives, Scientology "auditors" were doing that with e-meters. Decades before American Christianity made its full left turn toward "charismatic" abracadabra, people *feeling* and imagining they *saw* the supernatural, e-metered audits induced in Scientologists a comparable certainty that they were in touch with their godlike souls. What made Scientology so perfectly American was its emphasis on practical self-improvement of an entirely subjective kind: *If it makes you feel better, let alone omnipotent, it must be true.*

Hubbard had a brazen indifference to the line between nonfiction and fiction—specifically science fiction, and not just e-meters. Scientology's theological backstory is staggeringly ridiculous sci-fi, *2001* meets *Star Trek* meets *Star Wars* meets *The Matrix* meets *Prometheus*. In short, each of us contains a thetan, one of the ethereal beings who created the universe but each of whom, after being shipped to Earth and hit with nuclear bombs by the evil dictator of the Galactic Confederacy, was brainwashed to forget its godlike origins and believe in the false reality most people consider real.

I could devote an entire chapter to L. Ron Hubbard.

* * *

IN THE SPRING OF 1957, a few months before Wilhelm Reich died in prison, another persecuted, angry, reckless, middle-aged anti-Communist zealot died in a different federal facility, Bethesda Naval Hospital—Senator Joseph McCarthy, the man who had proudly given his name to McCarthyism.

Almost immediately after World War II, our most important ally, the Soviet Union, became our most serious adversary-cum-enemy. For Americans in 1950, it was not delusional to worry about international Communist aggression or Soviet espionage in the United States. But that's the problem with a conspiracist mindset. After some kernel of reality triggers exaggerated fears and a possible explanation, it grows into an imaginary labyrinth of all-powerful evil, an elaborate based-on-a-true-story fiction that passes for nonfiction, such as the fantasy that thousands of committed Communists were covertly using movies and TV shows to propagandize on behalf of Communism and the Soviet Union. Anti-Communism was realistic; McCarthyism was fantastical.

A year after the end of the war, before McCarthy had even been elected to the Senate, the Red Scare was launched in Hollywood. Being a Communist was not against the law. However, Congress had launched an investigation. The result of those House Un-American Activities Committee hearings was the refusal of ten subpoenaed screenwriters and directors to answer questions about their beliefs or associations; the Hollywood Ten, many of whom had been Communists in the 1930s, served prison terms for refusing to talk and were blacklisted by the entertainment industry. But among the people who eagerly testified was one who identified himself as "a producer of motion-picture cartoons" and another who'd just been elected president of the Screen Actors Guild, the Hollywood union. Both had particular axes to grind, and it is striking, a measure of the hysteria even before the Soviets had the atom bomb or China was Communist or the Korean War started, how fast and loose they played with the facts.

"In the past," Walt Disney told the congressmen when asked about subversives at his studio, "I had some people that I definitely feel were Communists." He was still pissed about the five-week strike by his animators six years earlier, which he told the committee had resulted in "smear campaigns" by "Commie periodicals" and "all the Commie groups." One animator he named, an "artist in my plant," had been "the real brains of" the strike. "I looked into his record and I found that . . . he had no religion." A congressman asked about two other animators who'd been leaders of the strike. "In my opinion," Disney said, "they are Communists. No one has any way of proving those things."

Nor did the new president of SAG, the young actor Ronald Reagan, have any hard evidence that his opponents in the union were Communists. "That small clique," however, "has been suspected of more or less following the tactics that we associated with the Communist Party. . . . I have heard different discussions and some of them tagged as Communists."

A few days later the owner of the *Hollywood Reporter* became a chief public instigator of the Red Scare, insisting the industry create a formal blacklist of left-wingers. He was a remarkable guy who married three of his six wives in Las Vegas and developed the Flamingo hotel-casino before bringing in Bugsy Siegel and other mobsters to take over. Just before publishing the *Reporter*'s first attacks on the Communist conspiracy, he went to confession at a Catholic church on Sunset Boulevard, where he got his priest's go-ahead to name names of people he figured were Reds.

"Any man or woman," he wrote, "who, under the guise of freedom of speech, or the cloak of the Bill of Rights, or under the pseudoprotection of being a liberal, says things, causes things to be said, or who actually is involved with many of the conspiracies that have now infested this great land of ours, has no place among us, be he commie or what." And a few weeks later the studios complied, issuing a joint statement in which they said that while "nothing subversive or un-American has appeared on the screen," the industry's leaders "deplore the action of the 10 Hollywood men" who hadn't cooperated with HUAC. Henceforth the studios wouldn't "knowingly employ a Communist" and would "invite the Hollywood talent guilds to work with us to eliminate any subversives."

An influential pamphlet called *Red Channels* listed 151 show business subversives, people responsible for "commercially sponsored dramatic series . . . used as sounding boards, particularly with reference to current issues in which the [Communist] Party is critically interested: 'academic freedom,' 'civil rights,' 'peace.'" Various blacklists eventually included more than three hundred names.

The Soviets tested their first atomic bomb. The anti-Communist hysteria quickened and spread. "Loyalty boards" were set up in every federal department, and thousands of U.S. government employees were fired or forced out. In 1950, after just three years in office, the junior senator from Wisconsin made the Communist conspiracy his issue. "Karl Marx dismissed God as a hoax," McCarthy explained in a speech. "Today we are engaged in a final, all-out battle between communistic atheism and Christianity." He said he had a list of dozens of State Department employees who were "members of the Communist Party," "names . . . known to the Secretary of State." His list, he variously claimed, consisted of 57 or 81 or 205 officials. It was not true. But the press continued covering the allegation—he was a U.S. senator!— and it became the most consequential piece of fake news in American history.*

McCarthy's fantasy grew more elaborate and absurd. A year later, during the Korean War, in which thirty-six thousand U.S. soldiers and Marines would die, he gave a speech on the Senate floor explaining that President Harry Truman was the puppet and "captive" of some of his Communist cabinet members, "the executioners" of "a conspiracy on a scale so immense as to dwarf any previous such venture in the history of man . . . a larger conspiracy, the world-wide web of which has been spun from Moscow." Preposterous, for sure, but Americans believed. Before long a Gallup Poll found that 50 percent had a favorable opinion of Joseph McCarthy.

After five years of such recklessness, the public and the Establishment finally had enough. McCarthy's fantasies were no longer just geopolitical: he was hospitalized for alcoholism, and at a social gathering in Wisconsin, he hallucinated that he was being attacked by snakes.† The Senate officially condemned him by a vote of 67 to 22.

The tendency to explain the world in terms of conspiracies, conspiracies on a scale so immense as to dwarf any previous such ventures in the history of man, didn't begin with McCarthyism. McCarthy as an individual was rather quickly discredited, and McCarthyism became a universal pejorative for false and hysterical and unfair accusation. Exaggerated fears of Communist subversion, however, lasted for the whole Cold War, letting modern Americans' antisubversion fantasies take root and spread and grow as never

* "Today the advent of McCarthyism has thrown real fear into the hearts of some," a young Washington reporter wrote a few months after McCarthy's speech in 1950, "fear of what a demagogue can do to America while the press helplessly gives its sometimes unwilling cooperation. . . . But who knows? One greater than McCarthy may come."

† Another moment of harmonic convergence in Fantasyland. This gathering was in his Wisconsin hometown, where Harry Houdini had also spent most of his boyhood, at the home of McCarthy's best man and former Senate campaign manager, Urban Van Susteren. Van Susteren's daughter Greta, then a toddler, grew up to become an anchor on Fox News for fourteen years—as well as a Scientologist, whose founder, L. Ron Hubbard, like McCarthy, lied about having been wounded in action during World War II.

before. The basic McCarthyist vision—a conviction that a powerful conspiracy of Americans in government, media, and academia, in alliance with foreign Communists, was hell-bent on the ruin of their own country—had several generations, from 1940s into the 1990s, to become an entrenched American habit of mind.

FOR INCITING BELIEF IN HISTORY'S greatest conspiracy, it didn't hurt that two-thirds of Americans were Protestants, a large and pious fraction of whom subscribed to a stark prophetic version of history and the future—divine virtue fighting it out with satanic evil. America was an exceptionally Christian nation; the Soviet and Chinese regimes were atheistic. So when the new superstar preacher Billy Graham reckoned that "over 1100 social-sounding organizations . . . are Communist or Communist-oriented in this country [and] control the minds of a great segment of our people," that was an American synergy. Even as McCarthy was being purged, Graham explained that Communism was "master-minded by Satan. . . . There is no other explanation for the tremendous gains of Communism . . . unless they have supernatural power and wisdom and intelligence given to them." It was just like with Satan's Native American warriors in the 1600s.

Since the 1920s, the new-old-school Christians, having gone off the mainstream radar, hunkered down, quietly building their own institutions to propagate their alternative reality. It was a counterculture willfully resistant (and mostly invisible) to the contemptuous mainstream. A hundred evangelical Bible institutes had opened, as well as full-fledged colleges and universities. Fundamentalist and Pentecostal churches multiplied.

And then came this new evangelical Billy, the perfect vessel for a resurgence of Christian fundamentalism lite in the 1950s. Billy Graham was young and tall and good-looking, with a great head of blond hair. He was Southern but no Elmer Gantry— upright, earnest, upper-middle class. He was a skillful speaker and performer who oozed conviction and sincerity—with none of the carny brashness of Billy Sunday or cultish creepiness of Aimee Semple McPherson. After attending two of the newly created evangelical colleges in the South, he'd graduated from Wheaton, an older, more respectable Christian institution in the North; he'd been ordained by the Southern Baptists, the largest and most venerable of the conservative denominations. He was in every way perfectly double-coded, fit for the embrace of the die-hard base as well as midcentury middle-American

Protestants and the media: Southern but no redneck, populist but with gravitas, apocalyptic but not wild or angry, simultaneously an outsider and an insider. And like all the megasuccessful American preachers before him, Billy Graham was filled with the spirit of entrepreneurship and of show business as well as of God.

At twenty-five, he left his job as host of a weekly Christian radio program in suburban Chicago to be the main preacher for a popular new evangelical road show called *Youth for Christ*—"Anchored to the Rock but Geared to the Times!"—playing to stadium audiences, bringing fundamentalist Christianity entirely out of its bunker and into the modern fantasy-industrial complex. The *Youth for Christ* performances were glitzy arena rock shows decades ahead of their time: a giant prop Bible carried to the middle of the Rose Bowl or Soldier's Field, stentorian religious narration blasted over loudspeakers, a charge of flash powder loudly detonated, a mushroom cloud produced, one hundred white doves released.

Graham started freelancing, staging several of his own days-long revival encampments in small cities. His breakthrough happened in Los Angeles, where dreams could come true on streets of gold and a zillion corrupted sinners needed saving. He pitched several circus tents in a downtown parking lot—that is, he created the Greater Los Angeles Billy Graham Crusade at the Canvas Cathedral. There was a searchlight, as at a Hollywood premiere—the Steeple of Light. Signs exhorted people to COME AND EXPECT A MIRACLE SUPERNATURAL EXPLOSION IN THE HOLY GHOST MIRACLE TENT. The L.A. crusade was scheduled to run three weeks and draw 125,000 people; it lasted eight weeks and played to 350,000. The national news coverage was extensive, some of it explicitly flattering ("Puff Graham," William Randolph Hearst had cabled the editors of his newspapers), all of it invaluable. *Time* reported that "nearly every prominent minister in Los Angeles had put in an appearance on Billy Graham's crowded platform. . . . 'Very rarely do I find an atheist,' Graham said. 'People aren't so smart-alecky any more.'"

Graham's crusades went national, attracting phenomenally huge crowds everywhere. He pushed no particular denomination and avoided doctrinal niggling. He declined to get into disputes over exactly how and when God created everything, and he downplayed the end-time. He carved out a new Christian space between liberals and fundamentalists: theologically backward and enthusiastic compared to the mainline Protestant denominations but apparently not too deranged.

He was clubbable and brilliantly political in all senses. Three weeks after the Korean War broke out—and just a year after he'd become famous—he was praying with Harry Truman in the Oval Office (then pissing off the president when he posed by himself for photographs kneeling in prayer on the White House lawn). He attended Eisenhower's inauguration and made a point of buddying up to the president after him, and the next and the next— giving each of them, unlike their thirty-one predecessors, the convenience of a single Protestant leader with whom the president of the United States could be publicly friendly. In a country both overwhelmingly Protestant and madly sectarian, he created and filled a new ad hoc national position of Pastor-in-Chief, our Archbishop of Mayberry. The year he turned thirty-five he appeared on the cover of *Time*.

In fact, all American Christian boats were rising. In his first year as president, at age sixty-three, Eisenhower was baptized. He appeared at the first National Prayer Breakfast, an event organized by a fundamentalist group, which became annual. The following year Congress and the president stuck "under God" into the eighty-seven-year-old Pledge of Allegiance, then gave America its first official motto, "In God We Trust," to be printed on currency. Eisenhower made prayer a regular part of cabinet meetings, the first one led by his agriculture secretary, a leader of the Mormon Church.

American go-getterism was also ripe for a certain kind of Christianizing in the 1950s. For two decades, the Reverend Norman Vincent Peale had been one of New York City's big-deal pastors, with a fancy Presbyterian church right off Fifth Avenue, CEO pals, and his own vaguely Protestant radio show and national magazine. In 1955 he published *The Power of Positive Thinking*, which stayed on the *New York Times* bestseller list for three years. Peale's approach was perfect for its American moment: breezy self-help motivational cheerleading mixed with supernatural encouragement, Dale Carnegie plus the Guy Upstairs.

In his book, Peale taught people to repeat bullet-point affirmations over and over and to suppress any doubts that might lead to an "inferiority complex." He shrewdly chose a nonreligious title, and chapters included "When Vitality Sags, Try This Health Formula" and "How to Get People to Like You" and "I Don't Believe in Defeat." But Christian faith is key to making the big sale, getting the great job, and being a winner. "A sure cure for lack of self-confidence is the thought that God is actually with you and helping you. . . . The secret is to fill your mind with thoughts of faith, confidence, and security." God had always tipped the scales for America economically and militarily, but now in the 1950s He was also looking out for *you*, the individual middle-class American busy bee. Peale mass-marketed two strains of thought that had wormed their way into American Christianity since 1900: magical thinking about wealth and success ("God's ability is mine," a prominent turn-of-the-century pastor had preached. "His success is mine. I am a winner") and *see no evil–hear no evil–speak no evil* as practical means of getting there. Lots of prominent Protestant theologians hated *The Power of Positive Thinking*—it was egocentric, materialist, and escapist, a cult. Billy Graham loved it.

The mainstream, for all its embrace of the Grahams and Peales, still considered the wilder and crazier Christians mortifying leftovers from another age. *The New York Times* discovered in 1955 that "fringe sects" such as Pentecostals, though "not widely known," were still around and practicing their "excessive emotionalism."

The following year, when the Pentecostal minister Oral Roberts bought time on hundreds of TV stations for a weekly show and faith-healed people on the air, the *Times* TV critic was appalled by this "gospel preacher making his own extemporaneous medical diagnoses and claiming magic results unsupported by the slightest shred of rational evidence. . . . To allow the enormously influential medium of television to be used week after week to allow undocumented 'miracles' . . . seems contrary to the spirit . . . of the industry's code governing mature and responsible broadcasting."

Growing up on the northwestern edge of the Bible Belt, most of the people I knew were churchgoing Christians, but I'm pretty sure none of them ever mentioned Jesus to me. During the 1950s, the fundamentalists and evangelicals started coming out of the closet, but they still looked like curiosities, marginal rearguard diehards, not the shape of things to come. At the end of the 1950s, big Hollywood movies explicitly disparaged redneck religion—adaptations of the satire *Elmer Gantry* and of *Inherit the Wind,* the Broadway hit about the Scopes Trial, with Spencer Tracy as Clarence Darrow. It was a victory lap for modern seculars. Everyone serious believed that crude, vestigial, old-time religion was about to fizzle out at last in America. Official Protestant belief and practice seemed to be evolving as they had in the rest of the developed world, toward something low-key, subtle, and amorphous that could comfortably coexist with modern reason and science and American optimism. In a 1961 *Redbook* magazine survey of students at seven leading American Protestant seminaries, only one out of a hundred expected Jesus to return.

As the 1960s arrived, the mainline Protestant churches absolutely ruled. Back then, in fact, nobody called those churches mainline—compared to what? *Mainline* was still a term reserved for discussions of railroads and electric power, not to distinguish the big, respectable denominations that kept supernatural fantasies on the down-low. Their attendance had increased by a third since World War II. They were thriving. As it turned out, they were also peaking.

PART IV

Big Bang: The 1960s and '70s

"We risk being the first people in history to have been able to make their illusions so vivid, so persuasive, so 'realistic' that they can live in them."

—Daniel Boorstin,
The Image: A Guide to Pseudo-Events in America (1961)

"If there is something comforting—religious, if you want—about paranoia, there is still also anti-paranoia, where nothing is connected to anything, a condition not many of us can bear for long."

—Thomas Pynchon,
Gravity's Rainbow (1973)

For more than a century, Woodstock, New York, has been a place where artists, utopians, and bohemians have settled. It was a town, a *New York Times* article explained in 1932, where "everybody takes art very seriously." As soon as he made a couple of records, Bob Dylan moved there. It became hugely famous in 1969, of course, when four hundred thousand young people attended the Woodstock Festival, even though that took place sixty miles away. By the following year, *the Woodstock Generation* was an all-purpose term for American youth. As a college freshman in 1973, I went to the town of Woodstock to visit my older brother, a rock musician who'd moved there from the Midwest with his band because . . . *Woodstock.*

One Saturday four decades later I went again, invited to give a talk about the 1960s. Most of the audience that morning consisted of people older than me who probably still thought of themselves as members of the Woodstock Generation. During the question and answer session, a bearded man with white hair pleadingly asked why, did I suppose, had the revolution they'd imagined been won in so many social and cultural zones—civil rights, women's rights, gay rights, ecology, sex, drugs, rock 'n' roll, natural foods and medicine, millions of old guys like him wearing jeans and long hair—but lost in the economic realm, with free-market ideas victorious?

There was a long pause. People nodded and shrugged and sighed.

I had an epiphany, which I offered, bumming out everyone in the room. What has happened politically, economically, culturally, and socially in America since the sea change of the 1960s and early '70s, I realized and haltingly explained, isn't really so contradictory or incongruous. It's all of a piece, for better and for worse.

Our Woodstock-branded popular understanding of what grew out of the 1960s is selective, cherry-picked to please and flatter one side and appall the other. People on the left "still swear by the values of the '60s," Charles Reich, author of *The Greening of America,* recently said. They focus only on the 1960s legacies of freedom that they define as progress. And people on the political and cultural right still demonize the decade from around 1963 to 1973 as the source of everything they loathe.

In fact, what the left and right respectively love and hate are mostly flip sides of the same coins minted around 1967. All the ideas we call countercultural barged onto the cultural main stage in the 1960s and '70s, it's true, but what we don't really register is that so did extreme Christianity, full blown conspiracism, libertarianism, unembarrassed greed, and more. Anything goes meant *anything* went.

A kind of unspoken grand bargain was forged between the anti-Establishment and the Establishment. Going forward, individuals would be permitted as never before to indulge their self-expressive and hedonistic impulses. But capitalists in return would be unshackled as well, free to indulge their own animal spirits with fewer and fewer fetters in the forms of regulation, taxes, or social opprobrium. "Do your own thing" has a lot in common with "Every man for himself." *If it feels good, do it:* for some that will mean smoking weed and watching porn—and for others, opposing modest gun regulation and paying yourself four hundred times what you pay your employees.

Legal equality definitely advanced in the 1960s. But beyond that expansion of equality, outside the statute books, was another more fundamental piece of Americanism: every individual became freer to be or believe *whatever* he or she wished. The idea that finally eclipsed all competing ideas was a notion of individualism that was as old as America itself, liberty and the pursuit of happiness unbound: *Believe the dream, mistrust authority, do your own thing, find your own truth.* In America from the late 1960s on, equality came to mean not just that the *law* should treat everyone identically but that *your beliefs* about anything are equally as true as anyone else's. As the principle of absolute tolerance became axiomatic in our culture and internalized as part of our psychology—*What I believe is true because I want and feel it to be true*—individualism turned into rampant solipsism.

This is something of a conservative view, but in a sense that *conservative* is seldom used these days. The 1960s enabled a deep and broad believe-anything-you-want ethos that has powered the political right more than the left—and that extends way beyond politics. The 1960s gave license to *everyone* in America to let their freak flags fly—superselfish Ayn Randians as well as New Age shamans; fundamentalists and evangelicals and charismatics; Scientologists, homeopaths, spiritual cultists, and academic relativists; left-wing and right-wing conspiracists; war reenactors and those abducted by Satan or extraterrestrials; compulsive pornhounds and gamblers and gun-lovers. *Do your own thing.* Our epistemological and ontological levees were blasted apart and never repaired thereafter. *Mistrust authority.* Nonfiction fantasies were no longer held back or filtered out from the mainstream as they used to be. *Find your own truth.* Henceforth reality will be whatever you—you inviolate individual, you empowered American, you priest of your own religion, you author of your own story—wish it to be.

More citizens than ever of a nation constructed on almost-anything-goes Enlightenment principles, having been shaped by centuries of peculiar American conditions—our follow-the-dream inception, our Protestant mental habits, our extreme populism and individualism and subjectivity, our sheer space—rejected the claims of reason and rationality once and for all.

At midcentury, reason had seemed to be triumphing in its long global post-Enlightenment competition with magical thinking. Modernizing cultures, it seemed, were steadily and irreversibly abandoning beliefs in the supernatural and the otherwise impossible. *The Sacred Canopy*, a 1967 book by one of the most esteemed sociologists of religion, affirmed the intellectual consensus as far as religion went. After Western religion paved the way for modernity, advanced modernity was now finally killing off religion. "Christianity," he wrote, "has been its own gravedigger."

But not in America, where the Protestant fires still burned brightly. And even for people who found themselves unable to believe the biblical tales (or associated fan fiction), there were suddenly new, additional ways to fill the post-God fantasy gap. The dreams of freedom and abundance in modern America include an unprecedented abundance of *choice*. And so in the 1960s, several disparate countercultures—left, right, and apolitical, high and low, variously eager to embrace the irrational, to reenchant the world, to believe in underlying and overarching master plans—launched their counterattacks on multiple fronts, battling America's rationalist fortresses as well as one another. And most of them won, or at least grew large and did not lose.

22

Big Bang: The Hippies

I DON'T REGRET OR DISAPPROVE OF MANY OF THE WAYS THE 1960S PERMA-
nently reordered American society and culture. It's just that along with the
familiar benefits, there have been unreckoned costs.

I was two months shy of my seventeenth birthday the first time I took a
psychedelic drug, mescaline, with one of my older sisters and two of her girlfriends. At some point, the girlfriends, both very pretty, took off their clothes
and remained naked for hours, which was awesome. Over the course of the
night, I had the kinds of holy-moly insights and hallucinations one is supposed to have—thermostats have a kind of consciousness, every living thing
on Earth is connected, and so on. In the morning, I sweatily, happily walked
home alone. In front of one house was a white plaster statue of the Virgin
Mary. As I looked at it, she seemed to come alive for a second or two, gripping
her gown and turning forty-five degrees—a sort of quick, sweet curtsy of
acknowledgment. Never again did I have a drug hallucination so religiously
specific. Yet not even later that day did I consider my vision of Mary a miraculous message from God, in whom I continued to have no real belief.

During the rest of high school and the first couple of years of college I took LSD maybe a dozen times. Once I thought I had telekinetically made the family cat vomit, another time that I'd willed pedestrians seven floors below me to drop their umbrellas repeatedly. Whenever the drug wore off, I always knew the supernatural episodes had been hallucinations, but the hundred flittering illusions and intuitions of the acid trips did change me, softened my brittle adolescent certainties, twigged me to the precariousness of perception and the accessibility of the mystical.

I grew my hair long, read Alan Watts, learned Transcendental Meditation, read and reread a giant paperback called *The Movement Toward a New America: The Beginnings of a Long Revolution (A Collage)—A What?* A few friends and I bought an old school bus that we drove down to Mexico and then up to Las Vegas (where some of us dropped acid) and to Disneyland (where some more of us did) and Big Sur. In college, I thought only pawns and automatons scrupled to attend every class.

The hundreds of older Beats begat thousands of beatniks. But in the 1960s and '70s, the whole baby boom generation came of age. Suddenly America had more teenagers than ever before, and a *much* larger fraction of young people living together on college campuses, plus prosperity, mass media reflecting the new youthquake back to the youth, and an escalating war that teenagers were drafted to fight.* The American bohemian idea could roll out and cross over and *scale,* from the angsty Beat beta version to the 1960s mass-market viral app fully compatible with the ever-expanding fantasy-industrial complex.

IN 1962 PEOPLE STARTED REFERRING to "hippies," the Beatles had their first hit, Ken Kesey published *One Flew Over the Cuckoo's Nest,* and the Harvard psychology teacher Timothy Leary was handing out psilocybin and LSD to students. And three hours south of San Francisco, on the heavenly stretch of coastal cliffs known as Big Sur, a pair of young Stanford psychology graduates, one of them pals with Kerouac and Ginsberg, founded a school and think tank they named after a tiny Indian tribe that had lived on the grounds long before.

"In 1968," one of its founding figures recalled four decades later,

Esalen was the center of the cyclone of the youth rebellion. It was one of the central places, like Mecca for the Islamic culture. Esalen

---

* In 1963, 16,000 U.S. soldiers and Marines were in Vietnam, 122 of whom died in combat; in 1968 the American deployment reached 540,000, of whom 16,592 were killed.

was a pilgrimage center for hundreds and thousands of youth interested in some sense of transcendence, breakthrough consciousness,
LSD, the sexual revolution, encounter, being sensitive, finding your
body, yoga—all of these things were at first filtered into the culture
through Esalen. By 1966, '67 and '68, Esalen was making a world
impact. At that time, many people came here looking for . . . the
golden elixir.

This is not overstatement. Essentially everything that became known
by the 1970s as New Age was invented, developed, or popularized at the
Esalen Institute. Esalen is a mother church of a new American religion
for people who think they don't like churches or religions but who still
want to believe in the supernatural. And who, like Anne Hutchinson in
Boston in 1636 and the revivalists at Cane Ridge in 1801 and the Pentecostals in Los Angeles in 1906, want their beliefs affirmed by ecstatically
feeling and *experiencing* the divine spirit. "It is a place," Esalen's website
declares today, "where miracles not only happen, but where they happen
all the time."

Esalen developed and popularized a wholesale reinvention of psychology and medicine and philosophy driven by a suspicion of science and reason and an embrace of magical thinking (also massage, hot baths, sex, and
sex in hot baths). Esalen was a headquarters for a new religion of no religion, as they came to say, and of "science" containing next to no science.
The idea was to be radically tolerant and undiscriminating of therapeutic
schemes and understandings of reality, especially if they came from Asian
or Native American or other shamanistic traditions. Invisible energies, past
lives, astral projection, whatever—the more exotic and wondrous and unfalsifiable the better.

The psychotherapist Fritz Perls, a German protégé and former patient of
Wilhelm Reich's, had moved to the United States after the war and, as the
1960s began, to California and Esalen. As an alternative to psychiatry's dominant Freudian mode—talking, recalling events, analysis—he and his wife
had developed "Gestalt therapy." Perls's approach was to focus entirely on
patients' *perceptions,* without judging. At Esalen, Perls distilled his approach
into four sentences, the famous Gestalt prayer:

I do my thing and you do your thing. I am not in this world to live up
to your expectations, and you are not in this world to live up to mine.

You are you, and I am I, and if by chance we find each other, it's beautiful. If not, it can't be helped.*

Fine. Except that in America, which *began* on a slippery slope of subjectivity, this new creed helped accelerate the giant slalom toward a concoct-your-own-truth culture and society.

Not long before Esalen was founded, the main cofounder suffered a mental breakdown and was involuntarily admitted to a private psychiatric hospital, where he spent a year. His new institute embraced the radical notion that psychosis and other mental illnesses were labels imposed by the straight world on eccentrics and visionaries, that they were primarily tools of coercion and control, not legitimate medical conditions at all. This was the big idea behind Ken Kesey's bestselling novel *One Flew Over the Cuckoo's Nest,* of course. (In the summer of 1964, one stop on his legendary transcontinental *ur*-hippie bus tour was Esalen, where he conducted a workshop called "A Trip with Ken Kesey.")

And within the psychiatric profession itself, this idea had two influential proponents, who both published unorthodox manifestos at the beginning of the decade—R. D. Laing (*The Divided Self: An Existential Study in Sanity and Madness*) and Thomas Szasz (*The Myth of Mental Illness*). "Madness," Laing wrote when Esalen was new, "is potentially liberation and renewal." Psychosis and schizophrenia are a "potentially natural process that we do not allow to happen," "an initiation ceremonial," and a "natural way of healing our appalling state of alienation called normality." The Esalen founders were big Laing fans, and the institute became a hotbed for the idea that madness was just an alternative and often superior way of perceiving reality.

These influential early critiques by the left-wing Laing, the libertarian Szasz, and the left-wing libertarians at Esalen had some bad consequences. Szasz opposed *any* involuntary psychiatric intervention and, along with the *Cuckoo's Nest* portrayal, paved the way for the disastrous dismantling of U.S. mental health facilities. But more generally they helped make popular and respectable the idea that much of science is a sinister scheme concocted by a despotic conspiracy to oppress the people. Mental illness, both Szasz and

* It's worth noting the big difference from the somewhat similar Serenity Prayer, written decades earlier by the Protestant theologian Reinhold Niebuhr—which aims for an ability to discriminate rationally, to accept immutable facts but change other facts and have "the Wisdom to distinguish the one from the other." Whereas Perls's 1960s prayer sends everyone off to inhabit his or her own custom-made reality.

Laing said, is "a theory not a fact"—now the universal bottom-line argument for anyone, from creationists to climate change deniers to antivaccine hysterics, who prefer to disregard science in favor of their own beliefs. The Esalen elder who called it the center of the youth rebellion cyclone has also said that its founders "gave refuge to the craziest characters in the Sixties," and during the 1970s "in rushed a bunch of charlatans promoting messianic cult visions."

Esalen was the main headwaters, but big-time non-Christian American magical thinking had other sources. Among the most important and least known is Jane Roberts. Like Scientology's founder, she'd been an author of sci-fi and fantasy fiction before she began claiming her fictions were real. After moving to western New York State, Roberts had an epiphany in 1963— "a fantastic avalanche of radical, new ideas burst into my head with tremendous force. . . . It was as if the physical world were really tissue-paper-thin, hiding infinite dimensions of reality, and I was flung through the tissue paper with a huge ripping sound." Using a Ouija board, she discovered a supernatural being called Seth, whose words she believed she spoke and her husband transcribed—channeling divine revelations at the south end of the Finger Lakes as Joseph Smith and the ghost-communicating Fox sisters had done a century earlier at the north end. "What we see in our lives," she reported, "is the physical picture of what we have been thinking, feeling and believing." In other words, *You create your own reality*—which would become one of the central tenets of New Age theology. The author of the several books she subsequently published, she said, was actually Seth. Roberts's prose is prototypical New Age–speak—physics-derived pseudoscience, hand-waving about consciousness, sneering at empirical reality. "The selves we know in normal life," she wrote in one of the books,

> are only the three-dimensional actualizations of other source-selves from which we receive our energy and life. Their reality can't be contained in the framework of our creature-hood, though it is being constantly translated through our present individuality. . . .
>
> Seth's books may be the product of another dimensional aspect of my own consciousness not focused in this reality, plus something else that is untranslatable in our terms, with Seth a great psychic creation more real than any "fact."

*   *   *

You KNOW HOW YOUNG PEOPLE always think the universe revolves around them, as if they're the only ones who really *get* it? And how before their frontal lobes, the neural seat of reason and rationality, are fully wired, they can be especially prone to fantasy? In the 1960s the universe cooperated and *did* seem to revolve around young people, affirming their adolescent self-regard, making their fantasies of importance real and their fantasies of instant transformation and easy revolution feel plausible. Practically overnight, America turned its full attention to the young and everything they believed and imagined and wished.

If 1962 was when the Sixties got going, 1969 was the year the new doctrines and their gravity were really cataloged by the grown-ups. Reason and rationality were *over*. The countercultural effusions were freaking out the old guard, including religious people who couldn't quite see that yet another Great Awakening was under way, heaving up a new religion with its priesthood of all believers, people "who have no option but to follow the road until they reach the Holy City . . . that lies beyond the technocracy . . . the New Jerusalem."

That line is from *The Making of a Counter Culture: Reflections on the Technocratic Society and Its Youthful Opposition*, published three weeks after the Woodstock Festival in 1969. Its author was Theodore Roszak, age thirty-five, a professor in the Bay Area, who thereby coined the word *counterculture*. Roszak, thoughtful and expert in history and literature, spent 270 pages, more or less reasonably and rationally, glorying in the younger generation's "brave" rejection of expertise, rationality, "all that our culture values as 'reason' and 'reality.'" So-called experts, after all, are "on the payroll of the state and/or corporate structure." A chapter called "The Myth of Objective Consciousness" argues that science is really just a state religion, scientists our culture's version of wizards—except that he hates the former ("bad magicians") and loves the latter ("good magicians"). In order to create "a new culture in which the non-intellective capacities . . . become the arbiters of the good [and] the true," he writes, "nothing less is required than the subversion of the scientific world view, with its entrenched commitment to an egocentric and cerebral mode of consciousness." Although thanks, science and technology, for making "economic security . . . something [youth] can take for granted," because "we have an economy of cybernated abundance that does not need their labor." Oh, the cybernated abundance of Big Rock Candy Mountain!

He disparages previous American fantasists—"Theosophists and fundamentalists, spiritualists and flat-earthers, occultists and Satanists"—yet in the same sentence pivots to extol the current ones, welcomes the "radical rejection of science and technological values . . . so close to the center of our society, rather than on the negligible margins. . . . Those who opt for rationality darkly warn us against the terrors that have come of submerging the intellect beneath a flood tide of feeling."

That same summer of 1969, a forty-one-year-old University of Chicago sociologist (and Catholic priest) named Andrew Greeley alerted readers of *The New York Times Magazine* that beyond the familiar signifiers of youthful rebellion (long hair, sex, drugs, music, protests), the truly shocking change on campuses was the rise of antirationalism, a return of the sacred—"mysticism and magic," the occult, séances, cults around the Book of Revelation. When he'd recently chalked a statistical table on a classroom blackboard, one of his students reacted with horror: "Mr. Greeley, I think you're an empiricist." A fellow scholar of religion at MIT, who had practiced mystical forms of Buddhism, Hinduism, and Islam and taken psychedelics with Tim Leary, described to Greeley one of his seminars. "I cannot recall the exact progression of topics" the MIT students wanted to discuss, "but it went something like this": the *Tibetan Book of the Dead*'s guide to the hypothetical state between death and reincarnation, "astrology, astral bodies, auras, UFOs, Tarot cards, parapsychology, witchcraft and magic. And underlying everything, of course, the psychedelic drugs." An impressed student marveled to Greeley that his woo-woo classmates "really believe that what they say is *true*," and all the students he interviewed "resolutely refuse to dismiss as foolish" anyone who really *believes* anything.

Three months later, right after Woodstock, the *Times Magazine* published another middle-aged intellectual's take on this "youth disturbance," which looked to him like a "turning point in history." Paul Goodman was a countercultural godfather who'd written *Growing Up Absurd,* a bestselling 1960 explanation of what's-the-matter-with-kids-today and who co-wrote Fritz Perls's *Gestalt Therapy*. He saw the diffuse surge of new belief as a "New Reformation," with all the anti-Establishment rage and righteous metaphysical certainty that had reshaped Christendom and generated the ultra-Protestants' would-be utopia in America. The younger generation in the 1960s, he decided, was defined "not, as I used to think, [by] their morality, political will and common sense," but by their "religion," their reflex to be "scornful of rationality."

Recall Jonathan Edwards, the fortyish minister out of Yale who in the 1740s saw and encouraged "a flash of lightning upon the hearts of young people." As 1969 became 1970 in New Haven, a forty-one-year-old Yale professor was finishing his book about the new youth counterculture. Charles Reich was a former Supreme Court clerk now at Yale Law School, tenured at one of rationalism's American headquarters. But hanging with the young people had led him to a midlife epiphany and apostasy. In 1966 he had started teaching a seminar called "The Individual in America," for which he assigned fiction by Kesey and Norman Mailer. He was feeling it, and he decided to spend the next summer, the Summer of Love, in Berkeley.

"Out here the atmosphere among the students is profoundly anti-intellectual," he wrote from California to a friend, but "one can't help admire some of their values. . . . On Sundays the park is full of great sights and sounds . . . electric bands with such names as . . . Big Brother and the Holding Company, and The Grateful Dead." On the road back to New Haven, he had his Pauline conversion to the kids' values. His class at Yale became hugely popular, and he let in hundreds and then thousands of undergraduates.

Just before publication of his book in 1970, *The New Yorker* published a third of it—at seventy magazine pages, the longest excerpt it had ever run. *The Greening of America* became the bestselling book in America, and remained on the *Times* list for most of a year. How huge and crazed was the attention paid? The *Today* show was so eager to hop on the bandwagon that when Reich turned down an appearance, they booked Yale's media-friendly left-wing chaplain to chat about his colleague.

At sixteen, I bought and read one of the two million copies sold. Rereading it today and recalling how much I loved it was a reminder of the follies of youth. Reich was shamelessly, uncritically swooning for kids like me. *The Greening of America* may have been the mainstream's single greatest act of pandering to the vanity and self-righteousness of the new youth. The first sentences appeared on the book jacket: "There is a revolution coming. . . . This is the revolution of the new generation."

In addition to the perfect timing and blue-chip imprimaturs, the book's underlying theoretical scheme was simple and perfectly pitched to flatter young readers. There are three types of American "consciousness," each of which "makes up a person's perception of reality . . . his 'head,' his way of life." Consciousness I people are old-fashioned self-reliant individualists rendered obsolete by the new "Corporate State"—essentially, kids, your grandparents. Consciousness IIs are the fearful and conformist organization men and women whose rationalism is a tyrannizing trap laid by the Corporate State—

your parents. And then there is Consciousness III, which "has made its first appearance among the youth of America," "spreading rapidly among wider and wider segments of youth, and by degrees to older people."

If you opposed the Vietnam War and dressed down and smoked pot, you were almost certainly a III. "Wrinkled jeans and jackets made of coarse material" are "a deliberate rejection of the . . . look of the affluent society." *Check.* "The violence with which some older people have reacted to long hair shows that they feel a threat to the whole reality that they have constructed and lived by." *Check.* And "in a society that keeps its citizens within a closed system of thought . . . marijuana is a maker of revolution, a truth-serum." *Check!*

In other words, simply by being young and casual and undisciplined, you were ushering in a new utopia. The "choice of a life-style is not peripheral, it is the heart of the new awakening." *Sweet.* It was like a smart, cool, successful uncle assuring you that, yes, your parents *are* miserable phonies, whereas you're revolutionary and heroic because, you know, you just *get it.*

Reich praises the "gaiety and humor" of the new Consciousness III wardrobe, but his book is absolutely humorless—because it's a response to "this moment of utmost sterility, darkest night and most extreme peril." Conspiracism was flourishing, and Reich bought in. Now that "the Corporate State has added depersonalization and repression" on top of the other injustices, "it has threatened to destroy all meaning and suck all joy from life."

Reich's magical thinking mainly concerned how the revolution would turn out. "The American Corporate State," having produced this new generation of long-haired hyperindividualists who insist on trusting their guts and finding their own truths, "is now accomplishing what no revolutionaries could accomplish by themselves. . . . The machine has begun to destroy itself." Once everyone wears Levi's and gets high, the "old . . . forms will simply be swept away in the flood."

The inevitable-imminent-happy-cataclysm part of the dream didn't happen, of course. The machine did not destroy itself. But for all his book's silliness, Reich was half-right. An epochal change in American thinking was under way and was "not, as far as anybody knows, reversible. . . . There is no returning to an earlier consciousness." His wishful error was to believe that once the tidal surge of new sensibility brought down the floodwalls, the waters would flow in only one direction, carving out a peaceful, cooperative, groovy new continental utopia, hearts and minds changed like his, all America Berkeleyized and Vermontified. Instead, Consciousness III was just one early iteration of the anything-goes, post-reason, post-factual America enabled by the tsunami. Reich's faith was the converse of the Enlightenment rationalists' hopeful fallacy two hundred years earlier: once granted complete freedom of thought, Jefferson and company assumed, most people would follow the paths of reason. Wasn't it pretty to think so.

IN THE EARLY 1970S, TWO of my siblings became devotees of a very young Indian named Guru Maharaj Ji, who led the Divine Light Mission, a large movement with tens of thousands of followers. He was known as the Perfect Master and Lord of the Universe, and the meditation technique he taught was called Perfect Knowledge. His followers believed he was about to usher in a magnificent new age, and my siblings devoted themselves to his mission in their twenties.

"This year," Maharaj Ji wrote in a 1973 letter to his followers, a lot of whom believed he was a god, "the most Holy and significant event in human history will take place in America. . . . This is a festival not for you or me. It is for the whole world and maybe the whole universe." So a week after Halloween that year, my parents flew from Omaha to Houston to attend Millennium '73, a three-day event at the Astrodome for Maharaj Ji's followers. Some of them believed the flying-saucer-esque Astrodome was going to lift off that weekend, literally rise from the Earth.

My parents sat in a special section reserved for parents of devotees. Rennie Davis, an antiwar celebrity turned Maharaj Ji apostle, announced that "honestly, very soon now, every single human being will know the one who was waited for by every religion of all times has actually come." They listened to the guru, who wore a bejeweled crown and sat in a throne atop a thirty-five-foot-high Plexiglas stage, deliver his sermons to enraptured followers. My mom and dad found it all very strange. Yet if their friends in Omaha remained their friends despite professing to believe all kinds of incredible things—the parting of the Red Sea, the virgin birth, the resurrection of Jesus, the blood and body of Christ sipped and eaten every Sunday morning—why wouldn't they cut the same slack for their own children's exotic new beliefs?

THE STRAIGHT WORLD'S DISCOMBOBULATED OMG reactions back then are understandable given how quickly everything had changed. Marijuana use is a good proxy for tracking the speed of the shift. In 1965 fewer than a million Americans had smoked pot; in 1972 the number was twenty-four million. In 1967 only 5 percent of American college students had smoked; four years later it was a majority, and a third were getting high every day.

Around the time I turned twenty, after I'd hallucinated voices a few times when I wasn't high, I mostly stopped using illegal drugs apart from cannabis. We all know that drugs can make you bonkers. Personally, I don't regret my own adolescent use, especially the acid trips, including the frightening ones. It was a highly instructive, character-building phase I passed through mentally intact, all part of my . . . *journey*. I'm convinced that plenty of people were improved and importantly inspired by smoking pot, dropping acid, eating mushrooms. Steve Jobs is only the best example.*

But I also think that the culture's sudden and enthusiastic embrace of psychotropics probably helped turn America into Fantasyland. Psychedelics and even marijuana obviously fog up the boundaries between reality and fantasy, make it easier to believe that all sorts of delusions and imaginary connections are true. Thirty-two million living Americans have used psychedelics; if they were members of a religion, it would be the second largest in the country. Americans' rate of lifetime use of cannabis is two or three or four times that of northern Europeans. For many people, drugs' fantasy-encouraging effects extend beyond the minutes or hours of being high, leaching into everyday thought, not always usefully.

THE GREAT CONTEMPORANEOUS FIRSTHAND ACCOUNT of this 1960s, I think, is *The Electric Kool-Aid Acid Test,* Tom Wolfe's book about Kesey and his acid-dropping Merry Prankster adventures. Eight years later, in the mid-1970s, as the Big Bang of subjectivity and hedonism blasted its new elements and energies through the American universe, Wolfe memorialized the larger transformation. He wrote an essay in *New York* magazine that's remembered today for coining a term, the Me Decade, still used as a catchphrase for the touchy-feely narcissism of the 1970s' newfangled self-improvement schemes. And while Wolfe did spend a lot of his twelve thousand words talking about est workshops and their ilk, the full title is "The 'Me' Decade and the Third Great Awakening." That is, Wolfe kept paying attention to the deeper continuities that Greeley and Goodman spotted in 1969, that what had been unleashed was a multifaceted American delirium, a complex shift with particular American sources and antecedents.

* "It was great," he told his biographer Walter Isaacson about a 1972 trip at seventeen in a wheatfield in what had just been named Silicon Valley. "I had been listening to a lot of Bach. All of a sudden the whole field was playing Bach. It was the most wonderful feeling of my life up to that point. I felt like the conductor of this symphony with Bach coming through the wheat."

As he wrote, "the ESP or 'psychic phenomena' movement began to grow very rapidly in the new religious atmosphere" of the late 1960s, because

> ESP devotees had always believed that there was an *other order* that ran the universe, one that revealed itself occasionally through telepathy . . . psychokinesis, dematerialization, and the like. It was but a small step from there to the assumption that all men possess a *conscious energy* paralleling the world of physical energy and that this mysterious energy can unite the universe (after the fashion of the light of God). . . . Even the Flying Saucer cults began to reveal their essentially religious nature at about this time. The Flying Saucer folk quite literally believed in an *other order* . . . under the command of superior beings from other planets or solar systems who had spaceships. . . .
>
> [Thus we had entered] the greatest age of individualism in American history! All rules are broken! . . . Where the Third Great Awakening will lead—who can presume to say? One only knows that the great religious waves have a momentum all their own.

I remember when fantastical beliefs went absolutely mainstream in the 1970s. I remember, for instance, when my mother bought and read *The Secret Life of Plants,* a big bestseller arguing that plants were sentient and would "be the bridesmaids at a marriage of physics and metaphysics." The amazing truth about plants, the book claimed, had been suppressed by the FDA and agribusiness. My mom didn't believe in the conspiracy, but she did start talking to her ficuses as if they were pets. In its Sunday review of *The Secret Life of Plants,* the *Times* registered the book as another data point in how "the incredible is losing its pariah status."

Indeed, mainstream publishers and media organizations were falling over themselves to promote and sell fantasies as nonfiction. In 1975 came the bestselling autobiography by the fraudulent young spoon-bender and mind-reader Uri Geller and *Life After Life,* by Raymond Moody, a philosophy Ph.D. who presented the anecdotes of several dozen people who'd nearly died as first-hand evidence for an afterlife. "The notion that these accounts might be fabrications is utterly untenable," Moody flatly declared. The book sold many millions of copies; before long the International Association for Near-Death Studies formed and held its first conference at Yale.

During the first six decades of the twentieth century, the popularity of homeopathy had declined as medical science won the battles against pseudoscience. But as the incredible suddenly lost its pariah status, homeopathy recovered from its own near-death experience, first in California and the Pacific Northwest, then everywhere. During the 1970s, U.S. sales of home-opathy's placebo medicines increased more than tenfold.

Real scientists got caught up in the mysticism as well. In 1965 a chemist designing life-detection instruments for NASA's Viking mission to Mars had a revelation: the entire Earth, he became convinced, its atmosphere and forests and seas and creatures, is a single organism perfectly and mysteriously tweaked to produce life—what he called "the Gaia hypothesis," Gaia being his name from Greek mythology for "this creature." He proceeded to develop the idea in collaboration with a microbiologist, publishing scientific papers and then in the 1970s a popular Oxford University Press book called *Gaia: A New Look at Life on Earth.** Gaia, he writes, "is now through us awake and aware of herself." And so on. An "aura of intention or planning . . . hung over the Gaia hypothesis," the main chronicler of Gaia has written, and led its developer for the rest of his life to try "to cleanse Gaia of its crudest . . . excesses." But the idea's popularity opened the door to a deluge of wishful and dubious understandings, including the new and improved creationism known as intelligent design.

* The NASA scientist was James Lovelock. His friend William Golding, author of *Lord of the Flies,* came up with the name Gaia. One of Lovelock's young NASA colleagues in 1965 was Carl Sagan, who didn't buy the Gaia idea (and later wrote a good primer on distinguishing science from pseudoscience called *The Demon-Haunted World*). At the time of Lovelock's epiphany, Sagan was divorcing his wife Lynn—the biologist who became Lovelock's collaborator on Gaia.

23

Big Bang: The Intellectuals

IN COLLEGE, I WAS ASSIGNED TO READ WILLIAM JAMES, THE PHYSICIAN AND philosopher and founder of American psychology after whom my main classroom building was named. I learned that the middle-aged James, while high on nitrous oxide and peyote, had had brilliant, poetic insights. "Our normal waking consciousness, rational consciousness as we call it, is but one special type of consciousness," he wrote in *The Varieties of Religious Experience*, published in 1902,

> whilst all about it, parted from it by the filmiest of screens, there lie potential forms of consciousness entirely different. . . . Looking back on my own experiences, they all converge towards a kind of insight to which I cannot help ascribing some metaphysical significance. The keynote of it is invariably a reconciliation. It is as if the opposites of the world, whose contradictoriness and conflict make all our difficulties and troubles, were melted into unity. . . . I feel as if it must

mean something. . . . Those who have ears to hear, let them hear; to me the living sense of its reality only comes in the artificial mystic state of mind.

James remained an empiricist and a rationalist, but he had come to understand the allure and significance of radically different, entirely subjective modes of perception. I realized that he'd figured out in the 1890s the sense of existential fluidity that was in the 1970s quickly becoming an everyday principle, the way modern Americans were supposed to think, whether or not they were high. *I have my truth, you have your truth, we each have our truth.*

For the first half of the twentieth century, it was traditionalists in America, such as the conservative Christians, who despaired at how rationalism and modernity were taking over, reshaping minds, wrecking everything. But after World War II, the academic Establishment also developed second thoughts about reason. Two German philosophers, Theodor Adorno and Max Horkheimer, fled the Nazis to live in America where (in poshest West L.A.) they wrote their 1947 magnum opus about the failure of the Enlightenment. Reason and rationality had led to an obsessive, excessive focus on efficiency and practicality and technology. "The Enlightenment's program," they wrote, "was the disenchantment of the world. It wanted to dispel myths, to overthrow fantasy with knowledge. . . . Yet the wholly enlightened Earth is radiant with triumphant calamity." Calamity such as the recent Nazi project.

During the 1960s, large swaths of academia made a similar turn, away from reason and rationalism as they'd been understood. Many of the pioneers were thoughtful, their work fine antidotes to postwar complacency. The problem was the nature and extent of their influence beginning at that 1960s moment, when all premises and paradigms seemed up for grabs. That is, they inspired lots of half-baked and perverse followers in the academy, whose arguments filtered out into the world at large.

In a nutshell: all beliefs and approximations of truth, science as much as any fable or religion, are mere stories devised by people to serve their own needs or interests. Reality itself is a social construction, a tableau of useful or wishful myths that members of a society or tribe have been persuaded to believe. The borders between fiction and nonfiction are permeable, maybe nonexistent. Superstitions, magical thinking, and delusions—any of those may be as legitimate as the supposed truths contrived by Western reason and science. The takeaway: *Believe whatever you want, because it's pretty much all equally true and false.*

This set of ideas emerged in two basic varieties, theoretical and applied—

the philosophers and sociologists in their offices cogitating, and people from psychology and anthropology out in the field, going native.

It really got started right at the beginning of the 1960s. In 1961 the French philosopher Michel Foucault published *Madness and Civilization*, echoing the new skepticism of the concept of mental illness, and by the 1970s he argued that rationality itself is a coercive "regime of truth," oppression by other means. Foucault's suspicion of reason became deeply and widely embedded in American academia. The following year a young UC Berkeley professor of science history, Thomas Kuhn, published a groundbreaking book called *The Structure of Scientific Revolutions*. In the way of Szasz and Laing, psychiatrists discrediting psychiatry, Kuhn had trained as a physicist. His book was not polemical like the antipsychiatrists', much broader in scope, both a popular bestseller and one of the most intellectually influential books of the age. Appearing when it did, it fed the new skepticism about science and scientists and, by extension, about rationality as propounded by elites, the mainstream, the Establishment.

Before Kuhn, the history of science had been understood as a steady march toward better approximations of the nature of existence, accomplished by observation, experiment, and scientists' habitual criticism of one another's work and all conventional wisdoms. But Kuhn argued that revolutions in science—the realization that the Earth circles the sun, or that subatomic particles behave according to different rules than larger objects—are not really just the result of better evidence piling up. Rather, "normal science" is conducted by drones doing "mop-up work," buttressing existing theories by working out the details (not unlike theologians working out the details of their religion's main beliefs). Then a Copernicus or an Einstein leaps way beyond the evidence with some radically new conjecture about the nature of reality (not unlike Martin Luther deciding the Catholics had it wrong). If and when enough scientists decide they agree with the new theory, and perform observations and experiments that seem to confirm it, a "paradigm shift" occurs and everybody changes their minds—until eventually too many inexplicable new facts come along and the next set of revolutionary revisions must be dreamed up.

Fascinating, provocative, bracing. But as that big idea spread into the public understanding, it caused a popular paradigm shift itself, making science seem iffier and sketchier, driven less by a dispassionate examination of facts than by . . . mere *beliefs*. Kuhn was Toto pulling back the curtain and exposing the Wizards of Oz: are our great and powerful scientists just dazzling humbugs whose power derives from persuading other people to *believe*?

Meanwhile in 1966, over in sociology, a pair of professors in their thirties published *The Social Construction of Reality,* one of the most influential works in their field. Not only sanity and insanity and scientific truth were somewhat dubious human concoctions, they explained; *so was everything else.* The rulers of any tribe or society do not merely dictate customs and laws; they are the masters of everyone's perceptions, defining reality itself. To create the all-encompassing stage sets that everyone inhabits, rulers first use crude mythology, then more elaborate religion, and finally the "extreme step" of modern science. "Reality"? "Knowledge"? "If we were going to be meticulous," Peter Berger and Thomas Luckman wrote, "we would put quotation marks around the two aforementioned terms every time we used them." "What is 'real' to a Tibetan monk may not be 'real' to an American businessman."

When I first read that at eighteen, I *loved* the scare quotes. It was the early 1970s, so this new paradigm made scales fall from eyes, and not just adolescents'. The book was timed perfectly to become a foundational text in academia and beyond. It just seemed so profoundly true that *nothing* was absolutely, immutably true. And if reality is simply the result of rules written by powers-that-be, then isn't everyone able—no, isn't everyone *obliged*—to construct their own realities?

A more extreme academic evangelist for all truths being equal, and a more ultra-1960s character, was a UC Berkeley philosophy professor named Paul Feyerabend. In the preface to *The Structure of Scientific Revolutions,* Kuhn had thanked him for his "most far-reaching and decisive" contributions. Feyerabend, an Austrian immigrant, had always been indifferent to and even excited by the world falling apart around him. He had been a teenager when the Nazis took over Austria, but to him, "occupation and the war that followed were an inconvenience, not a moral problem." He became a lieutenant in the Nazis' Wehrmacht, commanding tanks and infantrymen. He arrived in Berkeley in his early thirties, got tenure, then had a full 1960s conversion. Empirical proof and rationalism had nothing on irrational subjective belief. "It dawned on me," he wrote in a kind of memoir called *Farewell to Reason,* that the intricate arguments and the wonderful stories I had so far told to my more or less sophisticated audience might just be dreams, reflections of the conceit of a small group who had succeeded in enslaving everyone else with their ideas. Who was I to tell these people what and how to think?" He took the relativism that was mostly implicit in the new academic thinking and made it explicit, celebrating the chaos.*

---

* What is it with America's nineteenth- and twentieth-century imports from German-speaking Europe? In addition to Feyerabend, the authors of *The Social Construction of*

His best-known book, published in 1975, was *Against Method: Outline of an Anarchistic Theory of Knowledge*. "Rationalism," it declared, "is a secularized form of the belief in the power of the word of God," and science a "particular superstition." In a later edition of the book, published when creationists were passing laws to teach Genesis in U.S. public school biology classes, Feyerabend came out in favor, comparing creationists to Galileo.

And because science is just another form of belief, he insisted, the temples of reason must *own* that, making "the sciences . . . more anarchic and more subjective." Myth, revelation, astrology, witchcraft, *whatever*—because for anyone anywhere attempting to figure out how existence works, "only *one* principle . . . can be defended under *all* circumstances and in *all* stages of human development. It is the principle: anything goes."

What's more, the magical beliefs that modern reason had defamed and disgraced were often *superior*. For people without science and technology, he wrote, "there were no collective excursions to the moon, but single individuals, disregarding great dangers to their soul and their sanity, rose from sphere to sphere to sphere until they finally faced God himself in all His splendor while others changed into animals and back into humans again." This wasn't just poetic fancy. "Voodoo has a firm though still not sufficiently understood material basis," Feyerabend wrote, "and a study of its manifestations can be used to enrich, and perhaps even revise, our knowledge of physiology." He *believed*, seeking out shamans to treat his various illnesses, including the brain tumor that killed him.

Over in anthropology, meanwhile, where the exotic magical beliefs of "traditional" cultures were a main subject, the new paradigm took over almost completely—*Don't judge, don't disbelieve, don't flash down the street pointing your professorial plastic finger*. It was understandable given the times: colonialism ending, Native American genocide confessed, U.S. wars in the Third World. Who were we to roll our eyes or deny what these people believed? In the 1960s much of anthropology decided that oracles, diviners, incantations, and magical objects should be not just respected but considered equivalent to reason and science. If all understandings of reality are socially constructed,

---

Reality and Wilhelm Reich were from Austria. The inventors of mesmerism, phrenology, the water cure, homeopathy, and the patent medicine Microbe Killer were all Germans, as were the postwar Enlightenment-haters Adorno and Horkheimer and Esalen's Fritz Perls. Erich von Däniken, the swindler who popularized the ancient-extraterrestrial-gods idea in the 1970s, is German-Swiss, as was Hermann Hesse, whose Eastern-spirituality-soaked fiction was discovered by Tim Leary and company in the 1960s.

those of Kalabari tribespeople in Nigeria are no more arbitrary or faith-based than those of professors.

An enormously influential paper by a leading anthropologist laid it out clearly in 1967. Both science and shamanism are on a quest "for simplicity underlying apparent complexity; for order underlying apparent disorder," and both "make up for the explanatory, predictive and practical deficiencies of everyday, common-sense reasoning . . . by portraying the phenomena of the everyday world as manifestations of a hidden, underlying reality." One tells stories of a Big Bang, subatomic particles, gravity, and microbes, the other of gods, Water People, curses, and spells. We rationalist laypeople believe the incomprehensible things our scientists tell us the same way Third World magical thinkers trust their wizards. The hard distinctions we make between natural and supernatural are spurious. It's all good. Except that ours are more often bad.

In 1968 the University of California Press published the master's degree dissertation of a UCLA anthropology student who'd gone to Arizona to conduct a field study of southwestern Indians' medicinal plants. In the Yuma bus depot, the student, Carlos Castaneda, met an old guy named Juan Matus, who turned out to be a Toltec sorcerer. Matus fed him hallucinogens—jimsonweed, peyote, psilocybin mushrooms—and told him he would reveal the "secrets that make up the lot of a man of knowledge." Under the influence of drugs, Castaneda says he turned into a crow, talked to coyotes, and communed with the spirits. The M.A. thesis became *The Teachings of Don Juan: A Yaqui Way of Knowledge,* which was followed in 1971 and 1972 by two more bestsellers about Don Juan. Every with-it young American of the era was required to know these books. More followed, and tens of millions of copies were bought.* Margaret Mead, his celebrity anthropologist predecessor, had reported on so-called primitive people in the 1920s and '30s to persuade her fellow Americans that sex was natural and should be guiltless. In the 1960s and '70s, Castaneda, enthusiastically endorsed by Mead, reported on so-called primitive people to persuade Americans that magic was real.

Reviewing all three books in the Sunday *Times,* an important young anthropologist called them "a work which is among the best that the science of

---

* Castaneda had hung out at Esalen in the early 1960s before he published the first Don Juan book. He eventually published a dozen, all ostensibly nonfiction, in which he becomes a sorcerer and travels to other universes. He also recruited some female UCLA anthropology grad students, "the witches," with whom he led a cult in a house near the university for the rest of his life.

anthropology has produced," in part because Castaneda reveals "his personal struggle with standard Western reality whose thrall kept preventing him from accepting Don Juan's lessons on their own terms." The old man hadn't just *imagined* that a dog was Mescalito telling Castaneda that he was "the chosen one"—it was, the professor said, "what really happened." Moreover, the point of anthropology was no longer "finding out what other people's *conceptions* of the world are" but "learning . . . about the way the world really is."

Our tour of the 1960s academic pantheon began in psychiatry, proceeded through the departments of philosophy, history, sociology, and anthropology, and now returns finally to psychology. Back in the 1930s and '40s, a Duke University botanist-turned-psychologist established parapsychology as a U.S. academic discipline—that is, a field committed to proving telepathy, clairvoyance, psychokinesis, reincarnation, and ghosts are real. He founded the Parapsychological Association, and in the late 1960s (with Margaret Mead's encouragement) the American Association for the Advancement of Science (AAAS) certified it as an affiliate. One of his young protégés was a University of California psychologist named Charles Tart. Tart's first big claim to fame was a 1968 experiment in which, he wrote, a "young woman who frequently had spontaneous out of body experiences"—didn't *claim* to have them but *had* them—spent four nights sleeping in his lab hooked up to an EEG. Her assigned task was to send her mind or soul out of her body while she was asleep and read a five-digit number Tart had written on a piece of paper near the bed. He reported that she succeeded.

Other scientists considered the experiment bogus, but Tart got tenure at UC Davis and proceeded to devote his entire academic career to proving that attempts at objectivity are a sham and that magic is real. In an extraordinary paper published in 1972 in *Science,* he complained about "the almost total rejection of the knowledge gained" while high or tripping "by the scientific establishment." He didn't just want science to take seriously "experiences of ecstasy, mystical union, other 'dimensions,' rapture, beauty, space-and-time transcendence." He was explicitly dedicated to *going there.* A "perfectly scientific theory may be based on data that have no physical existence," he insisted. The rules of the scientific method must be revised. To work as a psychologist in the new age, Tart argued, a researcher should *be in* the altered state of consciousness he's studying, high or delusional or filled with the Holy Spirit "at the time of data collection" and during "data reduction and theorizing." Tart's new paradigm for research, he admitted, poses problems of "consensual validation," given that "only observers in the same [altered state] are able to communicate adequately with each other."

Tart popularized the term *consensus reality orientation* for what you or I would simply call *reality,* and around 1970 *consensus reality* became a permanent interdisciplinary term of art in academia. Later he abandoned the pretense of neutrality and started calling it the "consensus *trance*"—people committed to reason and rationality are the deluded dupes, not he and his tribe. His articles continued to appear in legitimate scientific journals and the *Oxford Dictionary of Psychology.*

Parapsychology established academic beachheads all over. In the late 1960s UCLA set up a lab, founded by a former actor and screenwriter who'd published a bestseller about her LSD experiences. In the 1970s Princeton University set up its Engineering Anomalies Research lab, also devoted to proving that paranormal phenomena are real. In the Age of Aquarius, make-believe became blue-chip.

EVEN PAUL GOODMAN, BELOVED BY young leftists in the 1960s, was flabbergasted by his students in 1969. "There was no knowledge," he wrote, "only the sociology of knowledge. They had so well learned that . . . research is subsidized and conducted for the benefit of the ruling class that they did not believe there was such a thing as simple truth." Ever since, it has been the American right that most insistently decried the spread of relativism. And that's because it has focused on relativism's most obvious and immediate origins and effects. The right hated how relativism undercut various venerable and comfortable ruling ideas—certain notions of entitlement (according to race and gender) and aesthetic beauty and metaphysical and moral certainty. Appalled by academia moving away from old-fashioned reason and by the uppity youth, conservatives conflated the phenomena. They saw only a single bratty, furry mob of bohemian barbarians inside and outside the gates.

But once the intellectual mainstream thoroughly accepted the notion that there are many equally valid realities and truths, once the idea of gates and gatekeeping was discredited not just on campuses but throughout the culture, *all* the barbarians could have their claims taken seriously. Conservatives are correct in pointing out that the anything-goes relativism of the campuses wasn't sequestered there, but when it flowed out across America, it helped enable extreme Christianities and consequential lunacies on the *right*—gun rights hysteria, black helicopter conspiracism, climate change denial, and more. The term *useful idiot* was originally used to accuse liberals of serving the interests of true believers further left. In this instance, however, postmodern intellectuals—postpositivists, poststructuralists, social constructivists, postempiricists, epistemic relativists, cognitive relativists, descriptive relativists—turned out to be useful idiots for the American right. "Reality has a well-known liberal bias," Stephen Colbert said, in character in 2006, mocking the beliefs-trump-facts impulse of today's right. Neither side has been aware of it, but large factions of the elite left and the populist right have been wearing different uniforms on the same team—the Fantasyland team.

24

Big Bang: The Christians

I STILL REMEMBER THE DAY AT THE END OF SIXTH GRADE WHEN I CAME HOME from school and saw the cover of the latest issue of *Time,* with no picture, just huge red letters against a plain black background: IS GOD DEAD? I didn't read it at the time, but it pleased me. Finally, the official publication of upper-middle Americanism was ratifying what the smart people knew but were too polite to say in public: in the modern world, religion had reached its sell-by date.

That 1966 story, written by a pious Roman Catholic who later became an editor of mine at *Time,* is a rueful, reasonable, intellectually subtle fifty-eight-hundred-word essay on metaphysics in the modern age. Its premise: as rationalism and secularization inexorably sweep the Western world, the only way for religion to thrive is to continue accommodating reason and intellectual subtlety. The article refers only once to fundamentalism and not at all to its rise as an important counterculture of increasingly florid magical thinking. "Nowadays not even fundamentalists are upset by the latest cosmological theories of astronomers," the writer asserted, and "even devout believers are empirical in outlook." The joke about *Time* was always that any trend making the cover was a sure sign the trend had peaked. "Is God Dead?" turned out to be one of the great whoppers of mainstream media myopia. Just a year later *Time* ran a cover story on "The Hippies"—so it's strange that the magisterial "Is God Dead?" article barely registered that rising tide of mysticism and magical thinking. "Is God Dead?" contains exactly one glancing reference: "In search of meaning, some believers have desperately turned to psychiatry, Zen or drugs."

Today's standard conception of The Sixties concerns youth and strife and hedonism. We remember the spectacular outbursts of spiritual *weirdness*—from Hare Krishnas to the Charles Mansonites to the Jonestown mass suicide in the 1970s—but that all rose and fell during those dozen cuckoo years and then ceased to matter, right? Meditation and yoga don't require any specific *beliefs*. The 1960s branding is not Sex & Drugs & Rock 'n' Roll & Irrational Belief in the Supernatural. In the popular understanding of the era, the most far-reaching and specifically religious craziness that detonated during those crazy years, extreme American Christianity, is omitted from the legacy.

In the late 1960s, especially in California, a small but conspicuous fraction of the multiplying hippies, aggressively convivial, were young Christian evangelists: the Jesus Movement or Jesus People, as they called themselves, or Jesus freaks, as everyone else called them. The Campus Crusade for Christ organized an "evangelistic blitz" in Berkeley and called Jesus "the world's greatest revolutionary." There was a Christian World Liberation Front and a Jesus Christ Light and Power Company. "At the outset practically all the Jesus People were young acid heads," Tom Wolfe wrote, "who had sworn off drugs . . . but still wanted the ecstatic spiritualism. . . . This they found in Fundamentalist evangelical holy-rolling Christianity of a sort that ten years before would have seemed utterly impossible to revive in America." Still, it seemed like a curious secondary sideshow to the true 1960s.

When evangelicalism and fundamentalism started blowing up bigger than ever in the 1980s, becoming synonymous with the political and cultural right, nobody remembered that Christianity had been revivified and crazified in the same 1960s that produced Esalen and Woodstock. The ascendant Christians mostly didn't look or talk very 1960s, but they shared the sense of unbound freedom to abandon reason and believe whatever they wished, some of them more fearful than hopeful, others radiating enchantment more than paranoia, some in the thrall of ecstatic experience and others, extreme doctrine. They amounted to a counterculture that emerged from one roiling postrational American sea.

Many American Christians, like hippies and New Leftists, also came to feel intolerably oppressed by the Man—culturally, politically, existentially. Since the turn of the century, American fundamentalists had reveled in their sense of persecution by an infidel elite, but in the 1960s the atheist tyranny became official. In 1962 and 1963 the Supreme Court decided in two cases, with only one dissenter in each instance, that it was unconstitutional for public schools to conduct organized prayer or Bible readings, and in 1968 the court finally ruled—unanimously—that states could not ban the teaching of evolution. Until the 1960s, biblical literalists (like white supremacists) had not been prohibited from imposing their beliefs on everyone around them. Losing that legal war added potency to their 1960s deliria. Thus the era turned out to be a curious win-win for extreme Christianity in America. The manifestations of the new anything-goes paradigm that appalled them, such as the hippies and blasphemy and sexual looseness, provoked a backlash that made them more fervently "traditional." Yet the anything-goes paradigm was simultaneously *enabling* their beliefs in magic to spread and become more extreme.

PENTECOSTALISM HAD GROWN SLOWLY SINCE its invention by Americans in America, but remained a fringe religion, with fewer than two million practicing U.S. believers—until the 1960s, when *all* the exotic and exciting fringes blossomed freely and started overtaking the main stems. "Young people today are simply craving for visions," said one of the most important Pentecostal leaders, David du Plessis, in the 1960s. "So they turn to LSD to get a 'trip.'" His religion let people experience real-seeming, life-changing hallucinations. Unlike the earliest Christians who'd witnessed miracles occasionally, people could now experience magic whenever they wanted, like taking a drug. American abundance knew no bounds.

In the 1960s the TV Pentecostalist Oral Roberts started producing (at NBC studios in Burbank) and airing (on hundreds of stations) regular prime-time specials that featured celebrity performers. He was appearing on Johnny Carson and Merv Griffin, *Laugh-In* and *Hee-Haw*. He'd gone mainstream, yet he remained a full-on nut: in addition to the central lunacy of speaking in tongues, he claimed his ministry had brought dead people back to life, and that Jesus had personally appeared and commanded him to build a medical center and, another time, to cure cancer.

The Pentecostal *brand* still had its déclassé, hillbilly, slum-dweller baggage; other Protestants looked down on *those people*. But beginning in the

1960s, that stigma stopped extending to its fantastic beliefs and practices. On Easter Sunday 1960, in middle-class San Fernando Valley, the priest at a big Episcopalian church—*Episcopalian,* no less—announced to his congregation that he possessed the gift of speaking in tongues. This was national news, and a traditionalist Episcopalian magazine ran an excited editorial: "Speaking in tongues is no longer a phenomenon of some odd sect across the street. It is in our midst, and is being practiced by clergy and laity who have stature and good reputation." Maybe, the high-church editorial figured, "God had chosen this time to dynamite . . . 'Episcopalian respectabilianism.'"

The respectabilian James Pike—for years head of the religion department at Columbia University and host of a weekly TV talk show on ABC, now the crusading liberal Episcopalian bishop of northern California—was among the most famous clergymen in America. Alarmed that a tenth of his Bay Area priests were speaking in tongues, he commissioned an official report, which found that the tongues craze "strikes a familiar note to the psychiatrist," deluded people taking the Bible way too literally. Bishop Pike himself was getting into trouble for not taking the Bible literally enough—he'd called the virgin birth a "primitive myth" and said he didn't "believe in the ascension of Jesus into heaven." Eventually he forced the Episcopalians to put him on trial for heresy, which in turn forced the church to declare the very idea of heresy "outdated."

In other words, he was a great man of reason—until he wasn't. When the full 1960s erupted, middle-aged Bishop Pike, living under the volcano in San Francisco, got carried away. He became close friends with Philip K. Dick, the author of brilliant speculative fictions in which reality is always uncertain and in flux. Dick, an enthusiast of psychedelics and amphetamines, had an increasingly hard time distinguishing fantasy from reality in life. Pike experimented with hallucinogens himself. He and his mistress (the stepmother of Dick's wife) believed they witnessed psychokinetic events in their apartment. In 1967 she used sleeping pills to kill herself there, and three months after that Pike used a psychic to try to contact his dead son during a séance broadcast on TV. In 1969, during a vision quest with his new, third wife in the Judean Desert—the wilderness where Satan tried to make Jesus prove he had superpowers and come to the dark side—Pike got lost and died.

But back to the glossolalia that he initially condemned. It started happening in all the mainline Protestant churches. Du Plessis, the guy who saw LSD as a gateway drug to tongues, became known as "Mr. Pentecostal," the ecumenical ambassador spreading it to other denominations. Scholars and religious writers referred to "neo-Pentecostalism," but such a ten-dollar term was never going to catch on, and it still contained the P-word. A mainline minister and public relations executive who'd spoken in tongues for years crafted the solution. The everyday magic sweeping churches, he declared, was a "charismatic renewal."

Charismata was an obscure religious word for the supernatural powers God very occasionally gave to certain humans, so it was theologically legitimate. But even better, *charismatic* had just become the new go-to adjective for people who were naturally exciting, like President Kennedy. The nondenominational Protestant rebranding of Pentecostalism as "charismatic Christianity" took off. In 1967 some Roman Catholic theology teachers started speaking in tongues, and charismatic Catholicism was born. However, the charismatics also created their own new churches and sects, because that's what Americans do. The most important early ones started in southern California.

In 1965 a minister left the L.A. Pentecostal faction founded by Aimee Temple McPherson to set up his own church in Orange County, not far from Disneyland. His Calvary Chapel specifically targeted youth. "The people in my generation," his baby boomer son-in-law explained recently, having succeeded the founder, "could relate to Calvary Chapel. You could wear your surf trunks, T-shirt, and flip-flops to church and carry your Bible." Also, a regular "afterglow" period followed each sermon, when people spoke in tongues. Calvary Chapel services became so popular, the founder had to buy a circus tent to accommodate the crowds.

Soon seven thousand charismatics a week were attending services, and the church started bursting forth spores, reproducing by the hundreds across the country. In the American Protestant way, these new churches were really franchises, sharing a brand—the name, the groovy music, and the belief that God is still granting ordinary folks magical superpowers. And because Calvary Chapel, a large denomination, was created in America during and after the 1960s, it insists it's "nondenominational"—like American politicians who began insisting at the same time they're antigovernment.

One of those Calvary spores sprouted nearby, in a fancier Orange County town. Its minister, John Wimber, was not just *targeting* unchurched young SoCal baby boomers: he was their cool older brother, a bearded rock 'n' roll keyboardist who'd played with the Righteous Brothers and been a Quaker pastor before turning evangelical and then neo-Pentecostal. In fact, for the more conservative Calvary Chapel founder, he came to seem too relaxed and nondoctrinaire. So Wimber split, aligning with a charismatic Christian group that held services featuring rock music on the beach in Santa Monica. (Bob

Dylan found Jesus there.) Wimber became the "spiritual father"—it seemed he could miraculously cure the sick . . . make the healthy crumple in ecstasy . . . and drive demons from the possessed. The church was called the Vineyard, and Wimber became known as Mr. Signs and Wonders, presiding over its rapid national franchising. Excellent post-1960s branding, *vineyard*: plenty of references in the Bible but also chic, natural, upscale, Californian.

Because the Vineyard and Calvary Chapel were both booming, and because neither called itself Pentecostal nor *obsessed* over tongues, they made it easier for Christians in established churches to adopt charismatic modes. *I'm weeping, I'm laughing, I'm falling to my knees or declaiming prophecy or speaking in tongues, my backache went away, the traffic jam suddenly cleared, God and Jesus are doing it all for me—I feel it's true, so it's true.* American Christianity was incorporating more magical realism and special effects than ever. By the end of the 1970s, even Billy Graham gave his okay to speaking in tongues.

The differences among Christian true believers in the late 1960s and '70s mirrored the differences among the new bohemian masses. The charismatics were like the hippies and New Agers, experiencing ecstasy and seeing signs and wonders, demanding cool music and clothes in church. The fundamentalists were like the New Left, insular zealots focused on arguing doctrine, hating the unrighteous, and awaiting the final battle. Charismatics were the Christian equivalent of the millions of circa-1970 hippies who didn't so much disagree with the radicals' critiques of the rotten world but were ultimately more interested in peace and love and awesomeness.

THE "CONSERVATIVE EVANGELICALS," AS FUNDAMENTALISTS were now calling themselves, doubled down on their literal readings of the Bible, on Heaven and Hell being as real as Disneyland and Las Vegas, and on the end of the world and Jesus's return coming soon. Because it was the 1960s, that dogma was about to get even more amazing.

From the Scopes Trial up to the 1960s, even many evangelicals had accommodated scientific findings concerning scientific questions: each "day" in Genesis lasted for aeons, Earth is billions of years old, plants and animals and humans came into existence gradually, God used chemistry and biology as His means of creation. But then in 1961 a pair of diehards, a Bible teacher at a fundamentalist seminary and a civil engineering professor, published *Genesis Flood: The Biblical Record and Its Scientific Implications.* The authors had graduated from Princeton and Rice, and their book was more than five hundred pages long, so it seemed legit. *Genesis Flood* almost single-handedly retrieved creationism from the dustbin of Christian intellectual history—just as the academic mainstream was starting to say that science couldn't necessarily be trusted as the arbiter of truth. The engineering professor cofounded the Creation Research Society in 1963 and the Institute for Creation Research in the early 1970s. Thus creationism in its most implausible form— *God made it all in six regular days six thousand years ago*—now had an institutionalized movement led by science-y Ph.D.'s. Within a generation, it would become a piece of American Christian orthodoxy.

Over creationism and other issues, hardline evangelicals began reasserting supremacy in the more conservative evangelical denominations. The most hidebound of the big Lutheran branches, the Missouri Synod, recommitted to the dogma that *everything* in the Bible is factually true. At its 1965 convention, over the objections of a reasonable president, it declared its "conviction that the events recorded in the book of Jonah did occur," that Jonah was a "real man" swallowed by a "real whale" until his prayers convinced God to make the whale spit him out. The head of its most prestigious seminary explained that no, the Jonah tale is like a lot of stuff in the Bible—a parable, not a factual account. Both men were purged, and the hard-liners took over.

The author of *The Message of Genesis,* which came out the same year as *The Genesis Flood,* was a Southern Baptist biblical scholar, and the Southern Baptists' press published it. His gist was that Genesis is all true-*ish,* but the famous early chapters—God creating Heaven and Earth, Adam and Eve and the serpent in Eden—are myth, divinely inspired but not strictly factual. Also, Noah's flood didn't cover the entire planet. Looking back from the twenty-first century, what's amazing is that this reasonable take seemed reasonable to evangelicals.

But the moderates were beginning to lose control. After a ruckus, the *Message of Genesis* professor was fired from his seminary, and official Southern Baptist doctrine had its first revision ever—now mentioning Hell and the end-time and being open to the possibility of dating Jesus's return. They elected a president who preached that Satan's Antichrist would literally take over the world before Jesus's return.

Outsiders didn't register the scale and scope of what was happening as it was happening. When the Supreme Court finally decided in 1968 that states couldn't outlaw the teaching of evolution, they figured they were just doing the judicial cleanup following the de facto die-off of primitive Christianity. "Only Arkansas and Mississippi have such 'anti-evolution' or 'monkey' laws on their books," the sniffy majority opinion noted, and nobody had been prosecuted under Arkansas's law, so these creationism laws were "more of a curiosity than a vital fact of life in these States."

To the confident, complacent midcentury Establishment, this didn't look like the tip of an iceberg, let alone what it actually was: the astounding peak of one mountain in a range rising from the American depths, part of the emerging continent of Fantasyland. Meanwhile other Christian alternate-reality institutions were popping up out of the murk like an archipelago.

In the 1960s, as entertainment became more and more a feature of every part of everyday American life, the old Sunday-morning ghetto of quasi-ecumenical religious TV came to seem impossibly dull. At the same time, the most aggressively entertaining forms of religion naturally thrived and grew and finally dominated. Evangelicalism and Pentecostalism and fire-and-brimstone fundamentalism are by their nature closer to show business than mainline Protestantism and Catholicism are: high-energy preachers, fantastic melodrama, superheroes and supervillains, amazing effects, over-the-top endings. The Christian Broadcasting Network (CBN), founded by the thirty-one-year-old Southern Baptist minister Pat Robertson, a Yale Law graduate and U.S. senator's son, began in the 1960s. In 1966 it launched its flagship program, a nightly two-hour variety-and-miracles show called *The 700 Club*, which soon starred Robertson. The first star of the show had been a Pentecostal minister—Jim Bakker, who hosted with his wife Tammy Faye, and promptly went on to become headliners for a new network founded by Pentecostals, Trinity Broadcasting.

To MANY AMERICANS IN MANY different ways, the 1960s and early '70s felt like the edge of an abyss. That feeling fed right into the revived Protestant preoccupation with Armageddon and the end-time. In 1967 Oxford republished *The Scofield Reference Bible,* the first fresh edition since it was created in the early 1900s—the Bible, but with parascripture about the six-thousand-year-old Earth and impending apocalypse and rapture built right in. In the 1960s this tendentious new improved American Bible was, so to speak, born again.

Starting in 1970, you didn't even have to bother with the confusing language of Ezekiel and Daniel and Revelation. Instead of ancient and cryptic poetic prose, *The Late, Great Planet Earth* was an easy-to-understand explanation focused on the exciting prophecies and studded with digestible bits from Scripture. The author was a knock-around Texas evangelical named Hal

Lindsey. The book's title gives a sense of his jolly approach to explaining the imminent apocalypse. Lindsey understood the new era in which he was pitching his Bible decoder kit. The opening epigraph would seem to undermine his entire project: "'We believe whatever we want to believe.' Demosthenes." He began by arguing that you should believe his book because nowadays people believe all kinds of nutty occult things. "Astrology is having the greatest boom in its history. . . . The hippy musical *Hair* has its own staff astrologer. . . . The Bible makes fantastic claims; but these claims are no more startling than those of present-day astrologers, prophets and seers."

With conspiracism suddenly on the rise, *The Late, Great Planet Earth* purported to reveal the details of the evil *über*-conspiracy—how Satan and the Antichrist and False Prophet and their minions in all their respectable disguises were taking over the world. For instance, those confusing references to "Gog" throughout the Bible? Obviously the Soviet Union. And the "beast coming up out of the sea, having ten horns"? The new European Economic Community! (Even though in 1970 it had only six members.) What's more, the EEC was created by the Treaty of *Rome*—and in Revelation, of course, "the great whore" Babylon *is* Rome! And so on. *The Late, Great Planet Earth* was the bestselling (so-called) nonfiction book of the entire decade, and it continued selling a million copies a year for the rest of the millennium. Its template was fill-in-the-blanks-flexible enough to incorporate all new satanic agents as they emerged—China! Iran! vaccines! Obama! Pope Francis! ISIS!

For Lindsey and American evangelicals generally, the creation of the state of Israel in 1948 was unmistakable evidence of the fulfillment of prophecies. Before the final events can play out, the Jews had to return to Israel. They had! And in 1967, with end-time fever beginning to rise in America, Israelis defeated the invading Arab armies and *retook Jerusalem*—"And they shall fall by the edge of the sword," it says in Luke 21:24, "and Jerusalem shall be trodden down of the Gentiles." In the 1960s and '70s, with the Middle East beginning to teeter on the edge of real-life Armageddon, this particular fantasy had a massive revival and eruption.

As the new modes of Christian hysteria boomed, Americans lost interest in the reasonable and nebulous on Sunday mornings. The Southern Baptists became the biggest American denomination around 1965 and kept growing. The ultrafantasy faction of Presbyterians broke away to form their own denomination and took off. By the end of the 1960s, most U.S. Protestants were evangelicals. Back in 1960, the largest Pentecostal denomination, the Assemblies of God, had 508,000 American members; by the end of the 1970s, its total U.S. members and "adherents" had grown to 2.6 million. The great pioneers in freakishly innovative Christianity, the Latter-day Saints, had grown slowly during the twentieth century. But the Mormons had a great 1960s and '70s, with U.S. membership almost tripling. In fact, their strenuous outward normality as individuals—so cheerfully hardworking, sober, and square, so *un-1960s*—was another way outré beliefs became normalized.

It was the evangelical Christians' involvement in national politics that finally, once and for all, made everyone pay attention to their ascendancy. And not, at first, Republican politics. In America, "the odd spectacle of politicians using ecstatic, nonrational, holy-rolling religion in presidential campaigning was to appear first . . . in 1976," Tom Wolfe wrote that very fall. (The ellipses are in the original.) The vehicle was "Jimmy Carter . . . absolutely aglow with mystical religious streaks. Carter turned out to be an evangelical Baptist who had recently been 'born again' and 'saved,' who had 'accepted Jesus Christ as my personal Savior'—i.e., he was of the Missionary lectern-pounding amen ten-finger C-major-chord Sister-Martha-at-the-Yamaha keyboard loblolly piny-woods Baptist faith." This was a major moment. In modern times, presidential candidates had been obliged to *downplay* their odd religions—George Romney his Mormonism, and Kennedy his Catholicism. But Carter's evangelicalism helped him win.

At his second National Prayer Breakfast as president, in 1978, he remarked that "the words 'born again' were [now] vividly impressed on the consciousness of many Americans who were not familiar with their meaning." Indeed so. A decade earlier, if a president had been Carteresque in this way—indeed, if any famous or powerful nonpreacher had been so religiously out of the closet—most people would've been weirded out.

Around the same time, as Robertson and Jerry Falwell moved into the right-wing political lane as well as their strictly religious lane, the news media began covering them as well. In the 1970s both founded their own universities, Regent and Liberty, as Oral Roberts had done in the 1960s. Unlike those brazen newcomers, America's most famous and beloved evangelical, Billy Graham, had avoided pushing too hard against reason and science and always made nice with powerful politicians of all persuasions. Even though Graham's basic religious beliefs were not much different from Robertson's and Falwell's, he now seemed even more moderate and mainstream by comparison.

For three hundred years in America, the overall Christian trendline had been in the direction of moderation, a long arc bending toward reason. The Puritans ejected Anne Hutchinson. The Methodists calmed down and became ordinary. The Mormons were quarantined in the desert, Pentecostals in hollers and slums. Creationism and end-of-the-world schedules became jokes. Midcentury American religion was like TV, respectable and bland.

But then during and after the 1960s and '70s, supernatural beliefs intensified, proliferated, and achieved permanent traction. This time as never before, America's renegade magical-thinking extremists won. False ideas from the past about the primordial past (creationism) suddenly had a huge dedicated constituency, as did wild ideas from the past about the predestined future (the end-time). And the conviction that the present is just like the magical past of Jesus's time—tongues, faith healing, personal messages from Heaven—spread like mad.

25

Big Bang: Politics and Government and Conspiracies

BELIEFS AND INKLINGS ABOUT HIGHER POWERS AND PURPOSES ARE FINE, within reason. Imagining alternate realities is fine, up to a point. Experiencing out-of-your-mind ecstasy is fine, every now and then. And rationalism is essential—but by the same token, it can also be carried to obsessive and excessive heights and depths. In the early 1960s, a mania for a certain kind of hyperrationalist abstraction had U.S. leaders in its thrall. It came along at just the right moment, as the Cold War and then the Vietnam War reached their horrific peaks, to help give reason itself a permanent taint in the American mind.

The mathematician John von Neumann, a father of both the digital and the nuclear ages, left Germany for the United States just before the Nazis took power. As a young man, he created game theory, the distillation of human decision making to its underlying, purely mathematical essentials. He helped to create the atomic bomb and to choose the Japanese cities to be incinerated, work about which he seemed blithe and unchastened. In the 1960s, once the United States and the Soviet Union were both armed with hundreds of nuclear launchers and a thousand megatons worth of warheads, each side capable of destroying hundreds of the other's cities, our central national defense strategy was reduced to a pure game theory notion that Von Neumann had helped craft: if rational player one believes that rational player two, no matter how massively attacked, will retain the ability to catastrophically counterattack, player one will never attack in the first place. Perfectly logical. The possible downside of the nuclearized "game" was hundreds of millions of deaths, however. People were appalled when they learned of Von Neumann's jocular acronym: Mutual Assured Destruction, or MAD.

President Kennedy had made a big campaign issue out of America's supposed nuclear missile inferiority to the Soviets—a complete fiction. He chose as his secretary of defense a caricature of the rational modern technocrat: the Harvard MBA, former accounting professor, and Ford Motor Company president Robert Strange McNamara. McNamara was infatuated with "systems analysis," the shiny new computerized approach, made possible by Von Neumann's mathematical work, that presumed to solve complex problems—especially military ones—by reducing them to quantitative data. The most important of McNamara's whiz-kid assistant secretaries had been a senior figure at the RAND Corporation, the original postwar think tank and the fountainhead of systems analysis. The problem was that the crunched data and equations made systems analysis *look* like pure science, and its self-confident brainiac practitioners and their clients certainly believed it was a form of perfect superrationality.

RAND's most public figure was Herman Kahn, who was also the most influential promoter of the idea that nuclear war wouldn't be *so* terrible. Kahn was a consultant to McNamara's Defense Department as the United States prepared to intervene militarily in Southeast Asia. McNamara and Kahn envisioned beating back Communism in Vietnam as a matter of feeding variables through the Pentagon's nifty new PPBS—that's Planning, Programming and Budgeting System—which made waging and winning a modern war look like designing and manufacturing new and improved Fords. "The Vietnam war," Reich wrote in *The Greening of America*, "represents a form of madness in which logic is carried to fantastic extremes." He had a point. In addition to the fact that moral calculus isn't reducible to actual calculus, the empiricism these best and brightest practiced was often faulty and fake. Enemy body counts are one very limited metric in war, seductive because they're simply quantifiable, and in this case grossly exaggerated as well. Furthermore, the American rationalists in charge didn't or couldn't recognize that the war in Vietnam was driven as much by emotion as by reason, by their exaggerated terror of Communism and their concern for America's superpower reputation.

At the same time, RAND had just revived war-gaming as a way for military leaders to manage real-life wars. But not that silly antique stuff with little models of ships and airplanes—now there were computers and game *theory*, with genius math underlying it all. Now wars that hadn't even happened yet could be imagined and planned and "fought" in advance. The emotionlessness made it all seem even more rational. Herman Kahn's RAND version of systems analysis, one of his biographers writes, amounted to "speculative fabrications" in which "Kahn's science became science fiction." War games were another entrancing and specifically American artifact in the 1960s that confused interesting fiction and the real thing.

ONE KIND OF LOGIC WAS carried to fantastic extremes by the war makers, and then another kind of logic was carried to fantastic extremes by some of the war's opponents. As the Vietnam War escalated and careened, the antirationalist 1960s flowered. "Over and over," the student radical and antiwar leader Tom Hayden wrote long afterward, "it came down to that question—what was reality in an unreal time?" The anti-Establishment deliria came in both scary and blissful versions, as always—the way some Christians are premillennialists, counting on a violent and cleansing Armageddon *now*, while some are postmillennialists, imagining a peaceful redemption of the world.

Both countercultural types were present at the March on the Pentagon to Confront the War Makers, the remarkable protests in Washington, D.C., in the fall of 1967, as the war approached its ferocious peak. In his book about those spectacles, *The Armies of the Night*, forty-four-year-old Norman Mailer wrote of "the generation [that] believed in LSD, in witches, in tribal knowledge, in orgy, in revolution," how "now suddenly an entire generation of acidheads seemed to have said goodbye to easy visions of heaven." He described chants—"'Out, demons, out—back to darkness, ye servants of Satan'"—and the circle of hundreds of protesters intending "to form a ring of exorcism sufficiently powerful to raise the Pentagon three hundred feet." They were hoping the building would "turn orange and vibrate until all evil emissions had fled this levitation. At that point the war in Vietnam would end."

In the modern age, purely happy fantasies tend to be apolitical and darker fantasies political—thus the difference between hippies and the New Left. And by the end of the 1960s, plenty of zealots on the left were engaged in extreme magical thinking. They hadn't started the decade that way. In 1962 a little campus group called Students for a Democratic Society adopted its founding document, drafted by twenty-two-year-old Tom Hayden. The manifesto is sweet and reasonable, decrying inequality and poverty and "the pervasiveness of racism in American life," seeing the potential benefits as well as the downsides of industrial automation, declaring themselves "in basic opposition to the communist system."

Then, *kaboom*, the Big Bang. Anything and everything became believable. Reason was chucked. Dystopian and utopian fantasies seemed plausible. Mailer had written that the New Left, feeling "the militancy of the blacks as a reproof," were "these mad middle-class children with . . . their lust for apocalypse." SDS became *the* New Left institution, and in 1969 its most apocalyptic and charismatic faction, calling itself Weatherman, split off and got all the attention. Its members believed they and other young white Americans, aligned with black insurgents, would be the vanguard in a new civil war. They issued statements about "the need for armed struggle as the only road to revolution" and how "dope is one of our weapons. . . . Guns and grass are united in the youth underground." And then they went to work making and setting off bombs. Some got a lot of attention—such as the ones in 1970 at New York police headquarters, in 1971 at the U.S. Capitol, and in 1972 at the Pentagon—but during an *average week* in 1969 and 1970, at least ten bombs were set off by the far left in America. In 1973 a dozen young fantasy revolutionaries formed the Symbionese Liberation Army in California, announcing they were "under black and minority leadership," even though all but one were white. They murdered the black Oakland school superintendent, then kidnapped the media heiress Patty Hearst—who became a comrade/character in the SLA's fiction, using the nom de guerre Tania, and stayed with them a year and a half robbing banks, driving getaway cars, and shooting up a store. If underground militant cells were setting off hundreds of bombs and robbing banks around the country these days, of course, America would be crazed, consumed, talking of nothing else, and probably under martial law. The bombings back then seldom made the national news because a reasonable and rational Establishment was still in charge of the media discourse, determined to help Americans remain reasonable and rational. "It is entirely possible," Wolfe wrote, "that in the long run historians will regard the entire New Left experience as not so much a political as a religious episode wrapped in semi military gear and guerrilla talk."

It wasn't only political extremists who became unhinged. In the 1970s the CIA and the Defense Intelligence Agency set up the infamous Project Star Gate to see if they could gather intelligence and conduct espionage by means of ESP.* Even before the Weathermen convinced themselves they were American Vietcong, officials at the FBI, CIA, and military intelligence agencies, as well as in urban police departments, convinced themselves that antiwar protesters and campus lefties in general were dangerous militants, and they expanded secret programs to spy on, infiltrate, and besmirch their organizations. Which thereby validated preexisting paranoia on the New Left and encouraged their wingnuts' revolutionary delusions. It was a symbiotic vicious circle, alarmed and overreaching government fantasists versus alarmed and overreaching antigovernment fantasists.

THE FANTASY FAR RIGHT HAD its own glorious 1960s moment. Right after Senator McCarthy died, one of his wealthy supporters, Robert Welch, founded the John Birch Society. According to Welch, both Republican and Democratic cabinets included "conscious, deliberate, dedicated agent[s] of the Soviet conspiracy" determined to create "a world-wide police state, absolutely and brutally governed from the Kremlin." In the early 1960s, the Birch Society started getting huge national media attention. It recruited tens of thousands of members, in chapters in dozens of states, and opened American Opinion bookstores and "reading rooms" around the country. The federal government was now "50–70 percent" Communist and was "under operational control of the Communist party," Welch claimed in 1961. Obviously academia and foundations and the news media were infiltrated, but the American Medical Association and the U.S. Chamber of Commerce were also "comsymps," in Welch's phrase.

The conspiracy came to be understood as extending well beyond American commies and comsymps serving Soviet and Chinese interests. Communism, according to the Birchers' new line, was just one piece of a global master conspiracy, a tool of a much grander plot by a "clique of international gangsters." It stretched back to the eighteenth-century European Illuminati— thus reviving that paranoid fixation in America for the first time in a century. For simplicity's sake, Welch wrote in 1966, "let's call this ruling clique simply the *Insiders*." For sure all the socialist innovations of the last half-century

* Charles Tart, the "consensus trance" professor, was a consultant. So were parapsychologists from the Stanford Research Institute who claimed to have validated the charlatan Uri Geller's psychic spoon-bending in the 1970s.

were their doing—"central banking, a graduated personal income tax," and the new "Medicare monstrosity"—but also fluoridating the U.S. water supply and expanding civil rights. The main bogeyman concerning racial integration was the chief justice of the Supreme Court, demonized on the Birchers' IM-PEACH EARL WARREN billboards that I remember from my childhood, some featuring Confederate flags. Warren was a former Republican governor and vice-presidential nominee who'd been appointed chief justice by President Eisenhower. And speaking of Eisenhower, Welch had "an accumulation of detailed evidence so extensive and so palpable" that he knew "beyond any reasonable doubt" that Ike—European Allied commander during World War II, beatified two-term Republican president—had been not merely "a stooge" of the commies but was "knowingly accepting and abiding by Communist orders, and consciously serving the Communist conspiracy for all of his adult life." A crazy fiction.

Because the John Birch Society's extraordinary rise happened in the *early* 1960s, before the forces of reason really started losing control, it could be effectively marginalized. The mainstream media did its part—a *New York Times* headline forthrightly called the Birchers SEMI-SECRET EXTREMISTS, to *Time* they resembled "a tiresome, comic-opera joke," and the *Los Angeles Times* published a multipart investigative series and a front-page editorial condemning them—but the decisive and telling rejection came from the Es-tablishment right. Leaders of the conservative movement, still new and still actually conservative, worried that these noisy crackpots might ruin their chance at the nomination and presidency in 1964.

In 1962 the movement's two key intellectual voices, William F. Buckley and Russell Kirk, his colleague and a syndicated columnist, met in Palm Beach with their would-be candidate, Senator Barry Goldwater of Arizona. "Every other person in Phoenix," the alarmed Goldwater told them, exagger-ating, "is a member of the John Birch Society. I'm not talking about Commie-haunted apple pickers or cactus drunks, I'm talking about the highest caste of men of affairs." They resolved to take down Welch and the Birchers. "I'll just say," Kirk proposed, "that the guy is loony and should be put away." For the next issue of his *National Review,* Buckley wrote a five-thousand-word hit piece: "How can the John Birch Society be an effective political instrument" with a leader whose "views on current affairs are . . . so far removed from common sense?" Goldwater piled on in a letter to the magazine, condemning "views far removed from reality."

Done and done. The leaders of the reality-based conservative movement and Republican Party led, declaring the John Birch Society beyond the pale and rendering it moot as an official player in the national political discourse. Within three years, the fraction of Americans with an unfavorable view of Birchers, according to Gallup, went from a minority to a majority, and when Ronald Reagan ran for the California governorship in 1965, even he called them "kind of a lunatic fringe."

But just because the Birch organization and brand was discredited, true believers in that mad vision of a global conspiracy involving Communists and liberals and elites didn't stop believing and multiplying. My parents were not much for conspiracy theories, but they were Goldwater supporters, and they owned one of the millions of copies of Phyllis Schlafly's pro-Goldwater polemic, *A Choice Not an Echo*. "Most of what is ascribed to 'accident' or 'coincidence,'" she wrote, "is really the result of human plans." The same year a guy in suburban St. Louis with a perfect name—John Stormer—self-published *None Dare Call It Treason*, which explained how the federal government and the press and the entire U.S. not-for-profit sector were dominated by treasonous stooges and co-conspirators. Stormer was a leader of the Missouri GOP. "Is there a conspiratorial plan," he asked, "to destroy the United States into which foreign aid, planned inflation, distortion of treaty-making powers and disarmament all fit?" It was a rhetorical question. *None Dare Call It Treason* sold a couple of million copies in its first year, and a million more a year for the rest of the 1960s. The ground was softened for another giant bestseller, *None Dare Call It Conspiracy*, published in 1972. "The conspirators come from the very highest social strata," the authors explained. "They are immensely wealthy, highly educated and extremely cultured," a conspiracy of "the *Insiders*," Rockefellers, Rothschilds, "the elite of the academic world and mass communications media," Illuminati, intent on creating a "world supra-government." One of its blurbs was from the same Eisenhower administration Mormon who'd led the first cabinet-meeting prayer. *None Dare Call It Conspiracy* sold five million copies.

THAT FURIOUSLY, ELABORATELY SUSPICIOUS WAY of understanding the world started spreading across the political spectrum after the assassination of John Kennedy in 1963. Dallas couldn't have been the work of just one nutty loser with a mail-order rifle, could it? Surely the Communists or the CIA or the Birchers or the Mafia or oligarchs or some conspiratorial combination must have arranged it all, right? The shift in American thinking wasn't registered immediately. In his influential book *The Paranoid Style in American Politics*, published more than a year after the president's murder, Richard Hofstadter devoted only two sentences and a footnote to it, observing that "conspiratorial explanations of Kennedy's assassination" don't have much "currency . . . in the United States." Elaborate paranoia was more of an established tic of the Bircherite far right, but because those folks fanatically despised Kennedy, they weren't motivated to believe in a conspiracy to assassinate him. The left needed a little time to catch up.

In 1964 a left-wing writer published the first American book about a JFK conspiracy, claiming that a Texas oilman had been the mastermind, and soon there were many books arguing that the official government inquiry—chaired by the far right's bête noire, Chief Justice Earl Warren—had ignored the hidden conspiracies. One of them, *Rush to Judgment* by Mark Lane, a lawyer on the left, was a *New York Times* bestseller for six months. Then in 1967 New Orleans's wacko district attorney indicted a local businessman for being part of a supposed conspiracy of gay right-wingers to assassinate Kennedy—"a Nazi operation, whose sponsors included some of the oil-rich millionaires in Texas," with the CIA, FBI, and Bobby Kennedy complicit in the cover-up. After NBC News broadcast an investigation discrediting the theory, the DA said the documentary was a piece of "thought control," obviously commissioned by NBC's parent company RCA, "one of the top ten defense contractors" and thus "desperate because we are in the process of uncovering their hoax." The notion of an immense and monstrous JFK assassination conspiracy became conventional wisdom in America.

As a result, more Americans than ever would become reflexive conspiracy theorists. Thomas Pynchon's novel *Gravity's Rainbow,* a complicated global fantasy about the interconnections among militarists and Illuminati and hashish, and the validity of paranoid thinking, won the 1974 National Book Award. In the early '60s, Hollywood released the Washington conspiracy thrillers *Seven Days in May* and *The Manchurian Candidate,* and by the 1970s conspiracy became *the* smart Hollywood dramatic premise—*Chinatown, The Conversation, The Parallax View,* and *Three Days of the Condor* came out in the same two-year period. Of course, real life at the time conspired to make such stories plausible. The infiltration by the FBI and intelligence agencies of left groups had just been revealed, and the Watergate break-in and its cover-up were an actual criminal conspiracy masterminded in the White House.

A revived will to believe in all-powerful conspiracies spread and grew from the 1960s on, an invasive species that became a permanent feature of the American mental landscape—like a new superkudzu that thrived everywhere, not just in the Southern heat and humidity. Within a few decades, the conviction that a web of villainous elites covertly seeks to impose a malevo-lent global regime made its way from the lunatic right to the mainstream. Delusional conspiracism wouldn't spread quite as widely or deeply on the left, but more and more people on both sides would come to believe that an ex-traordinarily powerful cabal secretly runs America, a dark conspiracy of in-ternational organizations and think-tanky groups and big businesses and politicians.

Each camp, conspiracists on the right and on the left, was ostensibly the enemy of the other, but they began operating as de facto tag-team allies. It's like relativist professors enabling science-denying Christians, and how the antipsychiatry craze in the 1960s appealed simultaneously to left-wingers and right-wingers (as well as to Scientologists). Conspiracy theories were more of a modern right-wing habit before people on the left signed on. However, the belief that the federal government had secret plans for detention camps for dissidents, for instance, sprouted in the 1970s on the paranoid left before it became a fixture on the right.

In fact, this left-right tag-teaming became a motif in the 1960s and '70s. The modern homeschooling movement, for instance, got going then in both fundamentalist Christian and Woodstockian iterations. The former sought to reduce children's exposure to ideas from outside the Bible-based bubbles of family and church. In left-bohemian milieux, parents decided that their chil-dren are not in this world to live up to expectations; that they must only and always do their own thing; and that tests and grades would turn them into drones of the corporate state. And in the 1970s the courts and state legisla-tures started deciding okay, whatever, do your own thing, Christian, hippie, it's all good, school's optional.

Retreating to self-sufficient rural isolation, living off the grid, became a hippie thing in the 1960s before it took off as a right-wing conceit in the 1970s. The back-to-the-land movement, with the *Whole Earth Catalog* as its official almanac and souvenir program, floated along on dreams of agrarian utopia. (For a year or two around 1970, I was a teenage Walter Mitty with my own Whole Earth dream.) Survivalism was the same but different. Both shared a vision of themselves as clued-in self-reliant ordinary heroes escaping the urban corporate-government hive because it was decadent, corrupt, and corrupting. One was more New England-town-meeting Transcendentalist, the other more sharp-shooting Idaho-wilderness mountain man. One had more in common with hopeful Christian postmillennials, building a new Eden, the other more like premillennials ensuring their own salvation in the violent end-time. But both were (and are) overcome by the long-running nostalgia for a dream of a purer, pastoral America they'd picked up from the fantasy-industrial complex.

Gun nut became a phrase in the 1960s because gun nuts really didn't exist until then—and they emerged on the far right and left simultaneously. The John Birch Society, Malcolm X, and the Black Panthers were our first modern gun rights absolutists. The Panthers' self-conception, as a heavily armed and well-regulated militia ready to defend Oakland's black community against the police, led quickly to a California law, sponsored by a Republican and signed by Governor Reagan, that made it illegal to carry loaded guns in public. Huey Newton, twenty-five-year-old cofounder of the Panthers, condemned it as part of "the plot to disarm" Americans.

Restricting the sale and use of guns became a salient political issue only after the assassinations of the Kennedy brothers and Martin Luther King, Jr. The gun control laws enacted or seriously proposed were modest. When Congress was passing gun regulation in 1968, the National Rifle Association's executive vice-president wrote that "the measure as a whole appears to be one that the sportsmen of America can live with." The GOP platforms of 1968 and 1972 supported gun regulation—and President Nixon, his speechwriter William Safire recalled, told him that "guns are an abomination" and that he would have *outlawed* handguns if he could. But violent crime had tripled in a decade, and in the late 1970s hysterics managed to take over the NRA, replacing its motto "Firearms Safety Education, Marksmanship Training, Shooting for Recreation" with the second half of the Second Amendment— "The Right of the People to Keep and Bear Arms Shall Not Be Infringed." Within a decade, the official Republican position shifted almost 180 degrees to oppose any federal registration of firearms.

In other words, fantasy was starting to hold its own against reason. *Three* national politicians had been gunned down over the course of a few dozen months. There were persuasive explanations for each assassination: three individuals each driven by his own fantasy to shoot a famous politician. And there was a reasonable political response: legislation to lightly regulate gun ownership. But the assassination victims were exciting and beloved celebrities whose spectacular killings made them seem still more like fictional characters. One of the assassins was himself assassinated, while in police custody, by a shady character, on live TV. Afterward, two fantasies became entrenched American idées fixes: conspiracies are the key underlying mechanisms of existence, and unlimited gun ownership is both the irreplaceable symbol and means of preserving one's liberty.

*   *   *

AMERICANS FELT NEWLY ENTITLED TO believe absolutely anything, to mix up
fiction and reality at will. I'm pretty certain that the unprecedented surge of
UFO reports was not evidence of extraterrestrials' increasing presence but a
symptom of Americans' credulity and magical thinking suddenly unloosed.
We *wanted* to believe in extraterrestrials, so we did. What makes the UFO
mania that started in the 1960s historically significant rather than just amusing, however, was the web of elaborate stories that were now being spun, not
just sightings and landings but abductions and government cover-ups and
secret alliances with interplanetary beings. Those earnest beliefs planted
more seeds for the extravagant American conspiracy thinking that by the
turn of the century would be rampant and seriously toxic.

As I've said, a single idée fixe like this often appears in both frightened
and hopeful versions. That was true of the suddenly booming belief in alien
visitors, tending toward the sanguine as the 1960s turned into the 1970s,
such as the ones that Jack Nicholson's character in *Easy Rider* earnestly describes as he's getting high for the first time. "We was down in Mexico two
weeks ago—we seen forty of 'em flying in formation. They've got bases all
over the world now, you know. The government knows all about 'em. . . .
These leaders have decided to repress this information. . . . So now the Venu-
tians are meeting with people in all walks of life, in an advisory capacity." In
the ultimate late-1960s movie, it was *whoa* truth telling as much as comedy,
a summary of an emerging American article of faith. The same year *Easy
Rider* came out, one evening in southern Georgia, a failed gubernatorial candidate named Jimmy Carter saw a moving moon-sized white or green light in
the sky that "didn't have any solid substance to it" and "got closer and closer,"
stopped, turned blue, then red and back to white, and then zoomed away.

The first big nonfiction abduction tale appeared around the same time,
in a bestselling book about a married couple in New Hampshire, recounting
the episode they believed happened to them while driving their Chevy sedan
late one night. They saw a bright object in the sky that the wife, a UFO buff
already, figured was a spacecraft. She began having nightmares about being
abducted by aliens, and more than two years later both of them underwent
hypnosis. The details of the abducting aliens and their spacecraft that each
described were different and changed over time. The man's hypnotized de-
scription of the aliens bore an uncanny resemblance to the ones in an episode
of *The Outer Limits* broadcast on ABC just before his hypnosis session.

Thereafter hypnosis became the standard way for people who believed they were abducted to recall the supposed experiences. And the couple's story established the standard abduction tale format: humanoid creatures take you aboard a spacecraft, communicate both telepathically and in spoken English, medically examine you, insert long needles into you, then let you go.

The couple were undoubtedly sincere believers. The sincerely credulous are also perfect suckers, and in the late 1960s a convicted thief and embezzler named Erich von Däniken decided to take advantage of as many Americans as possible. *Chariots of the Gods?* posited that extraterrestrials had come to Earth thousands of years ago to help build the Egyptian pyramids, Stonehenge, and the giant stone heads on Easter Island. That book and its many sequels sold tens of millions of copies, and the *Chariots* documentary had a gigantic box-office take in the early 1970s. Americans were ready to believe Von Däniken's fantasy to a degree they simply wouldn't have been a decade earlier, before the 1960s sea change. Certainly a decade earlier NBC wouldn't have aired an hour-long documentary in prime time based on it. And while I'm at it: until we'd passed through the 1960s and half the '70s, I'm pretty sure we wouldn't have given the presidency to some dude, especially a born-again Christian, who'd recently seen a huge color-shifting luminescent UFO hovering near him.

26

Big Bang: Living in a Land of Entertainment

THE LAST FOUR CHAPTERS WERE ABOUT HOW AMERICANS SUDDENLY RAMPED up their beliefs that all sorts of iffy and unreal things were actually, factually real and true. This chapter is about what happened in the realms that are *supposed* to be fictional—movies, novels, Disney World, Dungeons and Dragons, war reenactments, pop culture. And how in the 1960s and '70s we also began massively expanding the zone that *combined* fantasy with everyday reality—by making downtowns and suburbs more like Disneyland, theming restaurants, normalizing cosmetic surgery and gambling and pornography and so much more, turning American life into an exceptional hybrid of the authentic and make-believe. *Nothing is real*, the Beatles first psychedelic song instructed a generation in 1967. My point is that when the very definitions of reality were suddenly up for grabs on so many fronts—in science and social science, religion and politics—that extreme flux operated in synergy with all the unrealities being created and sold by the booming fantasy-industrial complex.

During the 1960s, we continued our great migration to the suburbs and the nostalgic, pastoral dream they fulfilled. For the first time, a plurality of Americans were suburbanites, on their way to becoming the majority. By 1970, 95 percent of households had television(s), most of them color, making the worlds inside the box still more entrancingly realistic. And we gorged, each of us spending more and more time watching TV, for many more hours than people in most developed countries (as we still do).

As the decade began, tellingly, American TV invented a curious new form of fiction passing-as-reality: comedies were now mostly filmed without audiences, but recordings of laughing crowds were layered into almost every sitcom soundtrack. And *what* we watched suddenly changed as well. For its first dozen years, prime-time network TV was more or less committed to realism—*Topper,* a sitcom about ghosts, was the memorable exception. But that unwritten law was repealed at the beginning of the 1960s—*The Twilight Zone, The Outer Limits, The Flintstones, The Jetsons*—followed by an immediate glut of the supernatural and otherwise fantastic. In the course of just three seasons, the three networks premiered *Bewitched, I Dream of Jeannie, My Mother the Car, Dark Shadows, The Flying Nun, Gilligan's Island, The Ghost and Mrs. Muir, My Favorite Martian, My Living Doll, The Time Tunnel,* and *Batman.* As well as *The Monkees,* a show about a fictional band that then turned into a real and hugely successful band.

Fantasy fiction was suddenly percolating all through pop culture. When I started sixth grade, in 1965, I remember very clearly how all at once half the teenagers I knew, including both my older sisters, felt obliged to buy and read and adore four newly reissued novels by some old English writer named Tolkien. Why did these obscure books, first published decades earlier, suddenly become enormous bestsellers among young Americans? Because we were young, and it was the 1960s. American baby boomers were hearing the dog whistle alerting them to alternate realities, and *The Hobbit* and *The Lord of the Rings* were supernatural stories with a benevolent magical bearded wise man; we had only just stopped believing in Santa and reading about Winnie-the-Pooh. Like Hermann Hesse's Asian-mystic stories, *The Hobbit* and *The Lord of the Rings* provided a means for the not-so-religious to feel a frisson of the spiritual and have a place in the 1960s national carnival of reenchantment.

A little over a decade later, I remember very clearly the moment when I realized fantasy would now *rule* pop culture. The first *Star Wars,* which a majority of Americans paid to see, was an epochal success for many reasons. But one of those reasons was that it wasn't just science fiction but had a *spiritual fantasy* at its core—the Force, the energy field that turned physics into metaphysics and vice versa, giving Jedis their telepathic and telekinetic powers. A mélange of affiliated New Age notions had just been mainstreamed, making 1977 the perfect moment to introduce an ecumenical new mysticism to the most religious rich country on Earth. The Force is very American, a spiritual discipline but also highly *practical,* a religion that lets you win battles, makes you *successful.* I remember walking out of the theater thinking the Force was the first faith with which I felt simpatico.

Because *Star Wars* and Tolkien's world were set, respectively, in the distant future and the apparently distant past, neither one connected directly to Americans' growing propensity to believe fantasies about real life right now. Then *Close Encounters of the Third Kind* appeared, very realistically depicting the extraterrestrials' twentieth-century arrival as an event as profound and glorious as Christ's Second Coming. The preceding decade of profligate belief—not just in UFOs but in government cover-ups and messianic prophecy—had primed us to love and *believe* in *Close Encounters.* (Spielberg would soon make another gigantically popular film about an extraterrestrial being, this one rescued from the malevolent U.S. government.) "The strange thing is," Philip K. Dick wrote right after *Close Encounters* came out, that "in some way, some real way, much of what appears under the title 'science fiction' is true. It may not be literally true, I suppose. We have not really been invaded by creatures from another star system. . . . The producers of that film never intended for us to believe it. Or did they?" It was one of the most lucrative movies ever, pop culture reflecting and energizing fantastical beliefs about our contemporary world.

In the past, Hollywood hadn't given Jesus Christ a lot of screen time. But as superliteralist Christianity revived, more Jesus-focused than ever, the fantasy-industrial complex enthusiastically waded in as never before. There were productions *starring* Him, full-on biopics like *The Greatest Story Ever Told* and the NBC miniseries *Jesus of Nazareth.* Between 1969 and 1974, two big musicals all about the Messiah (*Jesus Christ Superstar, Godspell*) and one about Genesis (*Joseph and the Amazing Technicolor Dreamcoat*) opened on Broadway, then became movies. All those, of course, were happy fantasies and period pieces. But there was also a market, heretofore untapped, for frightened Christian fantasies set in present-day America: Satan-among-us was a new Hollywood genre, either in the form of possession (*The Exorcist*) or his sons born to human women (*Rosemary's Baby, The Omen*). Outlandish supernatural belief was normalized.

*   *   *

DISNEYLAND BECAME A PARADIGMATIC PLACE, American culture perfectly distilled into a quarter square mile of southern California. Fantasies were rendered impossibly real, historical and mundane realities improved and glamorized, the two merged seamlessly, overseen by the strict but avuncular supreme being who'd created it all. By 1970, something like 40 percent of Americans had spent time there. In 1967 the Disney Corporation began building Disney World—in America's other confabulated paradise state, on a sunny emptiness a hundred times as big as Disneyland.

The Disney effect was at first just a matter of copycat tourist businesses chasing after the successful first mover. After Americans got a taste for Main Street USA and Frontierland, "living history" museums appeared everywhere, scores of them, so many that in 1970 at Old Sturbridge Village, they formed their own association. (There are now almost a thousand such places in America.) National Park Service rangers began dressing in period costumes to explain history, and by the 1970s they'd gone all the way, speaking with visitors as if they were historical figures—"doing first person."

Dedicated to blurring the lines between the fictional and the real, people in the living history world became focused on what they called the authenticity of their simulations. Living history boomed and acquired academic legitimacy, no longer just tourist traps but centers for "experimental archaeology" and "imitative experiments." In 1967 one of the foremost archaeologists of the American colonial era became assistant director of Plimoth Plantation, the built-from-scratch re-creation of the Pilgrims' village. Soon all the "interpreters" at Plimoth playing the parts of Pilgrims started doing full first person, speaking seventeenth-century English in the historically correct regional dialects of England and never stepping out of character. As the professor-in-charge said, they "actually build houses and outbuildings. . . . They cook food, and even eat it in period fashion" and "get dirty and tousled in their work in the fields." They are P. T. Barnum's descendants with advanced degrees and none of his winks about humbug.

Everywhere the living history fiction became more and more realistic, the blend of fake and actual more complete. The imperatives of show business often prevailed. When the new Pope John Paul II visited America in the 1970s, he touched down in the middle of Iowa. There he told the hundreds of thousands gathered for an outdoor mass that his "pastoral journey through the United States would have seemed incomplete without a visit . . . to a rural community like this." That rural community was, in fact, a living history theme park—a make-believe eighteenth-century Indian farm, a make-believe nineteenth-century farm and town, and a make-believe early twentieth-

century farm. It was a remarkable Fantasyland moment, as if the High Sep-
ton of the Faith of the Seven had come from Westeros to visit Middle Earth.

As everything started morphing into entertainment, more of America
became DIY mini-Disneylands. The centennial of the Civil War was the
perfect pretext at a perfect time for the emergence of a remarkable new
hobby. On a summer weekend in 1961 in Virginia, an hour east of Washington, D.C., where one hundred years earlier several thousand men had been
killed and wounded and hundreds more taken prisoner at the Battle of Bull
Run, several thousand men in Civil War costumes in ninety-degree heat pretended to kill and wound and capture each other. Among the make-believe
1860s soldiers were 2,200 real 1960s soldiers, National Guardsmen on loan.
At the battle reenactment in Manassas, not coincidentally, it was the victorious whooping yells of the pretend Confederate forces that got the big cheers
from the crowd of fifty thousand spectators. More Civil War reenactments
followed. The century-old fantasies around the South's Lost Cause had been
incarnated by this new mode of populist living theater.

Before long tens of thousands of Americans, almost all white American
men, had enlisted in faux Confederate *cavalry* companies and Union artillery
regiments, regularly going outdoors, fully kitted, to pretend to kill and die. It
was playing dress-up but manly dress-up. The most devoted, unlike the dilet-
tante *farbs,* became known as *hardcore authentics, stitch counters,* and *thread
Nazis* who insisted on cannons and fabrics and buttons and boots and eye-
glasses and hairstyles and pencils and food like the ones in the 1860s, in
order to perform perfect *impressions* in *total immersion events.* For those moments during the sham battles when a sham soldier most acutely feels it's the
real thing, reenactors call it a *period rush*—the phrase itself a 1960s period
piece.

Soon period rushes came from simulations of other kinds of events from
other periods, eventually any period. The big bohemian variants emerged in
California, created by young women. The first Renaissance fair—that is,
faire—took place in 1963 in Los Angeles, staged as a fundraiser for the local
Pacifica public radio station by a thirty-one-year-old and her artist husband.
Thousands of people came one weekend to their Laurel Canyon backyard to
pretend it was an English seaside town in the 1500s. "The Faire reminds us,"
the founder said, "of simpler times, more in touch with nature and the Earth."
It adopted the motto "Where Fantasies Rule." It then moved an hour west to
the Paramount Movie Ranch, where high-production-value pseudohistorical
stage sets made the fantasies seem more real. (Hallucinogens no doubt helped
too.) During the 1970s a dozen other impresarios started Renaissance fairs all

over the country. The founder of the original became a consultant to places in the blue-chip not-for-profit fantasy-industrial complex, such as Colonial Williamsburg.

Up north in Berkeley, a UC senior celebrated her 1966 graduation with an elaborate medieval-Europe-themed costume party and "tournament" attended by a couple of dozen of other sci-fi-fantasy geeks.* In their homemade tunics and tabards and jerkins, carrying broadswords and shields and long-bows and spears, they "fought," then marched up Telegraph Avenue "protesting the 20th century." They decided to repeat it every year and formed the Society for Creative Anachronism—which went national, with multiple "kingdoms" and thousands of members.

Starting in the early 1970s, millions more young Americans who were jonesing to fight and quest in a magical version of the late Middle Ages—but all the time, indoors, dressed normally—had Dungeons and Dragons. You play—role-play—a specific character (druid, barbarian, paladin, sorcerer). Role-playing had been a technique used by psychotherapists and educators for a while, but it was in the 1960s that *role-play* became a verb. The inventors of D&D were young war-gamers. With RAND and the Pentagon reviving and refining war games, war-gaming among ordinary Americans surged as well. The guys around a table in a Minneapolis living room felt their own military fantasies were a thrilling bit more like the real thing—even before they were using computers like actual generals.

American motorcycle gangs, suddenly a big deal in the 1960s as Americans wildly self-fictionalized, were all-in reenactors of a kind: Wild West outlaws instead of Civil War soldiers, with motorcycles for horses, colorful dime-novel names (Hells Angels, Bandidos), special bad-guy wardrobe and grooming, and deadly barroom brawls. When the Angels became branded celebrities, they naturally hung out with the Grateful Dead and Rolling Stones, celebrity performers who also played the parts of drug-taking outlaws. The Angels weren't the only American criminals at the time whose lives imitated art: only after a novelist and screenwriter *invented* a Mafia term in 1969—"the godfather"—did actual mafiosi start calling bosses "godfather" and discussing offers that people couldn't refuse.

Self-conscious fan fiction was another 1960s invention that permitted

---

* The host, Diana Paxson, became a successful author of fantasy fiction—and fantasy nonfiction, such as *Taking Up the Runes: A Complete Guide to Using Runes in Spells, Rituals, Divination, and Magic.*

consumers of fiction to *enter* fictions. It started with *Star Trek*. During the show's first season in 1966, young Americans began publishing homemade magazines that included their stories about the *Enterprise* and the Federation. Four years later, after the original show was canceled, there were dozens of such 'zines, and soon many more. Chekov and McCoy and Scotty and Spock actually corresponded with the 'zines—only the actors, but *still*—and appeared in costume at fan conventions. And in their stories, the young amateurs often included heroic and beloved and very young new characters—that is, fictional versions of themselves having adventures (and sometimes sex) in the twenty-third century with the *Star Trek* characters. Which became a trope in all fan-fiction genres as they emerged.

Before that moment, there had not been hordes of people living in their own private Disneylands or inserting themselves into familiar fiction and sharing their stories with the world. There were no Comic-Cons, the first of which took place in 1970 in southern California, when a few hundred people in love with comics and sci-fi met in the basement of a 1910 San Diego hotel that reeked of nostalgia—but that had also reeked of nostalgic make-believe when it opened, because it was built in a faux-old classical style popularized by the Chicago world's fair.

In 1967 YOUNG TOM STOPPARD had his breakthrough hit, *Rosencrantz and Guildenstern Are Dead*, a brilliant play about actors playing characters playing actors playing characters, and the amusing, confusing jumble of fiction and reality. Stoppard knew he was onto something new and important. "I have a feeling," he said at the time, "that almost everybody today is more trying to match himself up with an external image he has of himself, almost as if he's seen himself on a screen."

Exactly. That was the heart of what I'm calling the big bang in entertainment, when it rippled out into normal life and individuals' sense of reality. When you're consuming a particular cultural product, a piece of entertainment, the movie ends, you finish the book, you walk out of the theme park, you toggle back to reality, and everyday life resumes. But starting in the 1960s and '70s, lots more of everyday life was replaced by pieces of everyday fiction—fun, sexed-up confections that everyone agreed to consider real and normal, hardly any suspension of disbelief required. "In what was an entirely new concept, celebrities were self-contained entertainment," Gabler writes in *Life: The Movie*. "Every celebrity was a member of a class of people who functioned to capture and hold the public's attention no matter what they did or if they did nothing at all." The celebrity-focused news media ghetto that started in the early 1900s had remained mostly seedy and disreputable. After American teenagers were recognized as a distinct cohort in the 1950s, fantasy-prone and celebrity-mad, new magazines like *16* and *Tiger Beat* were created to let the kids feel an intimacy with the famous—girls could enter contests to win dates with singers and actors. And then the respectable media's resistance to celebrity obsession dissolved. After the circulation of the *National Enquirer* tripled in just a few years to several million, in 1974 Time Inc. created its final phenomenal success, the newsmagazine *People,* and *The New York Times*—the *Times!*—launched the celebrity magazine *Us.* All the big media companies recalibrated their self-respect compasses and plunged into the bog, making it entirely acceptable for all Americans to know too much and care too deeply about the lives of glittering strangers.

DISNEY'S GENIUS WITH MAIN STREET USA had been to conceive and build a big public space like a movie or stage set, but with no backstage in sight, an all-encompassing indoor-outdoor mise-en-scène that anybody could inhabit for twelve hours a day, every day. What happened in Disneyland did not stay in Disneyland, didn't even stay in museums and theme parks. Main Street USA's imitation of old-time small-town America was followed in 1966 by the three-acre simulation of a sexier, more cosmopolitan nineteenth-century *urban* downtown, New Orleans Square. They become the de facto models for large-scale builders and designers of shopping malls and much of the rest of real-life America. The Rouse Company, founded in Baltimore months after Disneyland opened, was a real estate development firm, but that's like calling Walt Disney an amusement park operator. Apart from Disney, no American had a more important role in refashioning America physically—that is, in Disneyfying it—than James Rouse. He more or less invented shopping malls (and coined the term) and definitely invented food courts (and coined that term). Before Rouse (and Disneyland), American shopping centers as we know them—big public spaces with single designers and owners, town squares in a can—barely existed.

Walt Disney was Rouse's visionary hero and friend. "I hold a view that may be somewhat shocking to an audience as sophisticated as this," Rouse said in a speech at Harvard's annual Urban Design Conference in 1963, "that the greatest piece of urban design in the United States today is Disneyland.

If you think about Disneyland and think of its performance in relationship to its purpose, its meaning to people—more than that, its meaning to the process of development—you will find it the outstanding piece of urban design in the United States. . . . It really has become a brand new thing."

By then Rouse had built a new town, Cross Keys, on the grounds of a defunct country club on the edge of Baltimore, because he wanted to "feed into the city some of the atmosphere and pace of the small town and village"—a century later reinventing the wheel of Olmsted and Vaux's prototypical suburb, their make-believe New England village outside Chicago. Just as Main Street USA was a nostalgic simulation of the Missouri town where Walt Disney had been a boy, Rouse was inspired to re-create a version of the old-fashioned little Eastern Shore town where he'd grown up. And then more: in 1967 in the countryside between Baltimore and Washington, Rouse's company opened the first of the old-fashioned "villages" that would constitute the new city of Columbia, then built seven more during the 1970s.

Simultaneously some of the most serious up-and-coming architects were rediscovering history, creating the first "postmodern" buildings, with classical columns and pitched roofs and pediments and colorful finishes, sometimes cartoonish and sometimes convincing reproductions—like Disneyland and Disney World. So why not nostalgically revise *existing* big-city downtowns, too? Why not, they decided in the 1970s, sprinkle this amazing new pixie dust of nostalgia on an abandoned two-hundred-year-old hulk in Boston and turn Quincy Market and Faneuil Hall into a colonial-themed shopping mall? And then the South Street Seaport in Manhattan? Both were Rouse projects. Thus the "festival marketplace" became the new middle-class mode of instant American urban renewal—dying or atrophied urban organs and limbs revivified as imaginary versions of themselves. *Themed* was becoming the standard MO for the creation of any and all new American places and spaces.

When I was born, restaurants were neither national businesses nor themed. That changed as suburbs fulfilled the old-timey small-town American dream and as Disney cracked the code for themed commerce. We got theming that indulged geographic nostalgia—Old West steakhouses, first Bonanza and Ponderosa (from *Bonanza*, the number-one TV show), then LongHorn and Outback, and Old South iterations like Cracker Barrel Old Country Stores. And then any and every fantasy source—a children's novel (Long John Silver), *Playboy* (Hooters), cartoon worlds populated by animatronic talking animals (Chuck E. Cheese, inspired by the founder's visit to Disneyland), or a clown (Ronald McDonald in McDonaldland). During the

1960s, the McDonald's founder said repeatedly his company was "not in the *hamburger* business, it's in *show business*."*

Unlike fast food, gambling and sex are not uniquely American pursuits. But both are obviously fantasy-fueled, and both were considered naughty for most of our history. And then the availability and cultural presentations of both changed radically.

In most places for most of U.S. history, gambling businesses had been outlawed. But after the anything-goes national ratification of fantasy in the 1960s, state government after state government decided to join the fantasy-industrial complex by operating lotteries—first New Hampshire in 1964, then New York, New Jersey, and ten more by 1975, eventually nearly every state. By the way, lotteries are gambling's *most* fantastical form, with worse odds than any casino game. The lottery business is all about selling ridiculous long shots to magical thinkers. What's more, government-run lotteries were specifically tweaked to exploit the psychology of fantasy. Scratch-card tickets—*Four correct, I almost won!*—essentially tricked bettors to keep buying, and computer-generated ticket sales gave the illusion of control over random chance.

Sex has probably been a fiction-reality blend for most of human history, but in America that all at once started becoming radically overt. The most common and incurable potentially negative consequence of heterosexual sex, producing children, had always inhibited the full flowering of make-believe. (If a random fraction of war reenactors used live ammunition in mock battles, for instance, "living history" would be less popular.) But once a contraceptive method of unprecedented effectiveness came along—the Pill, available everywhere by 1965—heterosexuality dramatically changed. People were freer to have sex more often and therefore more imaginatively, without the antifantasy buzzkill of possible pregnancy. Reliable contraception also meant they could do it with more people they found fleetingly attractive, and have sex unseriously, the way they might daydream about ravishing a character in a novel or a movie. When sex became far less consequential, it could become less "real" and more like exciting fiction.

---

* In his youth, Ray Kroc had had noteworthy brushes with Fantasyland past and future. A phrenologist examined him at age four and purportedly divined that Raymond would work in the restaurant business. At fifteen, during World War I, he lied about his age in order to enlist and served as a driver in the Red Cross Ambulance Corps—the same job in the same outfit that sixteen-year-old Walt Disney, a year later, lied about his age to join.

At the same time, as *guilty pleasure* started becoming an oxymoron, the sexual practice that was always completely fantasy-based, solitary masturbation, began losing its stigma. *Cosmopolitan,* after Helen Gurley Brown took it over in 1965, regularly ran articles about it. The slang term *stroke book* appeared. In 1969 *Portnoy's Complaint,* with a compulsive masturbator as its hero, spent three months as the bestselling novel in America. Portnoy was frank about how his sexual desire had been branded by show business: "I too want to be the boyfriend of Debbie Reynolds—it's the Eddie Fisher in me coming out," and what was more, he realized, "for every Eddie yearning for a Debbie, there is a Debbie yearning for an Eddie—a Marilyn Monroe yearning for her Arthur Miller." Philip Roth, thirty-five when he published *Portnoy,* understood that his popular breakthrough was a function of the zeitgeist shift at the heart of this history: "By the final year of the 1960s, the national education in the irrational and the extreme had been so brilliantly conducted," he wrote right afterward, "that for all its tasteless revelations about everyday sexual obsession . . . something like *Portnoy's Complaint* was suddenly within the range of the tolerable."

The first big business ever built on masturbation, Playboy Enterprises, had set the cornerstone in the 1950s for America's mainstreaming of erotica, but it was during the late 1960s and early 1970s that the smut wing of the fantasy-industrial complex really grew. Pornographic films had been around from the beginning of cinema as a groundbreaking mutant cross of fiction and reality—(bad) actors playing roles in (stupid) fictional stories but also *actually* fucking and sucking. However, most people seldom if ever saw them. Porn movies were a special taste, like liqueurs or sardines. The sexually explicit movie that began making porn respectable was hardly porn at all but a sweet, arty, black and white Swedish film called *I Am Curious (Yellow),* extensively covered in the news media when it was released in America in 1969. By 1972, *Playboy* was selling seven million magazines a month, one copy for every ten men and teenage boys in America. For women, *The Flame and the Flower* (1972) sold more than two million copies, turning "romance fiction" into an explicitly sexual ("His other hand cupped a breast and played with it to his pleasure . . . she felt his manhood deep within her") and hugely bestselling genre. The hardcore films *Deep Throat* and *Behind the Green Door* and *The Devil in Miss Jones* got enormous national media coverage when they opened in 1972 and 1973 and sold tens of millions of tickets. *Last Tango in Paris,* a serious drama released by a major studio starring Marlon Brando as an anal rapist, was the seventh-highest-grossing movie in the United States in 1973. Porn had been declared officially okay. Soon new technologies would make it ubiquitous, another American fictional realm that blurred with life and transformed it, providing a new model for sexuality.

Trying to appear younger and more sexually attractive wasn't the only reason a majority of American women suddenly started coloring their hair, but it was the main one. Dyed hair is a small fiction, a fib rather than a lie. But the dramatic cultural change on this score is a striking metric of the acceptance of make-believe in real life. When I was a child, it was unusual to encounter a woman over fifty whose hair was not gray or white. By the time I graduated college, it was unusual to see a woman between fifty and seventy whose hair was not blond or brown or black or red. When Clairol sold its first home hair-coloring line in 1956, maybe one in fifteen American women colored her hair. By 1970, two-thirds did. Everyone agreed to pretend that women's hair no longer turned gray. It was a cosmetological expression of the new paradigm that we quickly ceased to find odd.*

Cosmetic surgery was extremely rare before the 1960s. From plastic surgery's modern emergence during World War I through the 1950s, what plastic surgeons did was fix wounds from car crashes and fires and war and congenital problems like cleft lips. People who hadn't suffered some terrible piece of bad luck didn't ask surgeons to refashion their faces and bodies to make them prettier or sexier or younger-looking. And all but a few plastic surgeons would have refused. But then cosmetic surgery, heretofore disreputable, took off. Partly it was the result of new technologies—silicone breast implants appeared in 1962, that *annus mutabilitatis*—but it was mostly a matter of new thinking, often magical thinking. By the account of one pioneering New York practitioner, when he came along in the 1960s, there were only eight plastic surgeons in Manhattan. In 1967 the American Society for Aesthetic Plastic Surgery (ASAPS) was founded, followed in 1969 by the American Association of Cosmetic Surgeons.

ASAPS presidents talk about the paradigm shift as if it were a civil rights revolution. "Up until that time," says one, "face lifting was not considered a legitimate pursuit for any well-trained plastic surgeon and was done mostly behind closed doors." "Back in the 1960s," explains another former ASAPS president, who practices in Newport Beach, "when the major focus of plastic surgery was on reconstructive operations, . . . cosmetic surgery [was] 'in the

* During the same period, we never stopped to register that our food was suddenly becoming preternaturally colorful too: during the 1960s and early '70s, the food dyes consumed by the average American—tons of Red 40, Yellow 5, Blue 1—more than doubled, a bigger increase than any comparable period before or since.

closet,'" but a few heroes "had the courage and foresight" to sell boob jobs and tighter faces and smaller noses to any citizen who could afford them.

A friend of mine, the plastic surgeon Jay Arthur Jensen, started his medical education in the 1970s at Yale and now teaches at UCLA and practices in Santa Monica. "Patients [do] develop a fantasy," he told me. "I did a facelift on a woman who was not an attractive person. I think it was at least her second facelift. And when I was done, she screamed at me and said she did not 'look as good as Sophia Loren.' She was adamant that I could somehow change that. The patients are in a fantasy—they're imagining that somehow they'll become a different person or they'll have a different life."

Surgically renovated faces and bodies and artificially colored hair provided illusions of youth. They became widely available just as the first baby boomers entered adulthood—the generation, not coincidentally, that was the first to refuse to relinquish the perquisites of youth as they aged. Starting in the 1970s, adults were free and eager to behave and consume in ways previously the province only of teenagers and children.

A new national fantasy of permanent youthfulness kicked in.

No matter how old you got, you could continue dressing like a kid. You could continue riding your skateboard, continue listening to rock music and smoking pot, continue obsessing over ever more amazing ice cream and cookies, continue watching cartoons and comic book movies and reading comic books, continue going to Disneyland. In *The Making of a Counter Culture* in 1969, Ted Roszak noted and disparaged "the commercial world's effort to elaborate a total culture of adolescence based on nothing but fun and games," but he couldn't yet see that the new countercultural paradigm would meld perfectly and powerfully and permanently into that total culture of adolescence.

It was in the 1960s that we first learned of our *inner child*, that we should each attend to his or her wishes and aspire to be more childlike as adults. That was one of the heartfelt, enduring takeaways of the era, part of nearly all the therapeutic and pop-psychology strands spun out of Esalen and its kin. *If it feels good, do it*: invented by Americans barely past childhood, that motto made the inner child idea actionable, and although the phrase faded quickly, the ethos lived on.

Instead of taking the correct lesson from Bob Dylan's 1973 anthem "Forever Young"—to "grow up to be righteous" and "always be courageous"—way too many baby boomers chose to remain in Neverland, to keep believing they'd always have nothing but fun and never resemble mom and dad. The principle set forth in *Peter Pan*—"All children, except one, grow up"—was just another oppressive and unfair old-fashioned rule to be cast off.

IN THE 1970S, NOT LONG before he died, the sci-fi writer Phil Dick moved into an apartment in Orange County a few miles from Disneyland, an irony not lost on him. There he wrote a perfect summary of his dread about the transformation of American society and culture as the real and unreal became indistinguishable. "We have fiction mimicking truth, and truth mimicking fiction. We have a dangerous overlap, a dangerous blur. And in all probability it is not deliberate. In fact, that is part of the problem." I can't do better, so I'll quote him at length.

> The problem is a real one, not a mere intellectual game. Because today we live in a society in which spurious realities are manufactured by the media, by governments, by big corporations, by religious groups, political groups—and the electronic hardware exists by which to deliver these pseudo-worlds right into the heads of the reader, the viewer, the listener. . . .
>
> And it is an astonishing power: that of creating whole universes, universes of the mind. I ought to know. I do the same thing. It is my job to create universes. . . .
>
> I consider that the matter of defining what is real—that is a serious topic, even a vital topic. And in there somewhere is the other topic, the definition of the authentic human. Because the bombardment of pseudo-realities begins to produce inauthentic humans very quickly, spurious humans—as fake as the data pressing at them from all sides. . . . Fake realities will create fake humans. Or, fake humans will generate fake realities and then sell them to other humans, turning them, eventually, into forgeries of themselves. So we wind up with fake humans inventing fake realities and then peddling them to other fake humans. It is just a very large version of Disneyland.

PART V

Fantasyland Scales: From the 1980s Through the Turn of the Century

"Yeah, well, that's just, ya know, like, your *opinion*, man."
—THE DUDE,
The Big Lebowski (1998)

"What is real? How do you define 'real'?"
—MORPHEUS,
The Matrix (1999)

"But did it matter whether it was authentic or not? Hadn't this country been built on the promise of avoiding this very question?"
—KARL OVE KNAUSGÅRD,
in *The New York Times* (2015)

It seemed as if things had returned more or less to normal. We survived the late 1960s and their '70s aftermath. Civil rights seemed like a done deal, the horrendous war in Vietnam was over, and youth were no longer telling grown-ups they were worthless because they were grown-ups. Revolution did not loom. Sex and drugs and rock 'n' roll were regular parts of life. Starting in the 1980s, loving America and making money and having families were no longer unfashionable. Plus: whoa, *computers,* then the Web. It was all good.

The sense of cultural and political upheaval and chaos was over—which lulled us into ignoring all the ways that *everything had changed,* that Fantasyland was now scaling and spreading and becoming the new normal in America. What had seemed strange and amazing in 1969 or 1974 had come to be unremarkable and ubiquitous. The water in our national hot tub was still getting hotter and hotter—and most of us happy frogs, lah-di-dah-di-dah, didn't notice.

Extreme religious and quasi-religious beliefs and practices, Christian and New Age and otherwise, didn't subside but grew and thrived—and came to seem unexceptional.

Relativism, the idea that nothing is any more correct or true than anything else, became entrenched in academia—tenured, you could say. But it was by no means limited to the ivory tower. The intellectuals' new outlook was as much a symptom as a cause of the smog of subjectivity that now hung thick over the whole American mindscape. After the 1960s, truth was relative, and criticizing became equal to victimizing, and individual liberty absolute, and everyone was permitted to believe or disbelieve whatever they wished. The distinction between opinion and fact was crumbling on many fronts.

As the conservative elite positioned itself as the defenders of rigor against the onslaught of relativism, its members preferred to ignore the unwashed masses on *their* side, the reactionary hoi polloi activated by America's extreme new believe-whatever-you-want MO. Anti-Establishment relativism had erupted on the left, but it gave license to *everyone*—in particular, to the far right and in the Christian fever swamps.

The new ultraindividualism extended well beyond lifestyle choices. Finding your own truth and doing your own thing came to mean not just getting high and watching porn but objecting to irreligious public education and owning as many guns of any kind as you wished. It meant a revived American commitment to markets, amounting among some to an almost religious faith.

Belief in gigantic secret conspiracies thrived, ranging from the highly improbable to the impossible, and moved from the crackpot periphery to the mainstream.

Many more Americans announced that they'd experienced fantastic horrors and adventures, abuse by Satanists and abduction by extraterrestrials, and their claims began to be taken seriously. Parts of the Establishment—psychology and psychiatry, academia, religion, law enforcement—encouraged people to believe that all sorts of imaginary traumas were real.

America didn't seem as weird and crazy as it had around 1970. But that's because we had stopped *noticing* the weirdness and craziness. We had defined every sort of deviancy down. And as the cultural critic Neil Postman put it in his 1985 jeremiad about how TV was replacing meaningful public discourse with entertainment, we were in the process of amusing ourselves to death.

27

Making Make-Believe More Realistic and Real Life More Make-Believe

IT IS NOT MUCH OF A STRETCH TO SAY THAT IN THE 1980S AND '90S, OUR COUN-try became an amazing coast-to-coast theme park, open twenty-four hours. The boundaries between entertainment and the rest of life were definitively dismantled. America became addicted to the make-believe of drag—by which I mean everything from new buildings meant to look old or foreign to the geeks at Comic-Cons and Burning Mans dressing up as fictional beings. Casinos were suddenly ubiquitous. Celebrity-obsessed news media sprawled. Reality television was born.

And consider wrestling, the professional and fake kind, which suddenly became a huge, quintessentially American cultural phenomenon and busi-ness. To me, all professional sports exist adjacent to Fantasyland. Every NFL or NBA game is a televised adventure story, a narrative played out according to rules of strictly defined genre—but unscripted, the outcome unknown, entertaining spectacle and real life merged. The stars are as close to superhe-roes as reality has on offer.

Pro wrestling emerged during the entertainment boon times of the 1910s and '20s, when it had to compete both with ascendant sports like baseball and boxing as well as with theater and now movies and radio. Pro wrestling split the difference between the two: real people in physical competition, but the characters and action and outcomes all extreme works of scripted and improvised fiction. During the 1930s, the sensible American public registered and rejected the phoniness, and pro wrestling went into decline.

It had a brief renaissance in the 1950s, thanks to the new medium of TV, which needed content, and all the networks started airing matches. California's athletic commission officially agreed to keep pretending professional wrestling was real. If people preferred to believe an entertaining lie was true, that was their right as Americans. In 1957 matches were suddenly drawing Madison Square Garden's biggest crowds for any events in years, and one night, as a pair of "hero" and "villain" wrestlers kept "fighting" after their match finished, audience members started fighting over the outcome. Five hundred New Yorkers rioted, throwing punches and bottles. "Many of the fans," the *Times* incredulously reported, "believe the sport to be a true contest—of skill and strength." But that seemed like the swan song; pro wrestling's fakery was still a fundamental problem; it was a niche taste; as TV got flush and respectable, the networks moved on. During my youth in the 1960s and '70s, pro wrestling was a ridiculous, low-rent artifact quickly headed, everybody figured, for oblivion.

Until the 1980s. Cable TV programming had arrived, even more shamelessly willing than broadcast TV had been to sell *anything*. And then the networks, feeling threatened by cable and because the free market totally ruled, abandoned their old qualms about presenting fantasy as reality and began broadcasting wrestling once again. The new laissez-faire economic era also permitted a de facto monopoly to form what became the World Wrestling Federation and then the WWE. The businessman in charge of the monopoly, Vince McMahon, had a brilliant insight, realizing that America's Barnumesque strain had reasserted itself: fake versus real was no longer the point, because wrestling's audience was now fully habituated, as one scholar of the realm has written, to "believing and disbelieving in what it sees at the same time." And so during the 1980s, the WWF and other promoters were finally free to end the Big Lie. In the old days, wrestling always officially insisted it was real. Finally it could stop pretending, because "real" and "fake" were relative, because nobody really cared anymore.

In less than a decade, pro wrestling mushroomed from a business generating a few tens of millions to half a billion a year. The audience expanded beyond its old blue-collar yob niche to the middle classes, families, college kids. It was transgressive, a *fun* con. And the real and fictional parts of the wrestlers' lives were now indiscriminately mixed and merged. In professional wrestling matches, any occasional, inevitable bit of unscripted authenticity was known as a *shoot*—old-time carnival lingo for when the gunsight on a shooting gallery's rifle aimed accurately. The standard fakery of matches in pro wrestling was known as *work,* and in the 1980s WWF producers invented the *worked shoot:* as one historian (and fantasy novelist) explains, they started incorporating "the real events of wrestlers' personal lives as part of the story . . . alcoholism, cheating relationships, childhood trauma and problems with the law are fused from reality into the fantasy."

Is there a more apt metaphor for our recent cultural transformation? America became a worked shoot.

One of the WWF's lawyers who lobbied in the 1980s to get pro wrestling deregulated—to persuade the government it wasn't a real sport, even though for a century it had pretended otherwise—was elected to the Senate in the 1990s and has run for president twice. Rick Santorum disingenuously defends pro wrestling as a genre of "morality plays" that are "a non-elite artifact of our culture that has survived by trying to keep up with the envelope-pushers in Hollywood and New York." The last time Santorum sought the Republican nomination, in 2016, he lost to a much bigger figure in the wrestling world. Before entering politics, the current president of the United States had sponsored WWE events at one of his casinos, then became a WWE character pretending to slap and body-slam McMahon on stage, and finally got inducted into the WWE Hall of Fame.

This blending of entertainment fictions and real life was also a central feature of one of pop culture's only wholly new genres since the 1960s—rap and hip-hop. It makes perfect sense that hip-hop burgeoned at the same time as pro wrestling: gangsta rap in particular was a brilliant worked shoot. The raps and the musicians' public personae were highly embellished versions of their real lives. Eazy-E and Ice-T and Biggie Smalls really had grown up in horror-show neighborhoods and had been (minor) gangsters, some rappers genuinely hated each other, performers who got rich did consume ostentatiously, guns were carried and sometimes used, Biggie and Tupac were assassinated (the former on Miracle Mile in L.A., the latter on Las Vegas Boulevard). The mantra was *Keep it real,* but it was also all a show, fiction and reality a single fabulous melt sandwich, fans and sometimes the performers happy to forget the distinctions. Hip-hop superstars like Jay-Z are the Buffalo Bill Codys of modern Fantasyland.

At the same time, many more Americans knew much more about

many more celebrities—because celebrity-obsessed journalism and quasi-journalism expanded by an order of magnitude from the 1980s on. It became both glossier and more legitimate (*Vanity Fair*) and, on television every day, practically inescapable—*Entertainment Tonight,* then *Extra,* then *Access Hollywood.* Once again this was a new condition. One could now consume for hours a day a multimedia news diet consisting exclusively of information about and pictures of people in show business. The full-blown celebrity-obsession fantasy, of being *pals* with famous people and living like them, was taken a big step further in the 1990s by *InStyle,* Time Inc.'s last successful invention: a whole magazine of specific instructions—how *you* could use the same mouthwash as Madonna, wear the same underwear as Sharon Stone, sleep on the same sheets as Kevin Costner, and smell exactly like Jennifer Aniston. Starting at the turn of the century, the flip side of that fantasy was served up explicitly by *Us,* which now came out every week: paparazzi photos of famous people looking unglamorous and performing mundane tasks, previously unpublishable, were reframed as a way to let nobodies feel celebrity-esque: "Stars—They're Just Like Us!"

Feeding this vastly expanded celebrity-media maw required lots more famous people. Reality television came along in the nick of time. It had been invented twice before, with *Candid Camera* at the dawn of TV and then during the Big Bang, but nobody noticed. *An American Family* was a gripping, groundbreaking documentary series in 1971, shot over seven months, about an upscale Santa Barbara family unraveling. For TV executives, it was not a let's-copy-that eureka moment but a one-of-a-kind creation, a prototype for nothing. It was too highbrow, a sad documentary on PBS, just twelve episodes that took two years to produce. And it was also too lowbrow: back then, a genre based on milking the intimate everyday real lives of ordinary people would be *gross,* and a semifictionalized cross between documentary and game show literally unthinkable. But a generation later in the 1990s, as TV was becoming fully Barnumized, that suddenly seemed like a genius idea. MTV made *The Real World;* in 1999 and 2000 came *Survivor* and *Big Brother.* Sometimes there were prizes, but mainly what people won was a bit of fame. Reality television has *reality* in the name, but from the beginning, reality shows consisted of high-concept stunts, carefully cast, authored if not strictly scripted, and definitely performed. Transforming ordinary, mostly talentless people into celebrities became a television genre and then an industrial sector. TV was transformed.

*   *   *

As PROFESSIONAL BASKETBALL AND FOOTBALL and "wrestling" blew up by re-inventing themselves as larger-than-life, aggressively *contemporary* entertainment forms, baseball went the other way. Baseball is more like American sports used to be. Most of the players are still white. The games have their same old relaxed pace. More than any other sport, in other words, a haze of nostalgia hangs over baseball. So that nostalgia was indulged brilliantly in 1992 in decaying, depressing old Baltimore—with Camden Yards, a brand-new baseball stadium for the Orioles designed and built to look and feel exactly like an old-time baseball stadium. *Shazam: if you squint, it's 1951 again!* Camden Yards was instantly beloved by everyone. Other teams and cities rushed to copy it.

Camden Yards was inevitable because American architecture had been taken over by postmodernism in the 1980s and '90s. New skyscrapers and shopping malls and residential buildings were practically required to reproduce or refer to styles from other eras or continents. Some architects professed to hate the new tide of nostalgia and make-believe and imagined themselves heroically swimming against it. Yet most of those "modernist" resisters simply designed buildings that evoked styles of a *different* old days, Euro-flavored glass-and-steel retro instead of wood-and-masonry Americana retro, Tomorrowland rather than Main Street USA and New Orleans Square. This change struck informed observers as remarkable. A "shift has taken place in the way we perceive reality," the great architecture critic Ada Louise Huxtable wrote in 1992, "a shift so pervasive that it has radically altered basic assumptions about art and life. . . . The replacement of reality with selective fantasy has been led . . . by a new, successful, and staggeringly profitable American phenomenon: the reinvention of the environment as themed entertainment."

As I've described, America's suburbanization after World War II amounted to the first step in the absorption of real estate development into the fantasy-industrial complex. Then came the theming of suburban chain restaurants and the rest of retail, followed by nostalgically reinvented downtowns. After that, canny executives in other sectors came to understand that in America *their* businesses could also be understood as show businesses. In 1999 a renowned management consultant published a book about the "entertainmentization of the economy," explaining how the financial and automobile and other industries had joined the movie and TV and music and publishing industries as marketers of appealing fictions. It seemed unremarkably true.

"What you market in a car," the CEO of a car company finally admitted, "is not about what you use but about what you dream." Indeed, the American auto industry's signal success of the era was in selling an enormous toy that allowed people (especially men) to imagine they were tough, sexy, independent daredevils who might at any moment haul off into the uncharted wilderness for an adventure. In the early 1980s the market share for SUVs had been close to zero; by 1999, it was 19 percent. Adults who'd grown up watching *Combat!* and *The Rat Patrol* and *MacGyver* were now driving actual Jeeps (and Expeditions and—in my case—Land Rovers), playing army or cowboy every day.

The fantasy business of gambling grew much larger. Once state governments took over the numbers racket—that is, lotteries—they kept sliding further down the slippery slope. States colluded in the 1990s to create national lottery cartels that amped up the fantasy quotient; Powerball and Mega Millions encouraged even more wildly unrealistic dreams of even vaster wealth. Eventually *most Americans* would become regular lottery players, with the poorest third, probably not the least magical-thinking cohort, buying half the tickets.

And the states doubled down on the retailing of fantasy by legalizing casinos. Casinos are fantasy environments engineered to deny ordinary reality—no clocks, no views outside, plenty of booze. For most of a century, the industry had worked fine existing only out in the Nevada desert—and then in New Jersey. But after 1987, when the U.S. Supreme Court ruled that Indian reservations were exempt from gambling laws, states saw no reason why *white* businesspeople shouldn't also profit from citizen-suckers' fantasies. During the 1990s half the states legalized casinos. Some legislatures permitted gambling only under a special double-fantasy system: casinos had to *float on bodies of water,* as if that prevented the state from being sullied. So they were installed in nostalgic old-timey showboats and required to motor up and down rivers to sustain the fiction. But after a while they were allowed to remain docked, and finally they no longer even had to keep make-believe captains and crews. Despite the presence of casinos nationwide, Americans seemed to crave the full Nevada immersion even more, like believers making pilgrimages to Jerusalem or Mecca. As Las Vegas turned into a city posing as a theme park—with hotel-casinos that were huge new simulations of ancient Egypt (the Luxor), medieval England (the Excalibur), the seventeenth-century Caribbean (Treasure Island), Renaissance Italy (the Venetian), contemporary France (Paris Las Vegas), and New York City (New York–New York)—the number of visitors tripled.

At the other end of Nevada in the 1990s, a different adult fantasy theme park, chic and singular, was established for one week a year—Burning Man. On the Fantasyland family tree, Burning Man has deep roots in the late 1800s (the original world's fairs), but the main trunk is from the 1960s (hallucinogens, happenings, be-ins, Woodstock, costumes-as-clothes, worship of nature and the primitive), and adjacent stalks from the 1980s (live action role-playing) and '90s (cosplay). Every year since its founding, bohemian fantasists have assembled, as many as twenty-five thousand or more at a time, to spend a week in the desert several hours from Reno, camped in a mile-and-a-half-wide semicircle called Black Rock City. They spend a sum approaching $100 million for each of their Brigadoons. They dress as unicorns, birds, mermaids, geishas, chanteuses, time travelers, butterflies, anything, everything, or they wear no clothes at all. They roam around superb fantasy architecture—rococo polygons and furniture the size of small houses, glowing flowers as big as trees, bridges, log cabins, Shangri-La temples. At Burning Man, they step through the looking glass—that is, through the LED screen—to inhabit Azeroth or Tatooine or the fan-fictionalized *nice* section of the postapocalyptic *Mad Max* world.

Not so long ago, American adults never dressed up in costumes, certainly not as an annual ritual. When my daughters reached their early twenties, obsessing more than ever over their Halloween costumes, they were shocked when I told them that. The change happened recently, and it is another small expression of the new protocols. In the 1980s, after the Halloween parades invented by freshly out gay people in San Francisco and New York, dressing up on Halloween became a thing straight adults routinely did in every corner of America.

But why did Halloween have to be just a single day, and why couldn't the adult insistence on fictional *authenticity* become more narratively elaborate? Thus live action role-playing—LARP—took off, allowing people to become characters acting out stories in the real world, sometimes for days at a time. The founder was evidently a young actor in Manhattan who liked reading *Lord of the Rings* out loud by candlelight with his pals while high. When they went to the next level, staging a Hobbit War outdoors on somebody's parents' farm, it was the *ur*-LARP. But LARPing soon became a medium rather than a genre, a platform instead of a particular game. LARPs started as combat games, as participants used weapons made from sticks taped with foam, then more and more abandoned fighting. Every possible premise and milieu generated LARPs—Old West, detective noir and Nancy Drew, futures dominated by AI or zombies, fictional pasts based on H. P. Lovecraft or Nicola Tesla.

One of the points of LARPing is to remain in character, *to be* a fictional being for hours or days at a time. LARPers have a disparaging phrase for real life, *mundania*, and people who never LARP are called *mundies*, like muggles in Harry Potter. For players eager to blur the lines between their real and unreal selves even more, Nordic LARP arrived in the United States in the 1990s.* It de-emphasizes all the kid stuff, the combat and magic, and goes for more realism, with players aspiring to experience *bleed*, as they call it—to let their characters colonize their minds, to dream in character, to lose track of where real and fake begin and end.

---

* Fantasyland islets appear almost everywhere, and this particular one has arisen in northern Europe in a big way. According to *Time*, 2 percent of Danes LARP. But again: it was invented by Americans in America.

28

Forever Young: Kids "R" Us Syndrome

MIDDLE-AGED PEOPLE WEARING HALLOWEEN COSTUMES OR ATTENDING Burning Man are expressions of a phenomenon I described earlier—the commitment of Americans, beginning with the baby boom generation, to a fantasy of remaining forever young. The treacly term *kids of all ages* had popped up when baby boomers *were* kids. But its currency skyrocketed during the 1980s and '90s, when American adults, like no adults before them— but like all who followed—began playing videogames and fantasy sports, dressing like kids, grooming themselves and even getting surgery to look more like kids. It's what I call the Kids "R" Us Syndrome. It became pandemic and permanent. It ranges from the benign to the unfortunate.

As soon as all boomers were adults, half the buyers of comic books and tickets to superhero movies—the three *Superman*s and four *Batman*s just the beginning—were adults. As a result, both genres boomed. Video and computer games grew from nothing to a multibillion-dollar industry, not just because the technology got more powerful and the imaginary worlds more irresistibly realistic and immersive but also because by the end of the century, the great majority of consoles and cartridges and disks were bought by people who didn't have to ask their parents for money—the average player was in his thirties. Videogames, originally sold to boys to pretend they were grown-up action heroes, were soon bought mainly by grown men who wanted to play like boys.

I've played only one game at home for the many, many hours over many weeks and months required to become adept. It was the first *Goldeneye 007,* right after it came out in the 1990s. *Goldeneye* is what they call a free-roaming first-person shooter—that is, I was James Bond, looking for people to kill. I loved it. I loved the complex, 3D pictorial realism and the music. And I loved that the game transformed me when I was in its world, made me feel *actually* scared (the adrenaline) and *actually* as sharp as Bond (the dopamine), in ways that reading a novel or watching a movie generally don't. I played with my daughters, who were seven and nine at the time, each of us taking turns playing different characters. I called it quits after two years, however, because the Columbine massacre made our father-daughter pleasure in shooting and killing each other feel less fun.

The strictly children's hobby of collecting and trading baseball cards became a primarily adult thing in the 1980s, the same time that Rotisserie League Baseball was invented and became the prototype for fantasy sports. By 1988, there were half a million U.S. fantasy sports players. In any earlier era, to spend hundreds of hours a year on an elaborate game of make-believe—*I'm a team owner, buying and selling players*—would've been unthinkable for anyone but children.

With the Web, fantasy sports became fully industrialized, a new imaginary national pastime in which a third or more of American males would eventually participate. Fantasy sports are an expression of two underlying Fantasyland features that appear again and again. It's a *superrealistic* fiction, based on athletes' actual week-to-week performances and years of stats and a free market in make-believe assets. And it has *hyperindividualism:* each individual fantasy "owner" has a team composed of athletes whose individual performances are all that matter, rendering real teams' real wins and losses irrelevant.

Enthusiastic players can slide into outright delusion. In a documentary (called *Fantasyland*) about a fantasy baseball league, the main subject was a financial analyst who schemed to hang out in real life with "his" MLB players. "I think that the players really do play harder for you when they can see the face of their owner," he said, in the film's saddest moment, "when they know who's out there, who's the guy who's calling the shots." The real team owners naturally encourage the make-believe owners in their childlike obsession.

As a kid, I collected baseball cards and would've enjoyed fantasy sports. As a kid, I also went to summer camp, for three years during the late 1960s to a *themed* one—a "Spanish camp," where we took Spanish names and spoke the language and ate the foods and learned soccer and played in an Olympics against kids from the nearby Russian and German and French camps. Themed fantasy camps for *adults* got going in the 1980s, and by the end of the '90s, almost every team in every professional sport was inviting grown-ups to spend thousands of dollars a day to pretend they were pro athletes. The more imaginary celebrity proximity the better, so individual stars launched their own, from the Michael Jordan Fantasy Camp to the Dorothy Hamill Figure Skating Fantasy Camp. The San Francisco Giants Fantasy Camp sprouted a Sports Media Fantasy Camp so sports-loving weenies could pay to pretend to be broadcasters and photographers. Inevitably it spread to other glamorous fields, becoming its own little piece of the fantasy-industrial complex, more than a thousand camps in all. One such is the five-day Hollywood TV Star Fantasy Camp, where "you'll stay in the heart of tinsel town" with "your very own dressing room, cast chair, make-up artist, . . . call sheets with your name and character name, . . . a press interview like the ones you see your favorite stars doing, . . . [a] professional photo shoot to be put on your own personal industry magazine cover," and an "awards ceremony." By paying ten thousand dollars, "you'll not only rub elbows with working television actors, you'll be one!"

All at once in the 1980s, serious artists also embraced and embodied a new faux-childhood mode—Keith Haring's notebook doodles, Cindy Sherman's spook-house dress-up photos, and more. Jeff Koons would become the most famous and successful fine artist alive. Among his best-known works are a set of life-size statues from 1988 of forever-young Michael Jackson and his chimp Bubbles; *Puppy,* a forty-three-foot-tall terrier made out of flowers, the biggest, prettiest, cutest stuffed animal ever; and *Balloon Dogs,* a perfect mirror-polished stainless steel replica, twelve feet high, of the kid's party toy, one of which sold for $59 million. "The idea of boyhood is everything to Koons," a *New York* profile said of him, explaining that he gives a nonstop "Method performance of childlike mystic wonderment," never stepping out of character.

Going to *Star Wars* movies, playing *Goldeneye,* managing an imaginary NFL team, attending a counterterrorism fantasy camp, enjoying kiddie art: even if we've banished the thought that we're acting like kids and pretending to be young, we definitely know we're consuming fantasies and fictions. But without knowing it, we also started showing signs of Kids "R" Us Syndrome in our mundane everyday lives, the ways we ate and dressed and worked and talked.

When Ben & Jerry's introduced chocolate-chip-cookie-dough ice cream in 1991, only the first couple of times did eating it feel like a specifically childish indulgence. Adults who wore Starter-brand jerseys and jackets bearing the names and numbers of sports stars did not think of themselves as youth impersonators. Among women a "sexy schoolgirl" mode became fashionable: knee socks, short kilts, too-small sweaters, backpacks. One professional I knew started wearing a Curious George backpack, and another bought clothes for herself out of her daughters' Hanna Andersson catalog. Why did grown-ups start wearing sweatsuits in public? Why did chinos and jeans and polo shirts replace suits and ties in the office? Because our mothers no longer dressed us. Who wouldn't rather stay in play clothes all day long? In the coolest new offices, especially in California, bosses and employees weren't just *dressing* like kids, they actually stocked the places with toys and games, Slinkys and Mr. Potato Heads, Foosball and Halo. It was in the 1990s that I was asked for the first time about a new job, "Are you having *fun*?" Which became a standard form of the American work-satisfaction question.

FINE, YOU SAY, BUT WHAT *real harm* did any of that do? Apart from generally making it seem more and more okay for make-believe to leach into real life.

Well, Kids "R" Us Syndrome did have one extreme and hideous and tragic victim in Michael Jackson. Just before he entered middle age, he built Neverland Ranch, his own private fantasy camp. He had a steam locomotive pulling fake-old cars on the same narrow-gauge track as Disneyland's (but longer), and the brick pseudo-Victorian train station he built was practically a copy of the one at the foot of Main Street USA. There were a roller coaster and bumper cars, a petting zoo, a tree house with a ship's wheel, a rope bridge, and a candy shop where all the candy was free. He filled the place with real children, of course, and when grown-ups told him not to sleep with them, he'd cry. He'd wet himself and pee on the floor. He lived at Neverland with his chimpanzee, who slept next to him in a crib, attended recording sessions with him, traveled with him.

Jackson's desperation to look younger—to look *fantastic*—also drove his mania for cosmetic surgery, of course. During one period in the 1990s, he was reportedly having an operation every couple of months—which, no coincidence, was when cosmetic surgery really took off. Cosmetic surgery is mostly meant to make people look younger—and if not younger, more like fantasy figures from movies and TV and magazines. Breast augmentation surgeries for women tripled in five years, and eventually one in twenty-five American women would have pouches of silicone or saline implanted in her breasts.*

At the same time, images of fantastical sexuality were suddenly, shockingly everywhere. Thanks to home video players, then cable TV and then the Internet, pornography became ubiquitous. How did that make adults more childlike? Well, for one thing, in the old days, porn was a hobby pursued most avidly by teenage boys. But the normalization of pornography also affected women's behavior. I don't think it's a coincidence that pubic hair removal in its most extreme forms became fashionable in America during the early years of the porn glut. I think porn effectively encouraged women to groom themselves more like women in the videos—and thereby to look preternaturally younger, even prepubescent. By 2000 the Brazilian wax was a central plot device on *Sex and the City*. A University of Texas sociologist studied every *Playboy* centerfold in the magazine's first half-century. As the 1990s began, two-thirds of those mainstream pornographic fantasy figures still had apparently full, natural pubic hair; a decade later fewer than 10 percent did, and a quarter were hairless. Soon a majority of American women would experiment with or commit to removing all their pubic hair. And cosmetic surgeons started performing labiaplasties to make women's vulvas tidier, flatter, more childlike. A surgeon in southern California invented the most extreme version, the complete removal of the labia minora—"the 'Barbie' . . . labiaplasty," his website brags.

Americans began saying and wishfully believing about round-numbered ages that *X is the new Y*—thirty the new twenty, forty the new thirty, fifty the new forty, and so on. Yet in so many ways they all became the new twenty, the new fifteen. *Age-appropriate* used to be a term strictly for judging whether a particular toy or book or movie or activity was suitable for a child. Its application was reversed, but joshingly, and only concerning the age of adults' sexual partners; otherwise, there's no such thing as an age-inappropriate cultural or lifestyle taste for grown-ups. Because we really came to believe we were kids of all ages.

---

* This estimate is according to *Five Thirty-Eight*. Apart from postmastectomy reconstructions, around a quarter-million American women now get breast implants each year, including several thousand girls eighteen and younger. An additional 149,000 women a year have their breasts surgically lifted, a procedure that has become seven times more common since the 1990s.

29

The Reagan Era and the Start of the Digital Age

WHEN ALL THE BABY BOOMERS WERE STILL CHILDREN, IN THE EARLY 1960S, the final legal end of white supremacy came into sight. And as a result, certain white Southerners started displaying Confederate symbols, and Southern states retrofitted state flags to include them. It was a historical rhyme of what had happened a century earlier, when losing the war led Southerners to glorify Dixie and the Lost Cause. After the Civil War, historians started calling the decades before 1861 the *antebellum* era—for many white Southerners, a word connoting fantasies of a perfect Old South. *Antebellum* is Latin for "before the war"—any war. After the wars of the 1960s—after Vietnam, "the Negro revolt," the countercultural explosion—plenty of Americans mythologized the 1940s and '50s and early '60s as their own late lamented antebellum era.

The Republican Party saw an opportunity to play to that self-pitying, self-glorifying, ass-kicking nostalgia and adopted its so-called Southern Strategy to turn white Southerners, who had always been Democrats, into Republicans. It began working immediately. The historian Paul Gaston, a Southerner, was astonishingly astute about the social and cultural shift occurring as he wrote *The New South Creed* in the late 1960s. Many of the old "regional distinctions receded" after the Civil War, as expected. But nobody had counted on that becoming a two-way process starting in the '60s—that white people in the North and West would start feeling like Southerners, anxious sore losers more conscious than ever of their race. It was, Gaston wrote, "the nationalization of the race problem"—the Black Power movement, black riots, and skyrocketing rates of urban crime, all making white Americans all over feel besieged, their comfortable ways of life threatened, their whiteness no longer such an all-access VIP pass. It was, he detected as soon as it began, "the infiltration into the total American experience of the elements of pathos, frustration, and imperfection that had long characterized the South."

Wallowing in nostalgia for a lost Golden Age ruined by meddling liberal outsiders from Washington and New York, previously a white Southern habit, became more and more of a white American habit. And so the Republicans' Southern Strategy could be nationalized as well. When he first ran for president, Ronald Reagan popularized the term *welfare queen*—a powerful caricature, based on a single criminal case, that exaggerated the pervasiveness of welfare fraud and spread the fiction that black people were the main recipients of government benefits. In Vietnam, the United States had also just lost a war, which gave non-Southerners a strong dose of Lost Cause bitterness for the first time.

The next time he ran, in 1980, Reagan's fiscal big idea, cutting tax rates to expand the economy and thereby increase tax revenues, was famously mocked by his main GOP opponent as "voodoo economics"—crazy wishfulness, magical thinking. A few months later, after Reagan invited him to be his vice-presidential candidate, George H. W. Bush disavowed his voodoo line. And as President, Reagan didn't stick strictly to the voodoo path. He did dramatically cut some tax rates, but he also increased others and closed lots of loopholes to keep deficits from growing even larger. The government did not shrink.

But while Reagan had sensibly tacked back toward reality, his true believers on the right maintained total belief in the voodoo. For them, the ultra-individualist liberation of the 1960s and '70s had generated a kind of fundamentalist religious faith in markets, and thus an absolute knee-jerk opposition to any attempts by government to make markets work better or more fairly, and to taxes in general. If the new hypercapitalism was working well for *you*, even if you had no fervent ideological faith in markets, what had previously come across as simple selfishness could now be cloaked in righteousness. "*Greed* is *good*," the fictional Gordon Gekko declared in 1987, but now real people insisted that their moneymaking lust and skill were not merely useful in the aggregate but made them virtuous individually. The year after *Wall Street* came out, Reagan was reelected in one of the biggest landslides in history.

Oh, Ronald Reagan, lovable, shrewd, twinkly, out-of-it, blithe, brilliant Ronald Reagan. The transmutation of presidential politics and governing into entertainment had started a generation earlier, in the 1960s, with John Kennedy. JFK was like a movie star and like a fictional character. He was young and dashing, witty and sexy. He'd been a war hero, and Hollywood made a movie about those heroics, *PT 109*, while he was president, a production on which he gave notes. His glamorous patrician wife was even younger, only thirty-one when she became First Lady, and one of his girlfriends was a real movie star, Marilyn Monroe, the ultimate sexual fantasy figure. But that projection of youth and extreme vitality was a fiction, a lie, a fantasy presented to the public: he was secretly very ill with osteoporosis and Addison's disease, among others, and took painkillers, antianxiety drugs, sleeping pills, and stimulants.

As JFK was about to be elected, Norman Mailer wrote that "America's politics would now be also America's favorite movie, America's first soap opera, America's best-seller." Up until Kennedy, the wall between government and show business had been thick. His father had owned a movie studio, and not only did Jack pal around with Hollywood people, he agreed to go on stage at Madison Square Garden to receive the supersalacious "Happy Birthday, Mr. President" serenade from his mistress Marilyn. "In America," the great radio host Jean Shepherd said then about Kennedy, "everything becomes show business."

His murder was like the tragic, implausible denouement of a novel or movie—and his widow immediately recast his forty-six-month presidency as fiction, Camelot, after the recent Broadway musical about magical young King Arthur. For a few years, Kennedy had used television and the rest of the fantasy-industrial complex as a telegenic Cary Grant manqué; for a few posthumous days, it used him as the star of the most compelling television event ever.

After JFK, president-as-performer became more explicit. In the 1980s, as America kept turning the dial up toward full Fantasyland, we were ready for Reagan as we wouldn't have been earlier. "For Ronald Reagan," said Pat Buchanan, who served as his White House communications director, "the world of legend and myth is a real world. He visits it regularly, and he's a happy man there." Buchanan meant this as praise.

If Reagan's story were fiction, it would seem absurdly pat and over-determined, the irony too heavy-headed. Out of college during the Depression, he went straight to work for the new fantasy-industrial complex. In a Des Moines radio studio, he regularly pretended he was at Wrigley Field in Chicago, performing fake play-by-play broadcasts of Cubs games based on real-time wire-service descriptions. He visited Hollywood and got his first movie role—playing a radio announcer. During World War II, he was an officer in the army—serving in the First Motion Picture Unit, stationed in Burbank and Culver City, where he starred in *This Is the Army*, a movie in which he played a corporal who stages a piece of musical theater called *This Is the Army*.

After a so-so career playing fictional characters in movies, he became a superstar playing a politician in real life and on the TV news, first as governor of California. His winning presidential campaign in 1980 had policy specifics that jibed with his misty vision of a simpler, happier, more patriotic old-fashioned America—which in turn jibed with the simultaneous shift in Hollywood and architecture and elsewhere in the culture toward old-timey forms and subjects. As a vacationing president, he wore a cowboy hat and rode a horse at his ranch in southern California. He and his team concocted a brilliant fantasy narrative in which he was the convincing leading character. More than any previous presidential handlers, they staged and crafted his presidential performances specifically to make for entertaining television.

Reagan as fantasist had its cute side, in particular the multiple instances of movies blending into real life, such as his comment about the large fraction of the Pentagon's budget that went for "wardrobe." Then there was the story of American grit he repeatedly told about a World War II bomber crew, their B-17 going down, the terrified gunner unable to eject, his superior officer reassuring him, "Never mind, son, we'll ride it down together." The exchange did take place during World War II, but only in a movie called *Wing and a Prayer*, in which the star says to the other actor, "Take it easy, we'll take this ride together." Several times as president, once in a conversation with the Israeli prime minister, he told of being deployed to Europe at the end of the war to film concentration camps; it never happened.

In warning Congress not to enact a tax increase, he quoted Clint Eastwood's recent *Dirty Harry* line, "Go ahead—make my day." A few months later the United States and Lebanon negotiated the release of airline passengers hijacked and held hostage by Hezbollah. "Boy," President Reagan said, "I saw *Rambo* last night"—*Rambo: First Blood Part II*—and "now I know what to do next time this happens." *Star Wars,* the recent and ultimate Hollywood blockbuster, was both unprecedented and old-fashioned—like Reagan!— and he repeatedly used it. In the screen-crawl text of the first movie, the villains are described as "the evil Galactic Empire." Just before *Return of the Jedi* came out, President Reagan delivered a speech in which he referred to the Soviet Union as the "evil empire."* After he announced the development of technology to shoot down Soviet nuclear missiles, that not-quite-real technology became known as Star Wars, and Reagan said of it that "the Force is with us."

Nancy Reagan was also a former actor, and as First Lady she played "Nancy Reagan" both on the sitcom *Diff'rent Strokes* and on the prime-time soap opera *Dynasty.* It had always seemed as if she, ten years his junior, was the brains of the operation, coolly, anxiously, thoroughly reality-based. But then it turned out she employed an astrologer to schedule Reagan's important trips and meetings. "She feels there's nothing wrong in talking to her," Mrs. Reagan's spokesperson said of the astrologer. According to the astrologer, "Air Force One didn't take off without permission. [Nancy] set the time for summit meetings with Mikhail Gorbachev, presidential debates with Carter and Mondale . . . the timing of all the President's trips abroad, of his press conferences, his State of the Union addresses." "Good God," George H. W. Bush said when he learned of this operational voodoo near the end of his vice-presidency, "I had no idea."

Not so cute was a president of the United States expecting apocalyptic biblical prophecies to be fulfilled soon. Reagan was never much of a churchgoer, but he'd been enthusiastically connecting the Christian end-of-days dots at least since the late 1960s. "Apparently never in history," he'd said in 1968, "have so many of the prophecies come true in such a relatively short time." This was a consistent line before he ran for president—"We may be the generation that sees Armageddon," he said repeatedly. When Muammar Gaddafi took over Libya in the 1970s, Reagan saw it as "a sign that the day of Armageddon isn't far off. For the first time ever, everything is falling into

---

* Reagan delivered his "evil empire" speech in Orlando to the National Association of Evangelicals, an hour after he had been at Disney World. "I just watched a program— I don't know just what to call it—a show, a pageant . . . at one point in the movie Mark Twain, speaking of America, says, 'We soared into the twentieth century on the wings of invention and the winds of change.'" He'd seen Disney's *The American Adventure,* featuring an animatronic Mark Twain saying things Mark Twain never said.

place for the battle of Armageddon and the second coming of Christ. It can't be long now. Ezekiel says that fire and brimstone will be rained upon the enemies of God's people. That must mean that they'll be destroyed by nuclear weapons. They exist now, and they never did in the past."

He kept up the end-time chatter in the White House. A decade earlier such talk from a president would've been a shocking national embarrassment, but no longer.

"You know," President Reagan said in a conversation about the Middle East with the head of AIPAC, the main American pro-Israel lobbying group, "I turn back to your ancient prophets in the Old Testament and the signs of foretelling Armageddon, and I find myself wondering if—if we're the generation that is going to see that come about. I don't know if you've noted any of these prophecies lately, but believe me, they certainly describe the times we're going through."

At the final presidential debate in 1984, if the rest of us hadn't noticed before, there he went again. A moderator asked if it was true he "believe[d], deep down, that we are heading for some kind of biblical Armageddon." *Yessir.* Based on "some philosophical discussions with people who are interested in the same things," he did indeed take seriously "the prophecies down through the years, the biblical prophecies of what would portend the coming of Armageddon, and so forth, and the fact that a number of theologians for the last decade or more have believed that this was true, that the prophecies are coming together that portend that."

For Americans inclined to believe that prophecies definitely *were* coming together that portended the coming of Armageddon and so forth, the cheerful president of the United States had just confirmed it, as he would again and again. In the election two weeks later he won forty-nine states.

Beyond the mainstreaming of problematically batty beliefs, presidential politics was merging even more with the fantasy-industrial complex. Just as Bill Clinton wrapped up the Democratic nomination in 1992, he came on stage on a late-night talk show wearing Ray-Ban Wayfarers to play "Heartbreak Hotel" on sax. It was a memorable moment in the evolution of presidential campaigns into auditions for entertainer-in-chief, and on MTV two years later, he laid down the next milestone. Answering questions from an audience of young people, the president of the United States told a seventeen-year-old girl that he wore "usually briefs" rather than boxer shorts.

In early 1998, as soon as we learned that Clinton had been fellated by an intern around the Oval Office, his popularity *spiked,* according to the polls. Which was baffling only to those who still thought of politics as an autonomous realm, existing apart from entertainment. American politics happened on television; it was a TV series, a reality show just before TV became glutted with reality shows. A titillating new story line that goosed the ratings of an existing series was an established scripted-TV gimmick. The audience had started getting bored with *The Clinton Administration,* but the Monica Lewinsky subplot, including its cover-up, got people interested again. Fox News and MSNBC were both new start-ups, and because politics had become a low-production-value subgenre of show business, it was engaging only when it was entertaining. When serious journalists started asking Clinton about having extramarital sex with an intern, the public was not so much alarmed as amazed and thrilled.

Just before the Clintons arrived in Washington, the right had managed to do away with the federal Fairness Doctrine, which had been enacted to keep radio and TV shows from being ideologically one-sided. Until then, big-time conservative opinion media had consisted of two magazines, William F. Buckley's biweekly *National Review* and the monthly *American Spectator,* both with small circulations. But absent a Fairness Doctrine, Rush Limbaugh's national right-wing radio show, launched in 1988, was free to thrive, and others promptly appeared, followed at the end of Clinton's first term by Fox News.

Should the old federal broadcast rules have been abolished? Maybe, maybe not, but in any case, cable TV was making them iffy and the Internet was just about to start rendering them moot. In any case, when the Washington gatekeepers decided to get rid of that regulatory gate, it was a pivotal moment, practically and symbolically. For most of the twentieth century, national news media had felt obliged to pursue and present some rough approximation of *the* truth rather than to promote *a* truth, let alone fictions.

With the elimination of the Fairness Doctrine, a new American laissez-faire had been officially declared. If lots more incorrect and preposterous assertions circulated in our most massive mass media, that was a price of freedom. If splenetic commentators could now, as never before, keep believers perpetually riled up and feeling the excitement of being in a mob, so be it.

Rush Limbaugh, raised by a family of politically well-connected lawyers in southern Missouri, entered show business early. From his teens through his twenties, he was the radio deejay Rusty Sharpe, then the radio deejay Jeff Christie before he moved to talk radio using his real name. His virtuosic three hours of daily talk started bringing a sociopolitical alternate reality to a huge national audience. Instead of relying only on a magazine or a newsletter every so often to confirm your gnarly view of the world, now you had nationally broadcast talk radio drilling it in for hours every day.

As Limbaugh's radio show took off, in 1992 the television producer Roger Ailes created a syndicated TV show around him. The following year, just after Ailes became president of CNBC, I was reporting a *Time* cover story about talk radio, including Limbaugh. I had not yet had contact with either man when Ailes phoned me out of the blue to yell at me about the article that didn't yet exist. "How would you like it if I sent a CNBC camera crew to follow your kids home from school?" he said. My daughters were six and four. "Wow," I replied, "I'm sure Jack Welch"—the CEO of GE, which then owned NBC—"would be interested to hear that his new news executive is planning to stalk a journalist's children." I thought I could hear a gasp. "Are you *threatening* me?" Ailes shouted down the line. Two years later, when NBC News hired someone else to create and launch its cable channel, Ailes went off and created Fox News for Rupert Murdoch, and ran it until just before he died in 2017.

Fox News brought the Limbaughvian talk-radio version of the world to national TV, but it mingled straighter news with the news-ish commentary. It permitted viewers an unending and immersive propaganda experience of a kind that had never existed before. The new channel's trademarked slogan was a kind of postmodern right-wing inside joke: since the rest of the national news media *posing* as objective were unfair and imbalanced in favor of liberals, Fox News would be "Fair and Balanced." As the new right-wing multimedia complex was establishing itself, on radio and now on TV, in the White House were a pair of glamorous Hollywood-connected liberal yuppies out of Yale—perfect villainous foils, as political infotainment entered its WWF era.

For Americans, this was another new condition. Modern electronic mass media had been a defining piece of the twentieth-century experience that served an important democratic function—presenting Americans with a shared set of facts. Now those news organs, on TV and radio, were enabling a reversion to the narrower, factional, partisan discourse that had been normal in America's earlier centuries. The new and newly unregulated technologies allowed us, in a sense, to travel backward in time.

AND THE INTERNET. IN THE 1980s, before the Web, Usenet was a kind of cross between email and social media. In 1994 the first spam was sent, visible to everyone on Usenet: "Global Alert for All: Jesus is Coming Soon." Over the next year or two, the masses learned of the World Wide Web. The exponential rise of Fantasyland and all its dominions now had its perfect infrastructure.

It's hard to overstate the flabbergasting speed and magnitude of the change. In the early 1990s, when the Internet was still an obscure geek thing, fewer than 2 percent of Americans used it; by 2002, less than a decade later, most Americans were online. After the 1960s and '70s happened as they happened, it may be that America's long-standing dynamic balance—between thinking and magical thinking, reason and wishfulness, reality and fiction, sanity and lunacy—was broken for good. But once the Internet came along, we were definitely on a superhighway to a certain destination with no likely looking exits.

Before the Web, cockamamie ideas and outright falsehoods could not spread nearly as fast or widely, so it was much easier for reason and reasonableness to prevail. Before the Web, institutionalizing any one alternate reality required the long, hard work of hundreds of full-time militants—the way America's fundamentalist Christians spent decades setting up their own colleges and associations and magazines and radio stations. In the digital age, every tribe and fiefdom and principality and region of Fantasyland—every screwball with a computer and a telecom connection—suddenly had an unprecedented way to instruct and rile up and mobilize believers, and to recruit more.

Yes, we all know all about the extraordinary virtues and benefits of digital communication. You and I now have astounding access to information and ideas and cultural artifacts and people. In every pocket there is now a library, a phonograph, a radio, a movie theater, and a television, as well as a post office, a printing press, a telegraph, a still and video camera, a recording studio, a navigation system, and a radio and TV station. It is advanced technology indistinguishable from magic.

I'm not sure there ever would have been any effective or acceptable way to permit all the Internet's good parts and minimize the bad ones. By government fiat? By some spontaneous mass reactivation of our recessive American gene for restraint and moderation, like the Danes' *jantelov*? We're a populist democracy of individualists, so too much democracy and individualism were always going to be the directions in which we finally erred.

In any case, the way Internet searching was designed to operate in the 1990s—that is, the way information and belief now flow, rise and fall—is democratic in the extreme. On the Internet, the prominence granted to any factual assertion or belief or theory depends entirely on the preferences of billions of individual searchers. Each click on a link, trillions a year, is effectively a vote pushing *that* version of the truth toward the top of the pile of results, because every link to a page increases that page's prominence.

Exciting falsehoods tend to do well in the perpetual referenda and become self-validating. A search for almost any "alternative" theory or belief generates many more links to true believers' pages and sites than to legitimate or skeptical ones, and those tend to dominate the first few pages of results. For instance, beginning in the 1990s, conspiracists decided contrails, the skinny clouds of water vapor that form around jet-engine exhaust, are exotic chemicals, part of a secret government scheme to test weapons or poison citizens or mitigate climate change—and renamed them *chemtrails*. When I googled "chemtrails proof," the first page had nine links, the first seven of those linking to validations of the nonexistent conspiracy. When I searched for "government extraterrestrial cover up," in the first three pages of results, only one link *didn't* lead to an article endorsing a conspiracy theory. After a Cornell psychologist's widely reported experiment purported to show that people can telepathically know the future, a team of psychologists at the University of Pennsylvania and three other universities tried replicating it seven times—and found no evidence supporting precognition. When I googled the two papers, "Feeling the Future" and "Correcting the Past," the dubious and more exciting first one had seven times as many search results.

Before the Web, it really wasn't easy to find or stumble across false or crazy information that was convincingly passing itself off as true. Post-Web, however, as the Syracuse University professor Michael Barkun wrote in 2003 in *The Culture of Conspiracy,* "such subject-specific areas as crank science, conspiracist politics, and occultism are not isolated from one another," but "rather, they are interconnected. Someone seeking information on UFOs, for example, can quickly find material on antigravity, free energy, Atlantis studies, alternative cancer cures, and conspiracy.

> The consequence of such mingling is that an individual who enters the communications system pursuing one interest soon becomes aware of stigmatized material on a broad range of subjects. As a result, those who come across one form of stigmatized knowledge will learn of others, in connections that imply that stigmatized knowledge is a unified domain, an alternative worldview, rather than a collection of unrelated ideas.

*   *   *

THE APPARENTLY UNRELATED IDEAS ARE related by their exciting-secrets-revealed extremism, over the air and online, in paranormal and New Age and Christian and right-wing and left-wing political permutations. They form tactical alliances, interbreed, and hybridize. One thing leads to another. Ways of thinking correlate and cluster. Believing in one type of fantasy tends to lead to believing in others. The major general who commanded the army's paranormal R&D unit starting in the late 1970s—personally attempting to levitate, to dematerialize, to pass through walls, and to mentally disperse clouds—later became a 9/11 truther who's certain that hijacked planes didn't bring down the towers or hit the Pentagon. And it's not only a matter of the patently ridiculous coexisting with the patently ridiculous. Seventy percent of the "spiritual" third of U.S. college students, for instance, also believe the untrue claim that "genetically modified food is dangerous to our health," whereas among the "secular" third of college students, the majority know that GMO foods are safe to eat.*

Academic research shows that religious belief leads people to think that almost nothing happens accidentally or randomly: as the authors of some recent cognitive science studies at Yale put it, "individuals' explicit religious and paranormal beliefs" are the main drivers of their exceptional "perception of purpose in life events," their tendency "to view the world in terms of agency, purpose, and design." Americans have believed for centuries that the country was inspired and guided by an invisible, omniscient, omnipotent planner and that He and His fellow beings from beyond are perpetually observing and manipulating us. That native religiosity has led since the 1960s both to our special interest in extraterrestrials and to a Third Worldly tendency to believe in conspiracies.

Those Yale researchers also found that believers in fate, religious and otherwise, include a large subset of "highly paranoid people" who "obsess over other people's hidden motives." In a paper called "Conspiracy Theories and the Paranoid Style(s) of Mass Opinion," based on years of survey research, two political scientists at the University of Chicago have confirmed this special American connection. "The likelihood of supporting conspiracy theories is strongly predicted," they concluded, by two key pieces of our national character that derive from our particular Christian culture: "a propensity to attribute the source of unexplained or extraordinary events to unseen, intentional forces" and a weakness for "melodramatic narratives as explanations for prominent events, particularly those that interpret history relative to

* 2013 Trinity College American Religious Identification Survey.

universal struggles between good and evil." In fact, they found the single strongest driver of conspiracy belief to be belief in end-time prophecies. Belief in things such as ghosts and psychic healing also "significantly predicted belief in five specific conspiracy theories," according to the Chicago research. In other words, supernatural belief is the great American gateway to conspiracy belief.

Whether an individual's conspiracism exists alongside religious faith, psychologically they're similar: a conspiracy theory can be revised and refined and further confirmed, but it probably can't ever be disproved to a true believer's satisfaction. The final conspiratorial nightmare crackdown is always right around the corner but never quite comes—as with the perpetually fast-approaching end-time. Like Christians certain both that evolution is a phony theory and that God created people a few thousand years ago, conspiracists are simultaneously credulous (about impossible plots) and incredulous (about the confusing, dull gray truth). Conspiracists often deride arguments against their theories as disinformation cooked up by the conspirators—the way some Christians consider evolutionary explanations to be the work of the devil.

Researchers and experimenters have repeatedly demonstrated this pinball effect, in which fantastical beliefs lead to other, disparate fantastical beliefs. Once people decide a particular theory is true, they're apt to be open to another and another and another. In their 2013 paper on conspiracy believers, a team of German social psychologists summarized the research. "In fact," they found,

> this tendency even extends to beliefs in mutually contradictory conspiracy theories, and to beliefs in fully fictitious conspiracy theories. Thus, those who believe that Princess Diana faked her own death are also more likely to believe that she was murdered; those who believe . . . that John F. Kennedy fell victim to an organized conspiracy . . . are more likely to believe that there was a conspiracy behind the success of the Red Bull energy drink—a conspiracy theory that was purposely developed for a social psychology study.

A MAIN ARGUMENT OF THIS book concerns how so many parts of American life have morphed into forms of entertainment. From 1980 to the end of the century, that tendency reached a tipping point in politics and the political discourse. First a Hollywood celebrity became a beloved president by epitomizing and encouraging the blur between fiction and reality. Then talk radio and TV news turned into forms of politicized show business. And finally the Internet came along, making false beliefs both more real-seeming and more contagious, creating a kind of fantasy cascade in which millions of bedoozled Americans surfed and swam. Why did Senator Daniel Patrick Moynihan begin remarking frequently during the 1980s and '90s that people were entitled to their own opinions but not to their own facts? Because until then, it hadn't seemed like a serious problem in America.

With the Internet, our marketplace of ideas became exponentially bigger and freer than ever, it's true. Thomas Jefferson said he'd "rather be exposed to the inconveniences attending too much liberty than those attending too small a degree of it"—and it would all be okay because in the new United States "reason is left free to combat" every sort of "error of opinion." However, I'm inclined to think if he and our other democratic forefathers returned, they would see the present state of affairs as too much of a good thing. Reason remains free to combat unreason, but the Internet entitles and equips all the proponents of unreason and error to a previously unimaginable degree. Particularly for a people with our history and propensities, the downside—this proliferation and reinforcement of nutty ideas and false beliefs, this assembling of communities of the utterly deluded, this construction of parallel universes that look and feel perfectly real, the viral appeal of the untrue—seems at least as profound as the upside.

30

American Religion from the Turn of the Millennium

WHEN I WAS GROWING UP IN THE 1960S, MOST OF MY FRIENDS WERE CHRIS-
tian churchgoers, and all of those churchgoers were Catholics or mainline
Protestants—Episcopalians, Lutherans, Presbyterians, Methodists, Congregationalists. I'd never heard of anybody being "born again," and I'd never met
a Jehovah's Witness or Seventh-day Adventist. Until my brother married a girl
who'd been raised Pentecostal, I didn't even know that word.

The memberships of all the tried-and-true denominations were then at
their peak. By the 1970s, they were all shrinking and never stopped. Mainline churches are a lot like the nightly network news shows. The audiences
for both peaked at the same time and for analogous reasons have declined
since by around half. Episcopalians and Methodists and the others suddenly
seemed too sober and bland and elitist, especially given all the exciting alternatives: the new charismatic and fundamentalist churches were to American
Christianity as sensationalist two-hour local shows and talk radio and Fox
were to network news. Before long mainline Protestants would be outnumbered two or three to one by those who, as Tom Wolfe put it in the 1970s,

want "a little *Hallelujah! . . . Praise God! . . .* ululation, visions, holy rolling, and other nonrational, even antirational, practices."

The 1980s and '90s continued to be a boom time for all those alt-sects and denominations—the older ones like Southern Baptists and Assemblies of God, the ones invented in the 1960s and '70s like Calvary and Vineyard, and the latest freebooting start-ups. So many such churches had such enormous congregations we coined a word, *megachurch,* to describe them, and their number increased at least tenfold during the two decades after 1990. Holy-roller practices and beliefs, speaking in tongues and faith healing and the rest, went viral within established evangelical denominations. Most of the Protestant churches founded since the 1960s are growing; three-fourths of the ones founded before 1900 are not.

The newfangled Christianities rode the wave of newfangled entertainment technology. Cable television's rollout meant that by the mid-1980s, 40 percent of Americans were regularly watching religious shows—and *religious show* now essentially meant show-boating evangelical, fundamentalist, Pentecostal, and charismatic preachers. Robertson's *The 700 Club* on his CBN had an audience of seven million, three times as large as those of the top-rated prime-time Fox News shows today. CBN and the skeevier Trinity Broadcasting Network remain the largest, both serving as platforms for multiplying nondenominational churches and sects, many of which *exist only* electronically, virtually.

So how religious are we now, and how are we religious?

Much has been made of the increase in the fraction of people who aren't sure they believe in God or don't attend church. One in six Americans say their religion consists of "nothing in particular." The Pew Research Center lumps those people in with agnostics and atheists, but that's misleading. "Nothing in particular" isn't a proxy for disbelief. A large majority of them believe in God, and a plurality are "absolutely certain."

Compared to a decade ago, it's true, almost twice as many Americans say they don't believe in God. But consider the actual numbers: the total of agnostics and atheists has gone from extremely tiny (4 percent in 2007) to very tiny (7 percent in 2014). Those are percentages one otherwise finds in less-developed countries. If that is evidence for U.S. secularization, we are now just about as secular as, oh, Turkey.

In America, belief in the unreal seems to be very fungible. Individuals don't so much abandon religious fantasy in favor of reason as find *different* fantasies that better suit their particular excitement and credulity quotients—sometimes joining new churches, sometimes affiliating with amorphous movements, sometimes constructing bespoke packages of spiritual and worldly make-believe. People who *reject* institutional theologies are *more* likely to believe in New Age enchantments. Almost a third of the unaffiliated believe in "spiritual energy in physical things such as . . . crystals" or that they've communicated with the dead, according to Pew. Moreover, "religious and mystical experiences are more common today among those who are un-affiliated with any particular religion than they were in the 1960s among the public as a whole."

Women are much more likely than men to say they're "spiritual," whereas two-thirds of people who call themselves agnostic or atheist are men. So male seculars go elsewhere to satisfy their need to believe in the untrue—for in-stance, men constitute large majorities of devoted believers in nonexistent conspiracies. In America there are plenty of brands to satisfy everyone, of fantasy as with everything else. If you aren't crazy about Coke, there's always Pepsi; if not Coca-Cola Zero, then Pepsi Perfect or Pepsi Jazz Strawberries & Cream.

But for the moment we're talking about Coca-Cola Classic religion— God. And Americans remain exceptional. If you include belief in a diffuse "universal spirit" as belief in God, at least nine in ten of us are believers. Moreover, 80 percent of Americans say they *never doubt* the existence of God. When we set aside the iffier theists—the ones who say they believe but admit to doubts and the ones who think of God as "an impersonal force"— we're left with about half of us "absolutely certain" God exists as "a person with whom people can have a relationship." That's presumably the same half who say they often "receive a definite answer to a specific prayer request," the half who are also "absolutely certain" that Heaven exists and who "completely agree" that "miracles still occur today as in ancient times."

Sure, we're multicultural. However, those of us who identify with a spe-cific religious tradition but don't worship Jesus—American Jews, Buddhists, Hindus, Muslims, and others combined—make up less than 6 percent of the population.

We're still more than 70 percent Christian, and around 70 percent of those are Protestant.* People tend to talk about Protestants in a binary way, as belonging to either evangelical or mainline churches, with "historically black churches" off to the side. Which is okay if you're interested in the

---

* The data in the previous seven paragraphs are from the 2014 Religious Landscape Study by the Pew Forum on Religion & Public Life, based on interviews with thirty-five thousand Americans.

political implications of religious affiliation. But to get at the particulars of religion qua religion, that's too oversimplified. Instead, think of American Protestantism as a Venn diagram of four highly overlapping blobs— evangelical, fundamentalist, charismatic, and mainline.

Not very many *call* themselves fundamentalist anymore. Ever since antimodern Christians coined the term a century ago, *fundamentalist* has carried some taint. At midcentury, canny mass-marketers like Billy Graham rebranded by reviving the old term *evangelical*. Today the great majority of Protestants identify as evangelicals, the way all Americans call themselves middle class. Conservative evangelicals (né fundamentalists) believe that God created everything at once around 4000 B.C.E. and that Roman Catholics are going to Hell, whereas other evangelicals concede that He probably created Earth billions of years ago and that non-Protestant Christians might get to Heaven. As with America's denominational disputes from the beginning, the tendencies differ at least as much by temperament as by belief. "A fundamentalist," the religious historian George Marsden famously said, "is an evangelical who is angry about something."

Many clergy in these churches actually call themselves "pastorpreneurs."* It reminds me of the craft beer sector. There are all the different styles (IPA, brown ale, imperial stout, a dozen more) and breweries that run the gamut from thousands to millions of barrels per year. But the various nondenominational churches, like craft brewers, all emphatically push artisanal brand values—robust, authentic, anticorporate—no matter how similar they are or how big they get. Calvary Chapel and the Vineyard churches are the Sierra Nevada and Sam Adams. Over the last few decades beliefs among the biggest legacy denominations, Southern Baptists and United Methodists, have become more fundamentalist—the way Anheuser-Busch InBev and SABMiller now sell beers resembling those of the brewpubs and regional breweries.

The way *evangelical* replaced and subsumed *fundamentalist, charismatic* did the same for *Pentecostal*. Pentecostals are now just one old-school type of charismatic. The new coinage has made ecstatic outbursts and miraculous stunts—spontaneous shouting, shaking, and crying, hearing directly from God, channeling the Holy Spirit to get rich or cure illness or exorcise demons or speak in tongues—acceptable to Christians for whom Pentecostal has down-market white-yokel or black-ghetto connotations. Pentecostals are

---

* Anne Hutchinson, the Puritan whom the Puritans exiled because she said she received revelations directly from God and channeled the Holy Spirit, was America's original charismatic Christian pastorpreneur.

more or less fundamentalist charismatics who *insist* on speaking in tongues; for other charismatics, tongues are just one way to channel the Holy Spirit. Charismatic Christianity, both the term and the looser doctrines, gave respectable people permission to feast at the whole buffet of magical and miraculous signs and wonders. Especially respectable white people. Seven of the fifteen largest Protestant denominations are African-American, and *two-thirds* of black Protestants are Pentecostals or other charismatics who believe that tongues and faith healing are real.* Indeed, the black churches pretty much invented "charismatic" Christianity before that term existed.

UNTIL FAIRLY RECENTLY, MANY FUNDAMENTALIST Christians maintained a real antipathy toward the heretical Mormons. It subsided, I think, not exactly out of an outpouring of ecumenical fellowship but rather because Protestants' own beliefs and practices grew to be so peculiar that the Mormons' peculiarity became almost irrelevant. Indeed, in many ways evangelicals have been Mormonized during the last half-century without realizing it. Mormons were way ahead of Protestants in their rejection of evolution, their logistical preparations for the end-time, and their conviction that Jesus and the angels directly intervene in daily life. Theological deviancy was defined down.

But leaving the Protestant half of us aside (and Mormons and Greek Orthodox), what about the other two organized religions with which more than 1 percent of Americans identify? How much wild belief and practice exists among Roman Catholics and Jews?†

A fifth of Americans call themselves Catholic. The Roman Catholic Church is in every meaningful way mainline, with its stable hierarchy that shapes and enforces doctrine and practice. In this sense, America has been a four-hundred-year-long natural experiment testing how religion develops with and without a powerful central organization. In other words, a big reason American Catholics are more reality-based than Protestants is because tenured grown-ups, from the Vatican on down, have consistently been in command, tamping down and pinching off undesirable offshoots.

Only a quarter of American Catholics consider the Bible the actual word

---

* 2008 Barna Group survey.

† I don't discuss Islamic beliefs extensively in this book. But by the most basic metrics of religiosity and belief in the supernatural—certainty of the supreme being's existence, literalism concerning Holy Scripture, and so on—American Muslims are very much like evangelical Christians.

of God—as opposed to the half of Protestants who do.* In fact, Catholics have been fairly reasonable biblical interpreters from the beginning, before modern science even posed any problems, and they've stuck with it. Sixteen hundred years ago Saint Augustine instructed, basically, *Don't be stupid.* "Shall we say, then," he wrote about Genesis, "there was such a sense of hearing in that formless and shapeless creation, whatever it was, to which God thus uttered a sound when He said, 'Let there be light'? Let such absurdities have no place in our thoughts." In 1996 the conservative pope came out strongly in favor of the scientific consensus about how life works and humans came to be. "Evolution," John Paul II declared, given the "discoveries in different scholarly disciplines," is "more than an hypothesis." And as Pope Francis said in 2014, "When we read about creation in Genesis, we run the risk of imagining God was a magician with a magic wand able to do everything. But that is not so."†

There is the official Catholic doctrine about Communion, that the "bread and wine that are the Body and Blood of Christ are not merely symbols" but "truly are the Body and Blood of Christ." It's the single way in which Catholicism is more outlandishly literal than the doctrine of most American Protestants. However, 37 percent of practicing, mass-attending American Catholics admit they don't actually believe it.‡

Rationality and old-school sobriety, however, aren't selling. The church's only real growth sector is charismatic Catholicism. "In the early years of the Charismatic Renewal," Pope Francis told a gathering of them, "I did not love the charismatics: and I used to say of them 'they look like a samba school.' I did not agree with their way of praying and the many new things that were happening." But now? Go for it! "I began to understand the good that Renewal does for the Church."

His American clergy condone charismatic Catholicism today the way missionaries in the Americas centuries ago condoned bits of paganism their native converts incorporated into worship. More than a third of U.S. Catholics, including most Hispanic Catholics, are now charismatics. But only 12 percent of non-Hispanic white American Catholics are charismatics; like the

* 2014 General Social Survey.
† On the other hand, Catholics still defend their persecution of Galileo in the 1600s for saying the Earth circles the sun. "His problem arose," the quasi-official American site *Catholic Answers* explains, "when he stopped proposing it as a scientific theory and began proclaiming it as truth."
‡ 2011 *National Catholic Reporter* survey.

very white Southern Baptists and mainline Protestants, they are not yet surrendering en masse to this riptide.

As for American Jews—do I even need to stipulate how religiously reasonable they are? How little they fuss over the question of Heaven (although the fraction who believe in an afterlife has doubled since the 1970s), how few of them think a messiah is coming (although the small number who do has grown)? American Jews' great exception to assimilation, bless them, has been the national weakness for the supernatural. It's not only a matter of more education tending to make Jews more rational, although that correlation is striking: only one or two in ten Christian evangelicals, fundamentalists, and charismatics graduated college, versus six in ten Jews. An overwhelming majority of Protestants are fundamentalist, evangelical, or charismatic; maybe a sixth of Jews are Orthodox, ultra-Orthodox, or associated with the little New Age-y branch called Renewalist. American Judaism has not gone nuts.

31

Our Wilder Christianities: Belief and Practice

By *wild,* I don't mean, say, believing in an afterlife. Nearly all American Christians believe that Heaven (85 percent) and Hell (70 percent) are actual places. Rather, I'm focused more on the solid majority of Protestants, at least a quarter of Americans, who are sure "the Bible is the actual word of God . . . to be taken literally, word for word." As well as the larger number of Christians, more than a third of all Americans, who believe that God regularly grants them and their fellow charismatics magical powers—to speak in tongues, heal the sick, cast out demons, and so on.* I think it's important to understand the particulars of these extraordinary beliefs and practices and to realize just how widely and deeply they've now become embedded in American culture. I also find them fascinating.

*   *   *

* 2014 Pew survey and NORC General Social Survey.

IT WAS NEWSWORTHY IN THE 1960s when Billy Graham came out with a millennial prophecy, announcing like a Magic 8 Ball that "the signs indicate" "that these are the last days spoken of in the Scriptures," that Armageddon and Jesus's return were "at hand." By the 1980s, however, when President Reagan and members of his administration repeatedly promoted biblical predictions of Armageddon, it really didn't cause a big ruckus. So suddenly the evangelical and fundamentalist clergy who'd been pushing that line no longer seemed so wingnutty. Graham was free at last to put end-time beliefs front and center: his 1984 bestseller was called *Approaching Hoofbeats: Horsemen of the Apocalypse*.

This was a historic shift in American culture. After declining and plateauing since the early 1800s, references in books to *apocalypse* and *tribulation* and *Second Coming* rose significantly. In one generation, belief in an imminent apocalypse and the near-term return of Jesus became unembarrassed articles of faith for a large fraction of Americans. Every new war and rumor of war in Israel and the Middle East excited Christian zealots. They avidly consumed news reports about the places Jesus had lived and performed miracles and died, from which the Jews had been exiled and now returned, where all three of the big religions had armies arrayed. The prophecies were being fulfilled! Each outbreak of combat looked to a lot of American Christians like a foreshock or temblor leading up to the big one, the final showdown, Armageddon—an actual place, by the way, an hour's drive from Tel Aviv.

By 1990, there was a whole literature to explain and reinforce this current-events alternate reality, books like *The Last Days Handbook* and *The Coming Antichrist*. In 1990 and 1991, after Iraq invaded Kuwait, the evangelical theologian who'd run the Dallas Theological Seminary, considered a leading expert on the end-time and the rapture, was beside himself. The (Christian) United States was prepared to drive Iraq out! The (Muslim) Iraqis fired missiles on the Jews in Israel! He rushed out a new edition of his book *Armageddon, Oil, and the Middle East Crisis*. "I have never seen this kind of interest in prophecy before," he said, "and I've been at it a long time."

At the turn of the millennium, the great vehicles for popularizing Christian end-time prophecies, however, were works of *fiction* depicting characters in the near future—a future based on biblical fictions that a large fraction of Americans believed to be nonfiction. After the Gulf War, *Left Behind: A Novel of the Earth's Last Days* came out, about American Christians being raptured off the planet before the worst tribulations, leaving behind Christ deniers (and some Christians) to experience Hell on Earth and then Hell it-self. Its coauthor and front man was Tim LaHaye, a Bob Jones University graduate, Southern Baptist minister, cofounder of the Institute for Creation Research, and adviser to Jerry Falwell. A dozen sequels and prequels followed over the next twelve years, together with a YA series called *Left Behind: The Kids.* They sold seventy-five million copies.*

Protestants' millennial beliefs come in a variety of slightly different ver-sions. They disagree about timing and other details, but they all agree on the basic plot and characters. It's a drama that adheres to Hollywood's three-act formula: heroes' setup (the past), horrific villainy and setbacks (the present), special-effects-heavy battle and final heroic triumph (the near future). That script is now central to the faith of a majority of American Protestants, whether or not their churches officially agree. For instance, Southern Baptist doctrine avoids describing the Last Things in too much detail, but most Southern Baptists, like evangelicals and fundamentalists in general, believe that the end-time has already started or shortly will, that the Antichrist will be an actual person uniting the rest of the world under some satanic religion, and that around the time of the final seven-year period of tribulation, lucky Christians will be raptured away before the Messiah returns for the win. And most are also certain that the millennium that follows will be a thousand years of magical perfection here on the actual Earth, with Jesus literally pre-siding as king.

Minorities among Southern Baptists and other evangelical denomina-tions believe that the Antichrist and the millennium are metaphors, that the rapture is a made-up add-on, and that the state of Israel is not biblical Israel reborn. Differences are split: the largest American Lutheran church, for in-stance, warns its people against "succumbing to . . . feverish preoccupation with the 'signs of the times'" but also against "spiritual laxity based on the mistaken notion that Christ's coming is no longer imminent."

From the outside looking in, however, the disagreements amount to the narcissism of small differences. According to Pew, 58 percent of evangelicals believe that Jesus will return no later than the year 2050. (And only 17 per-cent of *all* Americans said they thought He definitely *wasn't* coming back during the next thirty-three years.) That expectation of an imminent Second

---

* LaHaye—a prince of Fantasyland retired in a place called Rancho Mirage, his hair pre-ternaturally dark brown at age ninety, his face plainly refashioned by cosmetic surgery—was "graduated to Heaven," as they say, in 2016.

Coming is surely more widespread and respectable today in America than at any time in three hundred years and vastly more than anywhere else outside the Third World.

JUST AS AMERICAN CHRISTIANS' BELIEFS about the near future have dramatically shifted since I was a child, so too have their beliefs about the distant past. A *New York Times* reporter in 1972 noted hopefully that the "vast majority of fundamentalists have adopted somewhat more liberal positions" concerning evolution, and "even the most avid Biblical literalists . . . seem to be reluctant to have their own view taught in the schools." That liberalism and reluctance wouldn't last long. In the early 1980s, Alabama, Louisiana, and Arkansas all passed "balanced treatment" laws that required teachers to give creationism equal time with evolutionary biology in public school classrooms. After the Supreme Court declared such laws unconstitutional in 1987, clever creationists revived a phrase from the 1800s, *intelligent design*, and rebranded their beliefs accordingly. *We're not saying the designer of Earth and all living creatures was* God—*just an unnamed all-powerful supernatural being.*

By the 1990s, creationism was downright respectable. Republican state party platforms started calling for "creation science" to be taught in public schools. Formerly it had been hard or impossible for Christian colleges that rejected evolutionary biology to be accredited, but in the 1980s they had their own new accrediting agency that required teaching "the inerrancy and historicity of the Bible" and "the divine work of non-evolutionary creation" as factually true. In 1991 the first Bush administration granted those creationist accreditors full U.S. government recognition. Intelligent design had a new blue-chip headquarters in Seattle called the Discovery Institute, a think tank and advocacy group dedicated to "revers[ing] the stifling dominance of the materialist worldview"—that is, science—and "replac[ing] it with a science consonant with Christian and theistic convictions." The founder recruited a former U.S. senator and Microsoft's former chief operating officer to join his board, and the Bill and Melinda Gates Foundation gave Discovery multimillion-dollar grants.

Nobody can disprove that certain miracles happened thousands or billions of years ago. Human souls distinct from human brains? Who can say for sure? And about supernatural events that might occur in the future, we'll have to wait and see. But concerning observable, testable matters where plenty of evidence exists—the creation of the Earth, the emergence of life, evolution—science has those covered to a fair certainty.

*   *   *

AND YET MOST AMERICANS DISAGREE. We're split into rough thirds: maybe a third who believe in God-free biology, not quite a third who think God took his time and possibly used evolution to create living things, and at least a third certain that "humans and other living things have existed in their present form since the beginning of time." Overall, we're becoming *more* dubious about the science. A Michigan State University metastudy of survey research found that since the 1990s, the super-open-minded in-between fraction of Americans "not sure about evolution" has *tripled*. Less than a quarter of evangelicals (and Mormons) believe in evolution.[*]

A large majority of evangelicals believe that humans and all other creatures have always existed in their present form.[†] But among Protestants there are degrees of misguidedness that cluster into two basic camps. So-called old-Earth creationism attempts to reconcile Genesis with the scientific facts that Earth was created 4.6 billion years ago and that it took another 4.599 billion years for humans to appear. Young-Earth creationists simply deny the science—earth and humans and all the rest appeared a few thousand years ago. More than two-thirds of pastors in nonmainline Protestant churches are young-Earth creationists.[‡]

In any case, creationism, in flavors and consistencies from nutty to extranutty, has been completely normalized and institutionalized in America. The nuttiest have invented an elaborate new pseudoscience. There are creationist research papers that look and read like real academic papers, written by scientists with advanced degrees, such as "Radioisotope Dating of Meteorites," which purports to explain why 4.5-billion-year-old rocks aren't actually old— "their 4.55–4.57 Ga 'ages' obtained by Pb-Pb, U-Pb, and Pb-Pb–calibrated isochron age dating are likely not their true real-time ages, which according to the biblical paradigm is only about 6000 real-time years." Their institutions grant master's degrees and doctorates in biology, geology, and geophysics. There are several dozen colleges and universities that feature strictly creationist curricula.

The Discovery Institute isn't *committed* to the six-thousand-year-old-Earth idea, but it's careful not to reject it, either. On its well-produced site *Evolution News and Views,* it regularly disparages astrobiology, the search

---

[*] 2014 Pew survey.
[†] 2014 Pew survey.
[‡] 2012 Barna Group survey.

for Earth-like planets and molecules elsewhere in the galaxy. "Organized Science longs to find extraterrestrial life" because it "has long banked on the faith that life started by accident," and "the thought that life on Earth might in fact be unique is unpopular, because that could mean that some source of intelligent design played a role." The institute's Harvard-educated founder and director has explained why so many Americans, unlike people in the rest of the developed world, deny biology. Our "high percentage of doubters of Darwinism" is because "this country's citizens are famously independent and are not given to being rolled by an ideological elite in any field."

OTHER SORTS OF EXTREME BELIEFS are less scriptural and more free-styling—how God and Jesus and Satan are tinkering with the world and people's lives tonight or next month. These come, as usual, in two versions, the scary horror story and the wonderful fairy tale.

Horror-story Christians insist that particular disasters and accidents are God's collective punishments for particular sins—the way Puritans sometimes explained attacks by Indians and smallpox in the 1600s. In the late twentieth century, the seventeenth-century vengeful-God idea became standard again. Pat Robertson, now eighty-seven, remains the most prominent blame-the-victims horror-storyteller.* In 2015 God made stock prices drop 3 percent because the government funded Planned Parenthood, the way he sent Hurricane Katrina as punishment for laws permitting abortion, sent tornadoes to the Midwest in 2012 because He wasn't hearing enough prayer, and killed a hundred thousand Haitians with an earthquake in 2010 because of their ancestors' "pact with the devil." September 11 was God's punishment of the United States for feminism, homosexuality, free speech, and paganism—ironic, given that the Muslim fantasists who hijacked the planes on 9/11 would've agreed totally.

Then there are the happy fairy-tale pastors, most prominently the charismatics who tell believers that prayer will bring them wealth now, in life, on Earth. This has never been as explicit, widespread, or respectable as it has

---

* Robertson is not all doom and gloom. "Where does Pat find the time and energy to host a daily, national TV show, head a world-wide ministry . . . while traveling the globe as a statesman?" His CBN site explains: an "age-defying protein shake . . . Pat developed." Also contributing are Pat's Age-Defying Protein Pancakes, miraculous pancakes that according to CBN provide protection against arterial plaque as well as breast, uterine, and prostate cancer.

become since the 1980s, the decade in which America renewed its commitment to manic materialism.

The Puritans regarded financial success as a possible signal from God—if He had made you wealthy, maybe you were a "visible saint," already elected to everlasting life. But in contemporary America, cause and effect have been switched. It is no longer just some dull Protestant work ethic that leads to success. As America's I'm-a-winner individualism extinguished belief in predestination, hopeful Christians decided that prayer could directly result in a high net worth. It was a way of reconciling two irreconcilable pieces of the American character—the extreme religiosity and the refusal to believe that success isn't up to each person individually. The solution: *you* can persuade *God* to make you rich.

In the 1920s and '30s the African-American ministers Father Divine and Sweet Daddy Grace got rich by preaching pray-for-prosperity, and their swanky lifestyles seemed like proof that it worked. In the 1950s and '60s, just as Southern white musicians and producers were turning black music into rock 'n' roll, Southern white Pentecostal preachers turned get-rich supernaturalism into a crossover phenomenon. Pentecostalism was invented as a black *and* white working-class religion devoted to wizardry, such as miraculous cures for illness. Getting rich by praying was just a miraculous cure for poorness. The Baylor University theologian Roger Olson, who grew up Pentecostal in the 1950s and '60s, says that for decades Pentecostalism's "'lunatic fringe' . . . promised physical and financial blessings in response to prayers of faith. . . . Almost to a person they prayed for people's teeth to be filled with gold." The TV Pentecostal Oral Roberts published *God's Formula for Success and Prosperity* in the 1950s, right around the time a young singer named Kenneth Copeland had one Elvis-y hit. Copeland found God, enrolled at the new Oral Roberts University in Tulsa, became Oral's chauffeur and pilot, and finally emerged as a godfather of what became known in the 1980s as the prosperity gospel.

A key passage for prosperity gospel preachers is the line by Jesus in Mark 11:24—"What things soever ye desire, when ye pray, believe that ye receive them, and ye shall have them." Of course, ironically, absurdly, it goes unmentioned that this comes just a few lines after the scene where Jesus performs his great act of militant anticommercialism, condemning and ransacking the tables of the moneychangers and salesmen in the Temple. Prosperity gospel ministers, Olson says, are promoting an idea of prayer that "makes God into a cosmic slot machine and turns salvation into a self-centered acquisition of physical blessings." America spent a century making Santa Claus its central

Christmas character because he *wasn't* a religious figure and adults could wink-wink *pretend* he was real; the new prosperity gospel makes God a real Santa in whom Christian adults actually believe.

At eighty, Ken Copeland still operates his nondenominational Christian multimedia empire, with hundreds of affiliated churches, out of Fort Worth, near the Kenneth Copeland Airport. The prosperity gospel megastar, Joel Osteen, also attended Oral Roberts University, but he's the very model of a *modern* major fantasy-monger—a young fifty-four, extremely fit, great-looking, stylishly dressed, always smiling, apparently sweet-tempered, well-spoken, a charismatic Christian who's also charismatic in the ordinary sense, totally ready for prime time. I find him mesmerizing. He runs America's biggest church, attended by forty thousand people every week, out of the Houston Rockets' former arena, which he fills with theatrical fog—every service is meant to look, as his former lighting director says, "like an awards show." Osteen's first book, *Your Best Life Now* (2004), stayed on the *Times* bestseller list for four years. Since then he has published dozens more, including the recent *You Can, You Will: 8 Undeniable Qualities of a Winner.*

He's as close as we have to a new Billy Graham. Graham mainstreamed evangelical Christianity by going lite, ratcheting back the anger, and Osteen goes further. He avoids involvement in political issues, but he's delivered the prayers in the U.S. Senate and House chambers and at the Texas inaugurations of a (lesbian) Democratic mayor and a (right-wing) Republican governor. He seldom talks about Hell.

"I get grouped into the prosperity gospel and I never think it's fair," Osteen says. "What it connotates [*sic*] is that you just talk about money. . . . I never preach that whatever you say, you can get—'I want five Cadillacs.'" No, but: "I do believe . . . that God wants us to prosper." So "when you pray big it shows God that, 'God I trust you,'" and conversely "if you pray small, ordinary prayers, then you'll live a small, ordinary life," because God will figure you're a loser. "I think God blessed me by writing this book and giving me a lot of money."

"Positive confessions" is the charismatic jargon for saying the specific things one wants—the better job, the business deal, the vacation, the five Cadillacs—in order to acquire them through God's intercession. So from Osteen's church you can get "Scripture-based positive confessions that we encourage you to speak over your life every day" in order to "build wealth . . . while you follow biblical financial principles." The verses are often paraphrased in fake-biblical language or are taken out of context in ways that change their meanings entirely. Several of the positive-confession mantras are from Proverbs—"The blessing of God makes me rich," "God traverses my way that He may cause me to inherit wealth and fill my treasury"—but ignore the preceding verses that make clear the riches in question are precisely *not* monetary. Osteen's older sister, who helps run the church, has said that "if you look through the Bible from Genesis to Revelation, . . . every person who served Him faithfully, God blessed financially."

What about Jesus, who wasn't really "blessed financially" and regularly hated on the rich in favor of the poor? When I searched Osteen's site for references to Mark 10:21 ("Go, sell what you own, and give the money to the poor, and you will have treasure in heaven") or Matthew 6:24 ("No man can serve two masters. . . . Ye cannot serve God and mammon") and 19:24 ("easier for a camel to go through the eye of a needle than for a rich man to enter into the kingdom of God") or any of the brutal first verses of James 5 ("Come now, you rich, weep and howl for the miseries that are coming upon you"), the result was No Results.

"God puts desires in your heart," Osteen says, and "there's nothing wrong with having a nice home." Each time an interviewer asks him how a focus on wealth and success and winning squares with Jesus's teachings, he delivers the same straw-man response with extraordinary message discipline. "There's a tradition that says you're supposed to take a vow of poverty if you're going to be a Christian," he told Katie Couric in 2013, "but I don't believe that." "There's a tradition that says you're supposed to take a vow of poverty if you're going to be a Christian," he told a Boston public radio interviewer in 2015, "but I don't believe that." His net worth is said to be $50 million.

IT USUALLY TAKES TIME TO become rich, even with God's help. But charismatics believe in and practice instant magic, in astonishing supernatural events happening *right now*, both fabulous and horrible.

Osteen's church services are euphoric and ecstatic for the ten or fifteen thousand people who attend each one, but he understands that the full-on public glossolalia of his Pentecostal youth might alarm charismatic-curious prospects. He and his believers do indeed speak in tongues; they're just discreet about it and don't do it on TV. Describing an introductory how-to session, the church explains that "you receive a supernatural language and a supernatural power. Come and join us and learn the five steps to . . . speaking in tongues." Osteen wants people to speak in tongues *every day*—by themselves. "It may sound strange to you," explains the guide, written by his sister, "but allow that supernatural language to flow out of you." It's a secret code that only God can decipher. More rarely, the primer explains, "the Holy

Spirit gives a believer a message in tongues to a congregation." This requires human de-encryption—and according to Osteenian teaching, public tongues are "always accompanied by the Gift of Interpretation of Tongues," which somebody present will miraculously and conveniently possess. "It is not a direct translation, but an interpretation."

When Osteen discusses Satan, the Prince of Darkness seems not so ghastly, more like a bothersome Debbie Downer. It's Satan who "brings you thoughts of worry, anxiety and fear," who "wants you to give up and quit so he can have the victory in your life." So if "we kick Satan out of our minds, everything clears up."

Osteen's father was a celebrity Pentecostal preacher who pioneered the idea of praying for money, but he also focused on battling Satan as if Armageddon were under way—"casting out devils" and exhorting believers to wage "spiritual warfare" against the "wicked spirits in high places." This old-school approach is thriving too, and it isn't only charismatics and Pentecostals who think Satan and demons are real. In surveys since the 1990s, between half and three-quarters of *all* Americans say they believe in the devil or that "it's possible for people to become possessed by demons." In one rigorous 2009 survey of Christians, more than a third agreed that Satan is "a living being."*

"Spiritual warfare," systematic demon-fighting, is another old Christian concept that had mostly faded away in America—until it revived in the 1960s and took off during the 1980s and '90s. It is now the animating notion across a broad swath on the darker side of American Christianity. A spiritual warfare Protestant is an evangelical or charismatic who's angry about something. They call their loud, belligerent prayers against Satan "violent intercession."

They focus on references in the four Gospels to "demon-possessed" people Jesus cured—individuals who happened to be blind, mute, or insane and thus were regarded as cursed. (According to John, of course, crazy Jesus himself seemed demon-possessed to much of the general populace.) Microlevel spiritual warriors try to root out the demons incarnated among their family, friends, and acquaintances. This is the Christianity of many thousands of American pastors and their many millions of believers, praying and grabbing and shouting and chanting to drive demons out of afflicted individuals. Ac-

---

* 1998 Harris, 2000 *Newsweek*, 2003 Fox News, 2007 Gallup, 2009 Barna Group, and 2012 Public Policy Polling surveys. "I . . . believe in the Devil," Supreme Court Justice Antonin Scalia, a Catholic, told Jennifer Senior of *New York* magazine in 2013. "You're looking at me as though I'm weird. . . . My God! . . . It's in the Gospels! You travel in circles that are so, *so* removed from mainstream America that you are appalled that anybody would believe in the Devil!"

cording to Pew, one in nine adults, 25 or 30 million Americans, are sure they've "experienced/witnessed the devil/evil spirits being driven out of a person."

So how do Christians know if they've got the sixth sense and magic touch to do this work? They take a quiz! That is, they complete a spiritual gifts inventory. There are many versions, but the original from which they derive is the Wagner-Modified Houts Questionnaire. It consists of a hundred-odd statements about one's ministerial aptitude and skills. People rate themselves from zero to three on each item.* For instance:

> "Through God I have revealed specific things that will happen in the future."
> "In the name of the Lord, I have been able to recover sight to the blind."
> "I have spoken an immediate message of God to His people in a language that I have never learned."
> "I can tell whether a person speaking in tongues is genuine."
> "I have actually heard a demon speak in a loud voice."
> "I have spoken to evil spirits and they have obeyed me."

As it happens, some of these unusual powers also appear on a checklist from a separate region of religious Fantasyland: according to the Vatican's official demon-hunting manual, "speaking in unknown languages" and predicting the future are—yes—signs of satanic possession.†

The Wagner of the Wagner-Modified Houts Questionnaire is C. Peter Wagner, now eighty-six, a major figure in the charismatic pantheon and a proud general in the wars against Satan. Wagner was a professor at the Fuller Theological Seminary in Pasadena, a major U.S. evangelical institution where he met John Wimber, the bearded preacher-to-hippies who was inventing the Vineyard movement at the time (see Chapter 24).‡ There are now around six

---

* There are many different kinds of "spiritual gifts." In one of his books, the co-creator of the test apologizes that he can't reliably determine which individuals will make good Christian martyrs: "I have not as yet come upon what I consider a decent way of testing for the gift of martyrdom, despite numerous attempts."

† Pope Francis is big on Satan, which is fine both with his growing charismatic wing and with his ultra-orthodox Latin Mass wing. "The Devil is present," Francis has said, even though people "have been led to believe that the devil is a myth, a figure, an idea, the *idea* of evil." According to *The Washington Post,* "a senior bishop in Vatican City" says "Pope Francis never stops talking about the Devil; it's constant."

‡ What is one to make of a miraculous healer who gets cancer and acute heart disease in his late fifties, then has a stroke, then falls and dies from a brain hemorrhage at sixty-three?

hundred Vineyard churches in the United States. Three-quarters of their members have spoken in tongues, and a majority say they've experienced miraculous healings.* They also believe that devils are among us.

Yet the Vineyarders come across as chill mainline Protestants: very white, lots of beards, many Democrats, European cars in the parking lots. They're clustered more in the North and the West than in the Old South. The clergy wear normal clothes. A decade ago Vineyard broke with the evangelical norm and started allowing women to be pastors, several of whom have risen in the clerical hierarchy. They seem *nice* and, to seculars, relatable.

Which is why the Stanford anthropologist Tanya Luhrmann, a nice baby boomer raised Unitarian, made them the stars of her highly sympathetic 2012 book about evangelicals, *When God Talks Back.* She spent several years among two Vineyard congregations and nailed the sort of magical thinking that makes the imaginary seem real, so that people think they've moved beyond wishful belief to another level, to *feeling* enchanted, to *knowing* the irrefutable truth. It's "more like learning *to do* something than *to think* something. . . . People train the mind in such a way that they experience part of their mind as the presence of God. . . . God wants to be your friend," and then "God will answer back, through thoughts and mental images he places in your mind, and through sensations he causes in your body." She encountered some who scheduled "date nights" with Jesus, setting an extra place at dinner and chatting with Him. They'd ask Jesus where to get a haircut or to arrange "admission to specific colleges, for the healing of specific illness— even, it is true, for specific red convertible cars."

Just because some *other* Christian demonologists are "odd ducks," I heard one Vineyard pastor say in a sermon on spiritual warfare, that doesn't mean demons aren't real. "We don't believe you have to be an expert on Satan," the Vineyard Church of Duluth explains in a guide called *Dealing with the Demonic,* "studying his ways obsessively, or looking for a demon behind every bush." Right. Cool. However, "once you know that, in fact, this probably is demonic activity," you proceed with the deliverance mission—"Pray in Jesus's name because the demons hate it. . . . If they do their part, demons will leave quietly and quickly in ten minutes, and that is how most deliverances that we do actually happen." If the de-demonization isn't quite so easy, there's a Troubleshooting section. The problem may be that your demon-possessed friends are hearing a satanic voice in their heads saying, "'This is a hoax, this

* Donald Miller, *Reinventing American Protestantism: Christianity in the New Millennium* (1999).

is ridiculous, this stuff isn't even real.'" According to Luhrmann, her Vine-yarders in Chicago and Palo Alto "would find themselves kind of going into restaurants and smelling for the demons and then having to pray to expel them." These, remember, are moderate, mainstream charismatics.

What's now called Strategic Level Spiritual Warfare, praying and chan-neling God's power to defeat satanic strangers and institutions, disappeared from America for centuries. The bit of the Bible that preoccupies these spiri-tual warriors, Ephesians 6:12, was obscure until recently: "Put on the whole armor of God. . . . For we wrestle not against flesh and blood, but against principalities, against powers, against the rulers of the darkness of this world, against spiritual wickedness in high places." To believers, the exhortation to wage war on the devil is not metaphorical. They ignore the "not against flesh and blood" passage and focus on the "wickedness in high places"—which to them means that particular VIPs (popes, presidents, supporters of marriage equality) are Satan's agents on Earth.* Which grants their political opinions and cultural tastes God's own antisatanic imprimatur.

Such warfare can be conducted after "spiritually mapping" one's region, so "intercessors" know exactly where to focus prayers on Satan's local "strong-men" and "territorial spirits" to "bind" them. These "demonic hotspots" are pretty obvious—Planned Parenthood clinics, Mormon temples, Catholic churches, Masonic lodges, meditation centers, LGBTQ gathering spots, strip clubs, and shops selling tarot cards or dreamcatchers.

Spiritual warfare can also take place on *extremely* strategic levels—Wagner, for instance, focuses on the entire nation of Japan. Satan personally enlisted Emperor Akihito on behalf of "the powers of darkness," Wagner ex-plained on NPR's *Fresh Air*—"the sun goddess visits him in person and has sexual intercourse with the emperor. . . . I don't know how that works be-tween a spirit and a human, but I know that's the case." Are Satan's represen-tatives "alive and functioning in America," Terry Gross asked—are U.S. politicians possessed? "Absolutely," he replied. "We like to use the word 'af-flicted' or the technical term 'demonized.'"

As charismatic practices become more popular and accepted, the evan-gelicals who subscribe only to unbelievable *theology* are on the defensive. Charismatics are the madcap descendants of Anne Hutchinson, and their

---

* Most translations of Ephesians make it even clearer that the supernatural evil is not on Earth at all—*not* in "high places" like the White House or the Vatican but "in the heavens" or "heavenly realms." Thus the further folly of biblical literalism: what some see as the obvious meaning—in a passage translated from ancient Hebrew to ancient Greek to Old Latin to New Latin to Middle English to Modern English—others will not.

remaining Christian opponents are like latter-day Puritans. The fundamentalist John MacArthur runs a megachurch in the San Fernando Valley and hosts a daily national radio show. Charismatics, he has declared, aren't channeling the Holy Spirit when they "look drunk . . . fall or flop, or roll, or laugh hysterically, or bark, or babble, or talk gibberish." These "emotional experiences, bizarre experiences and demonic experiences . . . visions, revelations, voices from heaven, messages from the Spirit through transcendental means, dreams, speaking in tongues, prophecies, out of body experiences, trips to heaven, anointings, miracles: all false, all lies." Not only that, but all the charismatic shenanigans are *the work of Satan,* whose "troops have taken over" evangelicalism.

That seems like a desperate last gasp by the old school. "The Charismatics and Pentecostals have already won the worship war," *Christianity Today,* the leading evangelical publication, declared in 2015. The Southern Baptists were the most important resisters, but even they are surrendering. Mike Huckabee, a pastor who was president of Arkansas's Baptists before he ran for president of the United States, says that "we tend to be a little Bapticostal where I go"—the new mix of Baptist and Pentecostal. "If you polled SBC churches across the nation," the Southern Baptists note officially, only a "very small minority might accept what is commonly practiced today in charismatic churches as valid." But in fact, their media division *did* poll their own clergy less than a decade ago, and fully half of them said they believe that speaking in tongues is real and okay if done in private. In 2015 the church gave way some more, deciding to let its missionaries speak in fictitious foreign languages when they were overseas—in order "to communicate the Gospel to foreign cultures."

32

America Versus the Godless Civilized World: Why Are We So Exceptional?

EXCEPTIONAL HAS TWO DIFFERENT MEANINGS—"HIGHLY UNUSUAL" OR "UN- usually good." America is both. But this book is about a set of ways in which we are peculiar. We are very different from the two or three dozen "advanced" countries that are otherwise like the United States, the most economically developed nations that aren't on the Persian Gulf, the societies mainly in Europe or created by Europeans that we used to call the civilized world or the First World and now call the Global North.

Americans invented and built and dominate the fantasy-industrial com- plex that mixed fiction and reality until they became indistinguishable. Peo- ple get surgically fictionalized everywhere, for instance, but we're third in cosmetic surgeries per capita (behind only Colombia and South Korea), and our boob-job rate (third to Venezuela and Brazil) is twice that of Canada and the U.K. Other developed countries have ascendant political movements driven by fantastical belief in conspiracies and a wish to go back in time, but we have given ours the national government to run. People in other developed countries have superstitious beliefs and practice every brand of religion and quasi-religion. But Americans invented and scaled all the most extravagant new species, and most believers in other affluent countries are irrelevant minorities or else quiet true traditionalists, such as pious Italians and Poles still attending mass and making confession.

The big, undeniable piece of American exceptionalism that helped launch this inquiry is our religiosity. One of the two developed countries that even come close is Israel, a religious state. The other, South Korea, has gone from being one of the poorest countries to one of the richest in just two or three generations, which makes the residue there of magic and superstition less surprising. It's thanks to the United States that the nation exists and that so many South Koreans are Protestant in our unusual fashion. A missionary who'd been present at the founding of Pentecostalism in Los Angeles planted an early church in Seoul, and then in the 1950s a U.S. Army chaplain imported teams of Pentecostal missionaries to start more churches.* Today about a tenth of South Koreans are Pentecostals or charismatics, an extraordinarily large fraction in the developed world and in East Asia—but a far distant second to the United States.

We've always been different in this way. A century after Tocqueville was struck by the religious enthusiasm he found here, a reporter asked New York's Catholic cardinal if Americans are more religious than Europeans. "We are certainly not *less* so," he carefully replied. At the time, the new Soviet Union was radically secularizing life there and later attempted the same in Eastern Europe.† But people in the rest of modern Europe were abandoning Christianity and supernaturalism voluntarily, absent any persecution by atheistic Communist regimes. According to a Gallup Poll in 1968, only 5 percent to 14 percent of Scandinavians said they attended church every week, as opposed to 43 percent of Americans at the time. And religious commitment in most of Europe has continued plummeting ever since. In the U.K. in 1985, for instance, a third of people said they had no religion at all; by 2012 it was up to

---

* The South Koreans also have the U.S. military partly to thank for their phenomenally fervent embrace of cosmetic surgery. Right after the Korean War, the U.S. Marine Corps' chief plastic surgeon, in addition to work mending war wounds, introduced the blepharoplasty, which makes Asian eyelids look more Occidental. "It was indeed," he wrote later, "a plastic surgeon's paradise."
† Marx famously called religion the opium of the people, and when Lenin founded the Soviet Union, he agreed, saying it was "used for the . . . stupefaction of the working class." But neither man had ever been to the United States, to see that for Americans it was as much or more a stimulant and hallucinogen than a stupefying opiate.

half. Unlike the Earth's other moderns, we have rushed headlong back toward magic and miracles, crazifying some legacy churches, filling up the already-crazy ones, inventing all kinds of crazy new ones.

The loosest measure of religiosity doesn't require any particular belief in the impossible. *Does religion play a very important role in your life?* is a survey question Pew asks respondents in dozens of countries. At the top of the rankings are African and Muslim and Latin American countries, as well as India and the Philippines—places where between 61 percent and 97 percent of the people say religion is very important in their lives. In the developed world, the percentages range from 11 percent in France to 33 percent in Britain—except, of course, for the United States, where it's 59 percent, right between Turkey and Lebanon.

The results are the same again and again, no matter how or where the questions are posed.

A majority of Americans tell Pew they pray every day; in the rest of the developed world, those fractions are one-tenth or one-fifth. Elsewhere in the developed world around half the people never pray; only one in nine Americans admit they never pray.*

Among the citizens of twenty-three countries surveyed in 2011 by the international research firm Ipsos, people in only three—Indonesia, South Africa, and Turkey—believe in Heaven and Hell more than Americans do. Our faith in an afterlife is greater, for instance, than that of Mexicans, Brazilians, and Saudi Arabians. While a majority of Americans think the devil is in some sense real, in nearly all other predominantly Christian countries, even the Philippines, devil believers are small minorities.

Is the Bible "the actual word of God . . . to be taken literally, word for word"? Although more than a quarter of Americans think so, in the rest of the rich world, the actual-word-of-God populations range from 4 percent to 10 percent.† Did God create humans in finished form at the start? Among people in thirty-four more-developed countries asked whether they accept evolution, the United States is second from the bottom, ahead only of Turkey.‡ On a different list of two dozen countries ranked by belief in evolution, Americans' disbelief is exceeded only by that of people in South Africa, Brazil, and three Muslim countries.§

---

* 2008 Pew surveys; 2012 WIN Gallup International survey.
† 1998 ISSP surveys and 2014 General Social Survey.
‡ 2006 metastudy by Jon D. Miller of Michigan State University.
§ 2013 Pew surveys.

Although the United States is by far the largest importer of *things,* we have become the world's great net exporter of fantasy. For the last century, we have created, defined, and dominated the ever-expanding, increasingly global culture industry—from advertising to movies to recorded music to television and digital games. Alongside the shiny pop-cultural fantasies, we're also phenomenally successful exporters of exciting fantasy *religion.* The market is the Third World, and we are saturating it. A century ago, right after Americans invented Pentecostalism, no more than one-tenth of one percent of earthlings were Pentecostals and charismatics. Today it's 10 percent, one hundred times as many, more than half a billion Christians—including a large majority of the world's Protestants—who believe they're routinely speaking in a mystical holy language, curing illness by laying on hands, hearing personally from God.[*] Since the 1960s, thanks to us, a third of Central Americans have become Protestants of the charismatic and Pentecostal kind.[†] America was always the modern country, the practical country, the country that solved problems, that inspired and pushed the rest of the world to cast off vestigial folk customs in favor of rational, sensible approaches to organizing society and life. Life and history are full of ironies, but this one's as big as they get.

WHY ARE WE SO PECULIAR? Why did Americans keep inventing religions and maintain so many beliefs that people in other affluent countries never took up or else abandoned?

The Protestants of capitalist Europe and Canada and Australia continued to do as Max Weber's sociology said they were doing—retain the work ethic but mostly remove the training wheels of religion. Why in America have we hung on to the magical beliefs *as well as* the industriousness and money love and individualism that our founding religion encouraged?[‡]

Some of the standard scholarly explanations seem correct as far as they go, but they're all limited by the scope and tools of their particular disciplines. They also tend to construct explanations that flatter Americans. Legalists focus on the Constitution and especially the First Amendment—that government wasn't permitted to mess around in religion, which made religion flour-

---

[*] 2011 Pew surveys.
[†] World Christian Database; 2013 and 2014 Pew surveys.
[‡] The way other Protestant countries have retained the practical legacies and jettisoned the other bits is analogous to what China did with its founding quasi-religion of Communism: they've kept the useful authoritarian part but jettisoned the economic utopianism.

ish and attracted persecuted believers from elsewhere. Other historians attribute it to our frontier past, where wilderness folk, untethered from social control, were more inclined and free to dream up new religions: they could, so they did.

But none that I've seen convincingly explains the persistence or extravagance of supernatural belief, or why during the last century and particularly the last half-century our divergence from the norm has grown so extreme. They don't look at our religions and spirituality in the context of the larger American predisposition to feel special and think magically. They don't register the connections between our religion and the rest of our giddy, uncertain grip on reality, the free-range wishfulness, the great American *all* of it. They try to be polite.

Europeans had highly developed regional and national cultures and societies before they bolted on Protestantism. America, on the other hand, was half-*created* by Protestant extremists to be a Protestant society. American academics accept the idea of American exceptionalism in one of its meanings—that our peculiar founding circumstances shaped us. "The position of the Americans," Tocqueville wrote in *Democracy in America*, "is . . . quite exceptional," by which he meant the Puritanism, the commercialism, the freedom of religion, the individualism, "a thousand special causes."

The professoriate rejects exceptionalism in today's right-wing sense, that the United States is superior to all other nations, with a God-given mission. And they also resist the third meaning, the idea that a law of human behavior doesn't apply here—scholars of religion insist that explanations of religious behavior must be universal.

The latest scholarly consensus about America's exceptional religiosity is an economic theory. Because all forms of religion are products in a marketplace, they say, our exceptional free marketism has produced more supply and therefore generated more demand. Along with universal human needs for physical sustenance and security, there's also such a need for existential explanations, for why and how the world came to be. Sellers of religion emerge offering explanations. From the start, religions tended to be state monopolies—as they were in the colonies, the Puritans in Massachusetts and the Church of England in the South. After that original American duopoly was dismantled and the government prohibited official churches, religious entrepreneurs rushed into the market, Methodists and Baptists and Mormons and all the others. European countries, meanwhile, kept their state-subsidized religions, Protestant or Catholic—and so in an economic sense those churches became lazy monopolies.* In America, according to the market theorists, each religion competes with all the others to acquire and keep customers. Americans, presented with all this fantastic choice, can't resist buying. We're so religious for the same reason we're so fat.

There is no doubt some truth in this. But I don't think it's anything close to the whole truth. You know how everything looks like a nail to somebody with a hammer? These rational-choice economists, calculating their input ratios and solving their equations, begin with a belief that individuals weigh the costs and benefits of this or that theology and choose the optimal one, deciding among the rapture and speaking in tongues and a six-thousand-year-old Earth the way they decide among makes of cars and types of pornography or potato chips.

A conclusion of some rational-choice theorists is that because we've had such a free religious marketplace for so long, and American Christianity is now so evangelical and charismatic, religion naturally "wants" to be more primitive, miraculous, and amazing. As two of the leading theorists have written, new sects emerge to "take the places of those withered denominations that lost their sense of the supernatural." But why only in America (and the Third World)? "The heart of our position is . . . that faced with American-style churches," one of those coauthors has written, "Europeans would respond as Americans do." But if Europe and the rest of the rich and open world constitute such a massive untapped market opportunity, why aren't religious entrepreneurs starting up more American-style churches abroad? In fact, there are charismatic and Pentecostal churches in Europe and Canada and elsewhere, just very few of them. And it's not because institutions like the withered Church of Norway are such hardball monopolists. It's because in the rich world, except America, *the product doesn't sell.*

What's more, if monopolistic state religions discourage religiosity, then how does one explain the higher rates of church attendance and prayer in Catholic countries and the thriving religiosity in officially Islamic countries? If it's the lack of government persecution that allows religious fires to burn freely, how to account for the powerful persistence of Catholicism in Communist Poland, or the success of Mormons during their difficult founding American century?

* Incidentally, the premise that the contemporary United States has nothing like state churches isn't entirely true. By the logic of the free-market theorists, shouldn't religious exemptions from U.S. taxes—state subsidy by other means—breed complacency and laziness among the leaders of every American church?

A different tack for explaining away America's exceptionalism is to compare the U.S. apple to a world of oranges. Peter Berger, coauthor of *The Social Construction of Reality* in 1966, took for granted the "widespread collapse of the plausibility of traditional religious definitions of reality." When those reports of religion's death turned out to be premature, he had an apostasy: "'secularization theory,'" he'd decided by the 1990s, "is essentially mistaken," given that "the world today . . . is as furiously religious as it ever was, and in some places more so than ever." His revised view makes unbelieving Europe the global exception. But of course, it's not just Europe—it's also Canada, Australia, New Zealand, Japan, and the whole modern world including China that has secularized. By treating all countries as one big data set, instead of dividing them among the several dozen economically advanced and the 150 less developed, this argument ignores the glaring and interesting deviation: America is the freak.

The economists also don't have much of an answer to a very specifically economic conundrum: the fact that, country by country, prosperity and a sense of security correlate with less religious belief almost everywhere— except America. As the political scientists Pippa Norris of Harvard and Ronald Inglehart of the University of Michigan explain in *Sacred and Secular: Religion and Politics Worldwide,* "religiosity persists most strongly among vulnerable populations, especially in poorer nations and in failed states. Conversely, a systematic erosion of religious practices, values, and beliefs has occurred among the more prosperous strata in rich nations."

Most of the scholars examining this question, because they're scholars and thus are expected to stay in their lanes and suppress tendentious speculations and hunches, exclude the X-factor, our peculiar and multifaceted American credulity that is the subject of this book.

Tocqueville's archetypal American in the 1830s stopped his frenzied making and selling to think impractical thoughts only when "his religion . . . bids him turn, from time to time, a transient and distracted glance to heaven." Over the next two centuries, as we ran out of New World forests and frontiers to clear and settle, as life kept getting easier (and for many of the least fortunate during the last couple of decades, gloomier), we've extended those occasional glances toward Heaven into a fixed and frenzied stare.

33

Magical but Not Necessarily Christian, Spiritual but Not Religious

FROM THE VENTURE-CAPITAL-BACKED PILGRIMS TO THE METHODISTS AND Baptists and Christian Scientists, from L. Ron Hubbard to the Christian Broadcasting Network and today's numberless nondenominational churches, American religion has always been entrepreneurial. By this, I don't mean it's therefore insincere or dominated by charlatans. I mean simply that American religious visionaries have always created independent enterprises to distribute and promote their magics as they see fit.

Therefore what I'm calling New Age, even though it consists of a zillion different small and large businesses (and nonprofits), still constitutes an American religion. Like our Protestantism, it's a movement that shares mystical and supernatural beliefs and attitudes, a basic ontology in pursuit of truth, bliss, self-improvement, and prosperity. Like our Protestantism, it's expansive and eclectic, variously subjective and experiential and doctrinal, with hundreds of different denominational start-ups, sects, practices, tendencies, and prophets. It thinks of itself as anti-Establishment even as it has become Establishment. New Age is a breath mint *and* a candy mint, part of the fantasy-industrial complex *and* a loose religious faith.

Unlike most standard religions, New Age doesn't have a single agreed-upon supreme being or messiah or creation myth—but that means it can coexist and cross-pollinate with Christianity and Judaism and other more formal religions. Although some Christians fight perpetual border wars against the Oprahs and Deepak Chopras, calling them the Antichrist's advance guard, there's also plenty of common ground. The American ecumenical mantra used to be *We all worship the same God.* In Fantasyland, it's essentially *None of us are sticklers for reason.*

The term *New Age* comes with pejorative baggage, so believers seldom call themselves that—just as Puritans and Shakers resisted identifying as Puritans and Shakers, and lately fundamentalists as fundamentalists. A great many say they're "spiritual but not religious." Like the evangelicals who aren't chronically angry and the charismatics whose supernaturalism isn't so demon-haunted, New Agers are mainly seeking personal happiness. In *Religion Explained: The Evolutionary Origins of Religious Thought,* the Washington University anthropologist and psychologist Pascal Boyer points out that providing bliss in the present and reassurance about the future hasn't been the main point of most religions. "Reassuring religion, insofar as it exists," he writes, "is not found in places where life is significantly dangerous or unpleasant, quite the opposite. One of the few religious systems obviously designed to provide a comforting world view is New Age mysticism. Note that these reassuring, ego-boosting notions appeared and spread in one of the most secure and affluent societies in history." Indeed, the emergence of all the American New Age precursors through the 1800s—homeopathy, phrenology, water cures, New Thought, spiritualism, Transcendentalism, Christian Science, theosophy—perfectly tracks our shift from a rough, poor start-up nation into a prosperous, secure one.

DURING THE 1980S AND '90S magically healing crystals, each associated with a particular invisible bodily *chakra,* became a thing. Non-Christian faith healing such as Reiki became a thing. Channeling the spirits of the dead once again became a thing. Unlike old-fashioned spiritualism, in which people believe they're communicating with dead relatives, celebrity channelers were possessed not so much by your late Uncle George as by *entirely fictional celebrities,* such as Seth and Ramtha. A woman in Washington State named Judith Darlene Hampton renamed herself Judy Zebra Knight, JZ for short, and became rich and famous by pretending to speak as Ramtha, a Stone Age warrior from the legendary land of Lemuria who'd fought a war against the legendary land of Atlantis and conquered most of the world before becoming an all-knowing demigod. JZ Knight attracted a ton of followers, including Shirley MacLaine.

"Harmonic convergence" became a thing. Over two days in the summer of 1987, a psychedelic visionary from Boulder, Colorado, had extraordinary success organizing big gatherings of people in many locations to engage in what he called Globally Synchronized Meditation, meant to neutralize bad vibrations and keep the planet from going haywire. The timing was derived from his understanding of ancient Amerindian calendars. The world did *not* end in 1987; therefore harmonic convergence must have worked; and so a Fantasyland fiefdom focused on Mayan and Aztec mythology and cosmology was fully launched.

By the 1990s, there was a big, respectable, glamorous New Age counter-Establishment. The late Jane Roberts and her cosmic entity Seth, their books republished, were now revered figures, on their way to becoming almost a Joseph Smith and angel Moroni of the movement. Marianne Williamson, one of the new superstar New Age preachers, popularized another "channeled" book of spiritual revelation first published in the 1970s, *A Course in Miracles*: the author, a Columbia University psychology professor who was anonymous until after her death in the 1980s, claimed that its 1,333 pages were more or less dictated to her by Jesus. Her basic idea, like her predecessors from Mary Baker Eddy to Roberts, was that physical existence is a collective illusion—"the dream." Endorsed by Williamson, the book became a gigantic bestseller.* Deepak Chopra had been a distinguished endocrinologist before he quit regular medicine in his thirties to become the "physician to the gods" in the Transcendental Meditation organization, and in 1989 he hung out his own shingle as wise man, author, lecturer, and marketer of dietary supplements.

Out of its various threads, the philosophy now had its basic doctrines in place: rationalism is mostly wrong-headed, mystical feelings should override scientific understandings, reality is an illusion one can remake to suit oneself. The 1960s relativism out of which all that flowed originated mainly as a means of fighting the Man, unmasking the charlatans-in-charge. But now they were mind-blowing ways to make yourself happy and successful by

---

* Williamson was present at a spectacular episode of Fantasyland convergence: just before Halloween in 1991 at Michael Jackson's Neverland Ranch, she officiated at Elizabeth Taylor's eighth marriage, to a man she'd met when they were rehab patients at the Betty Ford Center in Rancho Mirage. The wedding guests were almost outnumbered by a small army of one hundred security guards and Nancy Reagan's Secret Service detail.

becoming the charlatan-in-charge of your own little piece of the universe. "It's not just the interpretation of objective reality that is subjective," according to Chopra. "Objective reality per se is a concept of reality we have created subjectively."

Exactly how had Chopra and Williamson become so conspicuous and influential? They were anointed in 1992 and 1993 by Oprah Winfrey. Winfrey's daily show had started airing nationally in the mid-1980s. In the 1990s twelve or thirteen million devotees watched it every weekday. Through her magazine *O*, started in 2000, she reached millions more. More than any other single American by far, outside conventional religion and politics, Oprah Winfrey is responsible for giving a national platform and credibility to magical thinking, New Age and otherwise. In her broad domain, she is the Cotton Mather, John Wesley, Brigham Young, and Billy Graham, the first New Age pope. If Ronald Reagan was the first king of his Fantasyland realm, Oprah Winfrey is still queen of hers. Like Reagan too, I believe she's both sincere *and* a brilliant Barnumesque promoter of her dreamworld.

She has been an inclusive promoter of fantasies—extraterrestrial, satanic, medical, paranormal, all sorts of spiritual, sometimes Christian. When a Christian questioner in her audience once described her as New Age, Winfrey was pissed. "I am not 'New Age' anything," she said, "and I resent being called that. I am just trying to open a door . . . and perhaps be the light to get them to God, whatever they may call that. I don't see spirits in the trees, and I don't sit in the room with crystals." Maybe not those two things specifically; she's the *respectable* promoter of New Age belief and practice and nostrums, a member of the elite and friend to presidents, five of whom have appeared on her shows. (Billy Graham didn't speak in tongues, but he was fine with his fellow Christians doing it.) New Age, Oprah-style, shares with American Christianities their special mixtures of superstition, selfishness, and a refusal to believe in the random. "Nothing about my life is lucky," she has said. "Nothing. A lot of grace. A lot of blessings. A lot of divine order. But I don't believe in luck."

Williamson, Chopra, and most of the best-known prophets and denominational leaders in the realm owe their careers to Winfrey. Her man Eckhart Tolle, for instance, whose books *The Power of Now* and *A New Earth* sold millions of copies apiece, is a successful crusader against reason itself. "Thinking has become a disease," he writes, to be supplanted by feeling "the inner energy field of your body." The two of them conducted a series of Web-based video seminars in 2008.

New Age, because it's so American, so utterly democratic and decentralized, has multiple sacred texts. One of the most widely read and influential is *The Secret,* emphatically placed in the canon by Winfrey as soon as it was published a decade ago. "I've been talking about this for years on my show," Winfrey said during one of the author's appearances on *Oprah.* "I just never called it The Secret."

The closest antecedent to *The Secret* was *The Power of Positive Thinking* in the 1950s, back when a mega-bestselling guide to supernatural success still needed an explicit tether to Christianity. Reverend Norman Vincent Peale's book has a couple of hundred references to God and several dozen to Jesus. In *The Secret,* on the other hand, Rhonda Byrne mentions Jesus only once, as the founder of the prosperity gospel. All the major biblical figures, including Christ, she claims, "were not only prosperity teachers, but also millionaires themselves, with more affluent lifestyles than many present-day millionaires could conceive of."

The Secret takes the American fundamentals, individualism and supernaturalism and belief in *belief,* and strips away the middlemen and most of the pious packaging—God, Jesus, virtue, hard work rewarded, perfect bliss only in the afterlife. What's left is a "law of attraction," and if you just *crave* anything hard enough, it will become yours. Belief is all. *The Secret's* extreme version of magical thinking goes far beyond its predecessors'. It is staggering. A parody would be almost impossible. It was number one on the *Times's* non-fiction list for three years and sold around twenty million copies. Its sequels (*The Power, The Magic*) sold several million more.

"There isn't a single thing that you cannot do with this knowledge," the book promises. "It doesn't matter who you are or where you are, The Secret can give you whatever you want." Because it's a *scientific fact.*

> The law of attraction is a law of nature. It is as impartial as the law
> of gravity is. . . .
>
> Nothing can come into your experience unless you summon it
> through persistent thoughts. . . .
>
> In the moment you ask, and *believe,* and *know* you already have
> it in the unseen, the entire Universe shifts to bring it into the scene.
> You must act, speak, and think, as though you are receiving it *now.*
> Why? The Universe is a mirror, and the law of attraction is mirroring
> back to you your dominant thoughts. . . .
>
> It takes no time for the Universe to manifest what you want. Any
> time delay you experience is due to your delay in getting to the place
> of believing.

To be clear, she's talking mainly not about spiritual contentment but things, objects, lovers, cash. "The only reason any person does not have enough money is because they are blocking money from coming to them with their thoughts. . . . It is not your job to work out 'how' the money will come to you. It is your job to ask. . . . Leave the details to the Universe on how it will bring it about." She warns that rationalism can neutralize the magic—in fact, awareness of the real world beyond one's individual orbit can be problematic. "When I discovered The Secret, I made a decision that I would not watch the news or read newspapers anymore, because it did not make me feel good."

Right around the time *The Secret* came out, habitués of its general vicinity started buzzing about the year 2012. Ancient Mesoamericans, people were saying, had predicted that in 2012 humankind's present existence would . . . transition. The source of this hysteria had appeared in the late 1960s—a passing bit of speculation by a Yale anthropologist. "There is a suggestion," he wrote of the Mayans' belief about one of their calendar systems, that when the current 5,125-year-long period ends, "Armageddon would overtake the degenerate peoples of the world and all creation" and "our present universe [would] be annihilated." That apparently works out to December 21, 2012, which excited New Age religion makers: now they had their own ancient prophecy for their own dreams of something like a near-future Armageddon and supernaturally wonderful aftermath. Like the Christian prophecies, this branch of apocalypse belief also has its own history of cockeyed literalism, with accompanying debates about whether collapse will precede the happy ending and niggling pseudorational arguments about timing.

I'm sure it's only coincidence that Winfrey ended the daily *Oprah* broadcasts in 2011. A month before the final episode, she interviewed Shirley MacLaine for the millionth time and asked about 2012: "What's gonna happen to us as a species?"

"We're coming into an alignment," MacLaine explained. "It is the first time in twenty-six thousand years—*thirty-six* thousand years—*twenty-six* thousand years, I'm sorry, that this has occurred. . . . You have an alignment where this solar system is on direct alignment with the center of the galaxy. That carries with it a very profound electromagnetic frequency—"

"*Vibration,*" Winfrey interjected.

". . . *vibration,*" MacLaine agreed, "and gravitational pull. Hence the weather. What does that do to consciousness? What does that do to our sense of reality?" It's why people feel rushed and stressed, she said.

Winfrey asked her audience for an amen: "Are you all feeling that?" They were.

"So my stuff isn't really that far out. But what's actually happening, Oprah," MacLaine continued, explaining how the relevant astrology proved the supernatural inflection point was exactly 620 days away. "It's the end of that twenty-six-thousand-year procession of the equinox" and "the threshold of a new beginning. And I think what this *pressure*, this kind of psychic, spiritual *pressure* we're all feeling is about, is that your internal soul is telling you 'Get your act together.'"

When the "threshold" passed normally, 2012 Mayan end-time believers decided that the ancient prophecies must have been misinterpreted and misunderstood. American end-time Christians have had centuries to realize that setting particular dates is a bad idea; for their New Age equivalents, newer to the game, 2012 was a learning moment. Indeed, exactly like Christians who leap on every bit of bad news as proof of their end-time prophecies, the New Age millennialists still think that global warming and terrorism, for instance, are foreshocks of "the Mayan Apocalypse." Like the prophecy-Protestants, they simply *know* a glorious new age is inevitable. That was the take of Daniel Pinchbeck, a New Age evangelist-author who wrote *2012: The Return of Quetzalcoatl*—and then had a charming whoops-sorry essay ready to publish on December 21, 2012. Don't lose faith, Pinchbeck says, because we can all see there's a "growing realization" that "the rational, empirical worldview . . . has reached its expiration date."

——————

34

Blue-Chip Witch Doctors:
The Reenchantment of Medicine

It's one thing to try to experience more peace of mind or feel in sync with a divine order. Mixing magical thinking with medical science and physiology, however, can get problematic. A generation after its emergence as a thing hippies did, alternative medicine became ubiquitous and mainstream. As with so many of the phenomena I've talked about, it's driven by nostalgia and anti-Establishment mistrust of experts, has quasi-religious underpinnings, and comes in both happy and unhappy versions.

And has been brought to you by Oprah Winfrey.

In 2004 a very handsome heart surgeon, prominent but not famous, appeared on *Oprah* to promote a book about alternative medicine. His very name—*Dr. Oz!*—would be way too over-the-top for a character in a comic novel. After Harvard College, Mehmet Oz earned both an M.D. and an M.B.A. from the University of Pennsylvania, then became a top practitioner and professor of heart surgery at Columbia University and director of NewYork-Presbyterian Hospital's Cardiovascular Institute. Timing is everything—young Dr. Oz arrived at Columbia right after it set up its Center for Alternative and Complementary Medicine in the 1990s.

Soon he was bringing an "energy healer" into his operating room who placed her hands on patients as he performed surgery, and invited a reporter to watch. According to Dr. Oz, who is married to a Reiki master, such healers have the power to tune in to their scientifically undetectable "energies" and redirect them as necessary while he's cutting open their hearts.* When *The New Yorker*'s science reporter Michael Specter told Oz he knew of no evidence that Reiki works, the doctor agreed—"if you are talking purely about data." In Fantasyland, *purely about data* is a phrase like *mainstream* and *Establishment* and *consensus* and *rational* and *fact*, meaning *elitist, narrow*, and *blind to the disruptive truths*. "Medicine is a very religious experience," Oz told Specter, then added a kicker directly from the relativistic 1960s: "I have my religion and you have yours."

After that first appearance on *Oprah*, he proceeded to come on her show five dozen more times, usually wearing surgical scrubs. In 2009 Winfrey's company launched the daily *Dr. Oz* show, on which he pushes miracle elixirs, homeopathy, imaginary energies, and psychics who communicate with the dead. He regularly uses the words *miracle* and *magic*. A supplement extracted from tamarind "could be the magic ingredient that lets you lose weight without diet and exercise." Green coffee beans—even though "you may think that magic is make-believe"—are *actually* a "magic weight-loss cure," a "miracle pill [that] can burn fat fast. This is very exciting. And it's breaking news." He has encouraged viewers to believe that vaccines cause autism and other illnesses—as did Winfrey on her show before him. For a study in the British medical journal *BMJ*, a team of experienced evidence reviewers analyzed Dr. Oz's on-air advice—eighty randomly chosen recommendations from 2013. The investigators found legitimate supporting evidence for fewer than half.

The most famous physician in the United States, the man Oprah Winfrey branded as "America's doctor," is a dispenser of make-believe.

Let me be clear: not all alternative health beliefs and practices are quackery. Some deserve respect. Physicians *can* be arrogant hacks. The pharmaceutical business *is*, naturally, out to maximize profit. Sometimes medical science *has* been distorted by powerful corporate interests (smoking: cancer).

---

* Oz's healer, now practicing in Marin County, California, believes she has the power to "take people back to the origins of their disease and distress in early, hidden family trauma [and] take them down to the level of organ, tissue and cell to see how each responded to the shock and reprogram it."

I'm all for healthcare that is focused on prevention, proper diet, exercise, and overall well-being as well as on disease treatment.

I even spend a little time wading in the shallows of the New Age sea. I sometimes swallow capsules of echinacea, an herb American Indians used as medicine—because I read scientific studies that found it may help prevent colds and reduce flu symptoms. I've practiced yoga intermittently. And a few years ago I took up daily meditation. There's now a large scientific literature showing the power of meditation to alter everyday perception in useful ways. "These skills to steer the mind are not magical, otherworldly or transcendental," the distinguished neuroscientist Christof Koch has written.

Still, I couldn't read Gilbert Seldes's 1928 takedown of America's New Age moment around 1900 and not feel busted. "What then could be the appeal to Americans," he wrote when he was thirty-five, "of yoga . . . and the other forms of oriental mysticism?" Maybe it was "that satiety had set in, after all our grasping and possessing, and that we wished to rid ourselves of our encumbrances. . . . Mysticism would then be our escape from the implications of our own materialistic philosophy." But . . . not really. Instead, Seldes says, upscale America's original embrace of yoga and the like "served actually to soothe exasperated nerves" for people who

> had not the faintest intention of giving up the world. Yoga was for them a mystic way of renouncing whatever was irritating and preserving whatever was pleasing. It was an elaborate game of pretense by which noisy people went into silence and distracted people imagined that they were concentrating. The glamour of renunciation suffused the picture which they had of themselves. Actually nothing was renounced. . . . One was alone with the mysterious spirit and, breathing in a refined way, one returned to conquer the world.

In any case, the swing of the American pendulum toward unscientific medicine has been extreme and, it now seems likely, permanent. A big problem is that the rubric "complementary and alternative" is so expansive that a thousand bogus cures are legitimized by their popular-front proximity to a hundred useful practices and treatments. Twenty years ago an editorial in *The New England Journal of Medicine* was spitting mad about the growing respectability of alternative medicine, how it "largely ignores biologic mechanisms" and "disparages modern science," that it was "time for the scientific community to stop giving alternative medicine a free ride."

Nice try. Thanks to the coenabling usual suspects—academia, media, government, and business—we are living in two worlds at once, an amazing scientific present and a revived prescientific past, where robotic surgery and 3-D-printed bionic ears coexist with spurious folk remedies.

A century ago Congress passed the Pure Food and Drug Act, the first federal law regulating medicine and essentially outlawing fake patent medicines. It seemed like the definitive defeat of American medical quackery. But it only went underground, then erupted a generation after the tectonic shifts of the late 1960s and '70s. In 1991 the federal government established an Office of Unconventional Medicine within the National Institutes of Health. That faintly disparaging name was quickly changed to the Office of Alternative Medicine. (Deepak Chopra served as an adviser.) In 1998 it became a full-fledged NIH institute, the National Center for Complementary and Alternative Medicine, then chucked *Alternative* to become the National Center for Complementary and Integrative Health. This extraordinary apparatus was the work of Senator Tom Harkin, a Democrat, inspired by his belief that bee-pollen pills called Aller Bee-Gone had cured his allergies. The center has disbursed billions of dollars to fund research in homeopathy and long-distance spiritual healing, among other projects.

Harkin, when he retired in 2014, was chair of the Senate Health Committee, and during his last term he was cranky that the institution he'd created seemed *way too* science- and evidence-based. "One of the purposes of this center," he complained at a Senate hearing, "was to investigate and validate alternative approaches. Quite frankly, I must say publicly that it has fallen short. I think quite frankly that in this center and in the office previously before it, most of its focus has been on disproving things rather than seeking out and approving." Harkin also cosponsored a bill in the 1990s, along with two-thirds of the Senate, now a law, that removed supplements—not just vitamins but herbs and other botanicals, hormones, natural *whatever*—from regulation by the Food and Drug Administration. The author of the law was Orrin Hatch, the Republican senior senator from Utah; not coincidentally, America's nutritional supplement industry is concentrated in Utah, where Mormons are also concentrated. When federal deregulation was enacted in the 1990s, Americans were buying $9 billion worth of supplements a year; today they spend around $40 billion.

At the University of Arizona, the alternative health superstar Andrew Weil has his own Center for Integrative Medicine at the medical school, with a large faculty that includes a Reiki master/herbal practitioner/aromatherapist. Weil is a Harvard-educated M.D. who provides sensible health advice as well as nonsense about magical energies. Like the Ivy League–trained Oz, he is therefore harder to discredit. Weil's center and Duke University's have formed a confederation of woo-friendly divisions of other big-league medical centers, including those at Stanford, half the Ivy League, and dozens more.

Most alternative treatments and cures have failed to be scientifically confirmed. When they sometimes work to relieve pain or anxiety, the science-based people deride it as a mere placebo effect, a secular faith healing. So the believers who want a scientific imprimatur have changed tack and embraced a new, significant rebranding: *Okay, fine, it's a placebo effect*—and now placebo medicine and placebo studies are a discipline. They have the imprimatur of Harvard, which started a Program in Placebo Studies and the Therapeutic Encounter. (When I first heard about it, I actually thought someone was kidding me.) Its founder and director has a B.A. in East Asian studies and some kind of sketchy Chinese degree in traditional medicine; he had earned his living as an acupuncturist before Harvard made him a professor of medicine. If placebos can sometimes reduce pain and problems like anxiety, fine. But those are all *subjective symptoms,* sometimes remediable mentally because they're experienced mentally.

The problem comes when people jump much further, as they do, imagining and promoting all kinds of nonexistent "mind-body healing effects." If placebos can calm you down and pep you up and relieve aches, why can't they actually *cure diseases*? That's the bridge too far. The surgical oncologist who edits *Science Based Medicine* has written that he has "yet to come across a study that provides serious objective evidence that placebos change 'hard' objective outcomes, such as survival in cancer."

Arguments for harnessing placebo power are like arguments that it doesn't matter if the premises of Mormonism and conversations with Jesus and paranormal experiences are "real." They're like the arguments of Donald Trump's defenders who say it doesn't matter if he lies as long as what he says *feels* true. It's what the author of *The Secret* explained about her fundamental "law of attraction"—the life-changing fantasy that definitely isn't a fantasy, but if it is, so what: "The placebo effect is an example of the law of attraction in action. When a patient truly believes the tablet is a cure, he receives what he believes and is cured."

Maybe most of the millions of Americans who spend billions of dollars a year on homeopathic remedies for their asthma, depression, migraines, allergies, arthritis, or hypertension—six of the ten illnesses most commonly treated—do experience placebo effects and *feel* better. But some of them are failing to get diagnoses and take medicines that would actually treat their illnesses.

Maybe prompt surgical treatment of Steve Jobs's relatively curable form of pancreatic cancer would have made him live longer, maybe not. In any case, for most of a year, according to his biographer Walter Isaacson, he resorted to "fruit juices . . . acupuncture . . . herbal remedies . . . treatments he found on the Internet . . . a psychic," and so on. "I think that he kind of felt that if you don't want something to exist," Isaacson says, "you can have magical thinking" and make it go away. I think of Steve Jobs when I see my neighbors at Whole Foods flipping through the monthly magazine *What Doctors Don't Tell You* and the book *Herbal Medicine, Healing, and Cancer*, by an author whose advanced degree is an M.H.—master herbalist. And browsing the aisles full of homeopathic supplements and elixirs that promise to "build better blood." And buying expensive gluten-free snacks even though only a minuscule percentage of them have any medical reason to do so.

35

How the Mainstream Enabled Fantasyland: Squishies, Cynics, and Believers

As the old, clear distinctions between plausible and preposterous beliefs and assertions were fading at the turn of this century, Michael Barkun wrote in *A Culture of Conspiracy* that the Establishment still maintained the fundamental true-false boundary "in a variety of ways"—"by withholding access to the most powerful and prestigious channels of communication; by withholding institutional rewards and sponsorship from certain ideas; and by subjecting fringe ideas and those who hold them to scorn."

That list of the means by which leaders in any society try to maintain coherence and order sounds a bit evil and un-American: *withholding access, withholding institutional sponsorship, subjecting ideas and those who hold them to scorn, stigmatized knowledge.* That's why *elite* always has been a pejorative in this country, and why *mainstream* recently turned into one. It's also a big reason why, during the last few decades, so many in our boundary-drawing class yielded to so many varieties of nonsense.

Pre-Internet information systems, in which accuracy and credibility were determined mainly by experts or otherwise designated deciders, had terrible flaws and annoyances, including complacency, blind spots, snobbishness, and bigotry. But those gates and gatekeepers also managed to keep the worst hogwash out of our mainstream.

In religion, as I've described, the Protestant Establishment mainly had its power mooted by the rise of new denominations. In the secular Establishment, however, it happened differently. Among the gatekeepers in academia and media and government and politics charged with determining what's factually true and what's iffy and false, there has been much more capitulation, voluntary surrenders to the barbarians at their gates. It's a great irony: the institutional objects of so much Fantasyland scorn, all those mainstream elitists, have been essential to Fantasyland's growth and entrenchment.

Some of the capitulators are permissive, inclusive Squishies, people intellectually or temperamentally disinclined to "stigmatize knowledge claims" that deserve stigma—to tell people they're full of shit when they are. Some are Cynics, users or impresarios motivated by desire for renown or influence or money. Some are Believers who made their way into positions of gatekeeping responsibility. And some are Squishies or Cynics who simply lost their stomach for the fight against the multiplying and empowered Believers.

CAMPUSES HAD PLENTY OF SQUISHIES even before the rise of relativism made it impolite to distinguish between real and unreal, true and untrue. The work of a couple of French intellectuals, their gnomic murkiness part of the attraction to Americans, helped make relativism even more irresistible to intellectuals during the 1980s and '90s. After Michel Foucault had become an intellectual superstar with his critique of the concept of insanity, his rival Jean Baudrillard became a celebrity among American intellectuals by going further, declaring that rationalism was a tool of the oppressors that was tapped out as a way of understanding the world, pointless and doomed. In other words, as he wrote in 1986, "the secret of theory"—this whole intellectual realm now called itself simply Theory—"is that truth does not exist."

Yet for all his self-parodying European-intellectual shtick—the jargon, the bombast, the you-pathetic-fools contempt—in his 1981 book *Simulacra and Simulation* he was actually onto something: he coined the word *hyperreality* to describe contemporary American life (and Americanized places elsewhere). The concoctions of what I'm calling the fantasy-industrial complex, he said, had come to seem more real than reality and had twisted people's attitudes and behaviors accordingly.

At universities during the 1980s and '90s, the most committed relativists, convinced that all knowledge and especially science are merely self-serving opinions or myths, created their own disciplines and subdisciplines as various as Protestant denominations. Professors began proudly *identifying* as relativists. "For the relativist," two major figures in relativist sociology wrote, "there is no sense attached to the idea that some standards or beliefs are really rational as distinct from merely locally accepted as such," and they declared the ideal approach was being "impartial with respect to truth and falsity, rationality or irrationality."

In their perverse conviction that no particular understanding is superior to any other, many of these academics become de facto Believers. And some are also Cynics. "Black folks understand, just like white folks do," a Rutgers professor of Africana studies wrote in *Salon* in 2014, "that reason should be wielded as a tactic, not adhered to as a rule." But many more in the humanities and social sciences, beyond the confines of the hep postmodern isms, are simply nonjudgmental Squishies. Reason may be okay for *us* as far as it goes, in *our* privileged clan, but we may not presume to expect it of others.

These notions became standard on campus and were then taken out into the world by three generations of graduates so far, tens of millions of educated Americans, where they sifted into popular thought. It became uncool to disparage magical thinking and other irrationality. The very Americans who ought to be important fighters in the long war in defense of reason, professors and the graduates whose minds they shape, instead became enablers of Fantasyland.

It's all good, academia decided.

Berserk Christianity? *Fine.*

At the very high end is Tanya Luhrmann, the Stanford anthropologist who spent four years among charismatics. She acknowledges and approves of the wormhole between anything-goes academics and anything-goes Christians. "The playfulness and paradox of this new religiosity," she writes in *When God Talks Back,* "does for Christians what postmodernism, with its doubt-filled, self-aware, playful intellectual style, did for intellectuals. It allows them to waver between the metaphorical and the literal." She *wants* to doubt reality. ("I *want* to believe," as Agent Mulder said on *The X-Files* about a mysterious voice in his head.) Of her Christians who think God or Jesus talks to them, Luhrmann says, they're "not necessarily" making "a perceptual mistake" because—tautology alert—"someone's capacity to experience the supernatural . . . has something to do with their willingness to see more than is materially present before them."

Luhrmann was already going native at the start of her career in the 1980s. Her first book, *Persuasions of the Witch's Craft*, involved hanging out with "educated white [people] who practiced what they called magic." At a certain point in that research, she "began to feel power in my veins—to really feel it, not to imagine it. I grew hot. . . . I wanted to sing. And then wisps of smoke came out of my backpack, in which I had tossed my bicycle lights. One of them was melting." One day during that research, she awoke in her upper-floor bedroom and saw the faces of six Druids at her window, who then vanished. She's unhappy with how modern people have created "the concept of hallucination," because when "the seeing of ghosts became a psychological phenomenon, it also became a pathological one."

Then there's Steve Fuller, born and raised in New York, a graduate of Columbia, now a professor of the history and sociology of science. Scientific inquiry, he says, really is no different from or superior to religious belief. He's all for what he calls a "re-enchantment of science" and for letting anyone decide the factual truth of anything—the equivalent of "what happened in the Protestant Reformation, getting the Bible in your own hands, reading it for yourself." The pseudoscientific creationists behind intelligent design "are not anti-science," he says, "but they are anti-establishment." Which is a distinction without a difference that substitutes a thing everybody disapproves, *the Establishment*, for a thing academics are supposed to approve, *science*. At a famous 2005 federal trial in Pennsylvania, in which pro-science parents were suing to keep intelligent design out of their kids' high school biology classes, Fuller appeared as an expert witness for the school board. His testimony is extreme Squishiness in a nutshell. Intelligent design, he testified, isn't creationism in disguise or "inherently religious," and its "commitment to supernaturalism does not make it unscientific." For good measure, he stood on a piece of common ground shared by the left and the right, referring to "a tendency . . . for science to be governed by a kind of, to put it bluntly, self-perpetuating elite."*

The happy fantasies of pseudoscience and the paranormal? *It's all good.*

A leader of this counter-Establishment is Gary Schwartz. He got his psychology Ph.D. from Harvard and spent a decade at Yale as a professor of psychology and psychiatry. In middle age, he decided that souls exist and the

---

* The judge, a churchgoing Lutheran and Republican appointed by George W. Bush, didn't buy it. He ruled that intelligent design "is not science" and that the school board acted with duplicity and "breathtaking inanity"—as well as unconstitutionally. Some heroic gatekeepers are still guarding the gates.

living can communicate with the dead, and he set about trying to prove it. He moved from Yale to the University of Arizona and deep into Fantasyland. Although he has no M.D. or hard-science degree, he's now a professor of neurology, medicine, and surgery—and director of the university's Laboratory for Advances in Consciousness and Health, where the main research programs include Survival of Consciousness After Death and Other Worldly/ Higher Spiritual Consciousness. Among his hundreds of academic papers are two from 2014 and 2015, both entitled "God, Synchronicity, and Postmaterialist Psychology." In them he describes eleven coincidences that he found so "increasingly improbable," he figured God must have been signaling him, and then fifteen instances during one two-week period when he happened to encounter the words *giraffes* and *Paris*. To Schwartz, this showed that "'spirits' (e.g., the souls of people who have 'died') . . . collaborate with the Divine . . . for the purpose of orchestrating complex, creative, and personally meaningful synchronicities."

In 2014 he organized the first International Summit on Post-Materialist Science, Spirituality and Society in Tucson. The summit took place at Canyon Ranch, the $1,500-a-night resort where Schwartz is also corporate director of Development of Energy Healing. His conference co-organizer was a professor who runs Columbia University's clinical psychology program and its Spirituality and Mind-Body Institute. She's also co-editor of *Spirituality in Clinical Practice,* the APA's new peer-reviewed academic journal that published Schwartz's papers about supernatural coincidences involving giraffes and Paris.

Out of their summit came a "Manifesto for a Post-Materialist Science." By *post-materialist,* the manifesto makes clear, the signers mean postscientific. They reject the idea that "the mind is nothing but the physical activity of the brain," because *of course* "we can mentally influence—at a distance— physical devices and living organisms (including other human beings)," and we can "communicate with the minds of people who have physically died."

One of the subtlest thinkers in academia's magical-thinking camp is Jeffrey Kripal, a professor and former chair of religious studies at Rice University. He's the author of *Esalen: America and the Religion of No Religion,* a history of the place. Kripal wants to "put 'the impossible' back on the table again." He *believes.* He could write a fine Bizarro World version of this book.* He's happy about the erasures of boundaries between fiction and reality and

---

* Kripal co-wrote his most recent book, *Super Natural: A New Vision of the Unexplained* (2016), with Whitley Strieber, the extraterrestrial abductee I discuss in Chapter 38.

about the merger of science with religion and of both with fantasy entertainment. In a recent interview, Kripal said that when belief in the "paranormal is rejected by the elite scientific establishment . . . it goes where it can go—right into film, science fiction, and comic books. . . . The paranormal is such a popular subject *because it is real,* that is, because people actually have these sorts of experiences all the time" (emphasis added). When Kripal came out of an *X-Men* movie and found an X-shaped piece of jewelry in the parking lot, for instance, it wasn't a cool coincidence but a revelatory sign that "paranormal powers are the buds of our evolving supernature, that the X-Men are real."

In fact, according to some academics, any fictions and falsehoods passing for fact and truth are *all good, all fine,* as long as they come from the bottom up.

Jodi Dean is a political scientist, a Princeton graduate who took her advanced degrees at Columbia in the 1990s, as postmodernism achieved what she'd probably call hegemony. She's now a full professor with an endowed chair at Hobart and William Smith, a fine liberal arts college in upstate New York. In her book *Aliens in America: Conspiracy Cultures from Outerspace to Cyberspace,* she was delighted on principle "to defend the veracity of people claiming to be not just [UFO] witnesses but abductees."

However, her enthusiasm for untruths and her contempt for reason run much deeper and broader than that. She begins from a standard Squishy place. "There are myriad perspectives on the world, each with its own legitimate claim to truth," she says, and is "convinced that many contemporary political matters are simply undecidable." She uses academic jargon about "the fugitivity of truth" but goes further—"the meanings of 'belief' and 'real' aren't clear"—and still further. If there were a University of Fantasyland, she'd be a strong candidate for provost.

Dean celebrates practically every attitude and approach that appalls me. She rejects "the presumption that there is some 'public' that shares a notion of reality, a concept of reason, and a set of criteria by which claims to reason and rationality are judged." In fact, as far as "the rationality of the public sphere" goes, "the collapse of its very possibility" is all to the good. Naturally, she uses the late 1960s term *consensus reality* to disparage reason. The "norms of public reason are," she writes, "oppressive and exclusionary." Because the "antidemocrats" in the mainstream try "to contain the rest of us with their borders, sciences, traditions and truths," disbelief in science "makes sense" and "is potentially democratic. It prevents science from functioning as a trump card having the last word in what is ultimately a political debate."

Alternate realities engendered by the Internet and talk radio and cable news are fine by her. "Now," she writes, "the 'irrational' can get their message out. They can find and connect with those myriad others also dismissed by science. They can network and offer alternatives to official deployments or reason." Such as imaginary conspiracies: "democratic politics in an age of virtuality will need to turn to conspiracy theory as a way of making links," she says. "And, of course, to ask about the 'truth' of this information is to miss the point." *Of course.* To her, a particular feminist academic is foolish to warn against "epidemic hysteria" and distinguish between factual truth and "sensational news reports [and] rumors"—"as if we can know the difference." Rather, Dean says, the "approach to political action which is most likely to enhance freedom contributes to the production of paranoia." While she is exceptional, she's by no means unique.

How perfect that since getting tenure, Dean has declared herself a communist and says the USSR wasn't as bad as it has been portrayed—because she's also Orwellian in the *Animal Farm* sense, some of the equal animals being more equal than others. While every perspective has its legitimate claim to truth, she writes, we must consider the beliefs "of the oppressed as epistemologically superior."

During these last few years when I was immersed in postmodern academic texts, I was repeatedly reminded of a certain diary entry by a young Ph.D., a novelist and playwright, in 1924. "I believe that *The Protocols of the Wise Men of Zion* are a forgery," he wrote. "I believe in the intrinsic but not the factual truth of the *Protocols*." That was Joseph Goebbels, a decade before he became the Nazi Reich Minister of Propaganda.

MEDIA AND INFORMATION BUSINESSES WERE always businesses, but for much of the twentieth century with an asterisk—many corporations and especially families that owned major news outlets and publishers didn't expect to maximize profits. Belief in serving the public good really did privilege reason and sobriety in what they published and broadcast. The luxury of operating as oligopolies and local monopolies, of course, made it easier for broadcasters and newspapers to stick to straighter versions of the factual truth.

But then the economic, cultural, and political shields that had protected them from the market's full gravitational force started to disintegrate. The free market was the free market, America decided in the 1980s, and nobody got a pass. In the news and publishing businesses, making money became less a vulgar necessity and more the main point. The Cynics came out of the closet. Whatever sold, including fantasy nonfiction, they started selling.

NBC launched *Unsolved Mysteries,* which treated paranormal claims and counterfactual histories as if they were real. Back then, reality still mattered enough that the network felt obliged to preface each episode with warnings: "This is *not* an NBC News production" and "What you are about to see is *not* a news broadcast." During the 1980s too, television became cable television, and TV service in America turned from a shared public resource into another individually purchased product, its content freed from rules concerning truth or accuracy. The five-hundred-ring circus of cable TV became an important new piece of Fantasyland infrastructure, along with the Internet and talk radio.

I could fill pages with examples from the 1990s on, but a small sampling should do. *Crossing Over with John Edward,* a program purporting to let people communicate with the dead, was a big hit for the USA Network. Back then, when TLC was still called The Learning Channel, the taglines for a show during its Conspiracy Week were "Did they really catch the man behind the Oklahoma City bombing? Or was there a conspiracy?"

In this century, especially in the last decade, TV really gave itself over to the wanton retailing of fantasies as realities.* ABC News created brand extensions of its blue-chip shows, both *20/20: The Sixth Sense* and the limited series *Nightline Primetime: Beyond Belief,* with episodes including "Battle with the Devil" and "The Miracle Mysteries." After Time-Warner turned Court TV into truTV, one of its big shows was *Conspiracy Theory with Jesse Ventura,* on which the former governor and pro wrestler promoted 9/11 as an inside job, FEMA's concentration camps, the 2012 Mayan countdown, and the government electronically mind-controlling dissidents.

There were Scripps's *Ghost Adventures* and the History Channel's *Cryptid: The Swamp Beast.* Discovery Communications' various nonfiction cable channels have aired the documentaries *Mermaids: The New Evidence* and *Zombie Apocalypse* as well as the series *Angels Among Us, Amish Haunting,* and *Lost Tapes,* about werewolves and extraterrestrial reptilian humanoids on Earth. The National Geographic Channel aired a prime-time documentary, *Secrets of Revelation,* that featured a realistic digital enactment of Jesus's

---

* An irony: well after nonfiction TV freely began blending in fiction, the figurehead of one of the big organizations still attempting to adhere to factual reality was brought low for telling tall tales about himself. In 2015, in the reality-based zone inhabited by Brian Williams, it turned out that explicit public fabulism was still prohibited and punishable.

prophesied war with the Antichrist at Armageddon, and the History Channel followed with its *Revelation: The End of Days.*

For a generation, in other words, American television has trained Americans to treat fiction as nonfiction.

It's not just TV. During *Time* magazine's first quarter century, through 1947, Jesus appeared on the cover three times, all for stories about religious art. During the next forty-seven years, there were two Jesus covers, both illustrating actual news stories, about Christianity's revival in the 1960s and early '70s. Fast forward to the turn of this century, when *Time* put Jesus on the cover five times in less than ten years—plus two more about Genesis and the Virgin Mary.

The major publishers began issuing big nonfiction books about angels and the supernatural in the 1990s, and these days a bestselling account of the afterlife appears almost every year—*90 Minutes in Heaven, Heaven Is for Real, The Boy Who Came Back from Heaven, To Heaven and Back, Proof of Heaven.* The author of the last one, a neurosurgeon, says he rode around heaven "on a beautiful butterfly wing; millions of other butterflies around us . . . through blooming flowers, blossoms on trees, and they were all coming out as we flew through them . . . waterfalls, pools of water, indescribable colors, and above there were these arcs of silver and gold light and beautiful hymns coming down from them. Indescribably gorgeous hymns." He was the featured guest on two *Dr. Oz* episodes, and ABC News featured him on *Good Morning America, World News Tonight, 20/20,* and *Nightline.* His book sold two million copies. This genre hit a rough patch in 2015, however, when the boy who'd come back from Heaven at age six announced at sixteen that the book he'd co-written with his father was all lies.*

Rupert Murdoch's News Corp., the first big New York media company to enter the Christian book market in a big way, in the 1980s, has practically cornered it, selling half the true-believer books in the United States. Four of the five largest publishers now have their own Christian imprints. Time Warner calls its Warner Faith—an evangelical Christian publisher named after the Jewish brothers who founded the Hollywood dream factory out of which the company sprouted.

HOMESCHOOLING IS ONE WAY IN which government Squishies capitulated to Believers. After courts gave the go-ahead in the 1980s, homeschooling took

---

* The authors' surname, I swear, is *Malarkey.*

off. Like some alternative health practices, it can work; one of my nephews, homeschooled until high school, is among the smartest, best-informed, and well-socialized people I know. But as a general phenomenon, homeschooling is another instance of the Establishment's big green light to treating beliefs as facts and the imaginary as actual. Homeschools are part of the new infrastructure for enabling alternate realities.

About two million kids are now educated exclusively at home in the United States, a number that's more than doubled in this century. Two-thirds or more of the parents who homeschool say they do it "to provide religious instruction," and those are overwhelmingly evangelicals and fundamentalists—people trying to shield children from science (and history and philosophy and literature) at odds with their theological (and social and political) beliefs.* "Most home-schoolers," for instance, "will definitely have a sort of creationist component to their home-school program," according to a spokesperson for the Home School Legal Defense Association. Such as the textbook *Biology*, published by Bob Jones University Press, which teaches that unlimited CO_2 emissions are fine and that AIDS may have been God's means of punishing "sexual impurity." In other words, the Christian home-schooling movement consists of a million DIY mini-madrassas. It's a free country. But the Squishies (and Believers) in state governments have also failed to establish standards for parents who build epistemological bubbles for their children. Half the states require no standardized tests or other measures for homeschooled children, and fewer than a dozen require home teachers to be high school graduates. Doing otherwise would be elitist.

Homeschoolers with your creationist biology textbooks: go for it. But creationism is now also taught to many tens of thousands of children in public schools—that is, in publicly funded charter schools. For instance, a company called Responsive Ed is the largest charter-education operator in Texas, with dozens of schools around the state. "In the beginning, God created the Heavens and the Earth," Responsive Ed's science texts teach. Evolutionary biology, they say, consists of "dogma" and "unproved theory."

Then there is the craftier degradation of public school textbooks by a de facto coalition of co-enablers—the Cynics (and some Squishies) in publishing and the Believers (and Cynics) in state and local governments. If you're in the textbook business, and a third of the parents of your end users believe that evolution never happened (or that climate change isn't happening), selling accurate textbooks is a problem. So to mollify that large piece of your

* 2012 National Household Education Surveys Program.

market, you hedge. Texas is problematic both because it is (with California) the largest buyer of textbooks, and creationists have controlled its elected state board of education and many of its local ones. The chair of the state board in 2009 was a dentist who said that "evolution is hooey" and that he can "evaluate history textbooks [by] see[ing] how they cover Christianity."

The rest of us are supposed to relax because the Texas tail no longer wags the national textbook dog as much as it once did—and the big publishers have started custom-creating unscientific science and Christianized history texts just for public schools that want them. About global warming, for instance, the teachers' version of the sixth-grade *World Cultures & Geography* says that scientists "do not agree on what is causing the change" in "Earth's climate." The publisher is McGraw-Hill Education, one of the three largest educational publishers and a major capitulator to the science-denying forces. It was formerly part of one of the grand old American book and magazine publishers but is now operated by a private equity firm that also owns *American Idol,* Graceland, and Chuck E. Cheese's—not quite Disney but trans-Fantasyland corporate synergy nevertheless.

36

Anything Goes—Unless It Picks My Pocket or Breaks My Leg

AFTER EMERGING IN THE 1970S AS THE HAUNTED, WELL-ARMED COUSINS OF *Whole Earth Catalog* readers, survivalists steadily multiplied. They're betting on a complete breakdown of the U.S. economy and government that they can and will survive by living as they imagine Americans lived centuries ago, in rural isolation and off the grid. Theirs is a dystopia-ready lifestyle, a fantasy given vivid form and encouraged by the three *Mad Max* movies that came out between 1979 and 1985. A great selling point was the Y2K panic, the fear in the 1990s that our new digital systems would all go haywire as 1999 turned to 2000, and the newly digital-dependent world would collapse. That didn't happen, of course, but then the 9/11 attacks and new viral epidemics (SARS, avian flu) helped give survivalism its momentum. Once you *really believe,* you can always find new evidence to support your beliefs.

There are now millions of Americans counting on a nonsupernatural apocalypse. They got a bigger tent when the term *preppers* became common in the 1980s, a rubric encompassing everybody from hardcore survivalists to wannabes and lookie-loos, from that Ted Kaczynski–ish guy who carries his AR-15 into the diner to the nice couple down the block with a basement room full of whey powder and antibiotics. Preppers are to survivalists as evangelicals are to fundamentalists.

Of course, the premise of prepping and survivalism isn't necessarily delusional. It's possible some sudden catastrophic breakdown of systems could occur and last for months or years. But any of us could also win Mega Millions, too, and we don't rearrange our lives assuming it's going to happen. It's in this curiously wishful certainty of doomsday that prudence slides into fantasy.

Survivalists are an interesting case study because they combine so many Fantasyland strands into a single package. They've taken a couple of the role-playing hobbies that people acknowledge are fantasies—pretend war, simulated olden-times life—and make them *real*, a full-time fantasy game, a never-ending LARP.

The movement has a strong religious aspect. One of its most celebrated leaders, a former Army Intelligence captain named James Wesley, Rawles (he insists on that odd comma), has invited survivalists to the intermountain Northwest, what he calls the American Redoubt—an exodus "analogous to the Puritan exodus from Europe. They couldn't fit in and said, 'We're going to move to completely virgin territory and start afresh.' Christians of *all races* are welcome to be my neighbors."

Like American fantasists since the Puritans, preppers are highly invested in the *rationality* of their scenarios. They obsess over every riot and war and epidemic and uh-oh data point as confirmation that the sky really is falling this time, each news event a glimpse of our unavoidable every-man-for-himself near future. Their politics tend to be right-wing antigovernment, so government collapse and anarchy are dreams as much as fears.

Americans are *practical* people, and survivalists revel in the operational details. What were previously just lifestyle choices with fantastical aspects become life-or-death necessities—you'll depend on all those guns and ammunition, and alternative medicine will be the only alternative. Indeed, survivalist fantasy imbues ordinary hobbies—gardening, baking, canning, crafting, woodworking, camping—with *existential purpose*. It's American pioneer nostalgia pushed to the max, Frontierland meets *The Walking Dead*. Like the new patent medicine business, the survivalist freeze-dried food sector is a Utah-based Mormon oligopoly—Latter-day Saints have been end-time stockpilers for a century. ("While your neighbors are struggling to find food," one of the companies promised, "you will be dining on lasagna, beef stroganoff, and a variety of other delicious entrees.")

I'm reminded of myself at age twelve—with my beloved BB gun and the Big Ear surveillance device I bought at Radio Shack, camping out alone with packets of freeze-dried food and my secret notecard file of information about acquaintances, as I was earning Boy Scout merit badges. Preppers and survivalists love their jargon and acronyms that give their hobby/lifestyle a serious military feel. After the final SHTF (shit hits the fan) events, survivalists not yet in their *fortresses* will *bug out* and then cope with TEOTWAWKI (the end of the world as we know it), in which life is WROL (without rule of law). Each MAG (mutual assistance group) is urged to draft and ratify a constitution in advance.

And it's definitely another American phenomenon. In the whole of the United Kingdom, according to the *Guardian,* there is only a single shop, in a little nowhere land east of Milton Keynes, that specializes in gas masks and crossbows and machetes and tactical thumbcuffs for survivalists and preppers. The United States has scores of dedicated brick-and-mortar stores, as well as service businesses like American Redoubt Realty, which sells houses to survivalists "in the American Redoubt, or in one of the many Micro-Redoubt Safe Havens around the United States." The firm is actually not in *the* Redoubt but in a northern California ski town called Norden. As it happens, it's just a short walk from a perfect historic site, the spot where the single best-known group of freedom-seeking, risk-taking, self-reliant wagon train pioneers spent a winter in a snowbound mountain pass—the Donner Party, four dozen of whom survived, some by eating the corpses of their three dozen fellow pioneers.

SURVIVALISTS AND PREPPERS ARE WACKY and sad. But: *I do my thing and they do their thing, and if by chance we find each other, it's beautiful.* The fantasies they sincerely believe and elaborately enact don't really affect my life or yours.

And those fantasies are among the last I'll discuss at length that don't in some important sense, as our founding libertarian Thomas Jefferson put it, "pick my pocket or break my leg."

During the American Revolution, uniformed jackbooted tyrannical British thugs arrived at Jefferson's self-reliant (and slave-dependent) mountaintop Virginia fortress, Monticello. But he had run away in the nick of time, retreating to his second redoubt eighty miles away. There in hiding he completed his one great book, *Notes on the State of Virginia.*

In the chapter about religion, Jefferson reminded his readers that some of colonial America's official, government-sanctioned churches had persecuted and even executed heretics. Therefore, he declared, the new government must neither ban nor embrace any particular religion. Let people believe whatever they want, because "it does me no injury for my neighbour to say there are twenty gods, or no god. It neither picks my pocket nor breaks my leg."

I agree. I tend to agree too with Jefferson's assertion in the same passage that "reason and free enquiry are the only effectual agents against error," as well as his conclusion elsewhere that much of "our particular superstition," Christianity, is "made up of the deliria of crazy imaginations."

By my reckoning, way too many Americans now bother with reason hardly at all, give themselves over too much to the deliria of crazy imaginations, believe too many untrue and impossible things, and are losing the ability and the will to distinguish between real and unreal. Not that they don't have the *right*.

So: live in your bunker with a decade's worth of twenty-serving cans of teriyaki rice and beef. Pretend you live in a little house on the prairie and shop once a week on the make-believe Via Condotti nearby. When you're not managing your imaginary NFL all-star team, imagine you're serving as an officer in the Second Connecticut Heavy Artillery Regiment at the Battle of Cold Harbor. Get ready for Jesus's return. Impersonate mad Dr. Mundo's summoner in League of Legends, an aristocratic aesthete on Instagram, a truth-telling troll on Twitter. Fantasize that you were born with those perfect artificial breasts. Speak in tongues. Read and believe the books by people who say they died and went to Heaven. Dress like a wizard or a feudal baron. Believe that believing you'll get rich will make you rich, that burning sage cleared your house of evil spirits, that humans were supernaturally created in a flash the day before yesterday, that alien beings taught us to build computer chips. Go crazy.

You have every right. And snug and smug in my own Urban American Redoubt, I have every right to disapprove of my fellow Americans who've decided that reason and empiricism are just some of many ways of understanding the world, no better than any other, that everyone is entitled to *her* truth and *his* truth. I am free to practice what the liberal *New York Times* columnist Nicholas Kristof scolds writers for doing, to take a "sneering tone about conservative Christianity itself" even though "mockery of religious faith is inexcusable"—and then I can raise him one, sneering at his mockery of Christians who believe their faith requires them to oppose marriage equality. And he or they or whoever may all disapprove of me. We're Americans! Hurrah.

The great compromise between the American religious impulse and the

American Enlightenment in the 1700s permitted any and every conceivable sect to bud and blossom. Fine. But that principle isn't working so well anymore. The fanciful and religious and cryptoreligious parts have gotten overripe, bursting and spilling their juices over the Enlightenment-reason parts, spoiling our whole barrel. Holders of any belief about anything, especially and incontrovertibly if those beliefs are ascribed to *faith*, are now expected to be immune from challenge.

Most of the individual fantasies, Christian and New Age and those served up by the fantasy-industrial complex, don't pick my pocket or break my leg, as Jefferson put it—or yours, unless you choose to buy in. Who doesn't love the Amish? Their peculiar beliefs and lifestyles are odd but charming, picturesque, and bother nobody else. The new ubiquity of pornography and reality television has spawned the hybrid subspecies of amateur porn—sex between nonactors, or between actors pretending not to be actors.* Gross, depressing . . . but I don't have to watch. Porn addiction has apparently rendered millions of (male) pornhounds more disinterested, disappointed, and disappointing sexual partners, but that's not my problem. So what if there are lots of Americans with various screws loose? So what if they dream and stew in their own mad, mad, mad, mad dreamworlds? Ignore them, let them alone, let them be. Right? *Aye, there's the rub.*

There are real consequences in the real world.

Delusional ideas and magical thinking flood from the private sphere into the public, become so pervasive and deeply rooted, so *normal,* that they affect everyone. Some American fantasies have become weaponized, literally. In other words, our pockets *are* being picked and our legs *are* being broken.

Take the soft fantasies that underlay our monomaniacal suburbanization of the last seventy years. Aesthetics and the illusions of pastoral life aside, they wound up creating a highly problematic national dependence on cars and oil, made commutes too long and too many good jobs too far away from where workers live, and encouraged people to become unnecessarily overweight and therefore unnecessarily expensive for society to keep alive. As the more fantastical ideas of alternative medicine are mainstreamed, millions of

---

* And the sub-subspecies of sex between an actor and an amateur—the video that *Gawker* posted of WWE star Hulk Hogan (Terry Bollea) with a friend's wife. His testimony at the trial of his suit against *Gawker* is a milestone of Fantasyland jurisprudence as it tries to draw fiction-reality boundaries. Asked about media appearances where he'd cheerfully discussed the video and his penis, he replied: "We were discussing the length of *Hulk Hogan's,*" because "Terry Bollea's penis is not ten inches." But, he testified, "even . . . Hulk Hogan was embarrassed" by the video.

people are being cheated, which doesn't break your or my leg; but when their illnesses deposit them in the actual-doctor-and-hospital healthcare system late in the treatment game, paid for by insurance and the government, that does pick our pockets. The belief that childhood vaccines cause autism was a fantasy that directly produced disease and death among people who happened to be in the proximity of unvaccinated and infected children (see Chapter 41). As disbelief in science grows, our whole society may become less prosperous and more vulnerable. As religious belief drives government to make legal contraception and abortions more difficult to get, the rest of us will have our pockets picked in all kinds of ways for years to come.

That so many of our neighbors are saying so many loony things now *is* doing us real injury. More and more in lots of ways, Fantasyland has started to pick our pockets and break our legs.

PART VI

The Problem with Fantasyland:
From the 1980s to the Present and Beyond

"[You] in what we call the reality-based community . . . believe that solutions emerge from your judicious study of discernible reality. That's not the way the world really works anymore. We create our own reality."

—Karl Rove,
senior advisor to President George W. Bush (2004)

"You're saying it's a falsehood. And they're giving . . . our press secretary gave alternative facts."

—Kellyanne Conway,
counselor to President Donald Trump (2017)

37

The Inmates Running the Asylum Decide
Monsters Are Everywhere

You have to be of a certain age to recall the frenzy. Even if you're old enough to remember, you probably didn't register the extremity of what happened. But during the 1980s and '90s, Americans suddenly imagined that children—by the tens or hundreds of thousands—were being abducted and tortured and kidnapped and murdered every year.

These panics took several overlapping, mutually reinforcing forms. There was an element of overreaction, of mass hysteria that imagined actual but rare crimes to be epidemic. In a subjectivity of a new American kind, individuals were encouraged to believe they were victims and to elide the boundaries between imagination and memory—and were then believed because *they* strongly believed. The Christian focus on Satan was reviving. Americans' reawakened belief in conspiracies—conspiracies among evildoers, conspiracies in the government and elite professions to cover up the secret evil—provided fertile ground too. And prominent figures in those very institutions—the news media, the psychotherapeutic industry, law enforcement, churches—abetted the hysteria in ways they wouldn't have done before full-on Fantasyland was emerging.

Let me pull apart each element on each front of this particular perfect storm.

In the early 1980s, following the disappearances and murders of Etan Patz in New York City, Adam Walsh in South Florida, and two dozen children in Atlanta, a national missing-children panic ignited. Congress passed a federal Missing Children's Act, and milk cartons were plastered with photographs of missing children. News media pegged the number of abductions at between 20,000 and 50,000 a year, with estimates up to the hundreds of thousands.

I had just become a writer for the national affairs section of *Time,* and one day I did some simple arithmetic concerning the missing-children problem. If the low-end figure was true, if twenty thousand American children really were abducted by strangers each year, it meant that in New York City alone a dozen children would be disappearing every week. I found it improbable. I called half a dozen urban police departments around the country and asked each one how many cases it had had in the previous year of children taken by strangers. One here, none there, a couple in the next place. By extrapolation, it seemed clear that the correct national number was possibly in the hundreds, certainly not in the thousands, let alone tens of thousands. My editor at *Time,* however, declined to let me go forward with such a wildly skeptical story. A couple of years later some *Denver Post* reporters established that the vast majority of missing children were actually runaways or involved in parental custody disputes, and that the standard statistics were indeed exaggerated by orders of magnitude. They won a Pulitzer Prize. And indeed, a decade later the FBI estimated that the number of true kidnapping victims was no more than three hundred a year, most of whom were not murdered. The standard high-end figure of fifty thousand a year had been invented by Adam Walsh's father, who later admitted it was just his "guesstimate." The missing-children panic crested, but the myth became a permanent basis for a new American mode of anxious, frightened, overprotective parenting.

AROUND THE SAME TIME, THE culture recognized that the sexual abuse of children by adults close to them was more common than anyone had imagined—that it had been terribly underreported and underprosecuted. The exposure of sexual abuse and its prevalence—by victims, law enforcement, and the press—was important and heroic. There was, however, a panicked and extreme national overreaction as well, as the flurry of media coverage of legitimate revelations helped provoke a literal witch hunt. Instead of uncovering, for instance, the widespread sexual abuse of children by Roman Catholic priests, a story that wouldn't break until the 2000s, in the 1980s and '90s we focused instead on a terrifying but imaginary crime spree by demonic anti-Christians.

The psychiatry and especially the clinical psychology professions were essential enablers. For most of a century, psychotherapy was dominated by Sigmund Freud and his ideas. When he started, Freud had believed that many psychological problems were attributable to childhood sexual abuse, especially by patients' fathers—his so-called "seduction theory." But he soon decided that among his patients' memories of childhood sexual encounters, "the share of fantasy in it is far greater than I had thought in the beginning." This revised understanding, that children are prone to having sexual fantasies involving their parents, became an axiom of psychopathology. On the other hand, serious psychiatry and psychology abandoned the larger, collateral Freudian idea—that people in general automatically "repress" memories of sexual abuse and other traumas.

By the 1980s, Freudian psychotherapy was being eclipsed by other forms of treatment, therapies like those developed at the Esalen Institute and psychotropic prescription drugs. But Freud was still Freud. As a consequence of three big cultural changes wrought in the 1960s and '70s—sex now discussed openly, women demanding equality, fantasies taken seriously—his theories were ready to be selectively revised and revived. The new take was that Freud had been correct in the first place: fathers routinely *did* abuse their daughters sexually, and victims' memories of that abuse *were* repressed—and could be dredged up by therapists.

Among the most respectable promoters of this idea was Jeffrey Masson, a slick, Sammy Glick–ish young historian of psychoanalysis who worked for the Freud Archives at the Library of Congress. In the early 1980s, his book *The Assault on Truth* declared that "nobody had lied to Freud" when they'd described sexual abuse; rather, the original therapist had simply refused to believe his patients. The lies "came from Freud and the whole psychoanalytic movement," who suppressed the ugly social reality. In other words, Masson, a member of the elite, was exposing a century-long conspiracy and cover-up by the elite. His resulting rejection by his peers naturally made him seem like even more of a brave truth-teller to those who believed.

Scientists of the mind had long since abandoned the concept of repressed memories, but laypeople were primed to believe. The 1960s and '70s had taught them to obsess over sex, to credit conspiracy theories, and to believe that anyone who *feels* like a victim *is* a victim. Cinema also trained us to believe in repressed memories: a Harvard Medical School psychiatry professor has noted that "the flashback, in which a whole childhood trauma is suddenly recalled," is a fictional device that makes the fictional idea of repressed memory seem real. In the 1980s the notion of repressed memories came back big in the popular imagination, along with the new phrase *recovered memories*. We all supposedly had the power to unlock hidden truths about our pasts, and a hidden key had been revealed. A large and growing profession of caregivers had emerged for the unhappy and mentally ill—clinical psychologists, clinical social workers, and counselors, many of whom had limited training in or commitment to science. The number of clinical psychologists in America more than tripled during the 1970s and '80s—and many became repressed-memory therapists, recovered-memory therapists, and trauma-search therapists. They were devoted not only to believing and confirming the truth of any remarkable story any patient told them but sometimes to helping patients dream up and believe fictional memories.

One of the most influential recovered-memory books, first published in the 1980s, was written by a poet with one of her students who had been a childhood victim of sexual abuse. The message of *The Courage to Heal* was that if you felt bad about yourself and your life but couldn't figure out why, it was probably because you were molested or raped and had repressed those crippling memories. The book included a checklist of seventy-four possible symptoms of forgotten sexual abuse, including "You feel that there's something wrong with you deep down inside; that if people really knew you, they would leave," "You have no sense of your own interests, talents or goals," and "You have trouble feeling motivated." Even if a patient in whom suspicions of forgotten memories have been aroused "sometimes doubts it," the authors advised counselors and therapists that they "must believe that your client was abused . . . to stay steady in the belief that she was abused." *Because what they believe is always true.* The book sold a million copies.

Hypnosis became the prime tool for unearthing supposed memories of events that had been repressed—memories not just of possible real sexual abuse but also of alien abductions, "past lives," and other fictions. As with acupuncture, science has no real idea how or why hypnosis can help mitigate problems such as chronic pain and tobacco addiction and phobias, but it sometimes works. Fine. Hypnosis's increasing respectability became a problem, however, when therapists convinced themselves and patients that repressed memories from childhood could be recovered by inducing a trance state—

"regression hypnosis," which almost certainly isn't a real thing. But so what! "A memory retrieved under hypnotic age regression in therapy," a respected psychology professor declared in *Handbook of Hypnosis for Professionals* (1981), "may be quite useful to the therapeutic process *even if it is distorted, inaccurate, or a total fantasy as opposed to a real memory*" (emphasis added). From there it was a slippery slope to believing that fantasies were memories of real events.

In fact, the hypnotic state is a neurological sibling of fantasy states. Nearly all people who can be hypnotized most easily are those who have what psychology calls a "fantasy-prone personality"—for instance, people who think they possess paranormal powers, or who as (lonely) children tended to believe completely in their imaginary friends. So suppose you're an adult inclined to fantastical thoughts who starts imagining that some fantasy is real; under hypnosis, you're asked to provide details; the psychologist and you thereby become convinced it's real. A series of experiments at Harvard starting in the 1990s tested people who believed they recalled past lives or alien abductions to find how their minds worked when those "memories" *weren't* involved. Not surprisingly, the abductees "exhibited pronounced false memory effects" all the time, and the past-lives people had both "significantly higher false recall" and "scored higher on measures of magical ideation." In other words, they were fantasizers by nature.

So hypnosis is not a reliable tool for getting people to remember events they've forgotten. But the underlying idea—that we all have repressed memories that when retrieved can explain ourselves to ourselves—hardened into popular certainty despite fierce scientific consensus that it isn't true. Ulric Neisser is one of the founders of cognitive psychology. "False memories and confabulations are not rare at all," he said in the 1990s, as those fictional memories were being solicited wholesale. "They are still more likely to occur . . . where memories can be shaped and reshaped to meet the strong interpersonal demands of a therapy session. And once a memory has been thus reconfigured, it is very, very hard to change." The neurobiologist James McGaugh, another pioneer in the field, has in his half-century of research seen not "a single instance in which a memory was completely repressed and popped up again. There's absolutely no proof that it can happen. Zero. None. Niente. Nada. All my research says that strong emotional experiences leave emotionally strong memories. Being sexually molested would certainly qualify." And Richard McNally, a psychologist with his own research lab at Harvard, says these popular beliefs amount to "the most pernicious bit of folklore ever to infect psychology and psychiatry. It has provided the theoretical basis for 'recovered memory therapy'—the worst catastrophe to befall the mental health field since the lobotomy era." Indeed, his lab found the very opposite to be true—that instead of "possessing a superior ability to forget trauma-related material, the most distressed survivors exhibited difficulty banishing this material from awareness."

But science be damned; the clinicians and patients and other people desperate to believe had formed a movement, and they did not stop believing. Indeed, as ever, the repudiation by a rationalist elite reinforced belief, making it angrier and more righteous.

IN 1984, NOT LONG BEFORE he appeared on the cover of *Time* and ran for president, Pat Robertson published a book called *Answers to 200 of Life's Most Probing Questions*. Several of the questions were about Satan and his fallen angels currently posing as humans. "It is possible," Robertson wrote, "that a demon prince is in charge of New York, Detroit, St. Louis, or any other city."* Oh, America! I try to find some way to enjoy every crackling ember of your unhinged liberty, to channel Walt Whitman, to contain multitudes, to be pleas'd with the earnest words of the sweating preacher, impress'd seriously at the camp-meeting, to revel in the motley moonstruck hurly-burly of our exceptional, exceptionally strange nation. But beginning in the 1980s, the rising chorus of panicky Christian crazy talk had not just the rhyming *whiff* of Salem in 1692 but something like its actual horrible effect.

Legitimate concern over the sexual abuse of children spun off a new, almost entirely fictional subgenre. The idea that satanic cults were systematically and commonly subjecting American children to nightmarish abuse—by the thousands, by the tens or hundreds of thousands—was more or less invented by a young woman just across Puget Sound from Seattle. In her twenties, Michelle Proby, her life a mess, was treated by a psychiatrist named Lawrence Pazder. By means of hypnosis, he helped her "remember" that her late mother had been part of a satanic cult that had forced five-year-old Michelle to participate in its rituals: the Satanists had caged her with snakes, killed kittens in front of her, and physically abused her for months. All of which could have happened, theoretically—unlike her memory of Satan's "burning tail wrapped around her neck," and Jesus and the Virgin Mary personally erasing the physical scars of her abuse.

---

* *Or any other city,* but observant demon-hunters will note that the first two he named happen to be the large U.S. cities with the highest proportions of Jews and blacks, respectively.

Michelle and Dr. Pazder divorced their spouses, married each other, and co-wrote her memoir *Michelle Remembers,* released with fanfare in 1980. "Potentially the biggest nonfiction book I've ever published," said its editor, who'd recently published *Jaws,* "the true story of a little girl given by her parents to the Satanic church." *People* and other national media ran uncritical stories. It became a bestseller. Did New York editors and publishers and news producers actually believe? Did P. T. Barnum actually believe the fabrications he presented alongside his pure fictions and bona-fide artifacts?

When many of Michelle Pazder's supposed memories were specifically debunked, a reporter asked her husband if in his view the factual truth was irrelevant. "Yes, that's right," Dr. Pazder agreed. "It is a real *experience.* If you talk to Michelle today, she will say, 'That's what I remember.' We still leave the question open. *For her* it was very real." Other people "are all eager to prove or disprove what happened, but in the end it doesn't matter." True, false, whatever—it felt real.

After *Michelle Remembers,* Americans started "remembering" their own forced involvement in horrific satanic rituals. The details of their stories—drugs, sexual abuse with devices, torture, animal mutilation, human sacrifice, cannibalism—tended to bear an uncanny resemblance to the template established by Dr. and Mrs. Pazder. Rather than being a one-off artifact, *Michelle Remembers* was the prototype for a genre, for more books that inspired more copycat fabulists to undergo hypnosis and declare themselves victims of satanic cults that raped children and bred and killed babies.

A national panic was under way.

It immediately acquired a collateral go-to psychiatric diagnosis—which had the effect of making satanic cults seem more plausible, affirming the panic. At the time, some big-time American psychiatrists were successfully promoting multiple personality disorder as a diagnosis. The basic theory is that extreme childhood trauma causes people to repress the traumatic memories by developing "alters," characters they perform later in life as adults. Such cases were always exceedingly rare. But in 1980, psychiatry's bible, the *Diagnostic and Statistical Manual of Mental Disorders,* for the first time included multiple personality disorder as a full-fledged diagnosis.

Why the sudden extreme professional interest in this rare and controversial diagnosis? Another piece of pop culture, another powerfully influential artifact of the fantasy-industrial complex. In 1973 the book *Sybil* had been published, about a woman who said she'd been abused as a child and had sixteen different personalities. After selling six million copies in the United States, it became a four-hour Emmy-winning NBC *Big Event* movie that was one of the most watched shows of the year. During the previous centuries in the entire world, there had been perhaps two hundred reported cases of multiple personality disorder; during the 1970s, the decade of *Sybil*, there were around four hundred, mainly among American women, especially highly hypnotizable women. Twenty years later psychiatrists promoting the diagnosis estimated that at least two hundred thousand Americans had the disorder, or maybe more than a million.

In the next fully revised edition of the *DSM,* American psychiatry officially renamed the phenomenon "dissociative identity disorder." Despite the more scientific-sounding name, many experts in psychology and psychiatry continued to consider it bogus. Given that the multiple personalities usually appeared only in the course of therapy, didn't that suggest that therapists might be helping patients dream up the "alters"? And if childhood trauma produced the disorder, why were multiple personality cases in children almost nonexistent? It was another perfect modern American communion: from iffy case study to TV dramatization to experts-turned-activists pseudo-scientifically helping unhappy people "recall" trauma, to the respectable press agreeing it was an alarming epidemic reality.*

After Dr. Pazder appeared at a conference of the American Psychological Association and discussed "ritual abuse," that became the standard phrase for what satanists do. Among the psychiatrists and psychologists pushing the multiple personality epidemic was an influential faction who had their eureka moment: they decided they knew the source of multiple personality disorder in a quarter of cases—*satanic ritual abuse.* Cause and effect went topsy-turvy. It wasn't that some of their mentally ill patients had developed delusions about satanists but rather that the patients' actual victimization by actual satanic cults had generated tens of thousands of multiple personality disorders.

The psychiatrist Dr. Bennett "Buddy" Braun was one of the leading figures of the new field, and he couldn't have been more blue-chip. By the mid-1980s, he'd published twenty articles on multiple personality disorder, and he was on staff at one of the most prestigious hospitals in Chicago, Rush–Presbyterian–St. Luke's, where he set up a unit dedicated to treating "multiples." The annual conference of the International Society for the Study of Multiple Personality and Dissociation, which Braun cofounded, featured

* In her 2011 book *Sybil Exposed,* the journalist Debbie Nathan unearthed a letter written by the pseudonymous "Sybil" to her psychiatrist during treatment: "I do not really have any multiple personalities. I do not even have a 'double.' . . . I have been lying in my pretense of them."

sessions on satanism. Satanism was, in Dr. Braun's words, "a national-international-type organization that's got a structure somewhat similar to the Communist cell structure," and its coded messages were secretly embedded throughout American culture. More M.D.'s and Ph.D.'s from prestigious universities and hospitals signed on, and their conferences multiplied.

In 1986 Dr. Braun took on a new patient, a depressed twenty-nine-year-old named Patricia Burgus. She'd been treated for several years in Iowa by a psychiatric social worker who used role-playing techniques, instructing Burgus to speak in a child's voice and assigning names to each of her moods, such as Super Slow and Religious One. The social worker gave her an article about multiple personality disorder. "It was the first thing I'd ever seen in print on MPD," Burgus told a reporter for *Chicago* magazine years later. "This article was a sign from God." When she was referred to Dr. Braun by the National Institute of Mental Health, she believed she had twenty different personalities; after six years under his intensive treatment, two of those as a patient confined to his hospital, often hypnotized every day for hours and regularly dosed with powerful hypnotic drugs, she believed she had three hundred personalities.

Burgus read *Michelle Remembers*—and began "remembering" that her own parents had inducted her into a centuries-old satanic cult; that she'd been raped by panthers, tigers, and gorillas; that as a child, she'd had sex with President Kennedy; and that she'd taught her own two toddler sons, whom she decided she had sexually abused, to perform human sacrifices. One day during treatment, Burgus told the *Chicago* reporter, Dr. Braun "asked me if I'd ever cannibalized people. I said, 'Yes.' Well, he hit the door frame and said, 'Bingo.'" As a "high priestess" in the cult, she thought she recalled, she had "tortured, raped, murdered, and cannibalized 2,000 children a year while her husband was at work." Her children were also committed to Dr. Braun's psych ward for three years.

So those lives were ravaged. Meanwhile Dr. Braun testified widely as an expert witness in trials involving alleged satanic crimes. Episodes of *Oprah* featured both Michelle Pazder and the Pentecostal Christian author of the memoir *Satan's Underground*, a story that had all the main *Michelle Remembers* elements—orgies, rape, babies bred for sacrifice, satanic ritual murders, being saved by Jesus.*

---

* The author was an evangelical who published *Satan's Underground* under the pseudonym Lauren Stratford. After it came out, journalists for a Christian magazine debunked her stories as false. A decade later, the same journalists exposed its author again: she had taken yet another name and launched a new career retailing an entirely different

Dr. Pazder also had a new career as a go-to expert on recovered memories of the national satanic abuse conspiracy. In 1985 he was a talking head in an extraordinary report on ABC News's *20/20*, which had the largest audience of any prime-time American news program. "Tonight," the co-host said solemnly, "the startling, sobering results of a *20/20* investigation. Satanism, devil worship, being practiced all across the country . . . perverse, hideous acts that defy belief. Suicides, murders, and the ritualistic slaughter of children. . . . Yet so far the police have been helpless. . . . There is no question that something is going on out there." Then the reporter, ABC News's former White House correspondent, spoke: "Cannibalism. It's difficult to believe, but in every case we examined, children described it." *Defy belief* and *difficult to believe*: yes, but for the better part of half an hour, ABC News instructed America to believe. "That's terrifying," the show's other co-host, Barbara Walters, said at the end and asked the reporter why police weren't rounding up all the satanists. *Cover-up,* he suggested. "Police are very reluctant to investigate these crimes as satanic crimes, Barbara, because communities . . . don't want their reputations stigmatized as being the home of the devil"—*the home of the devil,* as if the devil exists. Even a decade earlier ABC News wouldn't have stooped so shamefully low. In fact, three years earlier, the distinguished ABC News veteran Av Westin had published a high-minded critique of his industry's new profit-driven decadence, scolding network news executives about their "responsibility to be fair . . . and accurate." Westin was executive producer of *20/20* when it aired the "Devil Worshippers" exposé.

The rest of TV joined in, whipping up and riding the hysteria. Geraldo Rivera hosted national specials on the satanic crime epidemic two years in a row. They were prime-time festivals of even more outrageous exaggeration and falsehood. "Estimates are that there are over one million Satanists in this country," Rivera said on the first program. "The majority of them are linked in a highly organized, very secretive network" dead set on a mission of "satanic ritual child abuse, child pornography, and grisly satanic murders. The odds are that this is happening in your town." His next one was on NBC. "Whether Satan exists," Rivera said at the outset, "is a matter of belief," as opposed to the supposed facts he was about to present: "the practice of evil in the devil's name . . . exists, and it's flourishing" in "a nationwide network of satanic criminals," some of them "born into satanic cults," who may be "desperate to flee but dread the penalty of grotesque death." That program was

---

make-believe nightmare girlhood—as a survivor of Josef Mengele's medical experiments at Auschwitz-Birkenau.

seen by a third of the Americans watching TV the night it aired, the largest audience in history for a two-hour NBC documentary.

Insane people have committed criminal acts they believed Satan wanted them to commit, and children are sometimes victimized in Grand Guignol fashion by sadists and lunatics. But this satanic crime spree and profusion of secret death cults *did not exist*. It was a mass delusion. Why did it happen at that moment? The precipitous rise in violent crime that began in the 1960s had not yet peaked. The supply of clinical psychologists, caregivers desperate to find the secret source of their clients' unhappiness, tripled from the mid-1970s to 1990. The national fantasy-industrial complex was giving people the perversity they wanted—TV news programs stoking fears as never before, Satan-themed bands like Mötley Crüe—and plenty of people now openly fancied themselves as Wiccans and devil worshippers.

Also, a large fraction of Americans believed that the devil was real and that all these witches and warlocks and satanists and Warner-Elektra-Atlantic recording artists were probably taking orders from him. For lots of people in the American Christian universe, bubbling with belief in Satan and super-natural experiences, the existence of a satanic megacult was hard evidence for the validity of the prophecies of Revelation. One Satan-obsessed Calvary Chapel in Los Angeles County took on ritual abuse as its special national battle. The author of *The Late Great Planet Earth* gave his enthusiastic endorsement to the panic and called *Satan's Underground* "absolutely incredible and true."

The supposed nationwide web of cunning Mansonesque groups and a satanic crime epidemic was being taken very seriously, and the hysteria spread. It was a remarkable episode of cascading Fantasyland synergy.

American law enforcement, accused of ignoring these organized packs of monstrous predators—*police have been helpless, police are reluctant to investigate these crimes*—naturally responded to the pressure. The FBI Academy's specialist on children's sexual victimization wrote a report during the panic:

> The information presented is a mixture of fact, theory, opinion, fantasy, and paranoia, and because some of it can be proven or corroborated (symbols on rock albums, graffiti on walls, desecration of cemeteries, vandalism, etc.), the implication is that it is all true and documented. Material produced by religious organizations . . . and videotapes of tabloid television programs are used to supplement the training and are presented as "evidence" of the existence and nature of the problem.

This special agent was like the good reverend in *The Crucible,* who comes to Salem looking for the devil but then realizes the panic is a fraud and tries to right the terrible wrong in which he'd been complicit. At the FBI Academy, he had organized the first national satanic abuse seminar; scores more followed. Training curricula warned about signs of cult abuse such as "candles" and "jewelry." A feminist astrologers' organization seemed suspicious. If a toddler showed a lot of interest in urine and feces, he or she might be under the spell of ritual abusers—that from a standard checklist of dozens of "symptoms characterizing satanic ritual abuse" created by a San Fernando Valley clinical psychologist associated with Dr. Braun and distributed to U.S. police and social workers. The "symptoms" also included "Preoccupation with passing gas," "Fear of ghosts and monsters," and "References to television characters as real people."

The national spiritual warfare ministry organized by the Calvary Chapel was behind a lot of the conferences. But many or most had secular auspices, such as the one concerning "C/S/DM"—Cults, Sects and Deviant Movements—at the University of North Florida's Institute of Police Technology and Management. At a homicide investigation seminar in Las Vegas, the chief clinical psychologist for the Utah State Prison told police that between forty and sixty thousand ritual homicides occurred in the United States each year. In fact, the *total* annual number of homicides in the United States at the time was around twenty thousand.

But who were cops to gainsay the certified experts, especially therapists treating miserable victims on the front lines? When the American Psychological Association surveyed its members, 93 *percent* said they believed the people claiming satanic ritual abuse were telling the truth. If the mental health professionals and journalists and police had become convinced it was real, so inevitably did prosecutors. In two national studies at the time, one by the American Bar Association and another by a team from the University of California at Davis, a quarter of prosecutors surveyed said they had handled cases of ritual abuse. From the early 1980s through the early 1990s, around two hundred Americans were indicted and prosecuted in dozens of states as satanic ritual abusers. More than eighty were convicted, some of them sentenced to long prison sentences for imaginary crimes.

The first big outbreak was in and around Bakersfield, a place known for extreme Christianity and for political and cultural conservatism. A new hardline county prosecutor was elected in 1983 and promptly created a ritual abuse task force. County social workers, including the one assigned to debrief the allegedly abused children whom the county had removed from their homes, had attended one of the law enforcement seminars about satanic crimes with *Michelle Remembers* on its syllabus—and soon the children were repeating the familiar story: blood-drinking, cannibalism, rape by chanting people in robes, babies bred for sacrifice. Local law enforcement guessed that thirty babies had been sacrificially slaughtered. No babies had been reported missing, no bodies were found, and all the prosecution witnesses to all the alleged crimes were children—including one who'd denied being sexually abused by his parents until his thirty-fifth investigative interview, and another who became an accuser only after being hypnotized during two months in police custody. Dozens of people were charged, of whom twenty-eight went to prison, some for more than twenty years. Another dozen people gave up their children in plea bargains.

The most infamous case of Satanic Panic began at the same time two hours south in a well-to-do L.A. County beach town. The mother of a boy attending the McMartin Preschool decided that his male teacher, the grandson of the school's owner, had been anally raping her son. She told the police and wrote a letter to the district attorney claiming the preschool's owner had taken the boy to an armory that had a "ritual-type atmosphere" with a "goatman," and to a church where she "drilled a child under the arms," and her grandson, the rapist, "flew in the air." Two years later the accusing mother was diagnosed with acute paranoid schizophrenia (and a year after that died of alcohol poisoning), but by then the bandwagon was rolling. A reporter at ABC's owned-and-operated L.A. station had broken and pushed the story during a ratings "sweeps" month in 1984. The district attorney had hired a team of therapists from one of the premier nonprofit L.A. child abuse agencies to interview several hundred children who'd attended the school. (Dr. Pazder was enlisted as part of this hunt as well.)

The questioning of the McMartin children became a literal textbook case of how such interviews should not be conducted. A child had never mentioned nudity or photographs, but an interviewer asked, "Can you remember the naked pictures?" Nope. "Can't remember that part?" Again, no. "Why don't you think about that for a while, okay? Your memory might come back to you." And when another child refused to say the teachers had done anything untoward, the interviewer asked, "Are you going to be stupid, or are you going to be smart and help us here?"

Children were persuaded that they had been flown on planes to other cities to be sexually abused and had watched a horse be beaten to death with a bat, a baby be decapitated in a church, and teachers dressed as witches. An extensive three-year investigation discovered no physical evidence. The prosecution's public theory of the case was that the school had operated as a child pornography production facility, but a global search by the FBI and Interpol found no films or pictures featuring McMartin children. The evidence consisted of eighteen children's dubious testimony, on which eight adults were indicted for sexually victimizing forty-eight children, a number later reduced to thirteen. But even the L.A. County district attorney admitted that most of his evidence was "incredibly weak" and eventually dropped charges against all but the original alleged perpetrator and his grandmother. The trial lasted three years, the longest criminal trial in U.S. history, and the two defendants, who between them spent seven years in jail, were found not guilty.

Despite the acquittal in Los Angeles, the hysteria continued raging both there and nationally: mainstream news still gave it credence, police still made arrests, prosecutors still prosecuted, and true believers among psychologists and psychiatrists (and their clients) still believed and proselytized, often with a government imprimatur.

Suspicions were voiced and accusations were cast practically everywhere, and dozens of prosecutions went forward. In a small town in Tidewater North Carolina, children testified that a satanic cult operating a daycare center had ritually abused them—and taken them in hot-air balloons to outer space and on a boat into the Atlantic where newborns were fed to sharks; several people were sentenced to long prison terms and served time before their convictions were overturned or charges dismissed.

In Austin a couple who ran a daycare center were accused by children of the standard horrors (including children airlifted to be raped elsewhere, abused by tigers and gorillas, babies fed to sharks) but with more chainsaws than usual. They were tried for raping a girl. When the prosecutor asked the alleged victim on the witness stand if either defendant ever "touch[ed] you in a way you didn't like?" she repeatedly answered "No" and "No, it didn't happen." The only physical evidence was the testimony of an emergency room physician who'd examined the girl and seen tears in her hymen. "I could've been wrong," that physician told a reporter after the couple were convicted and were serving forty-eight-year prison sentences. "Knowing what I know now . . . knowing how to do exams" properly, "I think that if I had that case now, I'd probably . . . decline to testify."

The Satanic Panic never really took off outside the United States. A historian in Norway found that until Rivera's 1988 NBC special was covered in the Norwegian press, there had been no public references to satanic ritual abuse. According to *The Day Care Ritual Abuse Moral Panic*, published in 2004 by a U.S. social psychologist specializing in trauma and mental illness, the few international prosecutions in the 1980s and '90s were generally "closed in a matter of months," which "made it difficult for the kind of improvised news that romped around in the shadows of the [U.S.] daycare cases . . . from getting a running start." The British cases, she writes, had "no chanting orgiastic Satanists . . . just ghosts, some of them pink, one eyed spirits; there was no cannibalizing of the flesh of dead babies, nor any drinking of their blood"—indeed, "there was no abuse . . . none of the rape, sodomy and torture that rendered the American master narrative so utterly appealing." And in no other developed country, of course, are so many citizens evangelical or fundamentalist Christians. America is exceptional.

IN THE 1990S, THIS NATIONAL episode of madness finally ended. After a dozen years, after people convicted of satanic abuse had collectively spent hundreds of years incarcerated, the judiciary and respectable opinion reimposed some sanity, child witnesses grew up and recanted, and convictions were overturned. "As I got off the medication and hypnosis," said Patricia Burgus, the satanic priestess in Chicago with three hundred personalities, "I started doing a little bit of math. Two thousand people a year I was supposed to be eating. If I was doing this for thirty years, where were all the people coming from?"

The professions that had enabled the panic tacked a bit back toward responsibility. "Repeated questioning," the American Psychiatric Association warned in 1993, "may lead individuals to report 'memories' of events that never occurred." The American Psychological Association formed a Working Group on Investigation of Memories of Child Abuse, but its equivocal findings, years afterward, still insisted that it's "possible for memories of abuse that have been forgotten for a long time to be remembered."

Many of the corrections of injustice and mea culpas didn't come until well into this century. Twenty years after she claimed in *People* that she'd remembered repressed memories of her parents molesting her thirty years earlier, Roseanne Barr admitted that, whoops, sorry, it wasn't true. She blamed *The Courage to Heal* ("It said, 'If you have the feeling that this happened to you, that means it did happen to you'") and psychotropics ("I was prescribed numerous psychiatric drugs") for the fact that she "totally lost touch with reality" and "didn't know what the truth was."

All but one of the two dozen convictions in Bakersfield were reversed. One of the men convicted was released in 2004 after nineteen years in prison; four children who'd testified against him had, as adults, finally recanted. One of the children who'd testified in the McMartin case admitted, at thirty, that those accused "never did anything to me, and I never saw them doing anything, I said a lot of things that didn't happen. I lied." The Austin couple convicted of raping a child were in prison for twenty-one years before their convictions were overturned.

History does not repeat, but it rhymes. In Salem in 1692 as in America in the 1980s and '90s, tales told by children drove the prosecutions and many of the accused copped pleas. In some ways, our late twentieth-century Satanic Panic was worse than the one in the late seventeenth century. Nobody was executed this time, but at least in Salem all the officials prosecuting and punishing their neighbors had the excuse of believing in satanic bewitchings. The Salem witch hunt was brief and local; just months after it began, the leaders of the Massachusetts Bay Colony regretted and then ended the prosecutions and punishments. By contrast, our recent satanism hysteria—thanks to mass media and the fantasy-industrial complex—swept the nation and lasted more than a decade. In New England in the 1690s, communal anguish and guilt kicked in immediately, and the awful overreach in Salem became the iconic cautionary tale of mad belief defeating reason—three hundred years later we're still retelling the familiar story. But ask Americans today about our Satanic Panic of just a generation ago, and you'll encounter a gaping memory hole: younger people know nothing about it, and almost nobody is aware of its scale and duration and damage.

The people responsible haven't paid much of a price or, in many cases, apologized. "Innocent people may have been accused at one point or another," said the Bakersfield district attorney a few years ago after being reelected six times. And sure, he granted, "if those cases came today we would have handled them differently. But what we had at the time, I think we handled them the best we could." In Illinois, after the Rush–Presbyterian–St. Luke's Medical Center closed its satanist-obsessed multiple personality unit and the state suspended the medical license of its mastermind, he moved to Montana, where he's a practicing psychiatrist, board-certified.

There are still regular satanic ritual abuse conferences. Dissociative identity (née multiple personality) disorder is still listed in the *DSM*, and its promoters in psychology and psychiatry still claim that millions of Americans suffer from it, undiagnosed. Psychologists more strongly committed to data and science formed their own national organization—but the main group, the APA, is five times as large. One of its presidents has complained that the pro-rigor faction has a "fervor about science [that] borders on the irrational."

After the Salem debacle, Christians mostly stopped discussing witches and demons. The recent episode, however, didn't temper American Christians' Satan-mania—and some, as in New England several hundred years ago, insist that the recent hysteria was Satan's doing, that he supernaturally *deluded* accusers and authorities into punishing those unfortunately innocent people.

In America, even people whose lives were mangled by this fantasy epidemic stick with magical thinking. Around the time Patricia Burgus was paid a $10.6 million settlement because her psychiatrist had convinced her she was a mass-murdering satanist cannibal who'd raped her children, she took them and her husband to the Vatican. "We wanted to thank God for seeing us through this ordeal," she explained, "and rededicate our lives to Him."

38

Reality Is a Conspiracy: The X-Filing of America

DURING THE DECADE AFTER *CLOSE ENCOUNTERS OF THE THIRD KIND* (1977) and *E.T. the Extra-Terrestrial* (1982), more and more Americans claimed they'd been personally visited, probed, and temporarily taken away by extraterrestrials—abducted. Many Americans with impressive credentials started to believe them. None was more impressive or important than a distinguished Harvard professor named John Mack.

Mack had been a New York City preppy who attended Harvard Medical School, where he remained, becoming a talented and beloved psychiatrist and professor of psychiatry. In addition to his work as a therapist and teacher, he won a Pulitzer Prize for his 1976 biography of T. E. Lawrence, the dashing British Establishment figure who became Lawrence of Arabia, galvanizing and quixotically leading a battalion of disrespected irregulars against oppressive powers-that-be. The theme of Mack's book, he said, was "Lawrence's need to be heroic," a need born of "childhood fantasies about the heroic past." It seems plain to me that Mack, a dashing American Establishment figure, finally indulged his own need to be quixotically heroic, to galvanize and lead a battalion of disrespected irregulars against oppressive powers-that-be, by plunging into a world of fantasy.

In 1987, in his fifties, Mack attended a small conference of "alternative" physicians and scientists at the Esalen Institute. There he met the creator of Holotropic Breathwork™, a technique for inducing supernatural consciousness by means of hyperventilation. When Mack tried it, according to its inventor, he "remembered" one of his past lives in Russia. Then at an advanced training session up the coast in Sonoma County, Mr. Holotropic and others told Mack "about UFO abduction experience as a trigger of spiritual emergency."

At the same moment, another member of the American elite, Whitley Strieber, a former advertising executive and successful author of horror fiction, published *Communion: A True Story*. It was his account of the nighttime visit, the day after Christmas 1985, by "non-human beings" with dark eyeholes and circular mouths who stuck a foot-long device up his anus. *Communion* was a number-one *Times* bestseller and sold two million copies. It encouraged many more Americans to announce they too had been visited and probed by aliens.

Soon Mack, still at Harvard, was dean of an alien-abduction truther movement. In 1992 he and an important physicist from down the street at the Massachusetts Institute of Technology organized an Abduction Study Conference. The premise of the five-day-long meeting at MIT was that the "abductees" were telling the truth—that creatures from outer space (or parallel universes) really had visited and examined and variously used them. The *New Yorker* writer C.D.B. Bryan attended and published a sympathetic book about the assembled true believers called *Close Encounters of the Fourth Kind*, further spreading the word and legitimizing the tales. With such luminaries now taking the storytellers seriously—and Mack's new research institute, the Program for Extraordinary Experience Research, was funded by Laurance Rockefeller—why wouldn't the supposed abductees and UFOlogists of every variety start taking their own beliefs more seriously? And why wouldn't millions more people start to believe as well? The MIT conference was a watershed moment, giving immense new credibility not just to this particular sector of fantasists but by extension to any and every group of fervid believers.

Mack based his 1994 book *Abduction: Human Encounters with Aliens* on the stories of dozens of supposed abductees he had treated as a psychiatrist—that is, whose apparent delusions he believed and encouraged. He called the people who imagined they'd encountered aliens not patients but "experiencers." To help them remember and flesh out their amazing stories, he used hypnosis as well as "deep, rapid breathing . . . evocative music, a form of bodywork, and mandala drawing." Many believed they had sexual interactions with the beings.

In *Communion,* Strieber wrote that any skepticism of people who believe they were abducted by aliens "is as ugly as laughing at rape victims"—and Mack never doubted. He *began* by regarding their subjective experiences as real, then groped to create some objective explanation that didn't involve psychiatric pathology: "Quite a few abductees have spoken to me of their sense that at least some of their experiences are not occurring within the physical space/time dimensions of the universe as we comprehend it. . . . The abduction phenomenon . . . I suspect, manifests itself in our physical space/time world but is not *of* it in a literal sense." That hedge is like one a subtle Christian theologian might use to explain to doubters how the Holy Spirit manifests supernaturally. And one is reminded of the New Age godmother Jane Roberts's pseudoscientific explanation of her imaginary friend Seth— how he might be a "dimensional aspect of my own consciousness not focused in this reality." But Mack himself definitely believed in the presence of otherworldly creatures on Earth, nosy beings who had "invaded our physical reality and [were] affecting the lives of hundreds of thousands, if not millions of people."

The *Boston Herald* called *Abduction* "a transcendent, landmark work," and *The New York Times Book Review* said Mack had "performed a valuable and brave service." The PBS science series *Nova* devoted an episode to Mack.

As academics and intellectuals and bohemians had been doing since the 1960s, he blamed modernity and rationality for blinding us to the true nature of existence. Only the narrow-minded cling to "the ontological framework of modern science" and "accepted laws of physics and principles of biology." Reason has created a "barrier between the spiritual and material worlds [that] has become so entrenched in the West. . . . this false dichotomy that makes our confrontation with beings who do not respect this gulf so shocking." Mack is a perfect exemplar of the mix 'n' match snowballing. He went from believing he'd remembered a past life to believing other people's alien-abduction tales and then down the slippery slope into a whole array of wishful woo. "What the abduction phenomenon has led me (I would now say inevitably) to see," he wrote in *Abduction,* "is that we participate in the universe or universes that are filled with intelligences from which we have cut ourselves off, having lost the senses by which we might know them" due to "the prevailing materialist/dualistic worldview." Those senses are restored during "near-death experiences . . . the use of psychedelic substances, shamanic journeys," and so on.

He had settled into Fantasyland, on common ground with more conventionally religious true believers—Christians clustered on one side, Mack and his New Age tribe mostly on another, but all of them variously disgusted with the world, leading them to abandon reason and evidentiary standards in favor of amazing stories of cosmic purpose and supernatural saviors. According to Mack, because we've messed things up, the mysterious superbeings, interplanetary or interdimensional angels, have come to set things right.

> Nothing in my work on UFO abductions has surprised me as much as the discovery that what is happening to the Earth has not gone unnoticed elsewhere in the universe. . . .
>
> The alien abduction phenomenon represents, then, some sort of corrective initiative. . . . My overall impression is that the abduction process is not evil, and that the intelligences at work do not wish us ill. Rather, I have the sense—might I say faith—that the abduction phenomenon is, at its core, about the preservation of life on Earth at a time when the planet's life is profoundly threatened.

THE POPULAR CERTAINTY THAT EXTRATERRESTRIALS are here among us seems like one of those thriving post-1960s fantasies we shouldn't fret about too much. It's a folk belief with some delusionally fervent believers—but it doesn't really pick our pockets or break our legs, does it?

In fact, it's an instance of complicated, consequential synergy— apparently harmless fictions blending and growing and spreading through the culture, combining with particular religious and political mindsets to become dangerous, with impacts in the real world. There is a line extending from flying-saucer obsessives to 9/11 truthers to Donald Trump.

As America's UFOlogy hothouse expanded, its exotic beliefs generating new types and subtypes, many of the most ardent believers didn't come from John Mack's happy, hopeful *Close Encounters* and *E.T.* place. Instead, they imagined the extraterrestrials as part of a malign secret apparatus of power and control, attaching this exciting and terrifying new cosmic fiction to their beliefs in a New World Order, the boundless national and global conspiracy of interconnected elite oppressors.

The first important bridge between the Fantasyland regions of UFO true believers and conspiracists appeared in 1991, just before the MIT conference. Its builder was a standard-issue middle-class southern Californian with the generic name Bill Cooper. Cooper had been an enlisted man in the navy in the 1960s, where he claimed he became privy to an elaborate U.S. government conspiracy involving extraterrestrials. After he started using Internet bulletin boards to disseminate his pseudoinformation in the 1980s, he claimed that federal agents tried and failed to kill him twice by running his car off the road. They kept tailing him until he flashed his pistol to an agent and threatened he "would not hesitate to use" it.

He described all this in *Behold a Pale Horse,* his remarkable 1991 magpie collage of personal reminiscence, interconnected conspiracy theories, congressional transcripts, letters, newspaper articles, maps, and photos. "We have been taught lies," he wrote. "Reality is not what we perceive it to be." Its excellent title comes from Revelation, yet the book doesn't spend much time on Christian exegesis; Mack's New Age spiritual-savior vision of extraterrestrials is far more religious. Unlike Mack, Cooper was a nobody—his postmilitary career consisted of running trade schools, not teaching at Harvard—but at the grass roots, *Behold a Pale Horse* became enormously influential.

One day in the Pacific during his navy service, he says he saw "a flying saucer the size of an aircraft carrier come right out of the ocean and fly into the clouds." He told his captain, and a commander from Naval Intelligence came aboard and ordered him to keep quiet about what he'd seen. Because Cooper followed that order, he was initiated into the cabal and given top-secret security clearance. And then began learning the unbelievable truth.

After the alien saucer crash-landed in Roswell, New Mexico, in 1947—and many more elsewhere in the United States over the next several years, Cooper reveals—a whole fleet of spacecraft arrived in 1953 and took up "very high geosynchronous orbit around the equator." Meanwhile two different sets of extraterrestrials landed at two different air force bases, one in South Florida and the other in southern California. Each entered into negotiations with the Eisenhower administration. The Florida ones warned that the orbiting aliens were bad guys and "offered to help us with our spiritual development" if the United States agreed to "dismantle and destroy our nuclear weapons." We declined. However, Ike met personally with the California extraterrestrials, struck a deal, and signed a treaty.

In order to finance building underground U.S.-alien military bases all over the West, the CIA took over the international illegal drug trade; one of its key early operators was the young private citizen and future CIA director George H. W. Bush—who was president when *Behold a Pale Horse* appeared. (According to Cooper, Whitley Strieber is also CIA.) Some Americans have visited the aliens' planet(s), and a secret executive branch group, exposed in the 1980s by other UFOlogists, oversees our extraterrestrial partnership. The conspiracy is international—by 1961, "a joint alien, United States, and Soviet Union base [already] existed on the Moon," years before the Apollo astronauts landed. President Kennedy, appalled by the CIA-drug-running part of the operation, told the conspirators he would "reveal the presence of aliens to the American people within the following year" unless the government got out of the narcotics business. Which resulted in his assassination—by his Secret Service driver.

By the way, it wasn't only in the navy where Cooper learned all these astonishing secrets: in *Behold a Pale Horse,* he reprinted what he said was a secret federal document that one of his sources happened to find stuck in "an IBM copier that had been purchased at a surplus sale." The supposed government memo spilled the beans about the conspiracy—in the fashion of Dr. Evil, with a lot of capital letters, referring to an "approach which is RUTH-LESSLY CANDID, with NO AGONIZING OVER RELIGIOUS, MORAL or CULTURAL VALUES," given its "extensive OBJECTIVES of SOCIAL CONTROL and DESTRUCTION OF HUMAN LIFE, i.e., SLAVERY and GENOCIDE."

Like Mack's evolution from Esalen breathwork to past lives to alien abduction to cosmic manifest destiny, Cooper's slide from fantasy to fantasy also illustrates the snowball effect—from belief in the Book of Revelation to belief in extraterrestrials' presence on Earth to belief in a mammoth conspiracy that combined both. The "aliens," he wrote, constitute "the true nature of the Beast. It is the only scenario that has been able to bind all the diverse elements."

The ultimate puppet masters, according to him, are the Illuminati—that secret society of eighteenth-century European intellectuals that frightened American conspiracy nuts two hundred years ago, got revived as a far-right obsession in the 1960s, then blew up bigger than ever in the 1980s and '90s. The master plan "as far back as 1917" had been to use the "threat from outer space in order to bring humanity together in a one-world government." And *everybody* has been in on it—"the Jesuits, the Masons . . . the Nazi Party, the Communist Party . . . the Council on Foreign Relations . . . the Trilateral Commission, the Bilderberg Group, . . . the Vatican . . . Skull & Bones . . . they are all the same and all work toward the same ultimate goal, a New

World Order" that "is beating down the door." Plus the Rockefellers, the RAND Corporation, the Federal Reserve, the CIA, and the United Nations. In fact, as Cooper noted, the masks were coming off—President Bush had started *speaking openly* about the plan to realize the Illuminati "dream of a new world order."

THE NEW WORLD ORDER. AT that moment, it was becoming *the* all-encompassing catchphrase for people who believed in a sinister conspiracy running the world, those elite entities named by Cooper as well as the ones—banks, news media, show business—McCarthyists and the John Birch Society had identified decades earlier. Now the American belief in globalist conspiracy was going wide, riding in the slipstream of extraterrestrial conspiracism, one fantastical suspicion leading to another. Previously, the political scientist Michael Barkun notes in *A Culture of Conspiracy,* New World Order beliefs had been "limited to two subcultures, primarily the militantly antigovernment right, and secondarily Christian fundamentalists concerned with the end-time emergence of the Antichrist. Their beliefs did not spread readily to outsiders. The extreme right constituted a pariah group whose viewpoints were systematically excluded from channels of mass communication and distribution." Once Harvard professors and mainstream journalists made belief in extraterrestrial visitors "semi-respectable, a quasilegitimacy was conferred," which in turn "advanced the process by which conspiracism was becoming culturally sanitized." As a large fraction of Americans came to agree that the U.S. government had covered up extraterrestrials' presence on Earth, "Ufology became . . . the vehicle for the New World Order to reach audiences otherwise unavailable to it."

Communism was the main focus of American conspiracists for most of the century. After the USSR and its empire finally fell apart between 1989 and 1991, however, they didn't calm down or give up. Instead they imagined a larger, not-necessarily-Communist conspiracy—as the Birch Society had pioneered in the 1960s—and redoubled and widened the focus of their fears. They required a fervent antifaith in *some* monumental scheme of evil. The first President Bush, Cooper wrote in *Behold a Pale Horse,* was "loyal only to the destruction of the United States and to the formation of the New World Order"—proving that "the Communists are not going to be much happier with the New World Order than we." That's the delirious beauty of an overarching master conspiracy believed with absolute conviction: contradictory new facts, rather than undermining or disproving the scheme, are recast as affirmations of the undeniable larger truth. Don't be fooled by the Communist collapse—the omnipotent overlords have just reshuffled and rebranded.

Revelation-fixated Christians were ready to go, post-Communism. They'd been blending global conspiracy ingredients into their end-time batter for a generation, and by the late 1980s and early '90s that cake was fully baked. When the fundamentalist preacher and media mogul Pat Robertson ran for the Republican nomination in 1988, he won four states. His politics were his theology and vice versa. His bestselling 1991 book *The New World Order* is essentially *Behold a Pale Horse* with more Christianity and no aliens: according to Robertson, the familiar conspiracy, running from the Illuminati to the Federal Reserve, was creating the satanic pre-Armageddon one-world government that Revelation predicted. New Age sorcerers were meanwhile creating the satanic replacement for Christianity. Like Cooper (and perhaps not unlike Vladimir Putin today), Robertson posited that the Illuminati contrived to make Russia Communist so that seventy-five years later it would fail and thus become dependent on the Illuminati-run global financial system—to which he added a neat plot twist: the Cold War was also contrived by the Illuminati to bankrupt the United States and thus make it ripe for their takeover as well.

It was no longer just a few powerless crackpots in the patriot and militia movements who believed the United States was about to surrender to the tyranny of the New World Order. Unregulated talk radio was instructing a large constituency full time, while respectable politicians were galvanized by and further galvanized those true believers. By the 1990s, the fear of a UN military takeover of the United States was so widespread and impassioned that the Indiana Department of Transportation, for instance, was obliged to abandon its internal system for tracking the age of highway signs. Indianans had become convinced the colored dots on the backs of the signs were coded navigation instructions for the impending invasion by the UN's armed foreigners.

Alarmed citizens decided that the federal government was massacring Christian gun owners for being Christians and gun owners. Seventh-day Adventists, you'll recall, were prophetically counting down to the end of the world and Christ's return a century before that became standard. Starting in the 1980s, one of their spin-off sects in Texas, the Branch Davidian Seventh-day Adventists, had a long-haired young folk-rock guitarist named Vernon Howell as its prophet and leader. He was in the Joseph Smith mode, a charming Heaven-sent alpha-dog outcast who holed up in the hot desolate West with a harem of believers and fathered a dozen children by multiple wives.

The name Vernon Howell wasn't a strong messiah brand, though, so he took the names of two biblical kings—David and Koresh. David Koresh prophesied that he would be martyred. And at thirty-three, just like Jesus, he was killed by the empire's henchmen. Unlike Jesus, he took four government agents and seventy-five of his disciples with him, all killed in a gun battle and fire after a federal team came to check out their arsenal of semiautomatic rifles.

I'm not suggesting Koresh and his followers are typical of Christians awaiting the supernatural end of the world, or of Americans whose gun love is driven by dreams of an armed citizen uprising against tyranny. But the Branch Davidians' theology is not so different from that of a large fraction of Americans. We call Koresh a "cult leader," which allows us to file him away reassuringly as a one-off nut, like Charles Manson or Jim Jones. But it's important to recognize that his church was a long-standing subgroup of a 150-year-old Protestant denomination that is one of the twenty largest churches in America, with six thousand U.S. congregations.*

The standoff in 1993 at the compound near Waco lasted seven weeks before its horrible end, so naturally a carnivalesque camp arose, with hundreds of journalists, gawkers, protesters, and souvenir hawkers. One of the latter, a government-hating vendor, was a twenty-four-year-old army veteran, a nomadic fixture on the national gun show circuit and compulsive gambler who'd made a pilgrimage to Waco to bear witness and stoke his anger. He sold bumper stickers off the hood of his car—BAN GUNS: MAKE THE STREETS SAFE FOR A GOVERNMENT TAKEOVER and A MAN WITH A GUN IS A CITIZEN, A MAN WITHOUT A GUN IS A SUBJECT.

"The government is afraid of the guns people have," he told a Dallas reporter who interviewed him there, "because they have to have control of the people at all times. I believe we are slowly turning into a socialist government. The government is continually growing bigger and more powerful, and the people need to prepare to defend themselves against government control." The fellow was also ferociously antitaxation and despised the United Nations—in other words, his views were standard talking points on the right.

For the overwrought millions of people who imagined themselves as the *real* Americans, whether besieged patriots or persecuted Christians or both,

---

* Including those attended by the current U.S. secretary for housing and urban development. "I mean, *Seventh-day Adventist*," President Trump said suspiciously of Ben Carson's religion when they were rivals for the 2016 nomination. "I don't know about, I just don't know."

the Waco siege and its finale were thrilling confirmations of every fear. A year afterward and a few hours north, the legislature in Oklahoma passed a bill demanding that Congress "cease any support of the establishment of a 'new world order' . . . either under the United Nations or under any world body in any form of global government" because that "would mean the destruction of our Constitution and corruption of . . . our way of life." Oklahoma wasn't the only state to pass such a resolution around that time.

And a year later right there in Oklahoma City, a couple of miles from where the state legislature had declared its opposition to a liberty-quashing New World Order, that young bumper-sticker salesman from Waco detonated a truck bomb that destroyed the city's main federal office building and killed 168 people. One response was to consider Timothy McVeigh a hero, a John Brown for his time; the more common public conclusion of his fellow travelers was to imagine he'd been a patsy of the government, which had surely staged the bombing in order to justify a crackdown on patriots.*

FULL-TILT EXPLAIN-IT-ALL CONSPIRACISM WAS BEING mainstreamed in America. Ross Perot, the first billionaire to make a creditable run for president, believed in highly unlikely conspiracies. During one of his debates with President Bush and Bill Clinton in 1992, the moderator politely wondered about his steadiness, given that he'd quit the General Motors board in a huff and suspended his presidential campaign in a huff. Perot's defense of his completely presidential temperament on national TV was very curious. "Again and again, on complex, difficult tasks," he said, "I have stayed the course. When I was asked by our government to do the POW project"—his unsuccessful freelance attempt to airlift food and medicine to POWs in North Vietnam—"within a year the Vietnamese had sent people into Canada to make arrangements to have me and my family killed." The assassins, he'd told a Senate committee a few months earlier, were Black Panthers. "And I had five small children, and my family and I decided we would stay the course, and we lived with that problem." By the way, Perot was certain the Vietnamese had kept and enslaved hundreds of U.S. POWs after the war—a belief shared by the 1990s by two-thirds of Americans.† So why had the CIA and

---

* Not long before he became famous, Timothy McVeigh traveled to gawk at the air force's so-called Area 51 in Nevada, the place UFO conspiracists believe the government keeps extraterrestrials and their downed spacecraft, and on death row he watched the movie *Contact*.

† 1991 *Wall Street Journal*/NBC News survey.

four presidents kept that terrible truth hidden? "When you look into the prisoner cover-up," he explained, "you find government officials in the drug trade
who can't break themselves of the habit." Perot won 19 percent of the vote in
the November presidential election.

If in the past a White House deputy counsel had gone to a park across
the Potomac from D.C. and shot himself in the head, it would've been a
small, tragic two-day story. But in 1993? Six months into the administration
of a president whom conspiracy theorists had already accused of being a cocaine trafficker? Vincent Foster's "suicide" *must* have been a murder arranged
by his old friends the Clintons as part of a conspiracy, so we were required to
have investigations by two different special prosecutors and two separate congressional committees in order to decide, officially, that he killed himself
because he was depressed.

In the 1990s too, a major character in the right's dark fantasies adopted
some of the mindset herself. "The great story here for anybody willing to find
it and write about it and explain it," Hillary Clinton said in 1998, when the
news first broke about her husband's affair with an intern, "is this vast right-
wing conspiracy that has been conspiring against my husband since the day
he announced for president." Calling the right's concerted opposition a "conspiracy" was unfortunate and did its little part to normalize such thinking
and such talk.

The fetish for grand conspiracies was a virus that spread more widely and
deeply on the right—much more—but the left had its growing constituency
of infected zealots. The CIA as global narcotics moguls, for instance, became
a certainty not just on the *Behold a Pale Horse* right and the Perotista middle
but among the elite and grassroots left. The belief was given permanent credence by a series of articles in the *San Jose Mercury News* in 1996. It posited
a mammoth and elaborate federal conspiracy to sell cocaine in the United
States, and even though other journalists promptly and persuasively discredited the story, it nevertheless swelled with affirmation on the new Web and
talk radio, especially among African-Americans. Southern California con-
gresswoman Maxine Waters promoted the idea that crack was a way for the
government to make money *and* enact its genocidal designs on black people.
Right and left agreed, too, that AIDS was a genocidal plot: a year after *Behold
a Pale Horse* asserted that the virus had been invented and spread by "the
ruling elite" to kill "the black, Hispanic, and homosexual populations," Spike
Lee said he was convinced that, yes indeed, "AIDS is a government-engineered
disease."

In 1996 a TWA 747 crashed near JFK airport after a short circuit made a fuel tank explode. However, a few months later Pierre Salinger—who had been John Kennedy's White House press secretary and for decades an ABC News investigative reporter—decided that a navy missile had brought down the plane and that the government was covering it up. Writing about it for *The New Yorker,* I called Salinger to ask about the source for his "scoop." He said he'd been given a document by "a top intelligence agent in France, a guy who's been a fantastic adviser to me." The basis of that document, it turned out, was a purely speculative scenario posted to the Internet by a retired airline pilot in Florida. And when Salinger had searched online himself for information about the crash—"You see," he told me, "I'm not a person who looks into the Internet"—he was impressed to find "forty pages of material." The missile and cover-up story therefore looked true to him, so he broadcast it. If a famous, award-winning, well-connected American journalist (and former presidential adviser) bought the exciting fictions he found on the Internet, why should we expect ordinary people to be any more scrupulous and skeptical?

Google didn't even exist yet, but already the Web was helping people to confuse fiction and reality in dangerous ways. The Internet was a particular boon to conspiracy-mongers. "One of the impressive things about paranoid literature," Hofstadter observed in the 1960s in *The Paranoid Style in American Politics,* "is the contrast between its fantasied conclusions and the almost touching concern with factuality it invariably shows"—McCarthy's ninety-six-page pamphlet had 313 footnote references, and the John Birch Society founder's attack on President Eisenhower had a hundred pages of notes. With the Web, this concern for pseudofactuality could be more elaborately expressed than ever.

In 1999, not long after the *New Yorker* journalist Michael Kelly coined the term *fusion paranoia* to describe how a conspiracist paradigm was increasingly shared by left and right, thousands of progressives assembled in Seattle for a few days to demonstrate their hatred of the global capitalist apparatus. They didn't chant about the gun confiscators and UN invaders, but their enemy was more or less the same shadowy, ruthless, omnipotent, multitentacled international conspiracy that had obsessed the far right for a long time. If you'd circulated a petition among the Seattle protesters consisting of unattributed passages from *Behold a Pale Horse,* who would've declined to sign? "We have been taught lies," Cooper wrote. "Reality is not what we perceive it to be." Right? Battlers in Seattle definitely would've bought into his outrage over "the Haig-Kissinger depopulation policy in Central America."

*   *   *

Broadcast mass media built two more crucial bridges between UFO-mania and conspiracism, in one case nominally nonfiction and in the other pure entertainment, both funneling millions more Americans into Fantasy-land.

A national news-talk radio program called *Coast to Coast AM* became a huge hit in the 1990s, syndicated on hundreds of stations. The creator and host was Art Bell, who talked for four or five hours every night from a studio near his home in the desert between Las Vegas and Death Valley. His guests were conspiracy theorists and promoters of the implausible and impossible of every sort, political and paranormal and pseudoscientific and apocalyptic. Compared to the strictly political new stars of talk radio, Bell sounded friendly and low-key, almost reasonable, not pushing one clear agenda but open to practically *any* claim or allegation or belief. *Coast to Coast AM* became the go-to broadcast venue for the excitingly untrue, and when celebrities appeared, the whole demented buffet seemed all the more legitimate. Of Americans awake each night between midnight and dawn, by my rough reckoning, during the 1990s as many as a fifth were listening to *Coast to Coast AM*.

I Want to Believe. Believe to Understand. Trust No One. The various tag-lines for *The X-Files,* which premiered in 1993, are perfect Fantasyland slogans. The makers of *The X-Files* weren't asked to justify themselves—it was straight-ahead entertainment, scripted fiction, with actors playing FBI agents and conspirators and aliens. But it and *Coast to Coast AM* were just different forms of infotainment distributed by adjacent branches of the fantasy-industrial complex, one on radio and the other on TV, tag-team propaganda vehicles for spreading and hardening belief in evil all-powerful secret government conspiracies and magical thinking. In the 1910s and '20s *The Birth of a Nation* had glamorized white supremacy and helped induce the rebirth of the real-life Ku Klux Klan; in the 1990s, *The X-Files* glamorously codified an important swath of the new conspiracist paradigm.

The symbiosis of *The X-Files* and *Coast to Coast AM* is especially clear in a half-hour segment of the latter featuring Chris Carter, the creator of the former. (Art Bell had recently played himself on Carter's *X-Files* spin-off series *Millennium.*) Bell discusses *The X-Files* as if it's a dramatization of actual events. Given that *X-Files* plotlines "brush so close to reality," Bell says, he wonders if Carter agrees that there is indeed "an ET presence on Earth." "Every time I get on a commercial airliner," Carter replies, "I ask the pilots if

39

Mad as Hell, the New Voice of the People

IN THE SUMMER OF 2001, SIX WEEKS BEFORE THE 9/11 ATTACKS, A TWENTY-
seven-year-old national radio host warned his listeners to wake up, implor-
ing and beseeching them. "*Please* call Congress," he said. "Tell 'em we *know*
the [Bush administration] is planning terrorism." He mentioned the World
Trade Center—and Osama bin Laden, who was not yet famous. "Bin Laden
is the bogeyman they need in this Orwellian, phony system." He called
George W. Bush "the bipartisan imperialist elite's front man." He later
executive-produced a documentary explaining that the 9/11 attacks were an
inside job by the U.S. government.

He's still around, ragging on the military-industrial complex ("sending
troops to die in illegal wars"), the horrors of the prison camp at Guantánamo
Bay, the Bilderberg Group ("the apex of the . . . power structure"), Goldman
Sachs, the World Bank, the International Monetary Fund, corporate America in general ("Madison Avenue makes us addicts of consumerism"). He has
been a supporter of Edward Snowden. In an on-air conversation with Noam
Chomsky, a towering intellectual avatar of the far left, the men agreed that

they've seen a UFO, and the flight attendants for that matter. . . . Almost always they say they have." When he's talked to "people who work in government in classified areas . . . [they] ask me where I get my information and say 'You don't know how close you are.'" When Bell asks if *X-Files* has been pressured by the government to keep certain truths hidden, Carter replies that the FBI abruptly and suspiciously froze out his researchers just before the series went on the air.

Time was correct to include Carter on its list of the "25 Most Influential Americans" in 1997, the year twenty-seven million people watched one of his episodes. And *The X-Files'* fusion paranoia was total, with plotlines to scratch every ideological itch: a character explains that the flying saucer crash at Roswell was "just a smoke screen" to serve the "global conspiracy of silence," the federal government's (real) Tuskegee syphilis experiment was part of the (fictional) master plot, the alien-government-corporate co-conspirators killed both JFK *and* Martin Luther King, Jr., and had a hand in the Anita Hill–Clarence Thomas affair. In the 1998 *X-Files* feature film, an apostate member of the conspiracy reveals the plan to have the president declare a state of emergency, after which "all federal agencies will come under the power of the Federal Emergency Management Agency—FEMA—the secret government."

By the end of the 1990s, this was no longer crackpottery dispensed only in self-published books. *X-Files* was a successful prime-time network television program on News Corp.'s Fox network. *Coast to Coast AM* was distributed by one of the biggest radio syndicators. The Web was exploding. Mainstream media and book publishers enthusiastically embraced and promoted the ostensibly nonfiction stories of alien conspiracies.

A decade after he put out *Behold a Pale Horse,* the movement's godfather Bill Cooper was killed in a shootout with sheriff's deputies at his home in rural Arizona. They'd come to arrest him for threatening a neighbor with a gun. It was 2001, and the police had originally planned to arrest him on . . . September 11. The coincidental timing naturally burnished his martyred-hero status among New World Order believers, for whom there are no coincidences. Not long after that, Fox stopped airing new episodes of *The X-Files.* Any more would've been superfluous, anyway. The show had already succeeded in training us to *Believe* and *Trust No One,* because *The Truth Is Out There.* In 2001, Americans reported seeing a lot of UFOs, but by 2015 they reported they were seeing 241 percent more.[*]

[*] Cheryl Costa and Linda Miller Costa, *UFO Sightings Desk Reference* (2017).

the elite imposes an illusion of consent on the people, that U.S. elections are mostly meaningless, that the Democrats and Republicans (as Chomsky remarked) are really just "two factions of one party." During the protests in Ferguson, Missouri, in 2014, he said that the National Guard was "clearly being given orders to brutalize the press . . . and to threaten to kill the press." "You're one of the only prominent leaders," he told Louis Farrakhan during their conversation in 2016, "that addresses that there is a conspiracy . . . [of] the power elite."

"We're on the march," he says again and again, the way Henry V said *unto the breach*, "and the empire is on the run." So who is this overwrought left-winger with an influential radio program syndicated on a hundred stations, live online TV shows beaming out for hours a day, eighteen YouTube channels (one of which has more than a *billion* views), a website with more traffic than lots of big daily newspapers? Why, that's no left-winger, it's Alex Jones, routinely described as "conservative" because he rants against gun regulation, government-subsidized healthcare, and taxes. Populist? Alt-right? Crypto-nihilist? Our language simply hasn't kept up with the new permutations.

He is the very epitome of cutting-edge political discourse, where outright fiction is presented and consumed as nonfiction. What's more, he's no longer a fringe freak; he's a freak who has both a huge following and the ear of the president of the United States.

In 1996, the year Fox News brought politicized talk radio to television, Jones started broadcasting on a radio station in Austin, encouraging darker, more fantastical fever dreams. Soon he was syndicated nationally, then on the Internet everywhere. He got attention by leading a team of patriots two hours up to Waco to rebuild the Branch Davidians' compound—a stunt that caused his station to fire him, producing a martyrdom that redounded to his national popularity and influence.

Growing up, he was schooled by "some neighbors who were members of the John Birch Society [who'd] come over for dinner. . . . The John Birch Society was right about everything." Reading his dad's old copy of *None Dare Call It Conspiracy* as a teenager was an aha moment. Coming of age in the early 1990s, just as Communism ended and the era of *Behold a Pale Horse* and *X-Files* began, he was a natural *omni*conspiracist, a native fusion paranoiac.

Long before Breitbart.com existed or Trump entered politics, Jones was ignoring the standard ideological lines to forge a confederacy of paranoids. JFK was "the last true president of the United States," and Lee Harvey Oswald was a patsy—just like Timothy McVeigh. "The Establishment," he has said, "they want to make it . . . right-wing versus left-wing." Glenn Beck, for instance, "spins it in a neocon-ish way that reinforces the controlled, left-right paradigm that divides people." Jones does consider the center-left more dangerous than the center-right—"the Democratic Party," he told Farrakhan in 2016, has "got black people in their web murdering your people and they love it." But whenever Jones's beliefs in the metaconspiracy contradict conventional conservative positions, he defaults to the former. His despised New World Order has always included the Republican donor class. Climate change is a hoax, but a hoax that serves the interests of the international financial elite. And when the stories the right tells aren't fantastical enough, Jones goes all the way: he doesn't just oppose firearms regulation, he has been a Sandy Hook truther, insisting two years after the massacre that it was "a synthetic completely fake [event] with actors."

The evil lurks *everywhere*. Life is a horror movie. "What's coming to take over," he says, "is your smart car taxing you by the mile, what's coming to get you is the smart meter frying you in your house, what's coming to get you is fluoride in the water, what's coming to get you is cancer viruses in the vaccines, what's coming to get us is the soft-kill New World Order."

The advertising on Jones's various media platforms illustrates the overlaps among regions of make-believe. Marketing Infidel body armor ("excellent protection that stops AK-47s") makes obvious sense. But on an ad for a natural medicine called Ancient Defense Herbal Immunity Complex, Jones himself does the voice-over: "the knowledge of the ancients, tried and true, trusted herbs and extracts fused with the latest neutraceutical science." He's also acutely attuned to a different overlap—between his fictional journalism and fictional prime-time depictions of it. The sixth season of the paranoid CIA thriller *Homeland* featured a character based on Jones. His site *Infowars* both complained—it was "propaganda" from the "establishment" conspiracy to "smear" him—and reveled: it proved that "Infowars is part of the cultural zeitgeist and cannot be ignored." The 2016 miniseries reboot of *The X-Files* also had a character modeled both on him *and* on his rival Beck. This triggered a perfect Jones harangue in which he struggled to parse the layers of fiction and reality: "Glenn Beck, who's a character based around me—*I'm* a real person, *he's* a *character* based around me," you see, and "now there's a TV show, the new *X-Files*." Yet a year later, his own lawyer in a child custody case was arguing in court that he's not *really* the frightening nut he appears to be all over the media. Rather, he's just "playing a character"—a character called Alex Jones, yes, but otherwise no different from Jack Nicholson playing the Joker in *Batman*. "He is a performance artist," Jones's lawyer said of his client.

* * *

JONES IS ONLY THE MOST important and prominent figure in a large and vibrant realm, where he and the other overheated conspiracy hounds must navigate their complicated networks of rivalries and alliances. It's like the situation among overheated Christians: they share beliefs in some basic narratives, but evangelicals are temperate compared to fundamentalists, and both may roll their eyes at charismatics. Somewhere between Jones and people who know that extraterrestrials secretly run the world is a fuzzy frontier—on one side, maybe a hundred million Americans with strongly conspiracist predispositions and ideas, and on the other, several million committed to beliefs that seem symptomatic of mental illness, way beyond the pale.

But the pale, the agreed-upon boundary line between reasonable and deranged, has moved by thousands of miles in Fantasyland. Fantastic beliefs that were beyond the pale twenty years ago are now mainstream. Alex Jones is deluded and hysterical, but he draws lines—between unbelievable and *really* unbelievable conspiracies, such as the one overseen by shape-shifting reptilian humanoids.*

He concedes that among his followers are some unfortunate loons. In his pity for them, he gets poetic. "Some unstable people are drawn to the bright flame of enlightenment that is so-called 'conspiracy culture,'" he said in 2011. "Some trees are going to become uprooted in a storm like this. But we can't stop telling the truth for fear of what telling the truth is going to do."

Thus he seems saner to his listeners and viewers and probably to himself. And he makes more middle-of-the-road conspiracists who *partly* agree with him—about the rigged system, elite puppet masters, consensus reality—feel reasonable and sensible because unlike Jones, *they* don't scream or sob in public or believe that the New World Order is deliberately frying their brains by means of home energy meters. His influence and celebrity are thus optimized.

In Fantasyland, everybody is graded on a curve.

* * *

* According to a 2013 Public Policy Polling survey, 10 percent or more of Americans who describe themselves as "very conservative" or "very liberal" believe in the reptilian conspiracy. The notion actually began as a piece of pulp fiction in a story in *Weird Tales* and was adapted by the fantasy writer H. P. Lovecraft before being recast as nonfiction and becoming the basis for the contemporary conspiracy theory.

JONES IS BOTH SYMPTOM AND cause of how knee-jerk, florid conspiracism has become rampant and normalized in America, a fixture of the way people now think and talk, eclipsing simpler Occam's razor understandings. Let me repeat once again: *I'm not saying that large secret plots haven't existed in the past and don't exist now.* For decades, people in the U.S. government, especially those whose work involves high-stakes secrecy, did a lot to make Americans start imagining conspiracies everywhere. The Warren Commission investigation of the Kennedy assassination was full of bungles and became a growth medium in the conspiracists' petri dishes for an infinity of bacterial theories—even though its essential conclusion was almost certainly correct. The government did lie about UFO sightings over the years—in order to cover up air force surveillance aircraft experiments. The Watergate burglary and cover-up were conspiracies—and promptly exposed, investigated, and punished. Among the most significant recent conspiracies, the cover-up by the Roman Catholic hierarchy and elite of its sexually predatory clergy was finally exposed—after we'd wasted vast resources and ruined hundreds of lives exposing and prosecuting a satanic sexual abuse conspiracy that didn't exist.

In fact, it was the sudden, shocking *exposure* of actual conspiracies starting in the 1970s that made Americans overcorrect, to assume that *anything* bad is the intentional result of some conspiracy. Which may make it harder, ironically, to expose and dismantle the rare real ones. Our news and Internet-enabled media discourse are clogged more than ever with conspiracy theories. All the fantastical noise obscures the occasional signals. I'm thinking, for instance, of the Russian government's interference in the last U.S. presidential election, to which too little attention was paid as it was happening. In the middle of 2016, it sounded like just one more wild speculation.

Donald Trump appeared on Alex Jones's show as a candidate and, right after the election, according to Jones, phoned him. "He said, 'Listen Alex, I just talked to the kings and queens of the world, world leaders, you name it, but . . . I wanted to talk to *you*. . . . We know what you did early on, throughout this campaign.'"

"It shows he's not the average elitist," Jones continued, still jazzed from his conversation with the president-elect,

> these stuck-up nobodies who believe they control the world, who believe everybody's an idiot . . . the people who tell you you have absolutely no rights or freedoms. . . . They stole five states on November 8th but still lost. And this whole criminal multinational enterprise . . . is now coming down. . . . We finally have people in

Washington that . . . don't buy the propaganda of the big mainline corporations that are using weaponized media to mind-control simple-minded people. . . . Once we restore the fact that it's okay for men to be masculine in America and defeat this big Ford Foundation program . . . people will become humans again and will be free. . . . [Trump won] because a lot of patriots, the Pentagon and you name it were part of the research program to carry this out—it was so horrifying they finally said, "No, we're not gonna do this to these people, we're not gonna turn them into cowardly jellyfishes." Your hoaxes did not work on us!

40

When the GOP Went Off the Rails

AS A THIRTEEN-YEAR-OLD, I WATCHED WILLIAM F. BUCKLEY'S *FIRING LINE* with my dad, attended Teen Age Republican summer camp, and during the 1968 Nebraska primary campaign, at the behest of a Nixon campaign advance man in Omaha, furtively ripped down Rockefeller and Reagan signs. Three years later I was a McGovern campaign volunteer, but I still watched and admired Buckley on PBS. Today I disagree about political issues with friends and relatives to my right, but we agree on the contours of reality. I never really loathed any president (until now), and over the years I voted for a few Republicans for state and local office.

People on the left are by no means all scrupulously reasonable—many give themselves over to the dubious and untrue. But the politics of Fantasyland are highly asymmetrical. That is, starting in the 1990s, America's unhinged right became much larger and more influential than its unhinged left. Moreover, it now has unprecedented power—as of 2016, effective control over much of the U.S. government.

Why did the grown-ups and designated drivers on the left manage to remain more or less in charge of their followers, while the reality-based right lost control to its fantasy-prone true believers?

One reason, I believe, is religion. The GOP is now quite explicitly Christian, the first time the United States has had such a major party. It is *the* American coalition of white Christians, papering over doctrinal and class differences—and now led, weirdly, by one of the least religious presidents in modern times. If more and more of a political party's members hold more and more extravagantly supernatural beliefs, doesn't it make sense that the party will be more and more open to make-believe in its politics and policy? The Southern Baptist minister and professor Roger Olson bemoans the fundamentalist takeover of evangelicalism. "An analogy," he wrote recently, "is what has happened to the Republican Party," where moderates were marginalized. But that isn't just an *analogous* dynamic: the transformations of Christianity and of the political right happened simultaneously and amplified each other.

I doubt the GOP elite deliberately engineered the synergies between the economic and religious sides of their contemporary coalition. But there it is nonetheless. As the incomes of middle- and working-class people flatlined, Republicans pooh-poohed rising economic inequality and insecurity; economic insecurity does correlate with greater religiosity; and for white Americans, greater religiosity does correlate with voting Republican. For Republican politicians and their rich-getting-richer donors, that's a virtuous circle, not a vicious one.

Another main way fantasists took over the GOP is with the flowering of conspiracism I described in the preceding two chapters. After 9/11, more Democrats than Republicans believed that the Bush administration allowed or arranged the attacks. Michael Moore's *Fahrenheit 9/11,* seen by twenty million Americans in theaters, nudged many liberals toward belief in an untrue conspiracy, but the mainstream left didn't push that fantasy. America simply has many more fervid conspiracists on the right, as research about belief in particular conspiracies confirms again and again.

Richard Hofstadter argued in the 1960s and many others have since that the right is inherently more fertile ground for such paranoia. Maybe. In any case, only the American right has had a large and organized faction *based on* paranoid conspiracism for the last six decades. As the pioneer vehicle, the John Birch Society zoomed along and then sputtered out, but its fantastical paradigm and belligerent temperament has endured and reproduced in other forms and under other brand names. When Barry Goldwater was the right-wing Republican presidential nominee in 1964, he had to play down any streaks of Bircher madness, but in his 1979 memoir *With No Apologies,* he felt free to rave on about the globalist conspiracy's "pursuit of a New World Order" and impending "period of slavery," the Council on Foreign Relations' secret agenda for "one-world rule," and the Trilateral Commission's plan for "seizing control of the political government of the United States." The right had three generations to steep in this. Its exciting taboo vapors wafted more and more into the main chambers of conservatism, becoming familiar, seeming less outlandish. Do you believe that "a secretive power elite with a globalist agenda is conspiring to eventually rule the world through an authoritarian world government"? Yes, say 34 percent of the people who voted Republican in 2012.*

Look at today's John Birch website: its concerns and spin are unremarkably Republican—abolish the Fed, pull out of the UN, kill Common Core, give moral support to the latest martyred right-wing lawbreaker who can't abide some government program or rule. Woodrow Wilson was in office when the Birch Society's founder came of age, and he demonized Wilson ever after—"more than any other one man [he] started this nation on its present road to totalitarianism." Which seemed quaint—until recently, when right-wingers like Glenn Beck revived that odd obsession with a president from a century ago.

Wilson pushed the League of Nations, the failed forerunner of the United Nations—and the UN, according to the far right in the 1950s and the mainstream right since the 1990s, is a headquarters of the globalist tyranny. In fact, of course, the UN has been a flawed but occasionally indispensable apparatus, and the right-wing vision of its villainous master plan for world domination is mad. The Republican Party's platform started depicting the UN as a bogeyman in 1996; the 2004 platform demanded that "American troops must never serve under United Nations command," but that document still had lots of references to the UN's utility and importance—the last one that did. (The 2016 GOP platform calls for a constitutional amendment to protect homeschooling "from interference by states, the federal government, or . . . the United Nations.")

This is not just symbolic wankery. It has had effects in the real world. Take Agenda 21, for instance. In 1992 the UN held an Earth Summit in Rio de Janeiro to start getting everyone on the same page concerning the environment and the new notion of sustainable development, especially concerning CO_2 emissions. It adopted a voluntary blueprint called Agenda 21. And then

* 2013 Public Policy Polling survey.

nobody outside the environmental do-good sector paid attention. From 1994 to 2006, there was exactly one reference to Agenda 21 in *The New York Times*.

But then the far right discovered it—exposed it!—and refashioned Agenda 21 as a secret key to the globalist conspiracy. (Conspiracists love learning the names of little-known government programs, especially if they contain numbers—the air force's Area 51, CIA's Operation 40, Special Ops' U.S. war games in 2015 called Jade 15—then repeating them until they become, dum-dum-*dum*, shorthand for shadowy evil.) By 2012, American right-wingers knew to be scared, *very scared*, of this vague, twenty-year-old international environmental plan. Agenda 21 and sustainable development, they say, were just totalitarianism and Communism by a different name. When the Obama administration created the White House Rural Council to promote economic development in places like Appalachia, a Fox News anchor warned that it was "eerily similar to a U.N. plan called Agenda 21, where a centralized planning agency would be responsible for oversight into all areas of our lives. A one-world order." When Newt Gingrich was the front-runner for the 2012 GOP presidential nomination and mentioned it during a debate, applause prevented him from finishing the thought. At that moment, Beck had just published his dystopian novel *Agenda 21,* and on his TV program one of the main Agenda 21 hysterics provided a perfect glimpse into the conspiracist mind: "You're not going to find anything that isn't Agenda 21 these days. . . . People recognize many, many things that are wrong but they don't realize that they're all connected."

By then, conservative activists all over the country were using Agenda 21 as the scary catchphrase to defeat ordinary county and city land-use plans, carbon-emission information programs, plans for high-speed trains, traffic decongestion, bike lanes, and home energy meters. The Republican National Committee called it a "comprehensive plan of . . . global political control" including "socialist/communist redistribution of wealth." The last two GOP platforms have had anti–Agenda 21 planks, and a dozen state legislatures passed resolutions decrying it.

IN THE LATE 1960S AND early '70s, the fantasy far left shot its wad and didn't leave many active cells. At the same time, the reality-based left more or less won: the retreat from Vietnam, the passage of civil rights and environmental protection laws, increasing legal and cultural equality for women, legalized abortion. Two leaders of the right, Milton Friedman and Richard Nixon, famously said at the time, "We are all Keynesians now"—meaning that, yes, the government does need to use taxes and spending to manage the economy.

But then the right wanted its turn to win: it more or less accepted racial and gender legal equality and learned to live with social welfare and regulation and bigger government, but it insisted on slowing it all down. The political center moved right—but in the 1970s and '80s not yet *unreasonably*. Most of America decided that we were all free marketeers now, that business was not necessarily bad, and that government couldn't solve all problems. It still seemed like the normal cyclical seesawing of American politics. In the 1990s the right also achieved two of its wildest existential dreams: the Soviet Union and international Communism collapsed, and as crime declined by half, law-and-order was restored.

But also starting in the 1990s, the farthest-right half of our right half, roughly a quarter of Americans, couldn't and wouldn't adjust their beliefs to comport with their side's victories and the dramatically new and improved realities. They'd made a god out of Reagan, but they ignored or didn't register that he was practical and reasonable, that he didn't completely buy his own antigovernment bullshit. After Reagan, his hopped-up true-believer faction began insisting on total victory. In a democracy, total victory by any faction is a fantasy, of course.

Pat Buchanan had been a senior official in three straight GOP administrations, making a career of bumptious nationalism and anti-Communism. As a teenager in the 1950s, his hero had been Joe McCarthy. The Soviet empire ended just as he began his first campaign for the GOP presidential nomination in 1992, so he simply substituted *New World Order* and *Davos* for *Communism* and *Moscow* in his talking points. He'd also praised his primary campaign opponent David Duke, the former KKK Imperial Wizard, for not being "intimidated into shucking off winning social issues" such as "discrimination against white folks." Buchanan won 23 percent of the national GOP primary vote against the incumbent Republican president, and in his campaign during the next cycle carried four states. Buchanan, running against a Bush in an effort to run against a Clinton, was a smarter, more sincere and ideologically coherent Trump twenty years ahead of his time.

Another way the GOP got loopy is by overdoing libertarianism. I have some libertarian tendencies, but at full-strength purity it's an ideology most boys grow out of. On the American right since the 1980s, however, they did not. Libertarianism used to have a robust left wing as well. Both disliked government. Both were driven by a fantastically nostalgic conviction that a country of three hundred million people at the turn of the twenty-first century could and should revert to something like its nineteenth-century self. Both had a familiar American magical-thinking fetish for *gold*—to return to gold as the foundation of U.S. currency because, they think, only *gold* is *real*.

However, as the post-Reagan Republican mother ship maintained extreme and accelerating antigovernment fervor—acquiring escape velocity during the 2000s, leaving Earth orbit in the 2010s—libertarianism became a right-wing movement. (Also helpful was the fact that extreme economic libertarians included extremely rich people like the Koch brothers who could finance its spread.) Most Republicans are very selective, cherry-picking libertarians: let business do whatever it wants, but don't spoil poor people with government handouts; let individuals have gun arsenals but not abortions or recreational drugs or marriage with whomever they wish; and don't mention Ayn Rand's atheism.

It's a political movement whose most widely read and influential texts are *fiction*. "I grew up reading Ayn Rand," Speaker of the House Paul Ryan has said, "and it taught me quite a bit about who I am and what my value systems are, and what my beliefs are." It was those fictions that allowed him and other higher-IQ Americans to see contemporary America as a dystopia in which selfishness is righteous and they are the last heroes. "I think a lot of people," Ryan said in 2009, "would observe that we are right now living in an Ayn Rand novel." I assume he meant *Atlas Shrugged*, a novel that Trump's secretary of state (the former CEO of ExxonMobil) has said is his favorite book. It's the story of a heroic cabal of men's men industrialists who cause the socialistic U.S. government to collapse so they can take over, start again, and make everything right.

For a while, realist Republican leaders effectively encouraged and exploited the predispositions of their fantastical partisans. That was the stone-cold cynicism of Karl Rove, like the Wizard of Oz's evil twin coming out from behind the curtain for a candid chat just before he won a second term for George Bush, explaining that the "judicious study of discernible reality" had been rendered obsolete. They were rational people who understood that a large fraction of Americans don't bother with rationality when they vote, that many voters *resent* the judicious study of discernible reality. Keeping those people angry and scared won them elections.

But over the last generation, a lot of the rabble they roused came to believe all the untruths. "The problem is that Republicans have purposefully torn down the validating institutions," says the political journalist Josh Barro, a Republican until 2016. "They have convinced voters that the media cannot be trusted; they have gotten them used to ignoring inconvenient facts about policy; and they have abolished standards of discourse." The right's ideological center of gravity careened way to the right of Rove and all Bushes, finally knocking them and their ilk aside. What had been its fantastical fringe became the GOP center. In retrospect, the sudden change in the gun lobby in the late 1970s, from more or less flexible to absolutely hysterical, was a harbinger of the transformation of the entire right a generation later. Reasonable Republicanism was replaced by absolutism: *no* new taxes, virtually *no* regulation, *abolish* the EPA and the IRS and the Federal Reserve.

As I've said, there are left-wing believers in nonexistent conspiracies and other fantasies, but they're not nearly as numerous or influential. During the 2016 Democratic primaries, after Bernie Sanders did better in some election-day exit polls than he did in the voting, some of his supporters were convinced a conspiracy had falsified the results. (In fact, exit polls always tend to oversample younger voters.) And while you might have considered Sanders's leftism unrealistic or its campaign rhetoric hyperbolic ("the business model of Wall Street is fraud"), the campaign wasn't based on outright fantasies. You may not want democratic socialism, but Denmark is a real country.

So WHILE POLITICIANS OF ALL stripes propagate politically useful make-believe, Republicans let this habit get the best of them in several consequential areas. Environmental science had the bad luck to recognize and start to publicize global warming in the early 2000s, just as full Fantasyland dawned. At first, Republicans were officially reasonable on the subject. As recently as 2008, their party platform mentioned "climate change" thirteen times, stipulating it was caused by "human economic activity," and they committed themselves to "decreasing the long term demand for oil" in order "to address the challenge." Four years later they had switched to denialism, the next platform mentioning "climate change" once, in scare quotes, only to disparage concern about it. The 2012 platform considered the UN's twenty-year-old global warming mission statement Agenda 21 a more dire problem than global warming.

The Republican position is now to oppose even *studying* climate change as well as any and all proposals to reduce carbon emissions. Rational people may disagree about how governments might minimize or prepare for the effects of global warming. You are entitled to your own opinion. But refusing to accept its reality is a new and unacceptable posture. You are not entitled to your own facts.

On this subject, some Republicans are Cynics, some are Believers, and many combine bits of both. The pure Cynics are doing the bidding of the fossil fuel industry, which has cynically and successfully raised doubts about the clear scientific consensus on the cause of global warming. In this, they repeated what the tobacco industry had pioneered starting in the 1960s, as soon as medical science established that smoking causes cancer. At the Brown & Williamson cigarette company in 1969, an internal memo was explicit. "Doubt is our product," it declared, "the best means of competing with the 'body of fact' that exists in the mind of the general public. It is also the means of establishing a controversy."

Senate Environment Committee chair James Inhofe is from Oklahoma, a big oil state, so he has rational political reasons to belittle climate change. But he also argues, in his book on the subject, *The Greatest Hoax: How the Global Warming Conspiracy Threatens Your Future,* that it's just God turning up Earth's thermostat a little, and he condemns "the arrogance of people to think that we, human beings, would be able to change what He is doing in the climate," which "is to me outrageous." Searching the records of the 278 Republicans serving in the Senate and House in 2014, the news organization PolitiFact found only eight who publicly acknowledged that global warming is real and caused by humans. We can't know, of course, how many of the others are Believers and how many are Cynics. The good news is that only 17 percent of Americans who don't call themselves Republican believe global warming is a myth.*

IN ADDITION TO HAVING BECOME a distinctly Christian party, the GOP is more than ever America's self-consciously white party. The nationalization of its Southern Strategy from the 1960s worked partly because it rode demographic change. In 1960, 90 percent of Americans were white and non-Hispanic. Only a few states had white populations of less than 70 percent—specifically Mississippi, South Carolina, Louisiana, and Alabama. Today the white majority in the whole country is down nearly to 60 percent; in other words, America's racial makeup is now more "Southern" than the Deep South's was in the 1960s.

For a while, the party's leaders were careful to clear their deck of explicit racism. It was reasonable, wasn't it, to be concerned about violent crime spiraling upward from the 1960s through the '80s? We don't want social welfare programs to encourage cultures of poverty and dependency, do we? Although

---

* 2008–15 biannual surveys by the Project on Climate Change Communication; 2013 Public Policy Polling survey.

the dog-whistled resentment of new policies disfavoring or seeming to disfavor white people became more audible, Republican leaders publicly stuck to not-entirely-unreasonable arguments: affirmative action is an imperfect solution; too much multiculturalism might Balkanize America; we shouldn't let immigrants pour into the U.S. helter-skelter. But in this century, more Republican leaders started cozying up to the ugliest fantasists, unapologetic racists. When Congressman Ron Paul ran for the 2008 GOP nomination, he appeared repeatedly with the neo-Nazi Richard Spencer, who was just coining the term "alt-right" for his movement. Senator Rand Paul employed as an aide and wrote a book with a former leader of the League of the South, an organization devoted to a twenty-first-century do-over of Confederate secession.

After we elected a black president, more regular whistles joined the kind only dogs can hear. Even thoughtful Ross Douthat, one of the *Times*'s conservative columnists, admitted to a weakness for the Old South fantasy. During the debate about governments displaying Confederate symbols after nine black people were shot dead by a white supremacist in Charleston, he discussed "the temptation . . . to regard the Confederate States of America as the political and historical champion of all . . . attractive Southern distinctives. . . . Even a secession-hating Yankee like myself has felt, at certain moments the pull of that idea, the lure of that fantasy."

Meanwhile the party Establishment was convincing majorities of Republicans of an entirely fraudulent fantasy it knew to be a lie—that rampant voter fraud required new ID laws to prevent (black and brown and young) people from casting ballots illegally. Moreover in all sorts of ways, the GOP, more than any other U.S. institution, helped convince white people of an extraordinary falsehood underlying the others. For almost a generation now, according to a new study by professors at the Harvard Business School and Tufts, the average white American has subscribed to the fantasy that anti-white bias is a more serious problem in the United States than antiblack bias.

AND THEN THERE WAS A new set of nonwhite people to fear. On September 20, 2001, President Bush made a point of saying that our enemy "is not our many Muslim friends . . . [or] our many Arab friends." But after that, many Republicans began explicitly encouraging and exaggerating fears of Muslims, especially after the election of a nonwhite president with the middle name Hussein. Why did half of Republicans—and two-thirds of Trump's primary voters—remain convinced that Obama is a Muslim?* Because GOP elected officials and other conservative leaders encouraged them for more than a decade. The hysterical fear of Muslims combines several familiar, long-standing American strains of fantasy-driven abomination: of secret conspirators in high places, of nonwhite people by white people, of non-Protestants by Protestants, of non-Christians by Christians, and of scary foreigners by everyone.

Sharia law uses the sacred texts of Islam as the basis for moral behavior, the way Jews are supposed to use the Talmud and Christians the Bible—and, in Muslim countries, it uses the Quran explicitly as the basis for legal codes. Just before we elected our forty-fourth non-Muslim president in a row, people on the right began fantasizing that American Muslims were scheming to supplant U.S. jurisprudence with Islamic jurisprudence. The definitive text is a 2010 book called *Shariah: The Threat to America*. Its nineteen authors included respectable hard-right conservatives and national security wonks. We're "infiltrated and deeply influenced," the book says, "by an enemy within that is openly determined to replace the U.S. Constitution with shariah." The movement took off, and in short order the specter of sharia became a right-wing catchphrase encompassing suspicion of almost *any* Islamic involvement in the U.S. civic sphere. The word gave Islamophobia a patina of legitimacy. It was a specific fantasy—not *I hate Muslims* or *I hate Arabs* but rather *I don't want to live under Taliban law*, and therefore it could pass as not racist but anti-*tyranny*. It was also a shiny new exotic term, a word nobody in America but a few intellectuals knew.

The coinventor of the fantasy and the ringleader and front man of *Shariah: The Threat to America* was Frank Gaffney, who'd been a Pentagon official in the 1980s. After 9/11, he claimed that Saddam Hussein's regime was behind those attacks—and that it had recruited Timothy McVeigh to bomb the Oklahoma City federal building. Gaffney became obsessed with his fantasy that the conservative antitax lobbyist Grover Norquist is a covert agent of the Muslim Brotherhood. As soon as Obama got elected, naturally, Gaffney was referring to the "mounting evidence that the president not only identifies with Muslims, but actually may still be one himself." None of this got Gaffney excommunicated from the right.

The antisharia movement lobbied states to pass statutes and constitutional amendments banning the use of sharia in their courts and legal systems, a fantasy solution to an imaginary problem, almost like a government plan to prevent a zombie apocalypse. Starting in 2010, nine states passed

---

* 2015 and 2016 Public Policy Polling and CNN/Opinion Research Corporation surveys.

such measures. And when candidate Trump first announced his proposed ban on Muslim immigrants—because sharia "authorizes such atrocities as murder . . . beheadings"—his backup data consisted entirely of bogus polling by Frank Gaffney.

WHEN I WAS GROWING UP, my Republican parents loathed all Kennedys, distrusted unions, and complained about "confiscatory" federal income tax rates of 91 percent. But conservatism to them also meant conserving the natural environment and allowing people to make their own choices, including about abortion. They were emphatically *reasonable,* disinclined to believe in secret Communist/Washington/elite plots to destroy America, rolling their eyes and shaking their heads about far-right acquaintances—such as our neighbors who opposed the fluoridation of Omaha's drinking water and considered Richard Nixon suspiciously leftish.* My folks never belonged to a church. Godless midwestern Republicans, born and raised—which was not so odd forty years ago. Until around 1980, "the Christian right" was not a phrase in American politics. In 2000 my widowed seventy-eight-year-old mom, having voted for fourteen Republican presidential nominees in a row, decisively quit a party that had become too religious for her.

The Christian takeover happened gradually, but then quickly in the end, like a phase change from liquid to gas. In 2008 three-quarters of the GOP presidential primary candidates said they believed in evolution, but in 2012 it was down to a third, and then in 2016 only one did. That one, Jeb Bush, was careful to say evolutionary biology was only *his* truth, that "it does not need to be in the curriculum" of public schools, and if it is, ought to be accompanied by creationist teaching.

Most people aligned with the white pan-Christian party today don't have a strong secular vision of America. A two-to-one majority of Republicans say they "support establishing Christianity as the national religion." (And a large majority of all Americans believe that the "Constitution establishes [the United States as] a Christian nation" already.)† I'm pretty sure we're never going to become a Christian version of Saudi Arabia or Iran, but are we not already close to something like Turkey, officially secular but with a distinctly

* The neighbors were the Lamps, whose youngest daughter Ginni graduated from my all-white public high school right after I did, then married a very conservative lawyer named Clarence Thomas.
† 1997–2007 First Amendment Center surveys; 2013 Public Policy Polling survey.

religious party in charge? When Megyn Kelly asked the GOP candidates during a 2015 primary debate if "any of them have received a word from God on what they should do and take care of first," it was strange, but she was just acknowledging the new Republican normal.

In fact, there are millions of American Christians trying to realize their fantasy of a fully theocratic nation. Their movement is called the Third Wave or dominionism, a term coined by Peter Wagner, the godfather of "spiritual warfare," who believes the satanic sun goddess has sex with the Japanese emperor (see Chapter 31). The movement is a loose confederation of churches, mostly charismatic and Pentecostal but some merely fundamentalist. They are endeavoring to acquire political and cultural power in order to battle and defeat demons and put fundamentalist Christians in charge.

They are, in other words, like the Muslim Brotherhood as the right-wingers imagine it, seeking to be long-run agents of influence in America. After the movement made news because of its links to national Republicans during the 2012 election cycle, Wagner wrote an essay in *Charisma News* about the criticism that his group has an "excessive fixation on Satan and demonic spirits. This is purely a judgment call, and it may only mean that we cast out more demons than they do. So what?" As for a theocracy, Wagner says, "There's nobody that I know—there may be some fringe people—who would even advocate a theocracy." *Fringe people*—as opposed to one member of Wagner's own Council of Prophetic Elders who, according to *Charisma*, "received word that a witch had applied for a job as chaplain of [Alaska's] prison system. 'As we continued to pray against the spirit of witchcraft, her incense altar caught on fire, her car engine blew up, she went blind in her left eye, and she was diagnosed with cancer.'" Hallelujah. In fact, a former Republican governor of Alaska, officially Pentecostal until she ran for statewide office, was a member of the prayer group led by her regional Wagnerian commandant and witch-buster—and Sarah Palin is now, of course, a prominent member of the GOP faction that runs the country.

Fantasyland is the result of one part of our national character overtaking the other part, and the new religiosity of Republican politics is a good example—there in the bloodstream forever but under control. Although constitutionally the United States can have no state religion, *faith* has always bordered on being mandatory. "Unbelievers are to be met with in America," Tocqueville wrote forty-two years after the Constitution came into force, "but, to say the truth, there is no public organ of infidelity." Only four presidents have lacked a Christian denominational affiliation, the most recent one in the 1880s. Two-thirds of Republicans today admit they'd be less likely to vote for a presidential candidate who disbelieves in God.*

As a matter of fact, the Constitution's key clause—"no religious test shall ever be required as a qualification to any office or public trust"—is kind of a theoretical freedom. Not only have we never had an openly unbelieving president, of the 535 members of the last Congress, exactly one listed her religion as "none." Among all 7,383 state legislators, there is apparently only one atheist.† Eight of the fifty state constitutions officially prohibit atheists from holding public office; of those, Pennsylvania and Tennessee specifically require officeholders to believe in Heaven and Hell; and in Arkansas, atheists are technically ineligible to have any state job or to testify in court.

The presence of so many Christian true believers holding office or otherwise wielding power has consequences in the real world, even leaving aside abortion laws. In Washington, D.C., they use their understandings of the Bible as guides to national security policy. Seven out of ten evangelical and fundamentalist Christians believe "the modern nation of Israel was formed as a result of biblical prophecy" and that "events in Israel are part of the prophecies in the Book of Revelation."‡ In other words, before the end-time battles can happen, as many Jews as possible need to be near Armageddon. The eleven-year-old Christians United for Israel, with 3 million members, is a primary vehicle of the American Christian Zionist movement. Its Pentecostal minister founder has preached that God sent Hitler to Earth as "a hunter" to exterminate Jews in order to herd and corral the survivors in Palestine—"to get them to come *back* to the land." The Christian Zionists' entire political focus is on lobbying for U.S. support of the hardest possible Israeli hard line—in order to be in sync, as they see it, with the Bible's apocalyptic prophecies.

These beliefs are an important source of the Republicans' policy toward Israel, and thus of America's, which is disturbing to me. Is that unfair? In a *New York Times* column opposing the nuclear deal with Iran, the right-leaning David Brooks argued that the United States should mistrust the Iranian regime specifically because of its religious beliefs about the end-time—because undoubtedly "Iranian leaders are as apocalyptically motivated . . . as their pronouncements suggest they are."

* 2015 Pew survey.
† Senator Ernie Chambers of Nebraska has actually said the Bible consists of "fairy tales."
‡ 2015 Southern Baptists' LifeWay Christian Resources survey.

I'm reminded of one of Mencken's dispatches from the Scopes Monkey Trial in 1925. "Civilized" Tennesseans, he wrote, "had known for years what was going on in the hills. They knew what the country preachers were preaching—what degraded nonsense was being rammed and hammered into yokel skulls. But they were afraid to go out against the imposture while it was in the making." In fact, what the contemporary Republican Party has done is worse, because it was deliberate and national and has more profound consequences.

41

Liberals Denying Science

REPUBLICANS AND EVANGELICAL CHRISTIANS ARE NOT THE ONLY PEOPLE who passionately believe in factual untruths that have unfortunate impacts on people.

Most Americans have been eating genetically modified foods since the 1990s, and nearly all our meat and chicken (and tofu and processed food) derive from GMOs. I understand why people tend to find the idea unsettling. Frankenfoods! Created by the agribusiness cartel! Identical majorities of liberals, moderates, and conservatives believe that foods containing GMOs are unsafe to eat—57 percent of all Americans.* But they are almost certainly mistaken.

After more than three decades and many hundreds of studies, the overwhelming scientific consensus is that GMO foods are safe to eat. The National Academies of Sciences, Engineering, and Medicine commissioned a comprehensive study of the science, and in 2016 their report declared GMOs

---

* 2014 Pew surveys.

both safe to eat *and* environmentally benign. Of the scientists in the American Association for the Advancement of Science, 88 percent think it's safe to eat GMO foods. This is almost exactly the same percentage of those scientists who say climate change is real and man-made, the latter a data point regularly used to demonstrate right-wing antiscience craziness.* In other words, people on the left occasionally choose to ignore evidence and disbelieve important science that they find upsetting.

But whipping up hysterical fears of GMOs does not pick your pocket or break your leg—although the millions of people in the Third World whose lives have been improved and saved by cultivating and eating GMO foods might beg to differ.† The movement that has made people afraid of vaccines, however, has unquestionably harmed Americans' public health.

When I was little, a thousand American children died from polio every year, and thousands more were permanently paralyzed. The year I turned three, a flu epidemic killed seventy thousand people in the United States, and I spent two weeks in the hospital with unstoppable diarrhea caused by a retrovirus, and nearly died. Back then, as many as a thousand American kids died every year from diphtheria, tetanus, and whooping cough. Several hundred Americans were dying every year from measles, and the disease rendered many hundreds more deaf or, as we said then, retarded. But during the 1950s and early '60s, vaccines appeared that prevented all those, and every kid got them. Many thousands of unnecessary deaths and cripplings were prevented. There was no antivaccine movement.

The false belief that vaccines cause autism and other terrible illnesses derives from familiar sources—a misplaced nostalgia for the past, excessive mistrust of experts, the conviction that some vicious conspiracy is behind everything bad, and the gatekeeper-free Internet.

The study that ignited the hysteria appeared in 1998, when diagnoses of autism had been increasing. A doctor studied ten children who showed autistic behavior after they were vaccinated against measles, mumps, and rubella, published his research in a medical journal, and instantly became the guiding light of a new movement.

His research could not be replicated by other doctors and scientists. Nor could the movement's other article of faith, that a mercury-based vaccine preservative was the autism trigger, be substantiated. Indeed, major study

---

* 2014 Pew surveys.
† Full disclosure: the insulin that keeps me and nearly all Type 1 "juvenile" diabetics alive is derived from GMO bacteria.

after major study after major study ever since has found stronger and stronger evidence that vaccines do not cause autism. Not until a dozen years after publishing the original paper—after the doctor was stripped of his medical license and found to have acted "dishonestly and irresponsibly"—did *The Lancet* finally retract his study, calling it "utterly false." The other major British medical journal called it an "elaborate fraud."

In the meantime, however, none of these reality checks mattered to the Americans who *believed.* A year after the original study came out, they got U.S. health authorities and the American Academy of Pediatrics to recommend that the preservative be removed from vaccines, just to be safe, and manufacturers did so. *See,* the believers said, *we must have been right—and vaccines must still be dangerous!* Google, which had just launched, enabled the panic to spread. Indeed, when the actress Jenny McCarthy became a public face of the antivaccine movement in the 2000s, she went on *Oprah* and gave the perfect defense of her credentials: "The University of Google is where I got my degree from!"

Robert F. Kennedy, Jr., became the movement's star, repeating his line that U.S. government scientists were "involved in a massive fraud." His big article on the subject was eventually retracted by both magazines that published it. *Part of the corrupt cover-up!* Among children born since thimerosal was removed from vaccines, autism-spectrum diagnoses continued rising. *Lies, disinformation and lies!* Still more studies appeared concluding vaccines are safe. *If not the mercury, then some other toxin! If not autism, then asthma or juvenile diabetes!* Their beliefs, like religious faith, are unfalsifiable by facts.

The media did their part too. In 2002 *The New York Times Magazine* ran a long article called "The Not-So-Crackpot Autism Theory." Kennedy, a liberal celebrity from a liberal celebrity dynasty, was endorsed all over TV, including in his appearance on *The Daily Show.* Oprah Winfrey: sure. But one doesn't expect America's great celebrity skeptic, the maker of a feature-film documentary mocking religion, to entertain and encourage provably false fantasies. According to Bill Maher, "Flu vaccines are bullshit"—in fact, getting vaccinated with a "flu shot is the worst thing you can do. . . . If you have a flu shot for more than five years in a row," he said on CNN, "there's ten times the likelihood that you'll get Alzheimer's disease." It wasn't the vaccine against polio that reduced its U.S. incidence from thirty thousand cases the year before he was born to several dozen when he was in grade school—it was just that better sanitation came along in the late 1950s. "I'm not into Western medicine," Maher says, and he means it—he denies the very basis of infec-

tious disease medicine: "It's not the invading germs. . . . It's not the mosqui-
toes, it's the swamp that they are breeding in." That's what scientists thought
in the early 1800s.

Millions of American parents stopped having their children vaccinated.*
States had always granted exemptions to people such as Christian Scientists
and Jehovah's Witnesses with theological objections. During the 2000s, exemptions for the new just-*because* reasons mushroomed. In a decade, Ohio's
exemptions tripled, and in California the number of nonimmunized kindergartners more than doubled. The unvaccinated fractions grew disturbingly
high in red states (Idaho, Arkansas), blue states (Vermont, Oregon), and
purple states (Colorado, Wisconsin), in religious enclaves (Orthodox Jews in
Brooklyn, Ohio Amish, Minnesota Muslims, Scientologists everywhere) and
in cosmopolitan Sodoms.

The antivaccine hysteria among well-educated, affluent parents I find
especially galling. A population's "herd immunity" starts to collapse and permit infectious epidemics when as few as 6 percent forgo immunization. In
dozens of New York City private schools, the rate rose to more than 30 percent. In the richest section of Los Angeles—Malibu to Santa Monica down
to Marina del Rey, through Beverly Hills and Brentwood to West Hollywood—
the fraction of preschoolers with Personal Belief Exemptions exceeded 9 percent, four times the rate in L.A. County at large. In plenty of West L.A.
private schools, especially "progressive" ones, *majorities* of parents stopped
vaccinating.

This natural experiment confirmed the science: diseases we had eliminated returned. If you'd nostalgically pined for a return to old-time America,
you got your way. U.S. cases of whooping cough had bottomed out at around
8,000 through the early 2000s; by 2012, we were up to 48,000—the 1955
level. The outbreak in California (as in Washington State) was the worst
since the 1940s—hundreds were hospitalized and ten were dead in one year.
Twenty of the Americans who got whooping cough in 2012 died, most of
them newborns. Measles cases increased tenfold within a few years.

Vaccine-phobia runs the ideological gamut, but lately it seems to be shifting rightward—where antiexpert and antigovernment derangement is more
intense. In all, almost a third of Americans believe that "vaccinations can

---

* As did parents in Britain and Ireland—it had been a British medical journal that published the original fraudulent study by a British doctor. Measles vaccination rates dropped
in France, Denmark, and Italy as well. America is the Fantasyland mother country, but it
extends beyond our borders.

cause autism" and that schools shouldn't require children to get them.* And the true believers keep believing, some more bonkers than ever. In a 2013 keynote address to a big convention of antivaccination activists, according to *Discover* magazine, Kennedy said that "this is like the Nazi death camps. . . . I would do a lot to see Paul Offit and all these good people behind bars." Offit is a distinguished pediatrician, professor, retrovirus vaccine inventor, and author of *Do You Believe in Magic? The Sense and Nonsense of Alternative Medicine*. "Is it hyperbole to say they should be in jail?" Kennedy asked his audience. *No.* "They should be in jail and the key should be thrown away."

* 2014 Pew and Harris surveys.

42

Gun Crazy

ONE SET OF FANTASIES HAS HAD MORE CURRENT, AWFUL, UNDENIABLE REAL-world consequences than any other: the one that recast owning guns as among the most important rights, as American liberty and individualism incarnate. During my lifetime, the love of guns has become a fetish. It is picking our pockets and definitely breaking our legs.

As a little kid, I was perpetually armed with cap guns until I graduated to BB guns and then, at YMCA summer camp and a great-uncle's farm, to .22 rifles. One of my fondest childhood memories is my dad and me turning an old three-inch pipe into an improvised cherry-bomb-powered mortar to fire tennis balls at grazing cows fifty yards away. One of my older brother's fondest childhood memories is ordering me to run across the backyard so he could shoot me with a BB gun from thirty yards and watch me crumple in pain to the ground, which he excitedly said at the time "was *just* like a *movie*." As an adult, I've enjoyed hunting turkey and shooting skeet, always feeling a little like Daniel Boone or Lord Grantham. And when my wife went to China and got to fire an Uzi at a shooting range, I was very jealous.

I get the fun of guns, and of the various fantasies that shooting makes possible.

But. Oh, but. I thought of my BB gun escapade not long ago, when I read an essay by the poet Gregory Orr. Just before, on a firing range outside Las Vegas, a nine-year-old had lost control of her fully automatic Uzi and shot her instructor dead. Orr is my brother's age. When he was twelve, the age my brother was when he shot me with a BB on purpose, Orr accidentally shot and killed his little brother while they were hunting. "To hunt," Orr wrote, "to fire a gun is to have your imagination tangled up with fantasies of power. A fatal accident makes a mockery of these fantasies."

Still, hunting isn't pure fantasy: you shoot a pheasant or a deer, and you eat it. But over the last few decades, Americans have lost their taste for hunting. Only 15 percent of us now say we ever hunt, less than half as many as in the 1970s. In any given year, maybe a third of those hunters among us, 5 percent of Americans, actually slog through fields and forests with rifles and shotguns.

In fact, fewer of us now own any kind of gun for any reason—even as the number of guns has increased phenomenally. In the 1970s about half of Americans had a gun, and it was almost always just *a* gun, one on average. Today only about a quarter of Americans own guns—but the average owner has three or four. Fewer than eight million people, only 3 percent of all American adults, own roughly half the guns. Members of that tiny minority of superenthusiasts own an average of seventeen guns apiece.*

Let me put a finer point on what I'm saying. Very, very few of the guns in America are used for hunting. Americans who own guns today keep arsenals in a way people did not forty years ago. It seems plain to me that that's because they—not all, but many—have given themselves over to fantasies.

The way I did as a child and still do on the rare occasion I shoot, they imagine they're militiamen, pioneers, Wild West cowboys, soldiers, characters they've watched all their lives in movies and on TV, heroes and antiheroes played by Clint Eastwood and Mel Gibson and the Rock, like Davy Crockett or Butch or Sundance or Rambo or Neo (or Ellen Ripley or Sarah Connor). They're like children playing with light-sabers, except they believe they're prepared to fight off real-life aliens (from the Middle East, from Mex-

---

* These two paragraphs are based on data from the National Opinion Research Center's 2015 General Social Survey, the U.S. Fish and Wildlife Service's 2011 survey, the Congressional Research Service, the Federal Reserve, research by Florida State University criminologist Gary Kleck, and a survey conducted in 2015 by Harvard and Northeastern University researchers.

ico) and storm troopers, and their state-of-the-art weapons actually wound and kill. Why did gangsters and wannabe gangsters start holding and firing their handguns sideways, parallel to the ground, even though that compromises their aim and control? Because it looks cool, and it began looking cool after filmmakers started directing actors to do it, originally in the 1960s, constantly by the 1990s.* Why are Americans buying the semiautomatic AR-15 and rifles like it more than any other style, 1.5 million each year? Because holding and shooting one makes them feel cooler, more like commandos. For the same reason, half the states now require no license for people to carry their guns openly in public places. It's the same reason, really, that a third of the vehicles sold in America are pickups and four-wheel-drive Walter Mittymobiles, even though three-quarters of four-wheel-drive off-road vehicles never go off-road. It's even the reason blue jeans became the American uniform after the 1960s. We are actors in a 24/7 *tableau vivant,* schlubs playing the parts of heroic tough guys.

Spectacular mass killings happen in America far more often than anywhere else, and not just because we make massacre-perfect weapons so easy to buy. Such killers are also engaged in role-play and are motivated by our besetting national dream of overnight fame. The experts say that most mass killers are not psychotics or paranoid schizophrenics in the throes of clinical delusion; rather, they're citizens of Fantasyland, unhappy people with flaws and failures they blame on others, the system, the elitists, the world. They worry those resentments into sensational fantasies of paramilitary vengeance, and they know that acting out those fantasies will make a big splash and force the rest of us to pay attention to them for the first time.

BEYOND THE FREE-FLOATING AMERICAN MYTHS underlying law-abiding American gun love—the frontier, badass individualism, action movies—there are the specific frightened scenarios driving the die-hard ferocity concerning gun regulation.

The least fantastical is the idea that if a criminal threatens or attacks tomorrow, you want a gun handy to kill him. Being prepared for a showdown with a bad guy is the main reason gun owners give for owning one, and that answer has doubled in the surveys since the 1990s. During the same period, the chance of an American actually having such an encounter has decreased by half. In New York City, where restrictions on owning and carrying guns

---

* It made it easier to frame the gun and the actor's face in the same tight shot.

are among the strictest in the United States, the chance of being murdered is
82 percent less than it was in 1990.*

Keeping a handgun for protection may be foolish, but it's not irrational.
Even though violent crime has dramatically declined, in a country where
every fourth person owns a gun, the hankering to be armed is understandable. Each of us runs life-and-death cost-benefit calculations differently.
Every year, according to the Justice Department's massive Crime Victimization Surveys, about one in six thousand Americans displays or fires a gun in
self-defense during an attempted robbery or assault. But the dozens of new
state laws that practically itch for make-my-day citizen showdowns—
Concealed Carry, Stand Your Ground—have been driven much more by fantasy and hysteria than by reason and prudence.

But beyond the prospect of protecting oneself against random attacks—
and by the way, among the million-plus Americans interviewed in ten years
of Crime Victimization Surveys, exactly one sexual assault victim used a gun
in self-defense—several outlandish scenarios and pure fantasies drive the
politics of gun control. One newer fantasy has it that in the face of an attack
by jihadi terrorists, armed random civilians will save the day. Another is the
fantasy that patriots will be obliged to *become* terrorist rebels, as Americans
did in 1776 and 1861, this time to defend liberty against the U.S. government
before it fully reveals itself as a tyrannical fascist-socialist-globalist regime
and tries to confiscate every private gun.

This uprising scenario, when it appeared in the 1960s, stirred people
only on the farthest fringes of American politics. It is now deep in the mainstream, thanks in large measure to the work of the National Rifle Association
and its affiliated hysterics. How did that happen?

When the Founders wrote the Constitution, they envisioned a very small
permanent national military. If Americans needed to fight wars, the states
would assemble their militias. And so the Second Amendment: "A well regulated Militia, being necessary to the security of a free State, the right of the
people to keep and bear Arms, shall not be infringed." For more than two
centuries, the Supreme Court avoided making any sweeping decision about
what the Second Amendment meant. It just didn't come up that much. Increasingly it seemed an artifact of another time.

The court okayed prohibiting certain kinds of firearms, such as sawed-off
shotguns. In 1980 a decision passingly noted that the Second Amendment

---

* 1999 *Washington Post*/ABC News and 2013 Pew surveys, FBI Uniform Crime Reports,
New York City Police Department CompStat 2016.

guarantees an individual's right to have a gun only if it bears "some reasonable relationship to the preservation or efficiency of a well regulated militia." But the constitutional can got kicked further down the road. States and cities that wanted to restrict gun ownership did, and occasionally Congress enacted modest regulations. Meanwhile people who loved owning guns could indulge their love in the United States more freely and fully than almost anywhere else on Earth.

But after the NRA's apoplectic-fantasist faction took control in the late 1970s, it turned its dial up to eleven and kept it there, becoming the center of a powerful new political movement that opposed any and all regulation of firearms—the types and numbers of guns and accessories and ammo people could buy, who could buy them and how easily, registration, licensing, even a requirement to use safety locks. Nevertheless Congress in the 1990s managed to enact two laws—one requiring most gun buyers to pass an FBI background check to screen out criminals and another banning the manufacture of certain semiautomatic guns and of magazines that hold more than ten rounds.

In response, the NRA sent a particularly hysterical, 2,600-word fundraising letter to its members. "President Clinton's army of anti-gun government agents continues to intimidate and harass law-abiding citizens," as in "Waco and the Branch Davidians." Today they're poking into a weapons cache, tomorrow they'll be taking away everyone's "right to free speech, free practice of religion, and every other freedom in the Bill of Rights." The new assault weapons ban "gives jackbooted Government thugs more power to take away our constitutional rights, break in our doors, seize our guns, destroy our property and even injure and kill us. . . . Not too long ago, it was unthinkable for federal agents wearing Nazi bucket helmets and black storm trooper uniforms to attack law-abiding citizens."

The letter was signed by Wayne LaPierre, the NRA's CEO. Growing up, LaPierre wasn't a young outdoorsman but a nerd, a politics nerd, and not even a conservative one. At twenty-two, he volunteered for the George McGovern presidential campaign, then went to work for a Democrat in the Virginia state legislature. From there, he happened to get a low-level lobbying job with the NRA in 1978, right after its extremist faction had taken over—and in 1991, the year *Behold a Pale Horse* was published, he became CEO.

The 1995 jackbooted-government-thugs letter was the moment the NRA inarguably settled in deepest Fantasyland. It seemed demented even to Republicans, dozens of whom had voted for the assault weapons ban in Congress. Former president George H. W. Bush resigned from the NRA in protest. Just days after the letter went out, the anti-gun-regulation activist Timothy McVeigh blew up the Oklahoma City federal building.

LaPierre and the gun rights zealots, however, did not rethink or walk it back. Although they dominated the political process concerning gun regulation, that wasn't enough. They sought total victory, unequivocal and unambiguous. They needed to convince a majority of the Supreme Court to ratify their new everybody's-a-freelance-militiaman interpretation of the Second Amendment once and for all. In the 1990s that still seemed improbable. No less a figure than Chief Justice Warren Burger, a conservative appointed by Nixon, complained after he retired that the Second Amendment "has been the subject of one of the greatest pieces of fraud—I repeat the word *fraud*— on the American public by special interest groups that I have ever seen in my lifetime."

But the winds were with the gun lobbyists. When the ban on semiautomatic weapons expired in 2004, it was not renewed. Even more amazingly, what Chief Justice Burger had denounced as a fraud in the 1990s had become respectable jurisprudence by the 2000s. In cases in 2008 and 2010, the Supreme Court finally agreed to decide the fundamental meaning of the Second Amendment. Four of the justices still interpreted it the old way. In the 2010 case, for instance, Justice Stephen Breyer wrote an opinion noting that back in 1791, "the Framers did not write the Second Amendment in order to protect a private right of armed self defense. There has been, and is, no consensus that the right is, or was, 'fundamental.'"

But in both cases, five justices went with the new reading. Now our Constitution does indeed guarantee each one of us the right to own firearms. We can argue all we want about how different guns were in the 1790s, when it took a minute to fire three shots, and about the correlation between the numbers of guns and gun deaths in the contemporary world, and how Australia's 1996 roundup program worked. Those debates are academic, however. In this instance, the Constitution apparently *is* a suicide pact, and not just metaphorically.

So that's how we got here. The NRA has won. Yet they and their compatriots seem no less paranoid or angry, still convinced that tyranny is right around the corner and that federal agents are coming for their guns. The wholesale confiscation of guns was never seriously bruited in the United States. Through the 1980s, even most conservatives considered the fear of confiscation to be screwball paranoia, relegated to self-published tracts like *Behold a Pale Horse*, which imagined a "patriot data bank" kept by the government, "consist[ing] of information collected about American patriots, men and women who are most likely to resist the destruction of our Constitution and the formation of the totalitarian police state under the New World Order." Now, however, thanks to the NRA, it's the rare Republican leader who *doesn't* encourage the confiscation fantasy.

LaPierre says that FBI background checks "are just the first step in their long march to destroying our Second Amendment–protected rights." Thus the NRA made sure that current federal law requires that the record of every gun buyer who goes through a background check be destroyed. Nevertheless one of LaPierre's lobbyists has noted that if the government *did* maintain "a database or a registration of Americans who are exercising a constitutional right"—that'd be "just like [if] they . . . maintain a database of all Methodists, all Baptists, all people of different religious or ethnic backgrounds." Extreme American gun love really is a lot like American religious faith.

So one unlikely possibility, a federal registry, leads to a supremely implausible fantasy, confiscation of guns. And that leads to an even more fantastical narrative—after the full police-state erasure of liberty, the final SHTF dream, well armed Americans obliged to launch an uprising against the U.S. government.

This chain of fantasies and ones like it have become respectable. It was a milestone when, at the beginning of this century, the NRA's president— a movie star famous for playing nineteenth-century American soldiers, including Buffalo Bill—ended a speech to his members by urging them "to defeat the divisive forces that would take freedom away," then lifted a replica of a Revolutionary War rifle and snarled "fighting words for everyone within the sound of my voice to hear and to heed . . . 'From my cold, dead hands!'" In other words, Charlton Heston was saying: *You'll have to kill me if you try to take away my guns.*

After that, the threat of armed insurrection became more explicit. Instead of ignoring or wishing away the first half of the Second Amendment, as it had always done, the gun rights movement *embraced* the idea that civilians needed guns for paramilitary purposes. And finally the Supreme Court agreed. One of the decisive opinions, written by Justice Scalia, says that the Second Amendment allows everybody to have guns so that they can spontaneously form militias when necessary—that is, to make "the able-bodied men of a nation . . . better able to resist tyranny," to join an armed "resistance to . . . the depredations of a tyrannical government," to shoot and kill members of a U.S. "standing army" they don't like. Scalia even acknowledged that such contingency planning is absurd, given that in this day and age "a militia, to be as effective as militias in the 18th century, would require sophisticated arms" and "that no amount of small arms could be useful against modern-day bombers and tanks." But so be it: the Constitution gives every American the right to amass an arsenal to prepare to enact that doomed fantasy.*

Are the gun zealots like dogs who catch the car but don't want to stop barking and snarling? Or the child who threatens to hold his breath until he dies? Despite their essentially total victory, they demand more: the freedom to fire dozens of rounds without reloading; to carry guns anywhere they please, like cops or soldiers; a still *greener* green light to shoot people if they feel threatened. They have to look hard for things that still outrage them, such as the bureaucratic protocol that prevented military veterans of "marked subnormal intelligence, or mental illness" from passing FBI background checks to buy guns. Or the Arms Trade Treaty adopted by the UN in 2013 to monitor the international weapons business and reduce the flow to bad actors, such as terrorists. "The tyrants and dictators at the United Nations will stop at nothing," LaPierre said, "to register, ban and, eventually, confiscate firearms owned by law-abiding Americans." The U.S. Senate refused to ratify the treaty.

REASONABLE PEOPLE HOPED THAT AFTER the massacre in 2012 of the twenty first graders and six adults at the Sandy Hook Elementary School in Newtown, Connecticut, the delirium might begin to break. The killer's mother, who homeschooled him, "had a survivalist philosophy, which is why she was stockpiling guns," according to her sister-in-law. The stockpile consisted of seven firearms, including the rifle with which her son murdered her. To murder the children and teachers, he used her semiautomatic "modern sporting rifle"—that's the term preferred by the national gun industry trade association, which happens to be headquartered in Newtown. The killer brought twenty-two high-capacity thirty-round magazines with him to the school.

All the guns had been legally purchased by his mom. According to a Connecticut state report, she "seemed unaware of any potential detrimental impact of providing unfettered access to firearms to their son," even near the end, "when [she] noted that he would not leave the house and seemed de-

* The relentless propagation of the confiscation fantasy paved the way both for the revised new understanding of the Second Amendment *and* for our three-hundred-million-gun stockpile. Both in turn make really meaningful gun control in the United States impossible: at this point, short of amending the Constitution and buying up guns—that is, fairly confiscating them, as Australia did—what else would do the trick? But doing any such thing, of course, is now a total political fantasy.

spondent." Yet the sister-in-law defended her on this count—she "wasn't one to deny reality. She would have sought psychiatric help for her son had she felt he needed it."

She wasn't one to deny reality. Right after the massacre and ever since, conspiracists have fantasized alternate realities about what happened. Maybe it involved an international banking scandal, and maybe Israeli intelligence was involved, but in any case the killings and cover-up were obviously undertaken by the government and media to gin up support for gun regulation. Some (such as Alex Jones) decided it hadn't actually happened at all, that it was all . . . a staged fantasy, with actors playing grieving parents on TV. Or else the shooter was a hireling, a pawn, a Manchurian Candidate or a Lee Harvey Oswald. The father of one of the murdered children devotes himself to debunking the Sandy Hook conspiracy theories; in 2016 one of the pro-gun fantasists was indicted in Florida for threatening to kill him.

Two months later, the same day President Trump spoke to the right wing's big annual Conservative Political Action Conference, Wayne LaPierre delivered an address too. They had completely won. So how could he keep the madness going? By presenting an even crazier *new* fantasy of armed patriots' self-defense. "Right now," LaPierre told them, "we face a gathering of forces that are willing to use violence against us . . . some of the most radical political elements there are. Anarchists, Marxists, communists, and the whole rest of the left-wing socialist brigade." Does he *know* this is madness? After thirty-nine years with the NRA, is he really itching for an actual civil war, or are his horrific movie-trailer visions just good for business? "Make no mistake, if the violent left brings their terror . . . into our homes, they will be met with the . . . full force of American freedom in the hands of the American people and we will win."

43

Final Fantasy-Industrial Complex

IF YOU LOOK AT THE OFFICIAL, CONVENTIONAL DIVISION OF THE U.S. ECON-omy into its ten or twenty sectors, you see only part of the fantasy-industrial complex, nothing like the sprawl that it actually comprises.

Arts, entertainment, and recreation is a small sector, down with *Mining* and *Utilities*. Of course, it includes Hollywood—the Hollywood that, before the 1990s, hadn't discovered reality television and wouldn't have released *The Matrix* or *The Truman Show*, expensive movies based on the premise that reality isn't real but the uncannily realistic product of a conspiracy to deceive us by an all-powerful fantasy-industrial complex.* They were movies that tens of millions of Americans instantly, deeply understood and adored but that, until then, would have been bewildering.

But the fantasy-industrial complex is a lot more than movies and TV and theater and advertising and publishing and theme parks and gambling. It's

---

* The directors and star of *The Matrix*, by the way, said they were inspired by Baudrillard's 1981 book *Simulacra and Simulation*.

much of information media, on the Internet and on TV and radio and in print, and not only the parts infatuated with celebrities and their products. It's not just videogames but large chunks of the Internet. It's the adults who go out in public dressed as soldiers and anime characters and superheroes and Santa as well as the people who pretend to own professional sports teams and fantasize online with strangers about committing horrific crimes. It's a lot of the firearms industry and more and more of the politics industry. It includes much of the real estate industry—themed housing developments, themed restaurants, themed shopping centers. America has a retail glut that drives sellers of indistinguishable commodities to speak of "retailtainment" and "entertailing." It's pieces of the healthcare industry—cosmetic surgery, psychopharmaceuticals—and, when and where it can get away with it, the financial industry. It ranges from the megaindustrial to the artisanal. It is the hearts and minds sector. It's the sector that punches way above its economic weight and dominates American life.

The fantasy-industrial complex has grown by enabling the suspension of disbelief more and more powerfully and ubiquitously: movies, then radio, then TV, then Disney's theme parks and all their amateur spin-offs—Renaissance Faires, war reenactments, cosplay—and then videogames. Each new wave of entertaining fiction was more immersive than earlier ones, seemed more real. As this output seeped and then gushed into everyday life, the old willing suspension of belief was joined by unconscious suspension of disbelief, all the unreality that we tend to forget is unreal. By that I mean everything from a brand-new Mediterranean villa in Wichita or an eighteen-room log cabin in Scottsdale, each with a lawn meant to evoke Currier & Ives or *Downton Abbey,* to the shopping centers simulating the simulations of Main Street USA and EPCOT, to surgically fictionalized faces and bodies.

Now there are casinos in forty of the fifty states (and other kinds of legal gambling in almost all the rest) where people sit for hours or days at a time magically thinking they're a moment away from becoming rich. We've made ourselves into one transcontinental gambling hall, each of our thousand casinos another room in the labyrinthine national casino occupied by millions of Americans all the time, Las Vegas only its magnificent center, Emerald City in our coast-to-coast Land of Oz.

In Fantasyland, it's hard for people to know where and when to draw lines or impose limits. Everything's relative. Everyone has her own truth. Imposing ours is judgmental and undemocratic and elitist. "Plastic surgical technology allows us to do things to distort reality," the Santa Monica plastic surgeon Arthur Jensen told me, "or to deny reality in ways that now be-come . . . is it fantastical? What *is* reality here? What is fantasy? The girl who has implants, that's *her* new *reality.*"

The digital revolution permits ever greater immersion in the unreal. There are the obvious malignancies, such as the new fictional news business, but the general blurring between true and untrue is pervasive. We no longer think of filtered Instagram or Photoshopped images as unreal. Google Photos can *automatically* combine separate images to generate new, improved pictures—that is, real-time revisionism to chronicle moments in your life that didn't happen that way. We can interact with phantom knights and super-Nazis and extraterrestrial robo-warriors, and we can pretend to be fictional characters as we interact with those software creations—or with actual hu-mans who, like us, may or may not be who they seem to be online. Now that most of human interaction is digital and potentially anonymous, we can co-vertly role-play whenever we want. We required new phrases, *catfish* and *sock puppet,* for people who masquerade online as romantic partners and fans of themselves, respectively.

We read messages and see the intimate visual details of celebrities' lives on social media; 15 million or 50 million or 86 million of us have identical unmediated connections with America's most famous people, including the president of the United States. Which makes us feel as if celebrities are our pals, in a way that *People* and the subsequent glut of celebrity media could not quite do. Meanwhile the American fantasy of *becoming* famous for real feels less fantastical than ever. Reality TV has turned hundreds of schmos (and Kardashians) into celebrities. There are almost as many reality shows on the air now as there were television shows of any kind in 2000. YouTube is a gateway to celebrity that has no gatekeepers at all.

The fantasy-industrial complex comprises, at one end, goods and services and experiences that we know are entertaining confections, and at the other end things we don't consider fantasies at all. In between is the large zone of fictions we probably know are make-believe but sometimes—we lose track, get immersed, become confused—almost, kind of, sort of, actually do believe are real.

Was the New York City cop Gilberto Valle *actually* preparing to kidnap, murder, and cannibalize women he knew when he was arrested in 2012? Or was his elaborate scheming with online comrades all in fun—his way of mak-ing the fictional "snuffplay" stories and pictures he consumed on the Internet feel more real? My guess is somewhere disturbingly in between. A federal jury convicted him, but on appeal Valle's lawyer argued for "the right [of fantasists] to fantasize about whatever and whomever they like," and the judge agreed, overturning the conviction. It was "more likely than not," he ruled, that "all of Valle's Internet communications about kidnapping are fantasy role-play," no different from what half of Americans do when they pretend they're killers in *Grand Theft Auto* or *Halo,* since "no real-world, non-Internet-based steps were ever taken to kidnap anyone." But hadn't Valle used the FBI's National Crime Information Center database to track the women? Isn't most of the Internet now the real world?

The case of the "cannibal cop" is extreme, but it is a cautionary tale. The more conscious we are of consuming any particular fantasy, the less problematic it is. I don't take the hard line of the biologist and professional atheist Richard Dawkins, who's practically Maoist on the subject. He argues that reading fairy tales to children may dangerously "inculcate a view of the world which includes supernaturalism."

Rather, I think a different Oxford don, J.R.R. Tolkien, had it right in the lecture he gave just after he published *The Hobbit.* "Fantasy," he said in 1939, talking about fantastical prose fiction, "is a natural human activity. It certainly does not destroy or even insult Reason; and it does not either blunt the appetite for, nor obscure the perception of, scientific verity. On the contrary. The keener and the clearer is the reason, the better fantasy will it make."

And yet . . . look at what's become of the culture industry lately. I don't think the explosion of fantasy fictions is unrelated to our general metamorphosis. It's not a coincidence that TV megahits of the last decade have been series about an ancient land where dragons and magic are returning (*Game of Thrones*) and a contemporary America beset by vampires (*True Blood*) and zombies (*The Walking Dead*). Or that *The Bible,* the 2013 miniseries about Jesus, was created by an inventor of reality TV (*Survivor, The Apprentice*), aired on the History Channel, and was watched by one hundred million Americans. Mark Burnett called his follow-up series on NBC, *A.D.: The Bible Continues,* "House of Cards meets Game of Thrones," and he was thrilled to see the "billboard on Sunset Boulevard, all across the Valley . . . [that] says, 'The crucifixion was only the beginning.' You go back to like ten years ago . . . what was the chance on network TV [that there would be a show] all about the resurrection? It's amazing! God is moving." It is amazing.

During the 1970s, a couple of each year's biggest movies at most were fantasies; nowadays only one or two are not. Only in the 2000s, a half-century after the Tolkien books appeared, did Hollywood finally turn them into a giant franchise. It's not a coincidence that in the last decade, more American adults read *Fifty Shades of Grey* than any other novel, or that it began as fan fiction pornofying the *Twilight* fantasy books. The most popular books of the last half-century, apart from the Bible and *Quotations of Chairman Mao,* are the *Twilight* and Harry Potter series, *The Alchemist, The Da Vinci Code,* and *The Lord of the Rings.*

"If men were ever in a state in which they did not want to know or could not perceive truth (facts or evidence)," Tolkien said in that same 1939 lecture, "then Fantasy would languish until they were cured. If they ever get into that state (it would not seem at all impossible), Fantasy will perish." It turns out he was half right. Many Americans now *are* in a state in which they don't want to know or can't perceive factual truth, yet the perishing of fantasy featuring elves and orcs and superheroes and zombies and angels is nowhere in sight.

THE WHOLLY NEW MEDIUM OF digital gaming—born in the 1960s and '70s, huge by the 1990s—is now uncannily pseudoreal and immersive as well as pervasive. No matter how immersed in a novel or a movie you become, there is no explicit, individual version of *you* in those stories; you can't affect the narrative; your fellow characters and the fictional landscapes don't respond to things you do or say. And gaming is dominated by fantasy fictions. Is that connected to the larger transformation? Or is it just because digital technology got so good at faking and transmuting reality? Those are different ways of asking the same question.

Starting in the 2000s, broadband Internet allowed for massively multiplayer online worlds populated by countless other real people in fantasy form, fellow émigrés from real life. The newer, more ultimate-Fantasyland business model for game makers involves making the commercial transaction itself part of the fantasy. You joined *Farmville* for free on Facebook because you were bored by life and real people, including yourself, so you killed time by pretending to be a farmer raising livestock and growing crops. But the standard production cycles of the pretend sheep and rutabagas were too slow— that is, too realistic, thus boring. So you spent real money to make your imaginary farming happen supernaturally fast.

Such "social gaming" often amounts to a breathtaking parody of the fantasy underpinnings of our consumer economy: inessential wants are conjured—for the first time, totally imaginary wants—and turned into lucrative needs. There's also the part that parodied the global sweatshop economy: American players started paying real money to low-wage workers in China, including labor camp inmates, to do online "gold farming" for them, the tedious game-world work that generates virtual currency.

Today *most* American adults inhabit digital game worlds some of the time, and a quarter of those are so seriously engaged that they devote at least five hours a week to playing with the best set of blocks ever (*Minecraft*) or angsting and living and dying in some supernatural netherworld (*Mortal Kombat, Final Fantasy*) or on Earth in a realistically violent past (*Assassin's Creed*), a realistically grotesque present (*Grand Theft Auto*), or a realistically ghastly future (*Halo, Fallout, Call of Duty*).

Virtual reality is finally, actually here, and the gear costs no more than a smartphone or a game console. I've tried a state-of-the-art version, with positional tracking sensors pasted to me, so I could physically move around inside the virtual reality. The experience was extraordinary. My half hour in virtual reality—walking on a narrow plank over a scary pit, flying like Superman through a high-rise cityscape—was something like taking hallucinogens for the first time. Unlike on an acid trip, not for a moment did I really think I had magical powers or faced death, but to my mind's more primitive, unconscious parts, the experiences seemed absolutely real.

The next step is augmented reality. It exists and works, and before long it will be available to everyone. Google, Warner Bros., and blue-chip Silicon Valley venture capitalists have shoveled $1.4 *billion* into the start-up Magic Leap, which has no products or revenues and almost a thousand employees. Its augmented reality technology won't encase your eyes in a headset's miniature-movie-theater mask. Instead, as you look around at the real world, teeny projectors will beam images directly into your eyes, onto your retinas. Reality and virtual reality will be seamlessly blended. All the imaginary things you see—the zombies or Ryan Gosling, the hovering Millennium Falcon or Jesus Christ—will appear to be there in the corner of your living room or in your backyard, in real life, right there with you. Microsoft has its own technology called HoloLens, versions of which have already shipped to developers.

I can't wait. It also gives me the heebie-jeebies. Who knows the consequences of these technologies? Will they be ridiculous, sublime, wonderful, or awful? Another immersive and breathtaking new medium for fiction, or . . . something weirder, deeper, more existentially transformative? All of the above, I'm guessing.

*   *   *

IN THE MEANTIME LOTS OF people are still so exceptionally committed to acting out their fantasies they want to be face-to-face and body-to-body with other flesh-and-blood humans, immersed physically as well as mentally, unable to escape by clicking a button.

Their prototypes and inspirations all appeared during the two decades encompassing my Big Bang, from the mid-1950s to the mid-'70s—Disneyland, living history, Renaissance Faires, Civil War reenactments, LARPing, retro obsessions of all kinds, BDSM clubs, Halloween costumes for adults. Millions of Americans now put on costumes and carry props and go out into the world to pretend for hours or days or a week at a time that they're not exactly or remotely themselves, that they're more interesting people living more extraordinary lives in more thrilling places or times—soldiers, comic book and movie characters, aristocrats, detectives, murderers, wizards, one-of-a-kind beings. The scale ranges from groups of friends who wander around in character to gatherings of thousands of strangers, the production values from kids-in-the-basement to *Waiting for Guffman* to chic extravaganza, the protocols from actual-life-with-a-twist to Method-acting-to-the-max. An elite corps of twenty-five thousand immerse in Burning Man each year, but a third of a million men and women now attend the two biggest annual Comic-Cons, in San Diego and New York City, many of them dressed as fantastical heroes and villains and creatures.

The original L.A. Renaissance Pleasure Faire from the 1960s now lasts for six weeks and attracts two hundred thousand visitors. Its owners operate three official spin-off versions. Indeed, there are three hundred annual Faires and Fayres and Festivals and Feasts and Gatherings and Wars and Mayhems around the country. Five million Americans a year attend one of those. The Society for Creative Anachronism (SCA) is still going strong—now with sixteen kingdoms in the United States, many tens of thousands of people dressing in their jerkins and chemises and armor to forge iron and eat roast peacock, ride horses, fence, shoot arrows, and throw spears and axes.

Civil War reenactors are the original gangstas in this realm, LARPers and cosplayers before those terms existed, but now they seem strangely—oh, what's the word?—right, *dated*. The Internet has made it much, much easier for reenactors—as well as cosplayers and LARPers and Burners and all the other outdoor fantasizers—to find costumes and gear and one another. Americans now reenact battles of *every* time and place. People pretend to be Vikings, Roman legionnaires fighting Celts, Catholics and Protestants fighting the Thirty Years' War, British soldiers fighting Americans in 1782 and

1812, Americans fighting Mexicans in 1847, Old West gunslingers, and especially Nazis fighting GIs. Although "SS troops may not have any facial hair,"
the WWII Historical Re-enactment Society does permit beards for Nazi al-
pine troops if they are "no longer than two (2) centimeters," but *everyone* in
the unit "must have beards in order for 1 person to wear a beard." The Vietnam War is reenacted as well. They call it "doing the Nam," playing recordings of Armed Forces Radio Service broadcasts from the 1960s and deploying
Huey helicopters. Some refer to their fake Vietnamese prisoners as "gooks"
and "dinks" and perform mock executions.

I get the appeal of playing army; I was once nine years old. I loved summer camp games of Capture the Flag, digging foxholes, and darting around
with a toy machine gun. More recently I spent an afternoon dressed in camo,
carrying an assault weapon and sneaking through the Connecticut woods on
an imaginary mission to search and destroy friends and family with paintball
bullets. Paintball, an American invention from the 1980s, is now passé, a
thing for unserious farbs like me. For people deeply committed to acting out
contemporary combat fantasies, it's now all about airsoft guns. Airsoft rifles
look exactly like the M4 rifles and MP7 submachine guns the U.S. military
use, and exactly like the AK-47s foreign bad guys use. The coolest ones are
gas-powered and have recoil, like the real things, and they can be set for fully
automatic fire, many plastic quarter-inch rounds per second. Nearly all the
imaginary soldiers forgo the fluorescent orange barrel tips meant to signify
that the guns aren't deadly weapons.*

Like survivalists, airsoft soldiers love using real and fake Pentagon acronyms. Instead of the children's term *playing army*, they use the neat-o
made-up word *MilSim* for what they do, and talk about their plans for
MOUT (military operations on urban terrain) and CQB (close quarters
battle). Thousands of uniformed, locked-and-loaded players "enlist" for
each of the biggest events, which consist of multiple "scenarios" over several
days. Some bring their own armored vehicles, prop tanks, and APCs. They
wear helmets with audio headsets so they can say "Enemy down!" when
they pretend to kill somebody. One of the main MilSim operators hires
"VIP commanders," such as an Army Ranger lieutenant colonel from the

---

* Every year U.S. police kill someone carrying an airsoft gun without the fluorescent
markings. Tamir Rice, the twelve-year-old shot and killed by a Cleveland police officer
with a real Glock nine-millimeter in 2014, was carrying a perfect airsoft replica of a semiautomatic Colt .45.

Somalian *Black Hawk Down* debacle, and a former Soviet army sergeant who occupied Afghanistan.

But almost no big MilSim events are *re*enactments. Instead, the battles are improvised and happening *now*, fictional but in their Syrian and other Middle Eastern specifics entirely plausible. The wars are enacted in private police and military training facilities, in defunct factories and mines and amusement parks—and on army and National Guard bases that the government lets them use for their make-believe. Because, of course, the U.S. military operates its own combat theme parks where soldiers can train before they deploy to places where the bullets and bombs are lethal. The Indiana National Guard has a full-scale fake town that civilian simulators use, with a "governor's mansion," a "culture-specific farm," "collapsed structures," and an "engineered rubble pile." A couple of hours south, a fake town at Fort Knox that also hosts MilSim combat has "burn on command" buildings and cars, a subway entrance, falling telephone poles, an exploding gas station, and simulated odors of rotting flesh. The guy who created the Fort Knox effects made official visits to the name-brand public theme parks and debriefed their designers, but "in the realism department," he has said, "we have both Universal and Disney beat."

The most serious MilSim enthusiasts form their own units, invent their own gadgets, and travel the country from imaginary conflict to imaginary conflict. Probably the best known is a squad in New York State, the Green Mountain Rangers, who think of themselves as elite commandos who sometimes go rogue. Their fantasy, they say, is "a lifestyle rather than hobby or sport," not "the normal airsoft 'game.'" The language of their official history is a simulation of military pride that I'm sure to them is absolutely earnest and real. A dozen years ago, after "many of the founding members weren't able to continue the commitment level the lifestyle called for," the few good men who remained "built a hard forged unit structured on new cutting edge principles of training," conducting "weekly trainings for months that [took] them to a new level of integrity and honor." Their fake-war stories sound like war stories, such as the "final assault that culminated on a 10KM ruck deep into enemy territory, undetected to deliver a dawn lit airstrike package and direct assault to the Russian Base camp."

There's a lot of manly-man *grrrrr*-ing. The big MilSim operator Lion Claws refers to the people who play enemy combatants as *hajis*—the Islamic religious term that has become something like the contemporary version of *gooks*. Their backstory-writers can't resist slipping in tendentious bits of pseudoreality, such as Operation Lionclaws XII in 2013, in which "we have a

Commander in Chief"—unnamed—"who is adverse [*sic*] to utilizing a boots on the ground force."

A company based in Oklahoma, American Milsim, doesn't stage foreign wars. And it combines superrealistic airsoft combat with what LARPers call "campaigns," enacting one continuous, evolving story over years. They put on a weekend battle every couple of months around the South and Southwest. Their premise is an armed American insurgency that broke out in 2012 after an infrastructural breakdown that led to increased federal taxes and regulation. Texas, Louisiana, and Alaska seceded from the United States and formed a confederacy. The American Milsim players have been *pre*-enacting a contemporary U.S. civil war.

In their battles, real "helicopters provid[e] touch and go OP's [*sic*]," and military cargo trucks and armored personnel carriers rumble around; there are night-vision goggles, lasers, robots, drones, rockets, suicide vests, grenades that really explode. When players take certain fantasies too far, "staff may ask for your name when a War Crime is recorded, [but] this information will not be made public." Depending on which side prevails in each weekend's battles, the Washington, D.C., regime or the confederacy (the Coalition of Sovereign Territories) can win or lose states. Online "news service" reports appear that insert new fictional twists into the narrative, such as the emergence of a separate force ("The Patriots"), soldiers and veterans "worried about violations of the constitutional rights of US citizens," and the independent secession of western states in reaction to "the increasing [federal] tax burden."

All these guys are aware that they're *playing* army. In Fantasyland, however, as art imitates life, so does life imitate art, and boundaries blur.

Consider Eric Frein, for instance, who was an extremely devoted MilSim reenactor in rural eastern Pennsylvania for nearly his whole adult life. He sometimes pretended to be a Nazi, but he *really* geeked out over the Yugoslav civil wars of the 1990s, when he was a boy. His special thing was pretending to be a Serbian soldier, a member of the particular real-life unit involved in the massacre of thousands of Bosnian civilians.

Do all MilSim dudes hate the government and have survivalist fantasies? No, but Frein did, so in 2014, living in his parents' basement at age thirty-one, he decided to take it to the next level. Instead of his airsoft replica AK-47, he picked up a real one and became a real sniper, ambushing two Pennsylvania state troopers, one of whom died. *How awesome*, he must have thought when they fell. He lit out for the woods, smoked his special Serbian cigarettes, lived off the land, and outsmarted a battalion of cops, some of them in full combat gear, for seven weeks.* *How totally awesome.* "I almost think that some of this is a game to him," said the state police colonel in charge of the operation. "A war game, if you will." As that phase of his greatest game ended and Frein was arraigned for murder, a citizen screamed at him, "You're not a *real* soldier!" But that was just one interpretation, one person's opinion, one truth.†

Isn't Lion Claws' slogan "Building a New Generation of Patriots," and don't they partner with the U.S. Army Recruiting Command to convince potential soldiers that war fighting is cool? Surely some of the American Mil-Sim gamers have understood their games to be training for a fantasy that they don't consider a fantasy—the secession and patriot insurgency and civil war that may arise after the tyrants in Washington, D.C., finally give the order to confiscate their guns and open the FEMA concentration camps.

Let me quote once more from Tolkien's lecture, which he delivered a few months before the fantasy-besotted Nazis started World War II. "Fantasy can, of course, be carried to excess. It can be put to evil uses. It may even delude the minds out of which it came."

---

* The uniquely American militarization of police was also inspired by playing-army fantasies. The Los Angeles Police Department created the first police SWAT team in the late 1960s, training on Universal Studios' back lot. As police all over the United States militarized, *The New York Times* reported in 1975 that "some departments have been stimulated into adopting a SWAT strategy by the [new] weekly network television program [*S.W.A.T.*] that erroneously depicts SWAT teams getting involved in almost every phase of police operations." Before long, SWAT teams everywhere *were* getting involved in every phase of police operations.

† In 2017, Frein was convicted and sentenced to death.

44

Our Inner Children? They're Going to Disney World!

MOST AMERICAN ADULTS DO NOT WANT TO PLAY THE PARTS OF SOLDIERS OR villains or ghouls. Most Americans want to play characters who are beautiful, sexy, cute, fun, beloved, safe, and happy. But like the villains and ghouls who go too far, people tend to forget some fantasies are fantasies. Instead of toggling in and out, the Suspend Disbelief button clicks into place permanently.

From the earliest days of the American fantasy-industrial complex in the 1850s, snooty critics used *Barnumized* as a term of disparagement—in 1854 *The New York Times* called a celebrity conductor's concert of classical music attended by forty-five thousand New Yorkers a Barnumized spectacle; in 1922 a movie director was said to have Barnumized classic works of literature. A few decades ago we coined the successor synonym: *Disneyfication,* to denote how urban America had started to resemble theme parks. Starting in the late 1960s and '70s, pieces of cities were spiffed up and turned into reimagined reproductions of themselves—SoHo in Manhattan, Pioneer Square in Seattle, and the Old Market in Omaha, then Times Square and the imitation SoHos everywhere (including Tribeca, directly south of SoHo), each with its own Starbucks or four. *Disneyfication* is different from *Bar-numized*: it's a noun referring to an ongoing process and permanent condition rather than a one-off creation, the rule and not the exception. Practically every big city now has its own Main Street USA or New Orleans Square implant, historical fictions and quasi-fictions in which people live life.

Which isn't an altogether bad thing. Absent the total theater modeled by Disneyland and Disney World, modern America might never have started saving old buildings or rediscovering the charms of urban life. I'm delighted to live on a Brooklyn block that looks very much like it did a hundred years ago. I love it when the old man parks his old-fashioned little truck and rings his bell and we take our knives out to be sharpened, as the people who lived here in the 1920s must have done. My favorite neighborhood bar is the one that took over a dark, anonymous old Italian social club and did almost no renovating. One of my favorite neighborhood restaurants is a simulated nineteenth-century steak and oyster house where most of the waiters are mustachioed and side-burned young men. Disneyfication has its irresistible aspects.

Walt Disney foresaw the next American century, this one, and built the prototypes. We aren't living under climate-controlled plastic bubbles, but the visionary pastiche of Walt's first EPCOT rendering—no more dirty factories, pedestrianized faux-1800s neighborhoods, plus pagodas, plus strolling bagpipers—has become a go-to American model for living. Even, for instance, hunting for photo ops and compulsively taking pictures of ourselves and our surroundings—didn't that used to be something people did only at places like Disney World? We don't yet say "Have a magical day!" to people we meet on the street. But whatever we're pretending to be—a costumed or digital commando, a magical creature at Burning Man or Comic-Con, an artist in a million-dollar loft in downtown Denver, or a writer-angler living in a brand-new fake-old million-dollar cottage in Florida, whether our wardrobe comes from Anthropologie or our props from Restoration Hardware—we are guests *and* cast members (as Disney calls its employees) in America.

THREE YEARS AGO, FOR MY radio show *Studio 360,* we made an hour-long documentary about the Disney parks. We interviewed a girl named Anabelle at Disneyland in California. Her explanation of why she loves it could be an epigraph for this book. "Well," she said, "at my age you know they're not real. But just the whole experience of it makes it *seem* so real that you go along with it and play along. The school, science-y, math-y part of you is being like, 'Oh, that's not real, you have to stay strong, that's not real.' But another part

of your mind, that's I guess the dream-maker part and the fantasy part . . .
actually is telling you, 'Oh, but it *seems so real.*' It's like living in a fantasy
book." Coming from a nine-year-old, it was so smart and perfectly charming.

But these days at least a third of the people at theme parks are adults
without children. These days thousands of couples get married every year at
Disney theme parks—women imagining their weddings as the final scenes of
Cinderella or themselves as Ariel or Belle or Jasmine in character-specific
gowns purchased through Disney's Fairy Tale Weddings division, attended by
strangers in royal-servant getups.

To produce our documentary, we also went to Walt Disney World—and
to Celebration, Florida, where I'd been before. Celebration is the real town
that Disney built at the south end of Disney World in the 1990s. It's an example of New Urbanism, the movement among architects and planners, beginning in the 1980s, that considers the development of cities and suburbs
since World War II disastrously misguided. America abandoned the accumu-
lated wisdom of centuries and built streets too wide, houses too far apart,
driveways and garages too dominant, and homes too far from jobs and shopping, with too much dependence on driving and too much incoherent sprawl.
The houses Americans built are architecturally inferior not because they ape
old styles but because they're *inauthentically* nostalgic. Most New Urbanists
want new houses and neighborhoods to be more accurate simulations of
houses and neighborhoods from the past. New Urbanism was upscale Disneyfication before the people running Disney called themselves New Urbanists.

Celebration is a self-conscious reproduction of some fictional but ideal
American town circa 1945, population 7,500, coherent, stylistically consistent, walkable, bikable, and charming. It isn't gated, and it's not just a bunch
of McMansions plopped around a golf course. It looks like an actual
community—although one transplanted from Ohio or Connecticut to the
tropics. It's a fantasy. But if I had to move to central Florida, I might choose
to live in Celebration.

The Siegels are a Celebration family. When Jim Siegel took early retire-
ment as a Ford executive, he and his wife, Marita, wanted to move someplace
warmer than Michigan. "My wife said to me, 'Well, I don't know where you're
going to live, but I'm going to live at Disney World.' Meaning Celebration." He
had his doubts. "Some people think of this as a fantasy place. It seems like
the back lot of a movie studio. Some of my friends, their initial reaction when
they came down and saw this was 'Oh, you live in *Pleasantville*.'"

He was outvoted by Marita and their younger daughter, Julie, who was

just graduating from college. She announced she'd be joining them in Celebration. Julie and her mother have always been extreme Disney devotees. During the twenty years before they moved to Celebration, they'd made thirty-three visits to Disney World. The decorations on two of the several Christmas trees Marita put up each year in Michigan were Disney-themed, as was Julie's apartment during and after college—"all decorated, all Mickey Mouse, all of it. Dishes, silverware, placemats, sheets, Mickey Mouse toys everywhere." The Siegels originally called their two teacup poodles Chip and Dale, but then changed the names to Lilly Disney (after Walt's wife) and Fozzie Bear.

When we spent the day together, Julie was thirty-three and unmarried. "Disney," she told me, "was a huge influencer for me to kind of shape who I am. I just remember always loving Walt's dream. I think it's really fun and magical. It's very magical. And Tinker Bell flying from the castle at night—it's just . . . the feeling you get from watching the parade is so—I get chills just now just talking about it. I was blessed enough that I had a place of escape that I could call my own."

When Julie and her older sister were kids, Jim and Marita took them on vacation to Europe two summers in a row. At the Piazza San Marco in Venice, the parents asked the girls what they thought. "I was eleven at the time. And I said 'Gosh, it's really beautiful—it looks *just* like EPCOT.' And then I said, 'But I like EPCOT better because it's cleaner.'" Jim fondly remembers the moment too. "'Dad,' they said, 'we really appreciate the opportunity to be in Europe, but we'd just as soon go to Walt Disney World.'"

During our conversation, Julie used the word *escape* again and again. She grew up in a big house in a nice suburb with loving parents and did well at school. Escaping what? "I was escaping life. My mom picked me up from school one day because she just felt the frustration that I was feeling with being bored at school and not wanting to go. 'Come on, I got our tickets already, pack your bag, we're going to Disney World tomorrow.' And that was not the only time that had happed during my high school. If I was frustrated with school, my mom would just pick me up and take me out of school. I had the highest absence record in my high school's history because we came down to Disney so much."

But as an adult, what is *so great* about being at Disney World? "I feel like I'm someone special. Even though there's tens of thousands of other people around me. *I am someone special,* and I matter. And seeing the fantasy of Mickey Mouse and Minnie Mouse, and the magic and wonder that just kind of bubbles up in me."

As soon as Julie moved to Celebration, she went to work at Disney World. I asked what her job was. "I got to help out the characters, mostly Mickey and Minnie, but other characters I helped out, including Suzie and Perla from Cinderella, Pinocchio, Timon. I also helped Max, who's Goofy's son, Robin Hood, Pooh and Piglet, Mushu, Uncle Scrooge, Turk from Tarzan."

Exactly what do you mean, I asked, by *help out* the characters?

"I was very close friends with them," she replied, "and I helped them get ready for whatever show they were doing—or if they needed help when they were meeting and greeting with guests."

I was still confused, didn't yet know the rules. Although when we spoke Julie had not been an employee for nine years, she still adhered to the coy Disney corporate omertà: the people who play characters in the parks aren't supposed to say, ever, that they *play* Snow White or Donald Duck. Because then the fictional beings might seem less real.

I wondered if she'd moved on because, living next door at Celebration, she'd finally had her fill of Disney. "*No!* There is never enough Disney. It never gets boring." Her feelings about Celebration, however, were more mixed. Tourists ask, "'Does it ever rain here? Do they put the dome up?' People have stopped me and asked 'Is this a real town?' They look at you a little bit like you're imaginary, [like] I'm just a Stepford Wife, I have a microchip in my head. They act almost as if I'm part of the facade and part of the story."

However, she likes all the *deliberate* make-believe in Celebration. Each evening for a month in autumn, every hour on the hour, tissue-paper leaves fall in the town center, and each evening in December every hour on the hour, snowlike soap flakes drift from the sky onto the street. "There's music"— official strolling Charles Dickens Carolers—"Santa's house, and you can do carriage rides with horses. During those times, when it tends to be a little bit more Disneyesque rather than just a regular old town, that's when it makes me really happy." Although the fake snow, which Disney calls snoap, "gets very filthy and dirty. Snow up north gets dirty and gross, [so] in that sense it's very realistic."

In fact, for Julie, Celebration's problem is that it isn't Disney enough. "I don't like being stopped by a gang of turkeys, a herd of wild turkeys standing in the middle of the road. I don't walk Lilly"—her poodle—"because I never know what's going to come out of the bushes, a snake or even if a hawk comes swooping down and I'm not able to see it because there's so much vegetation above me or if there is going to be an alligator that comes out of the swamp and starts chasing us. At the Animal Kingdom, [the animals are] all secretly and invisibly barricaded so they can't get to you. But here in Celebration, it's the real deal. It's ironic." And then there are the free-range humans. "There's mean people here in Celebration too. I don't walk at night. I don't feel safe anywhere. There's crime that happens here. I've seen some sketchy characters."

If the town weren't a Disney creation next door to Disney World, it wouldn't be *quite* such a breathtaking example of America's transformation. "People had the impression that if they moved to a Disney town," the executive who masterminded it says now, "their lawns would never get weeds and their children would never get anything but As." Exactly. But even without that provenance and proximity, Celebration is a perfect modern hybrid of real life and nostalgic make-believe, the original fake-small-town idea of the American suburb from the 1860s evolved to its ultimate state. It is also apt that in the 2016 election, Donald Trump lost the county and congressional district by landslides but carried Celebration.

The Siegels seem emblematic because they're *not* cosplayers or MilSim fetishists but ordinary upper-middle-class Americans. Whose intelligent, self-aware daughter Julie is on the Kids "R" Us Syndrome spectrum— somewhere between Michael Jackson and most of the rest of us. "I haven't had an annual [Disney World] pass now for several years now," she told me, "and I really am going through withdrawal—it's hard." She quit working in the park, dressing up as cartoon characters, only because "I needed to get what my mom called a 'big-girl job.'"

CELEBRATION DOES NOT PICK MY pocket or break my leg. Kids "R" Us Syndrome isn't close to the worst thing about Fantasyland, and adults in love with Disney World are not close to the most troubling symptom of the syndrome.*

However, I do think American adults have come to *think* more fundamentally like children, and that does get problematic.

Waiting to get what you want is a definition of maturity; demanding satisfaction this instant, on the other hand, is a defining behavior of seven-year-olds. The powerful appeal of the Internet is its instantaneity as much as the "community" it enables—you can send a message *now*, get any question answered *now*, buy anything you want *now*, meet a stranger for sex *right now*. Telecommunications satisfy one kind of inner child, the impulsive one with

---

* Although it is weird that Walmart alone sold $200 million worth of coloring books for adults in 2016.

zero tolerance for waiting. As a result, over the last couple of decades, delayed gratification itself came to seem quaint.

What do the brattiest children do? They shout and name-call and exaggerate, like the new generation of political commentators, like Internet trolls, like Trump. They cover their ears and refuse to listen to unpleasant facts and tell ridiculous lies. They're selfish, and anytime they're thwarted or someone else gets something they want, no matter how justly or reasonably, they scream *That's not fair!*

In politics and elsewhere, this childish *style* often goes hand in hand with childlike *beliefs*—that is, fantasies. The original child psychologist, Jean Piaget, believed that the minds of children and adults were fundamentally different, that kids were egocentric magical thinkers and adults were rational and reasonable, and that growing up consisted of shifting from one mode to the other. Psychology has revised Piaget's big idea. Now they cast the difference between children and adults as a continuum, not a sharp break. As Fantasyland emerged, more Americans moved away from the adult end of the continuum. Not coincidentally, psychology has also recast schizophrenia as a point at one end of a spectrum running from delusional to rational.

The UC Berkeley psychologist Alison Gopnik studies the minds of small children and sees them as little geniuses, models of creativity and innovation. "They live twenty-four/seven in these crazy pretend worlds," she says. "They have a zillion different imaginary friends." While at some level, they "know the difference between imagination and reality . . . it's just they'd rather live in imaginary worlds than in real ones. Who could blame them?" But what happens when that set of mental habits persists into adulthood too generally and inappropriately? A monster under the bed is true *for her,* the stuffed animal that talks is true *for him,* speaking in tongues and homeopathy and vaccines that cause autism and Trilateral Commission conspiracies are true *for them.*

Gopnik says the mental state of young children is similar to that of adults when they're consuming fiction. "You are not in control, your consciousness is not planning, your self seems to disappear—that's part of what's great about being absorbed in a movie. . . . The events in the movie are very, very vivid in your awareness." Now that we spend so much of our lives immersed in the worlds of the fantasy-industrial complex, it seems we have become more like little children mentally. "There is no inevitable march toward objectivity or enlightenment," the Harvard child psychologist Paul Harris writes in his book *Trusting What You're Told: How Children Learn from Others.* "The endpoint of cognitive development is not objectivity and equilibrium. It is a mix of the natural and supernatural, of truth and fantasy, of faith and uncertainty."

In the psychology of American adults, I think, the mix has become an unusually unbalanced one. This is an area where Kids "R" Us Syndrome can be more disquieting. Despite Harris's point, there is *some* inevitable march toward reality-based understandings of the world: most American three-year-olds believe in Santa Claus and the tooth fairy, for instance, while most nine-year-olds do not. Indeed, until they're about ten, children naturally think everything that exists or happens has a purpose, designed and arranged by somebody or something to fulfill particular roles—hippos to be on display at the zoo, clouds to make rain, Mommy to be nice. Then they get older and are supposed to learn the various truths, counterintuitive and disappointing though they may be.

However, if the adults around them still cling to childlike beliefs, as so many do in America concerning religion, children don't necessarily grow out of the beliefs. A study by a University of Michigan psychologist found that between ages eight and ten, nearly everyone has a creationist explanation for how life emerges; biological evolution doesn't yet make sense. But by age twelve in the United States, her study found, it's pretty much only children in fundamentalist Christian households who still believe that animals and people were created supernaturally and simultaneously.

Young children, in the phrase of one eminent child psychologist at Boston University, are "intuitive theists" who naturally tend to believe that some kind of God must be running the whole show. A major argument of this book is that Americans are not just exceptionally religious but that our dominant religion has become exceptionally literal and fantastical—childlike—during the last fifty years in particular. The fantasies of perpetual youth, Kids "R" Us Syndrome, also appeared fifty years ago, when American adults started becoming more than ever like adolescents and children in our tastes and ways of thinking. These simultaneous spikes could be a coincidence, but they look to me like another case of cultural symbiosis.

And childlike magical thinking synergy isn't limited to *Christian* kinds. "How do you get yourself to a point of believing?" Rhonda Byrne asks in *The Secret,* the Oprah-endorsed New Age guide to success-by-wishing-and-pretending. "Start make-believing. Be like a child, and make-believe. Act as if you have it already. As you make believe you will begin to believe you have received. . . . Your belief that you have it, that undying faith, is your greatest power. When you believe you are receiving, get ready, and watch the magic begin!"

45

The Economic Dreamtime

FROM THE 1980S THROUGH THE '90S AND INTO THE 2000S, THE FINANCIAL AND economic fantasies that got such traction were happy happy happy. In addition to our uniquely entrepreneurial approach to religion, America also developed an unusually religious approach to entrepreneurialism, especially since the 1960s. At Amway, Mary Kay, Walmart, Chick-fil-A, Apple, the Oprah Winfrey empire, Martha Stewart in her heyday, Whole Foods, and Amazon—among employees as well as customers—those businesses cultivated a cultish, evangelical vibe. And maybe most of all at Apple, one of my own brand faiths, where the acid-tripping megalomaniac Steve Jobs famously radiated a "reality distortion field" that made people believe whatever he wanted them to believe. "In his presence," said the Apple underling who borrowed the idea and phrase from a *Star Trek* episode, "reality is malleable." Another employee explained her boss to Jobs's biographer in terms of the Bay Area religious entrepreneur Jim Jones, who became famous when Apple was also a Bay Area start-up: "It didn't matter if he was serving purple Kool-Aid. You drank it."

Entrepreneurialism that produces useful, innovative new products and processes is one thing. Bravo to Jobs and these entrepreneurs. But the free-market fundamentalism that became our governing paradigm starting in the 1980s had unfortunate consequences when it extended into wholesale wishfulness and denial of reality. Near the end of a speech he delivered at a conservative think tank around Christmastime in 1996, during the long boom, our libertarian chairman of the Federal Reserve, Alan Greenspan, wondered, "How do we know when irrational exuberance has unduly escalated asset values?" *Irrational* exuberance: in other words, were we in danger of slipping off the reality tether, becoming so financially delirious we were heedless of our delirium?

Yes, as it turned out.

The bubbles in technology stocks and real estate were classic American phenomena. We'd been there before—with the Virginia gold hunters in the 1600s, overbuilt railroads in the 1800s, rocketing Florida real estate prices in the early 1920s, and the value of U.S. stocks tripling in four years in the late 1920s. As the prime interest rate fell from 20 percent in 1981 to 4 percent in 2004, however, credit had never been so easy for so many Americans. The irrational exuberance, the national fantasy of good times rolling forever, had never lasted longer or been shared more widely. The Great Depression had chastened people in the 1930s, but that was *then*—by the 2000s, everyone who'd lived through it was elderly or dead. We were ready and hungry to believe in financial and economic fantasies again.

In less than a decade around 2000, the value of the average home almost doubled. Many, many middle-class Americans suddenly felt rich. The country seemed to be on some incredible Vegas winning streak or at a multigenerational rave that went on and on. (Actual raves, no coincidence, also emerged in the 1980s and '90s.) We decided that Mardi Gras and Christmas are so much fun, we should make them year-round ways of life. Maybe some people knew deep down it couldn't last forever, just as some people found the incredible performances of Barry Bonds and Roger Clemens . . . incredible. But no one wanted to be a buzzkill. The fantasies were more fun, and in the financial domain self-fulfilling.

To the technology and real estate and financial businesses, the years on either side of 2000 were like what the years on either side of 1970 were to the rest of American life: the prudent old rules no longer applied, anything seemed possible.

In Silicon Valley, a few clever and lucky people occasionally found a pot of gold, which encouraged everyone else to keep believing and wishing. The odds of any individual entrepreneur becoming a megawinner are vanishingly small, as they are for buyers of lottery tickets, and the jackpots in tech are capricious. The first generation of digital entrepreneurs to get *amazingly* rich, in the 1980s and '90s—Gates, Jobs, Bezos—became billionaires in early middle age. In this century, before and after burst bubbles and meltdowns, it happened to younger, digital billionaires at thirty (Larry Page of Google) or twenty-five (Evan Spiegel of Snapchat) or twenty-three (Mark Zuckerberg). Which serves only to make the dream all the dreamier. What's the new term of art for the most financially successful tech start-ups? *Unicorns,* after the magical creatures in which only children believe.

It's correct to say that the financial meltdown of 2008 resulted from too much deregulation, too many arcane Wall Street innovations, and some fraud. But that's just one way of explaining it, the one that comfortingly focuses *all* blame on government and a small class of the rich and powerful and deceitful. The deeper causes were more widespread and unconscious, the fantastical wishfulness affecting at least a large minority of Americans, maybe a majority.

In the late 1990s, the smart people decided the old rules didn't apply because digital technology had created a New Economy. Companies with no revenues were worth billions of dollars, and paying 175 times earnings for a share of the *average* tech stock didn't seem mad. Why not buy bigger and bigger houses, why save money, why not go deeper into debt? The price of the average house was bound to just keep doubling every ten years. To keep Tinker Bell alive, Peter Pan sent out a magical alert to everyone in the world "who might be dreaming of the Neverland. . . . 'Do you believe?' he cried. . . . 'If you believe,' he shouted to them, clap your hands.'" For two decades we clapped our hands and believed in fairies.

One undeniable virtue of markets is that eventually they reflect hard facts. The financial world isn't prone to permanent fantasy. During the 1990s and the early 2000s, however, Wall Street "honed the art of creating and selling financial products with an increasingly tenuous connection to reality," Nick Paumgarten wrote in *The New Yorker* right after the 2008 crash. "It was more like what anthropologists and psychologists call magical thinking—the tendency to believe that wishing it so makes it so." Americans

> clung to the conviction that you can have outsize returns with little risk, leverage without recoil. This is what the clever financiers claimed that their inventions could do. Their colleagues and clients

wanted to believe them. They all wanted to believe that their credit-default swaps could continue to insure against debt defaults. . . .

Magical thinking enables you to see good where there may be only bad.

The financiers were a mixture of Cynics and Believers. When their faith in the financialized magic ended in 2008, they promptly chucked those wishful beliefs, of course, and defaulted to pure, reality-based Cynicism.

What ended that period of extreme financial make-believe? It wasn't grown-ups in charge stepping up and announcing it was crazy and doomed, that enough was enough. Rather, we finally ran through the supply of greater fools willing to pay a premium for the houses and other things the last group of fools had just bought. When America and the rest of the world were spanked by reality's invisible hand, we got the meltdown and crash and Great Recession, the inevitable results of Fantasyland economics.

In 2009, I sincerely argued that our national near-death experience, in which we glimpsed the economic abyss, could sober us up and put us back on the reality-based straighter and narrower—a national reset! It was pretty to think so. Our voracious national craving for fantasy, however, when denied in one area, quickly finds other places to satisfy itself.

46

As Fantasyland Goes, So Goes the Nation

AFTER THE FINANCIAL MELTDOWN, IN SPITE OF OUR GOVERNMENT'S ACTIONS
to contain the damage and prevent a full-fledged depression—and *because*
of those emergency actions—a rabid fraction of us, hysterical true believers
as well as the merely pissed-off, could no longer be controlled. Some called
themselves the Tea Party and even engaged in cosplay, appearing at protests
and community meetings in eighteenth-century American military drag.
Dozens were elected to Congress and became the convulsive tail wagging
the Republican dog. They hate or think they hate the status quo, including
government itself, so they've been delighted to make the federal government stop working when they couldn't force it to give them total victory—
for them government dysfunction is an end, not just a means. The
reality-based Republican elite who'd kept the fantasy-based communities
as their useful idiots had been playing with fire. The idiots finally understood that the people in charge considered them idiots—and grabbed the
matches.

Consider the experience of one prominent Republican congressman from California's Central Valley. When he arrived in 2003, at twenty-nine, he was among the most conservative elected officials in Washington. The right-wing Heritage Foundation now ranks him in the most "liberal" third of House Republicans. "I used to spend 90 percent of my constituent response time on people who call, e-mail, or send a letter" about some real issue, he told *The New Yorker.* His typical constituent back in the 2000s had an opinion about "actual legislation. Ten percent were about 'Chemtrails from airplanes are poisoning me' to every other conspiracy theory that's out there. And that has essentially flipped on its head," he said, during the last dozen years or so. Now only a small fraction of the messages from constituents are "based on something that is mostly true. It's dramatically changed politics and politicians, and what they're doing." The congressman who sounded so sensible in 2015 was Devin Nunes, who chairs the House Intelligence Committee. By 2017, he was a stalwart defender of a president whose specialty is passing along untrue conspiracy theories, such as the one about having been wiretapped in Trump Tower.

During the two decades leading up to the financial and economic crash of 2008, the right and far right built out an unprecedented new multimedia infrastructure. There are now ten times as many talk radio stations as there were in the 1980s. Of the several shows with the largest audiences, all but one are about politics and government by and for right-wingers, with a combined daily audience of forty-five million. (The other show provides "biblically based" financial advice aimed at evangelicals, and directly behind those is *Coast to Coast AM,* the nightly conspiracy-and-magic-and-falsehood clearinghouse.)

In a decade, from 1996 through 2007, we got Fox News, the *Drudge Report, Infowars,* and *Breitbart,* with Facebook, YouTube, and Twitter as free global platforms for all of them, their followers and wannabes. At least until it fired its most popular anchor in 2017, Fox News's audience has been not just bigger than that of the other news channels—more people watched it than *any* cable channel in 2016. During the month before the 2016 election, as many people "interacted" with Fox News stories on Facebook as they did with stories from CNN, *The New York Times, The Washington Post,* and *The Wall Street Journal* combined.

Skepticism of the press and of academic experts has been a paramount fetish on the right for years, which effectively trained two generations of Americans to disbelieve facts at odds with their opinions. "For years, as a conservative radio talk show host," Charlie Sykes wrote in early 2017, "I played a role in that conditioning by hammering the mainstream media for its bias and double standards. But the price turned out to be far higher than I imagined. The cumulative effect of the attacks was to . . . destroy much of the right's immunity to false information." The conservative talk-radio host John Ziegler made a similar confession in 2016: "We've effectively brainwashed the core of our audience. And now it's gone too far. Because the gatekeepers have lost all credibility in the minds of consumers, I don't see how you reverse it."

The loss of immunity to false information is the big problem. Fox News's conservatism is fine, but the channel's tendency to present fiction as news is definitely not. For instance, in 2012 a San Diego PR man self-published a book called *"White Girl Bleed a Lot": The Return of Racial Violence to America and How the Media Ignore It,* positing an epidemic of young black people punching random white people on city streets, in what he called the "knockout game." Over the next two years, the author wrote more than one hundred posts for the influential far-right site *WND,* aggregating reports of assaults by black people, especially when their victims were white; a typical headline was WHY DON'T BLACKS BEHAVE? In 2013, just after a pretend Florida police officer (George Zimmerman) was acquitted of murdering an unarmed black seventeen-year-old (Trayvon Martin) whom he imagined was a criminal, Sean Hannity was informed of the fantastical epidemic of black-on-white violence that the news media had failed to report. He put the author on the air, at which point all of Fox News (along with talk radio) flooded the zone with discussions of the "horrifying and deadly new trend sweeping the country.'"* The rest of the news media were obliged to cover this urban myth as if it might be real.

It kept happening. In 2014 Fox News reported that Bowe Bergdahl, the army sergeant who went AWOL in Afghanistan, had "converted to Islam . . . and declared himself a 'mujahid,' or warrior for Islam" while he was imprisoned by the Taliban, according to "secret documents" created by a private security firm. Neither Fox nor any actual news organization discovered any further confirmation of this claim, but right-wing media has treated it ever since as established fact. For a week after the jihadists' massacre of the *Charlie Hebdo* staff in Paris, Fox News anchors and guests painted a portrait of urban Europe that spiraled beyond mere exaggeration and hyperbole into hysterical counterfactual fiction—*a multinational parallel government with*

---

* "The scum that gets high on badly hurting old ladies and others through knockout assaults wouldn't feel that way with a gun at their head!" the reality-show host Donald Trump tweeted at the time.

ISIS in charge! Days before the 2016 election, the channel's ostensibly fair-and-square news anchor Bret Baier reported that FBI agents had evidence that five foreign intelligence agencies had hacked Hillary Clinton's email server and also that she would be indicted soon for Clinton Foundation corruption. And then, whoops, forty-eight hours later he admitted he was mistaken—as Fox also finally did about its "regrettable errors on air regarding the Muslim population in Europe" in 2014. In 2017, for a week, Fox News promoted the conspiracy theory that Democrats had rubbed out a party functionary for leaking material to WikiLeaks. Fox finally retracted that story too.

Yet compared to the Breitbart News Network and Infowars, and leaving Sean Hannity aside, Fox News is fair, balanced, and reality-based. Once again, the residents of Fantasyland get graded on a curve. There are different degrees of egregious.

Until recently most of us were unaware of the new global cottage industry that knowingly concocts and publishes false news stories, each optimized to be clicked, shared, and viralized. Facebook had been the most important platform for this species of clickbait "news," just as it is for genuine news. It's a digital version of what the tabloid *Weekly World News* was doing just before the Internet took over, a curious sideshow that wasn't worth worrying about—until it suddenly was, during the last presidential election campaign.

At the end of 2016, *BuzzFeed* analyzed the year's political stories—the twenty most viral articles from publications such as *The New York Times* and *The Washington Post,* and the twenty most viral published by false-news peddlers. During the last three months of the presidential campaign, the top fictional articles—"Pope Francis Endorses Donald Trump," "Wikileaks Confirms Hillary Sold Weapons to ISIS"—were much more widely shared and commented on than the top genuine ones. The direct democracy of Internet search algorithms is a stark example of Gresham's law, the bad driving out—or at least overrunning—the good.

DURING THE FIRST FIFTEEN YEARS of the twenty-first century, the GOP turned into the Fantasy Party, with a beleaguered reality-based wing. A far-right counterculture empowered millions of followers and took over the American right, as their extremist predecessors succeeded in doing to evangelicalism and the gun lobby three decades earlier.

This book had been under way for a couple of years when the 2016 presidential campaign began. The fact that Fantasyland candidates were the consistent front-runners for the Republican nomination (Donald Trump and Ben

Carson at first, then Trump and Ted Cruz) was surprising and appalling but also, I have to admit, a little gratifying to me—empirical proof of my theory as it applies to politics. The day after the Republicans' second primary debate in 2015, at the Reagan Library, before the debates became completely cartoonish, a shocked *New York Times* editorial called it

> a collection of assertions so untrue, so bizarre, that they form a vision as surreal as the Ronald Reagan jet looming behind the candidates' lecterns.
>
> It felt at times as if the speakers were no longer living in a fact-based world where actions have consequences, programs take money and money has to come from somewhere. Where basic laws—like physics and the Constitution—constrain wishes. Where Congress and the public, allies and enemies, markets and militaries don't just do what you want them to, just because you say they will.

I read that and said out loud, "Welcome to Fantasyland." After his election, another *Times* editorial granted that "Trump understood at least one thing better than almost everybody," that the "breakdown of a shared public reality built upon widely accepted facts represented not a hazard, but an opportunity."

I started paying close attention to Donald Trump a long time ago. In *Spy* magazine, which I cofounded in 1986 and edited until 1993, we devoted many hundreds of hours to reporting and researching and writing three cover stories and countless other articles about him, dozens of pages exposing and satirizing his lies, brutishness, egomania, and absurdity. Now everybody knows what we knew then. In the pre-Twitter age, whenever he sent threatening letters and called us names in public—"It's a piece of garbage," he said of the magazine—it was amazing, trippy, as if Daffy Duck or Roger Rabbit had turned from the onscreen cartoon universe and *replied*. It was kind of providential that he came along just as we were creating a magazine to chronicle America's rich and powerful jerks. And I guess it's sort of providence redux that Trump became the center of all attention as I was in the middle of writing a history of America jumping the shark.

Donald Trump is a pure Fantasyland being, its apotheosis. If he hadn't run for president, I might not have mentioned him at all. But here he is, a stupendous Exhibit A. To describe him is practically to summarize this book.

He's driven by resentment of the Establishment. He doesn't like experts because they interfere with his right as an American to believe or pretend that fictions are facts, to *feel* the truth. He sees conspiracies everywhere. He exploits the myths of white racial victimhood. His case of Kids "R" Us Syndrome—spoiled, impulsive, moody, a seventy-year-old brat—is extreme.

And he is first and last a creature of the fantasy-industrial complex. "He *is* P. T. Barnum," his sister, a federal judge, said to his biographer Tim O'Brien in 2005. Even as a teenager in the early 1960s, Trump himself told O'Brien, he understood that any racket in America could be turned into an entertainment racket. "I said, 'You know what I'll do? I am going to go into real estate, and I am going to put show business into real estate. I'll have the best of both worlds.'" Back then, in 1961, the historian Daniel Boorstin already saw what was coming in politics, what would make Trump president. "Our national politics has become a competition for images or between images, rather than between ideals," because we live in a "world where fantasy is more real than reality," Boorstin wrote. "Strictly speaking, there is no way to unmask an image. An image, like any other pseudo-event, becomes all the more interesting with our every effort to debunk it."

Although the fantasy-industrial complex had been annexing presidential politics for more than half a century when candidate Trump came along, his campaign and presidency are its ultimate expression, like nothing we'd witnessed in real life or imagined we ever would. From 1967 through 2011, California was governed by former movie stars more than a third of the time, and one of them became president of the United States. But Trump's need for any and all public attention always seemed to me more ravenous and insatiable than any other public figure's ever, similar to an addict's for drugs. Unlike Reagan or Schwarzenegger (but like Barnum, who also entered politics in middle age, between the two halves of his show business career), Trump was as much or more of an impresario as a performer, and not just in his real estate hucksterism and his deals with the WWE. Before the full emergence of Fantasyland, Trump's various enterprises would have seemed an embarrassing, ridiculous, incoherent jumble for a businessman, let alone a serious candidate for president. What connects a Muslim-mausoleum-themed casino in New Jersey to a short-lived sham professional football league to an autobiography he didn't write to hotels and buildings he didn't build to a mail-order meat business to a beauty pageant to an airline that lasted three years to a sham "university" to repeatedly welshing on giant loans to selling deodorant and mattresses and a vodka and toilet waters called Empire and Success to a board game named after himself to a TV show about pretending to fire people?

What connects them all, of course, is the new, total American embrace of admixtures of the fictional and real and of fame for fame's sake. Trump's reality was a reality show before that genre or term existed. His home in Palm Beach, a Mediterranean-fantasy castle built at the height of the first Florida real estate bubble, is also a private club that costs $200,000 to join. "It's like going to Disneyland and knowing Mickey Mouse will be there all day long," says one of the members, a local billionaire. Trump has always played the character Donald Trump, the way William Cody played the character Buffalo Bill, but more so, because now there is no offstage.

When he entered political show business, after threatening to do so for most of his adult life, his portrayal of that character was an unprecedented performance—presidential candidate as insult comic with a ridiculous artificial tan. And the hair—colored gold like a clown's in a farce, shamelessly unreal and whipped into shape as if by a pâtissier. Successful presidents and candidates have had to be entertainers for a while, but Trump went all the way. He used the pieces of the fantasy-industrial complex as nobody had before. He hired actors to play enthusiastic supporters at the kickoff of his candidacy. And unlike the other candidates, he was an exciting *star,* so TV shows wanted him on their air as much as possible—and as people who worked on those shows told me, they were expected to be careful not to make the candidate so unhappy he might not return.

As he began his campaign, a nine-year-old in Iowa he'd brought aboard his helicopter asked, "Are you Batman?" and Trump replied: "I am Batman." Before any votes were cast, he bragged compulsively about his polling numbers—not even ratings, like on TV, but hypothetical votes, virtual votes. The campaign turned from a *Batman* subplot to a new postmodern genre that broke the fourth wall. Like no candidate ever before, Trump riffed in campaign speeches *about* the campaign, *about* his performances and box office. When a longtime PR man for tyrants took over, he followed suit, commenting on the Trump character and script and show as part of the show. "When he's out on the stage," Paul Manafort said, "he's projecting an image that's for that purpose. The part that he's been playing is evolving into the part that now you've been expecting, but he wasn't ready for, because he had first to complete the first phase." Act one had finished, he said, and during act two, "the image is going to change." It did not then and has not since. "We're in more of a WWE brawl stage as a nation right now," Ben Carson explained. "This is the ultimate reality show," Manafort said before the national convention, a show where the prize would be "the presidency of the United States." Then, as on a reality show, Manafort was abruptly asked to leave the tribal council area, chopped, fired. For two months between the election and the inauguration, contestants competing to win cabinet seats paraded past a bank of cameras in the shiny pink lobby of Trump Tower one at a time, past displays of Trump-themed merchandise. One of them was the cofounder of the WWE, Linda McMahon, who won her cabinet-level position. And then his administration put out word that the two finalists for the open Supreme Court seat were coming to Washington for the finale, exactly as on a reality show.

Before Trump won their nomination and the presidency, when he was still "a cancer on conservatism" that "must be . . . discarded" (Governor Rick Perry) and an "utterly amoral" "narcissist at a level I don't think this country's ever seen" (Senator Ted Cruz), what upset and bewildered Republicans was his performance style, like that of a villain in a bad movie. Back then they were genuinely shocked not by his racism but by the shameless ways he indicated he was a fellow traveler of the straight-ahead racists who cheered him on. Serious Republicans also hated Trump's ideological incoherence—they didn't yet understand that his campaign logic was a new kind, the consistency of exciting tales and showmanship that transcends ideology. Super Bowl halftimes and Disneyland are crazily eclectic too, but they're *entertaining*.

Serious Republicans followed the unwritten rule that candidates were to let the right-wing media entertainers savage the rest of the news media, not do it themselves—but in 2016 Trump made his lying-press shtick a theatrical campaign staple, shocking Republicans twice, when he kept doing it and when it worked. It's telling that the only important institutional piece of the Republican coalition that never distanced itself from him was its most recklessly fantastical one, the NRA. They and he were in sync on more than just the Second Amendment; both called out the reality-based enemies of the people. "One of America's greatest threats is a national news media," the NRA's Wayne LaPierre said at CPAC back in 2014, because the press's "intentional corruption of the truth is an abomination."

Fantasyland medicine? Trump touched that base too. During the campaign he regularly repeated the falsehood that vaccines cause autism. And instead of undergoing a normal medical exam from a normal doctor and issuing a press release, the way nominees always have, Trump went on *The Dr. Oz Show* and handed him a sheet of test results that his own wacky doctor had performed. "If a patient of mine had these records," Dr. Oz obligingly said, "I'd be very happy, and I'd send them on their way."

Did his supporters know his hogwash was hogwash? Do they now? Yes and no, the way people buying tickets to Barnum's exhibitions 175 years ago did and didn't know (and certainly didn't care) that the black woman on display wasn't really Washington's 161-year-old former nanny and the stitched-together fish and ape wasn't actually a mermaid. Trump waited to run for president until he sensed that a critical mass of Americans had decided politics were *all* a show and a sham—that a conspiracy consisting of "the press, the talk-show experts, the campaign strategists, the political parties, even the candidates themselves—has rigged the game," as Louis Menand put it in *The New Yorker*. "Everyone knows that what you see in politics is fake or confected." Yet that article in the summer of 2015 did not even mention Trump, who was still an impossible joke candidate. If the whole thing is an insincere charade, rigged, Trump's brilliance was calling that out in the most impolitic ways possible, deriding his earnest competitors as fakers and losers and liars—because *that* bullshit-calling was uniquely candid, excitingly authentic in the age of fake.

Who but a preternaturally *honest* man would say in his announcement speech that Mexican immigrants are "rapists"? Or, as he said a few months later, that Muslims should be prohibited from entering the United States? A ban on Muslims is "very important and probably not politically correct, but I don't care."* Fuck the dog whistles, you fucking pussies.

Trump took a key piece of cynical wisdom about show business—*The most important thing is sincerity, and once you can fake that, you've got it made*—to a new level: his *actual* thuggish, un-PC sincerity is the opposite of the old-fashioned goody-goody sanctimony that people hate in politicians. And when Trump does do his obligatory bits of patently faked niceness, they get a pass, because the rest of the time he's implying that most public niceness is fake.

If he were just a truth-telling wise guy, however, he wouldn't now be president. Trump's genius was to exploit the extreme skepticism about politics—too much equivocating, democracy's a charade—but *also* pander to Americans' extreme magical thinking about national greatness. "I play to people's fantasies," his ghostwriter, on Trump's behalf, warned Americans thirty years ago in *The Art of the Deal*. "People want to believe that something is the biggest and the greatest and the most spectacular. I call it truthful hyperbole. It's an innocent form of exaggeration."

When you're about to be president, it's not innocent at all—such as the fantasy of a new healthcare system that will be "something terrific, "something great." "We're going to have insurance for everybody," Trump guaranteed. "There was a philosophy in some circles that if you can't pay for it, you

* Back in 2010, that had been one of the eight specific recommendations in *Shariah: The Threat to America* (see Chapter 40).

don't get it. That's not going to happen with us. . . . I am going to take care of everybody. Everybody's going to be taken care of much better," and the new system will appear "Immediately! Fast! Quick!"

Not just healthcare. "I will give you *everything*," Trump actually promised. Yes: "every dream you ever dreamed for your country" will come true. Another version of that big, magical fantasy he continuously served up was the general idea of *winning*. "We will have so much winning," he said in front of the Capitol at the very start of the campaign, "that you may get bored with winning. *Believe* me." His crowd cheered. "I agree. You'll never get bored with winning. You'll never get bored! We never get bored!" By the time of his Nevada primary victory speech at the Treasure Island Hotel & Casino, the *winning* had dissolved into pure mantra: "And now we're winning, winning, winning the country—and soon the *country* is going to start winning, winning, winning." Then he miraculously *won*, seeming to prove that *The Power of Positive Thinking* and *The Secret* are true.

There have been all his component subfantasies, alternatively happy and hateful, many of them born of nostalgia for the days when lots more Americans were white and lots fewer spoke with foreign accents, when white *guy* guys totally ruled and slicked-back ducktails were cool—when America was Great. The assorted fantasies of how a belligerent superhero president would destroy or defeat villains—ISIS, the Chinese government, U.S. corporations that build factories abroad. The fantasy that on 9/11 "thousands and thousands of people" in New Jersey from "the heavy Arab population . . . were cheering as the buildings came down," and the fantasy that Mexico will pay for building a high concrete wall along the border. What about the fact that the number of illegal immigrants from Mexico has been declining for years, a fact that makes the case for a wall even weaker? "We will build the wall no matter how low this number gets," President Trump told the NRA convention at the end of his first hundred days in office. "Don't even think about it. Don't even think about it. . . . We'll build the wall. Don't even think about it. Don't even think about it. Don't even think about it."

The single major item on the Fantasyland checklist we can check off only nominally is the one for religion. Among the many shocking things about Trump is his irreligiosity—that our Christian party chose the candidate who was the least Christian of the lot, and that white evangelicals nonetheless approve of President Trump overwhelmingly. During the campaign he tossed a few special fantasy crumbs their way, promising he'd make sure they would again feel free to say "Merry Christmas" to strangers of every faith. And his shameless-sinner style is still more proof of his astounding *honesty*—he's not pandering to them, not feigning piety or saintliness. When asked about his religious affiliation, Trump regularly describes himself as "Protestant"—an odd tell, sort of like saying he's a *Homo sapiens* of the Western Hemisphere instead of an American man.

The one influential religious figure in his life was Norman Vincent Peale, author of *The Power of Positive Thinking,* with its instructions to "never think of yourself as failing" and to banish any "negative thought concerning your personal powers." (See Chapter 21.) The Trump family attended his Presbyterian church, and the first of Donald's three weddings took place there, the Reverend Peale officiating. Now that a version of Peale's autohypnotic self-confidence scheme is at the heart of a hot charismatic Christian sector, Trump can almost pass for a prosperity gospel lay preacher. Sure, he's ignorant of religious particulars (like when he called a book of the New Testament "Two Corinthians" instead of Second Corinthians), but he's ignorant of the details of government policy and U.S. history as well—so what? White born-again Christians and Trump also really do share a contempt for (and from) the so-called elites. As I've said, Fantasyland's regions have open borders: specifically Christian make-believe isn't part of Trump's make-believe, but both he and they definitely do make believe and *feel* the truth regardless of facts. *Don't even think about it.*

First the Internet enabled and empowered full Fantasyland, then it did so for candidate Trump in 2015 and 2016, feeding him pseudonews on his phone and letting him feed those untruths directly to followers on social media. He is the poster boy for the downside of our digital world. "Forget the press," he advised people as a candidate—just "read the Internet." After he wrongly declared during the campaign that a certain anti-Trump protester "has ties to ISIS," he was asked if he regretted tweeting that falsehood. "What do I know about it?" he replied. "All I know is what's on the Internet."

But then he decided the Internet is a doubled-edged sword. On the one hand, it allows him to find and circulate conspiracy theories easily. "It gives a forum for people to express their ideas," a senior minion explained, so "when he sees an idea that he thinks is worthy of having a discussion about," he can immediately tweet it. On the other hand, Trump read on the Internet (*Breitbart, Infowars*) that his elite enemies operating the Internet (Google) conspired to spread lies to hurt him. "Google's search engine," he announced at a rally just before the election, was "suppressing the bad news about Hillary Clinton. How about that?"

Fantastical conspiracy theories, a recurring Trump motif, have also been a recurring motif in this history of Fantasyland—the supposed schemes of witches and Catholics and Masons and Jews, now of Muslims and liberals and internationalists. Trump launched his political career by embracing a brand-new conspiracy theory twisted around two other deep American taproots—fear and loathing of foreigners and nonwhites. In 2011 Trump became chief spokesperson for the fantasy that President Barack Obama was born in Kenya, a fringe idea that he brought into the mainstream—he wasn't a nut, he was *Donald Trump!*—so that it could be regularly promoted on Fox News and by an anchor on CNN. A dozen House Republicans cosponsored a federal bill that would require presidential candidates to submit a birth certificate and other proof that he or she isn't a secret foreigner; similar bills were introduced in state legislatures. After the Hawaiian bureaucrat who released a copy of the president's birth certificate died in a private plane crash, Trump tweeted: "How amazing. . . . All others lived"—suggesting the official had been murdered by the Obama conspiracy. Finally, in the fall of 2016, he grudgingly admitted the president was indeed a native-born American—at the same moment that an *Economist*/YouGov survey found a majority of Republicans still believed Obama probably or definitely was born in Kenya.

A conspiracy of scientists, journalists, and governments perpetrated the false idea of climate change, Trump has said for years. "Global warming has been proven to be a canard repeatedly over and over again," he declared, "mythical," "nonexistent," "bullshit" "based on faulty science," "a total, and very expensive, hoax!" He tweeted, "The concept of global warming was created by and for the Chinese in order to make U.S. manufacturing noncompetitive." On that last one, he later claimed he'd been kidding.

Conspiracies, conspiracies, still more conspiracies. "Scalia," the rightwing host of the *Savage Nation* asked him on the radio in 2016, "was he murdered . . . ?" Well, Trump replied, "they say they found the pillow on his face, which is a pretty unusual place to find a pillow."* On *Fox and Friends,* he discussed, as if it were fact, the *National Enquirer*'s suggestion that Ted Cruz's father was connected to JFK's assassination. "What was he doing with Lee Harvey Oswald shortly before the death, before the shooting? It's horrible." The Fox News anchors interviewing him neither challenged nor followed up. He revived the 1993 fantasy about the Clintons' friend Vincent Foster—his death, Trump said, was "very fishy," because Foster "had inti-

---

* In fact, the pillow was found on the mattress, not on Scalia. By the way, that show's host, Michael Savage, is another exemplar of Fantasyland's open borders: as Michael Weiner, Ph.D., he is the author of more than a dozen alternative medicine books, such as *Herbs That Heal* and *The Complete Book of Homeopathy.*

mate knowledge of what was going on. He knew everything that was going on, and then all of a sudden he committed suicide. . . . I will say there are people who continue to bring it up because they think it was absolutely a murder." He has also promised he's going to make sure "you will find out who really knocked down the World Trade Center." And it has all worked for him, because a critical mass of Americans is eager to believe almost any conspiracy theory, no matter how implausible, as long as it jibes with their opinions and feelings.

Not all lies are fantasies, and not all fantasies are lies; people who *believe* untrue things can pass lie detector tests. Trump's version of unreality is a patchwork of knowing falsehoods and sincerely believed fantasies, which is more troubling than if he were just a liar. His insistence that he didn't grab or kiss any of the dozen women who in 2016 said he had, unbidden—"Nothing ever happened. Didn't exist. This was all fantasyland"—is a lie, I'm close to certain. But he probably really believed that "the murder rate in our country is the highest it's been in forty-seven years," the total and dangerous falsehood he told leaders of the National Sheriffs Association in the Oval Office. Whatever he believes or doesn't, he makes untrue assertions more frequently than any U.S. leader in recorded history. The fact-checking organization PolitiFact looked at four hundred of his factual statements as a candidate and as president and found that 50 percent were completely false and another 20 percent mostly false. After he became president, according to *The Washington Post,* he issued an average of more than four falsehoods or "misleading claims" per day.

He gets away with this as he wouldn't have in the 1980s and '90s, when he first talked about running for president, because now factual truth is just one option, the *consensus* reality, and Americans feel entitled to their own facts. After he won the election he began routinely referring to *all* unflattering or inconvenient journalism as "fake news." Trump's White House counselor was explicit about that their first weekend in the White House, when the inauguration crowd estimate was at least 75 percent smaller than the president wished it to be. "Our press secretary," she said on *Meet the Press,* "gave alternative facts to that." When his public approval declined during his first months in office, Trump simply refused to believe it: "Any negative polls," the president tweeted at dawn one morning from Mar-a-Lago, "are fake news."

In Fantasyland, refusing to be fact-checked is celebrated—"his brazenness is not punished," the *Economist* noted, "but taken as evidence of his willingness to stand up to elite power." Lying works for Trump even when he's denying that he told lies he was recorded telling. "From the point of view of political psychology," the University of Connecticut philosophy professor Michael Lynch explains, "the more blatant the contradiction, the better. . . . If I simply deny what I earlier affirmed and act as if nothing has happened, then *you* are left having to decide what I really meant. . . . The most disturbing power of contradiction is that its repeated use can dull our sensitivity to the value of truth itself." If our sensitivity to the value of truth is dulled, it's easier for everyone to become more like him and those in his thrall.

Did he *really* think he lost the popular vote because of a conspiracy that arranged for millions of noncitizens, "illegals," to vote for Clinton? "I'm a very instinctual person," President Trump said when a *Time* reporter challenged him on this claim, "but my instinct turns out to be right." Did he *really* think President Obama ordered his telephones to be tapped and that a conspiracy of government officials covered it up? My hunch is that both of those conspiracy theories were as much sincere beliefs as lies.

The people who speak on Trump's behalf to journalists struggle to defend or explain his assertions. They'll sometimes point out that a fantasy was asserted by somebody else, too—as when the press secretary quoted a Fox News commentator who'd said, without evidence, that British intelligence spied on Trump at Obama's behest. Or they'll ask that Trump be graded on a curve: because he's new to politics, the things he says mustn't always be taken *literally*. Asked about "the President's statements that are . . . demonstrably not true," the White House counselor asked the reporter to please remember all "the many things that he says that *are* true."

According to *The New York Times,* the people around Trump say his baseless certainty "that he was bugged in some way" in Trump Tower is driven by "a sense of persecution bordering on faith." And indeed, their most honest defense of his false statements has been to cast them practically as matters of religious conviction—he deeply *believes* them, so . . . end of story. That's what the press secretary did concerning the nonexistent three to five million illegal voters: in a single encounter, he earnestly reminded reporters that Trump "has believed that for a while" and "does believe that" and "it's been a long-standing belief he's maintained" and "it's a belief that he has maintained for a while."

Which is why a quarter of Americans subscribe to that preposterous belief themselves.* And in Trump's view, *that* overrides any requirement for facts.

* 2017 *Washington Post*/ABC News and *Politico*/Morning Consult surveys.

"Do you think that talking about millions of illegal votes is dangerous to this country without presenting the evidence?" the anchor of *ABC World News Tonight* asked President Trump.

"No," he replied, "not at all! Not at all—because many people feel the same way that I do."

THIS BOOK HAS TRACED THE route that our exceptional country has taken to arrive at this latest version of its exceptional self. Now we can see how each fork in the road tended us toward the next, and the next, and then the next.

If the Roman Catholic French or Spanish had been more successful in making more of North America theirs, maybe we would be less rogue-utopian and individualistic. If the Dutch had extended their influence beyond New York and beyond the 1600s, the sensible and cosmopolitan strains of our national character might be more dominant. What if those first hundred radical Puritan extremists hadn't leased the *Mayflower* and had stayed instead on their side of the Atlantic? What if we hadn't been so tolerant of slave labor? What if the American Revolution had failed, or the Confederate secession had succeeded? What if California had remained part of Mexico, or the United States hadn't fought a war in Vietnam? What if Joseph Smith and P. T. Barnum and Walt Disney and Ronald Reagan and Oprah Winfrey and Donald Trump and a dozen other key channelers of these American tendencies had never appeared? What if Internet search had been designed differently or if, in 2009, some senior Wall Street executives had been imprisoned for their recklessness and fraud? There were so many inflection points along the way. We might now be a warmer Canada, a massive Netherlands, a lumbering Argentina, or the United States the way it was until recently—that is, a country with a penchant for fantasies, but the penchant mostly under control.

Instead, it all happened as it happened. We are what we are, in all our sui generis splendor.

America was the dreamworld creation of fantasists, some religious and some out to get rich quick, all with a freakish appetite for the amazing. Beyond our passionate beliefs in various kinds of magic and destiny, our particular religious DNA, supercharged, was the source of other defining American habits of mind as well, such as the craving for the mysterious to be literal, and the hair-trigger sensitivity to persecution by elites. In addition to being the first designed-built Protestant nation, America was also the first designed-built Enlightenment nation. The two fed each other—and sometimes became toxic in combination.

Mix the Protestant impulse to find the meaning and purpose in *everything* with the Enlightenment's empiricism, and you get our American mania for connecting all the dots,* irrationality in rationalist drag. You get phrenology and homeopathy and intelligent design. You get complex data-rich schemes calculating the dates that God created the world and everything on it and the dates when God or Quetzalcoatl will erase and reboot it. You get books packed with facts and factlike assertions proving that this or that omnipotent conspiratorial enemy—witches! Masons! extraterrestrials! Muslims!—has infiltrated America to enslave or destroy us.

Our special American alloy of Protestantism and the Enlightenment also generated our extreme, self-righteous individualism. *I have searched for the truth and discovered it* (Protestant and Enlightenment). *My intuitions are equal to facts* (Protestant). *My skepticism is profound* (Enlightenment) *except concerning my own beliefs* (Protestant). *Who I am is whatever I imagine myself to be* (both), and *You're not the boss of me* (both).

As we did with our founding religious legacy, we've taken from our Enlightenment legacy certain pieces of the program—skepticism, freedom of thought, mutable truth—and selectively amped them to extremes at the expense of other Enlightenment virtues, such as reasonableness and rigorous self-doubt. It's what pathologists call hypertrophy, when an organ or muscle grows too big, or like an autoimmune disease, when an essential process that normally keeps us healthy runs amok and makes us sick.

It wasn't only our peculiar amalgam of new sixteenth- and seventeenth-century religion and new seventeenth- and eighteenth-century philosophy that laid Fantasyland's groundwork. Other American idiosyncrasies had roles. Ours was a country created by wildcatters and entrepreneurs, hustlers of every kind. Wide open spaces made for solitude as much as for community, which in turn made for still more extreme individualists—people alone for months on end marinating in their own thoughts and feelings and fancies. The spaciousness also made it easy for Americans, especially at the start and again more recently, to sort themselves into homogeneous, self-reinforcing geographic clusters where all the inhabitants share the same script.

Fantasies were always synergistic in America. The wild new religions prepared people for wild new pseudoscience and vice versa. If serious people took mesmerism seriously, why shouldn't other people regard homeopathy and phrenology and cure-all pills as state-of-the-art science? If Yale professors believed there were winged men on the moon, why shouldn't other peo-

---

* I realize: given this book, I'm one to talk.

ple believe it was possible to communicate with the dead? If America's great men were convinced of a hidden government of occultists and a Vatican plot to destroy liberty, who could gainsay the claims of *any* vast scheme of evil genius?

Our nostalgia tic also explains a lot. Americans have always been apt to think of America as the best place on Earth—but also that it *used to be* so much better, more pioneering, more charming, more virtuous, more authentic. People imagined in the 1700s that it was better in the theocratic wilderness of the 1600s, then in the 1800s that it was better back in the 1700s, before the racket and speed of factories and railroads; in the 1900s we imagined it had been so much better back in the 1800s, when we still depended on guns, before we moved from farms and small towns into noisy crowded cities; today, on top of most of those older nostalgias, we miss the good old days when Americans worked at secure well-paying jobs for years on end. In 1900 a lot of people were nostalgic for the time when Americans were all Protestant, later for when Americans were all Christian, and now for when we were practically all white—*and* when men were men and women were women and the love that dared not speak its name didn't speak it.

Like other fantasy-flavored impulses, American nostalgia can express itself happily or fearfully, as wishful stage-set charm or they've-wrecked-our-stage-set rage. Nostalgia enacted and gratified by the fantasy industrial complex is mostly the happy kind. The kinds of nostalgia that drive our politics can either be fond, like Ronald Reagan's, or angry and scared; lately it's the latter.

In fact, our political culture sometimes comes in happy *and* scary forms inside the same big tent. The late 1960s were experienced simultaneously as the threshold of violent revolution and as a romp through cloud-cuckoo-land. Most of the Americans who have recently been most certain that America is both wrecked *and* the best place *ever* call themselves Republicans. Our tendencies to fear the new and to reject reason have appeared on the left as well as the right, often in a tag-team fashion—first Transcendentalists and utopian communards in the mid-1800s, then Protestant fundamentalists in the early 1900s. But during the last half-century, the cycles got faster. The right-wing conspiracists of the 1950s were followed in the 1960s by conspiracists on the left, then the hippies of the 1960s appeared almost simultaneously with extreme Christians.

The spectrum from madly full of dread to madly optimistic also applies to our spiritual beliefs. There are the believers in irremediable human depravity, Armageddon any day, most people bound for hell, in the meantime persecution of the virtuous by Satan's agents. Then there are the more hopeful—instant E-Z salvation, imminent global alakazam, plenty of room in Heaven. And finally the *super*hopeful, believing that angels are here improving the world right now, that shamans and healers channel mystical energies, that actionable magic can increase your net worth or in the afterlife send you to your own planet as an immortal. Then there are people with strong beliefs in both supernatural terror *and* bliss, bipolar optimist-pessimists—they can chat with God or Jesus or ancient spirits but may also be possessed by demons; they believe that chants and diluted poisons give them virtual superpowers but also that an evil corporate-government conspiracy is out to sicken them with vaccines and genetically modified food.

By the mid-1800s, entertainment was bigger here than anywhere (theaters, popular music, superstar singers, circuses, dime museums, magicians), but the new wrinkle was that *other* businesses and professions were becoming *show* businesses—religion, medicine, journalism at first—and that real-life heroes (Daniel Boone, Buffalo Bill, Sitting Bull) morphed into fictionalized show-biz versions of themselves. The zone between make-believe and true was expanded and became a quintessential product of entrepreneurial America.

The fantasy-industrial complex invented and dominated by Americans continued to sprawl exponentially, taking over parts of every conceivable realm—politics, real estate, retail, "hospitality," lifestyle, life. We have encased ourselves in a wall-to-wall 24/7 collage of fantasy and fantastic reality. Sure, at Disney World or an IMAX theater or playing *Mortal Kombat,* we know we're in fictional domains. But otherwise? In so much of the rest of our lives, the nominally authentic parts—the ways we look and dress, where we live and eat, the world depicted by infotainers and news commentators and Internet exhorters—many, many distinctions between fake and real have been erased. A lot of American reality is now virtual. We're often unaware whether we're inside or outside of Fantasyland.

FOR THREE CENTURIES, IN CULTURE and religion as well as in politics and economics, the fantasist and realist impulses existed in a rough balance, with a powerful animating tension between the two tendencies. That dynamic balance was key. We were like an internal combustion engine, a great machine powered by endless little explosions—every idiosyncratic vision and dreamy ambition permitted to ignite—but with control mechanisms and gaskets and a sturdy engine block, all keeping the contraption from blasting apart. Or if you will, the American id was kept in check by a strong ego and superego.

For instance, when the U.S. government was created, the Founders invented a cautious Senate to overrule the House fiends when necessary—Washington told Jefferson it was like a saucer to cool impossibly hot coffee. Jefferson's nemesis Alexander Hamilton hoped the Electoral College would do something similar every four years, that a sober, deliberative group could have the final say in case the People ever elected some unacceptable charlatan or demagogue with "talents for low intrigue and the little arts of popularity."

Renegade religious sects emerged, then calmed as they grew and matured. We submitted our faith in free markets to constraints so that the system seemed fair enough to continue operating successfully. Dream the impossible dream, build it and they will come, put the pedal to the metal, let your freak flag fly—but play by the rules, and don't drink and drive. Being an American always meant having a chip on your shoulder about fancy-pants know-it-alls, but when push came to shove, the know-it-alls who actually knew important things remained firmly in control. Most of the time it worked okay.

As life became easier, however, the easier climate was more conducive to the loosey-goosier parts of the American psyche. A tipping point came in the 1960s, when our yin began to be overwhelmed by our yang. We discarded the good residue of our founding Puritan ethos—discipline, austerity, hyperliteracy—and doubled down on the old Puritan beliefs in magic and an imminent apocalypse and utopia. After 1970 certain ingrained American habits—individualism, righteous conviction, open-mindedness—were all at once out of control, like flora and fauna in a newly tropicalized climate, blooming luxuriantly and shooting out seeds.

Then the economic climate changed again. Postwar prosperity had afforded fantasy-prone Americans the luxury of indulging more and more fantasies, and the Internet allowed them to inhabit more all-encompassing fantasies even more of the time. But around the turn of this century, the economic balminess ended for at least half of America. As a chilly dead-end dusk and gloom descended on the disappointed and newly disempowered, we did not as a nation cope by reverting en masse to old Yankee virtues—self-restraint, realism, pragmatism, and compromise. Too many of us had become too habituated to our various forms of magical thinking. As the American dream of endless upward economic mobility came to seem increasingly like myth, all sorts of pure myths and fantasies became still more appealing and seemed more real. The unprecedented and broadly shared affluence of our twentieth century—with its go-go blowout starting in the 1960s—was a prerequisite to Fantasyland, but the arrival of full Fantasyland was accompanied by the *end* of those economic glory days for most people.

According to psychologists, stress can trigger delusions, and engaging in fantasy can provide relief from stress and loneliness. According to sociologists, religion flourishes more in societies where people frequently feel in economic jeopardy. According to social psychologists, belief in conspiracy theories flourishes among people who feel bad about themselves; they may be powerless to improve their lives, but knowing about all the alleged secret plots gives them a compensatory jolt of what feels like power.

When Barack Obama first ran for president, his most memorable campaign gaffe was to describe this dynamic. "You go into some of these small towns in Pennsylvania," he told a group of supporters in San Francisco in 2008, "and like a lot of small towns in the Midwest, the jobs have been gone now for twenty-five years and nothing's replaced them. So it's not surprising then that they get bitter, they cling to guns or religion, or antipathy to people who aren't like them, or anti-immigrant sentiment . . . as a way to explain their frustrations." Sure, it was condescending, but it was also true. The political scientists who wrote *American Conspiracy Theories* (2014) found that the least educated are almost twice as likely as the most educated to be highly predisposed to believing conspiracies.

For half a century, several generations of Americans lived with a binary view of the world, totalitarian bad guys versus the Free World. But after the Soviet Union collapsed and China became a normal country, global geopolitical reality was exposed in all its messy, confusing, shades-of-gray complexity. Russia is no longer Communist or much of a superpower, but it's still evil or . . . what, no, maybe not? China still calls itself Communist and is now our fellow superpower, but . . . economically it's even more unequal than we are *and it's also* our indispensable economic partner? Muslim countries used to be either pro-American or pro-Soviet, but now they're either secular (good) or fundamentalist (bad) . . . but wait, the United States is allied with *and* fighting regimes and rebels in *both* categories?

As a way to make the world seem understandable again, to focus on a single enemy, the idea of the existence of some kind of elite cabal became irresistible to more and more Americans. Somebody *must* be pulling the strings. It can be simultaneously terrifying and comforting to believe that bad people are tyrannizing you. So conspiracists squint at the real world and see the exercise of power as both ridiculously simple and brilliantly complex.

They fictionalize reality. Instead of the real-life Rube Goldberg contraption with no single designer or operator, they imagine a few puppet-masters in charge of a global Borg in which all the circuits and software operate in perfect synchrony. It's the way religious fundamentalists see physical reality as God's perfectly designed masterwork rather than as it really is, a somewhat kludgy but astounding accumulation of happy accidents with nobody in charge.

I've referred repeatedly to *full Fantasyland* and to events and phenomena (such as President Trump) that wouldn't have happened before it emerged. Until now I've avoided setting a precise date. When did it begin? Obviously after the 1960s and '70s, and after Ronald Reagan. The 1990s were the hinge decade: Oprah and *Behold a Pale Horse* and the Satanic Panic and Limbaugh and *The X-Files* swept the nation, the NRA called law enforcement officers jackbooted thugs, a wrestler from the booming WWF was elected governor of Minnesota, Disney built its perfect make-believe town in Florida, the federal building in Oklahoma City was blown up, the Pats Robertson and Buchanan ran for president, President Clinton was investigated for murdering his White House counsel before being investigated for lying about adultery, *Final Fantasy* was launched, and so were the National Institutes of Health's alternative medicine center and reality TV and Fox News. And, of course, the Internet: starting in 1995 everyone could browse the Web, so let's call 2000, the first year a *majority* of Americans were online, the unequivocal first year of full Fantasyland.

I GREW UP IN THE 1960s in a family that was as irreligious as both my parents' families had been in the 1920s and '30s, Protestant only culturally—not Catholic, not Jewish, so what else was there? Christmas was a big deal, and when we were little, we hunted for dyed eggs every Easter morning. My parents spent time in churches almost exclusively for weddings and funerals, but we were not taught to think of believers as fools. Most people we knew went to church, and that was fine. We were just . . . indifferent. Back then in Nebraska—in America—religious belief was a private matter.

My folks weren't antireligious, but they were anti*dogmatic*. They didn't even enforce their religious unbelief on us. When some of my siblings and I decided we wanted to try out Sunday school, first the Congregationalists down the street and then the Unitarians (where my mother sometimes played piano), we were neither discouraged nor encouraged—and then each of us stopped going on our own. One day when I was about eleven, I tried to get my mom to admit, finally, that she didn't believe in God. She carefully and cutely hemmed and hawed until I probed and pushed so much she surrendered.

Since the 1970s, when my siblings went through their intense exotic-Eastern-religious phase, I've wondered if that was some kind of recoil from our secular childhoods, or an extrapolation of the family's Transcendentalist strain. My parents did seek to experience deep wonder and contemplate the exalted mysteries of existence. It's one reason they took us camping across the northern Great Plains and the mountain West every summer. The trips on which we got to see the aurora borealis had the feel of successful religious pilgrimages. One of my mother's favorite writers was the poet John Neihardt, whose book *Black Elk Speaks* is the biography of an Oglala Lakota shaman.

I still seek out unfathomable and fathomable mysteries and wonders of existence that render me dumbstruck. I enjoy having my mind boggled. When our two daughters were growing up, my wife and I didn't take them to church services, but often we'd all go outside on clear nights to lie on the ground and look up at the stars, marveling and discussing the scale and complexity and the amazing good luck of this planet and our species and our very selves. On the greatest family vacation ever, as my wife and children and I drove one dusk through the East African bush, where the first humans lived a hundred thousand years ago, we spotted a troop of chimps walking in the distance, and I teared up.

"I'm not an atheist," the great Harvard biologist E. O. Wilson said in 2015, "I'm a scientist. Atheism is the belief that there is no god, and you declare there is no god: 'Come, my fellow atheists, let us march together and conquer those idiots who think there is a god—all these other tribes. We're going to prevail.' I would even say I'm agnostic *because* I'm a scientist."

In this he echoes the greatest scientist of the last century. "In my opinion," Albert Einstein wrote, "the idea of a personal God is a childlike one . . . but I do not share the crusading spirit of the professional atheist. . . . I prefer an attitude of humility corresponding to the weakness of our intellectual understanding of nature and of our own being." Indeed, he wrote,

> the most beautiful thing we can experience is the mysterious. . . . He to whom this emotion is a stranger, who can no longer pause to wonder and stand rapt in awe, is as good as dead: his eyes are closed. . . . To know that what is impenetrable to us really exists, manifesting itself as the highest wisdom and the most radiant beauty which our dull faculties can comprehend only in their most primitive forms— this knowledge, this feeling, is at the center of true religiousness. In

this sense, and in this sense only, I belong in the ranks of devoutly religious men.

Yes. My life isn't one of pristine, lab-pure rationalism, unleavened by emotion or superstition. Superrationalists are often prone to arrogance, hubris, a blindered devotion to markets or technology, an abandonment of the wholehearted search for meaning beyond science and economics. Flecks of fantasy are charming condiments in everyday existence. Like so much of life, it's an instance of the Goldilocks Problem, avoiding the too-cold and the too-hot in favor of the just-right. But despite my dull faculties and primitive comprehension of the impenetrable mysteries of existence, I do try hard not to surrender to magical thinking.

I'm agnostic about God, always ready but never expecting to be persuaded.* America's tiny population of agnostics and atheists is growing briskly, doubling in the last decade to 7 percent. Back in 1972, the entire nonreligious fraction of Americans, disbelievers plus doubters plus nothing-in-particulars, was just 5 percent—and now it's 23 percent. (That's partly a function of education. Almost half of Americans who didn't get beyond high school think every bit of the Bible is literally true, while only one in six college graduates do.) If that rate of growth were to continue, in another forty years we would be more like a normal rich country, half of Americans religiously unaffiliated, and half of those agnostics and atheists.

The recent American secularization, such as it is, has been led by the young. A third of millennials say they're atheist or agnostic or nothing in particular, and fewer of them than their elders say they believe in God with absolute certainty. The small fraction of all Americans who regard the Bible matter-of-factly—as "an ancient book of fables, legends, history and moral precepts recorded by man"—has increased a lot since 1990, as has the group convinced of a God-free process of creation and evolution.†

But here's the thing: the fraction of Americans who believe that the Bible is "the actual word of God . . . to be taken literally, word for word," is unchanged—33 percent in 1990, 32 percent now. Beyond that hard core, religiously affiliated Americans say they're praying more, reading the Bible more, and "sharing faith with others" more. And the younger a Christian is, for in-

---

* According to a 2014 Pew survey, the Americans who most frequently "feel a deep sense of wonder about the universe" are agnostics.
† Data in this paragraph and the previous one are from the General Social Survey 1990–2014 as well as Gallup, Harris, Pew, and Ipsos surveys.

stance, the more likely she or he is to "believe that the charismatic gifts, such as tongues and healing, are valid and active today"—including a large majority of Christians under thirty-five.[*]

As far as religion goes, then, America isn't so much secularizing as splitting into two distinct societies, one more secular and reality-based, one much less so. Rationalism and reasonableness are gaining some ground, but the true believers, still the bigger cohort, are sticking to their guns. We are polarizing religiously the way we have been polarizing politically. As I've said, that's not coincidental, it's synergistic.

Which makes America exceptional in a curious new way. Instead of the Puritans' shining city upon a hill, a newly invented model society to which the rest of the world should aspire, we've become a warts-and-all model *of* the messy, mistrustful rest of the whole world—split between cosmopolitan seculars and tribal fundamentalists, between educated people hopeful about possible futures and others desperate to return to some dreamy past.

DURING THE EARLY MONTHS OF the Trump administration, I was reminded of a George Orwell essay from 1943 about the civil war in Spain, four years after the fascists won. One subtle but profound effect of the fascist regimes in Spain and Italy and Germany, he wrote, was how their propaganda "often gives me the feeling that the very concept of objective truth is fading out of the world. After all, the chances are that those lies, or at any rate similar lies, will pass into history."

His contemporary Hannah Arendt escaped Germany as a young woman in 1933, when the Nazis took over, and emigrated to America, where she became one of the most important political philosophers of the age. Her first big book, in 1951, was *The Origins of Totalitarianism*. I'd never read it until 2016, around the time Trump made "rigged elections" a recurring theme of his campaign. "The essential conviction shared by all ranks" in a totalitarian movement, Arendt wrote, "from fellow-traveler to leader, is that politics is a game of cheating." When I read the next paragraph, I was staggered. I stopped and read it again. It gave me goosebumps.

A mixture of gullibility and cynicism have been an outstanding characteristic of mob mentality before it became an everyday phenomenon of masses. In an ever-changing, incomprehensible world the

---

[*] General Social Survey 1990–2014, Pew 2014 survey, 2010 Barna Group survey.

masses had reached the point where they would, at the same time, believe everything and nothing, think that everything was possible and that nothing was true. . . . Mass propaganda discovered that its audience was ready at all times to believe the worst, no matter how absurd, and did not particularly object to being deceived because it held every statement to be a lie anyhow. The totalitarian mass leaders based their propaganda on the correct psychological assumption that, under such conditions, one could make people believe the most fantastic statements one day, and trust that if the next day they were given irrefutable proof of their falsehood, they would take refuge in cynicism; instead of deserting the leaders who had lied to them, they would protest that they had known all along that the statement was a lie and would admire the leaders for their superior tactical cleverness.

Arendt published *Origins of Totalitarianism* when Stalin was in power and Hitler only six years gone. I don't think the most important U.S. institutions are about to collapse. History doesn't repeat. But *damn,* this rhyme is chilling.

The idea that progress has some kind of unstoppable momentum was always a very American belief. But it's really an article of faith more than a historical law—the Christian fantasy about history's happy ending was reconfigured during the Enlightenment into a set of secular fantasies about inevitable improvement. One version was our blithe conviction that America's forms of freedom and democracy and justice and affluence must prevail in the end.

I can imagine, for the first time in my life, that America has permanently tipped into disarray and decline.

I wonder if it's only America's destiny, exceptional as ever, to unravel in this Fantasyland fashion. Or maybe we're early adopters, the canaries in the global mine, and Canada and Denmark and Japan and China and all the rest will eventually follow us down our tunnel. The German historian Oswald Spengler, author of *The Decline of the West,* a complete pessimist about our civilization, wrote in 1931 that "only dreamers believe there is a way out. Optimism is cowardice."* I'm not there yet, but why should modern civilization's

---

* "Hitler is a fool," Spengler said in 1932, then voted for him for president anyway, because he thought that only strong leaders on the model of the Caesars might save the West from further decline.

great principles—democracy, freedom, tolerance—guarantee permanently great outcomes? Just as Christian believers think God granted humans free will to sin, the Enlightenment granted us the freedom to create the Dark Ages all over again.

"Keeping an open mind is a virtue," Carl Sagan wrote in *The Demon-Haunted World,* the last book he published, but "not so open that your brains fall out. . . . I have a foreboding of an America when, clutching our crystals and nervously consulting our horoscopes, our critical faculties in decline, unable to distinguish between what feels good and what's true, we slide, almost without noticing, back into superstition and darkness." That was twenty years ago.

The historical period of superstition and darkness that looms in our rearview mirror is the closest one, the Middle Ages in Europe, preceding the Enlightenment and the Renaissance. *Renaissance,* of course, means "rebirth"— the rediscovery six hundred years ago of much *earlier* golden ages of intellectual clarity and rigor and brilliance, in ancient Rome and Greece. For a moment this cheers me: give us some time, and we'll have another renaissance!

But then I look at the rise and fall of ancient Greece. The seven centuries of Greek civilization are divided into three eras—the Archaic, then the Classical, then the Hellenistic. During the first, the one depicted by Homer, Greeks' understanding of existence defaulted to supernaturalism and the irrational. Then suddenly science and literature and all the superstar geniuses emerged—Aeschylus, Sophocles, Euripides, Socrates, Plato, Aristotle—in the period we canonize as "ancient Greece." But that astonishing era lasted less than two centuries, after which Athens returned to astrology and magical cures and alchemy, the end. Why? According to *The Greeks and the Irrational,* by the Oxford classicist Eric Dodd, it was because they finally found freedom too scary, frightened by the new idea that their lives and fates weren't predestined or managed by gods and they really were on their own. Maybe America's Classical period has also lasted two centuries, 1800 to 2000, give or take a few decades on each end.

In any case, our circumstance doesn't seem altogether new. Fantasyland has been the norm for the run of humanity; the unusually rational and scientific centuries here and there along the way, like the last few, are exceptions. Dominant cultures have had their enlightenments and golden ages before, then returned to primitivism and murk.

*   *   *

BECAUSE I'M AN AMERICAN, a fortunate American who has lived in a fortunate American century, I remain more of an optimist than a pessimist. I haven't abandoned hope. Even as we've entered this winter of foolishness and darkness, when too many Americans are losing their grip on reason and reality, it has been an epoch of astonishing hope and light as well.* During these same last three decades, Americans accomplished the miracle of reducing murders and other violent crime by more than half. We decoded the human genome, elected an African-American president, recorded the sound of two black holes colliding a billion years ago, and created *Beloved, The Simpsons, Goodfellas, Angels in America, The Wire, The Colbert Report, Transparent, Hamilton,* and, in my extended family alone, a dozen excellent babies. Since 1980, the fraction of Earth's people living in extreme poverty has plummeted from more than 40 percent to 10 percent. I do despair of our devolution toward unreason and magical thinking, but not everything has gone wrong.

What is to be done? I don't have an actionable agenda, Seven Ways Sensible People Can Save America from the Craziness. But I think we can slow the flood, repair some dikes and levees, maybe stop things from getting any worse.

If we're splitting into two different cultures, we in reality-based America must try to keep our zone as large and robust and attractive as possible for ourselves and the next generations. We need to adopt a guiding principle, based on those aphorisms of Daniel Moynihan and Thomas Jefferson I've quoted so often: *You're entitled to your own opinions and your own fantasies, but not your own facts—especially if your fantastical facts hurt people.*

We need to become less squishy. We must call out the dangerously untrue and unreal. That may sound impractical, but a grassroots movement against one kind of cultural squishiness has taken off and reshaped our national politics—the opposition to so-called political correctness. Antifantasy is different, because PC is more in the eye of the beholder, ranging from the dopey and annoying to expectations of common decency, and everyone in a culture as diverse as ours is bound to draw those lines differently. However, distinguishing among the factually true, the dubious, and the false, at least

---

* Charles Dickens, *A Tale of Two Cities*: "It was the best of times, it was the worst of times, it was the age of wisdom, it was the age of foolishness, it was the epoch of belief, it was the epoch of incredulity, it was the season of Light, it was the season of Darkness, it was the spring of hope, it was the winter of despair, we had everything before us, we had nothing before us, we were all going direct to Heaven, we were all going direct the other way—in short, the period was . . . like the present period."

outside of religion, doesn't involve many judgment calls about taste or "appropriate" and "inappropriate." This struggle should be less fraught.

But it will require a struggle to try to make America reality-based again. We few, we happy few, we band of sisters and bothers—in fact, we're not really *so* few. Fight the good fight in your private life. You needn't get into an argument with the stranger who claims George Soros and Uber are conspiring to make his muscle car illegal, but do not give acquaintances and friends and family members free passes. If you have children or grandchildren, teach them to distinguish between true and untrue as fiercely as you do between right and wrong or between foolish and wise. We need to adopt new protocols for information media hygiene. Would you feed your kids a half-eaten casserole a stranger handed you on the bus, or give them medicine you got from some lady at the gym? Do you have unprotected sex with people you just met? Remember when *viral* was a bad thing, referring only to the spread of disease? The same goes for what you read and watch and believe.

And fight the good fight in the public sphere. One task, of course, is to contain the worst tendencies of Trumpism and cut off its political-economic fuel, so that a critical mass of fantasy and lies doesn't turn it into something much worse than nasty, oafish, reality-show pseudoconservatism. Progress is not inevitable, but it's not impossible either.[*]

Cultural predispositions and national characters are real, and societies do come to crossroads and make important choices. But while our Fantasyland tendencies were present from the beginning, the current situation was not *inevitable,* because history and evolution never are. Nor now is any particular future. We could regain our national balance and composure. These last decades may turn out to have been a phase, one strange act of our ongoing epic, an unfortunate episode in the American experiment that we will finally move past and chalk up to experience. Nations and societies have survived and recovered from far more terrible swerves, eras that felt cataclysmic as they were happening. The good news, in other words, is that America may now be at peak Fantasyland. We can hope.

---

[*] For instance, the state of California eliminated Personal Belief Exemptions from vaccination for schoolchildren as of 2016, and the vaccination rate for California kindergartners is already higher than it has been in a decade.

Acknowledgments

One day in 2013, I had breakfast with Gina Centrello, who runs Random House. I told her that when I finished the new novel I'd just started, I had a nonfiction book in mind. I gave my half-baked pitch. She reacted positively—in fact, she suggested, given how timely it sounded, maybe I should pause the novel and write the nonfiction book first? So I did. I'm grateful for Gina's many years of cheerful enthusiasm and support—and now for her uncanny prescience as well.

Andy Ward took a humongous, baggy draft and helped me turn it into the book it needed to be. He was a hedgehog *and* a fox, with one brilliant big idea and thousands of excellent small ones, all of them adding clarity and rigor. I expected a good editor, but I got an indispensable collaborator as well.

Once again I've depended on the talent and collegiality of my other abettors at Random House, especially Rachel Ake, Janet Biehl, Andrea DeWerd, Benjamin Dreyer, Greg Kubie, Allyson Lord, Steve Messina, Paolo Pepe, Tom Perry, Chayenne Skeete, Susan Turner, and Jessica Yung.

Even though I advise writers they don't need to be friends with their agents, I fail to practice what I preach: Suzanne Gluck is my smart and delightful pal as well as my ideal professional facilitator.

Among the many other friends (and relatives) whose conversations sparked ideas or sent me down useful paths are Ari Andersen, Bruce Birenboim, Art Jensen, Melik Kaylan, Rob Kutner, Guy Martin, Seth Mnookin, Susanna Moore, Susan Morrison, Lawrence O'Donnell, David Samuels, Chris Schultz, Harry Shearer, Adrás Szántó, Emily Thorson, James Traub, and Kit White.

Thanks to the Siegels of Celebration—Jim, Marita, and Julie—for their hospitality and openness. Jenny Lawton was my essential partner at Celebration and Disney World (as was Matt Holzman at Disneyland).

I began writing *Fantasyland* in an ideal fantasyland—on the grounds of a fifteenth-century Italian castle among a dozen writers and artists and musicians. Thank you, Civitella Ranieri Foundation.

The generosity of professors Paul Bloom and Konika Banerjee at Yale and Joseph Uscinski at the University of Miami was a happy reminder of how much I admire and enjoy the reality-based academic community. Thanks also to Stefan Cornibert of the Pew Research Center for his help, and to Stephen Bruno (and the Hunter College MFA program) for his. I relied on my sister Kristi—Kristi Andersen, political science professor emeritus at Syracuse University—again and again, from beginning to end. My old friend Jack—the Reverend Jack Gilpin of the Episcopal Church—was a helpful reader of my chapters on Christianity.

I'm grateful to Kate and Lucy Andersen for allowing me to know for sure that something—love for one's children—transcends reason and rationality. And to Anne Kreamer, my beloved daily collaborator and first reader, who enables it all.

Index

About the Author

Kurt Andersen is the bestselling author of the novels *Heyday, Turn of the Century,* and *True Believers.* He contributes to *Vanity Fair* and *The New York Times,* and is host and co-creator of *Studio 360,* the Peabody Award–winning public radio show and podcast. He also writes for television, film, and the stage. Andersen co-founded *Spy* magazine, served as editor in chief of *New York,* and was a cultural columnist and critic for *Time* and *The New Yorker.* He graduated magna cum laude from Harvard College, where he was an editor of *The Harvard Lampoon.* He lives in Brooklyn.

kurtandersen.com
Facebook.com/kurtandersenbooks
Twitter: @KBAndersen

About the Type

THIS BOOK was set in Fairfield, the first typeface from the hand of the distinguished American artist and engraver Rudolph Ruzicka (1883–1978). Ruzicka was born in Bohemia (in the present-day Czech Republic) and came to America in 1894. He set up his own shop, devoted to wood engraving and printing, in New York in 1913 after a varied career working as a wood engraver, in photoengraving and banknote printing plants, and as an art director and freelance artist. He designed and illustrated many books, and was the creator of a considerable list of individual prints—wood engravings, line engravings on copper, and aquatints.